Software Process Improvement and Management:

Approaches and Tools for Practical Development

Shukor Sanim Mohd Fauzi
Universiti Teknologi Mara, Malaysia

Mohd Hairul Nizam Md Nasir
University of Malaya, Malaysia

Nuraminah Ramli
Universiti Pendidikan Sultan Idris, Malaysia

Shamsul Sahibuddin
Universiti Teknologi Malaysia, Malaysia

T0338693

Information Science
REFERENCE

Managing Director:	Lindsay Johnston
Senior Editorial Director:	Heather Probst
Book Production Manager:	Sean Woznicki
Development Manager:	Joel Gamon
Development Editor:	Michael Killian
Acquisitions Editor:	Erika Gallagher
Typesetters:	Mackenzie Snader
Print Coordinator:	Jamie Snavely
Cover Design:	Nick Newcomer, Greg Snader

Published in the United States of America by
Information Science Reference (an imprint of IGI Global)
701 E. Chocolate Avenue
Hershey PA 17033
Tel: 717-533-8845
Fax: 717-533-8661
E-mail: cust@igi-global.com
Web site: http://www.igi-global.com

Library of Congress Cataloging-in-Publication Data

Software process improvement and management: approaches and tools for practical development / Shukor Sanim Mohd Fauzi ... [et al.], editors.
        p. cm.
   Includes bibliographical references and index.
   ISBN 978-1-61350-141-2 (hardcover) -- ISBN 978-1-61350-142-9 (ebook) -- ISBN 978-1-61350-143-6 (print & perpetual access) 1. Software engineering--Case studies. I. Fauzi, Shukor Sanim Mohd, 1980-
   QA76.758.S65619 2012
   005.1--dc23
                                        2011043142

British Cataloguing in Publication Data
A Cataloguing in Publication record for this book is available from the British Library.

All work contributed to this book is new, previously-unpublished material. The views expressed in this book are those of the authors, but not necessarily of the publisher.

Editorial Advisory Board

Table of Contents

Detailed Table of Contents

The industrial revolution transformed the cottage industry into mass production. In this chapter, the authors trace the recent advancement of the software industry and establish that it is following a similar route followed by the manufacturing industry towards industrialization. The chapter positions the concept of Software Product Lines (http://www.sei.cmu.edu/productlines/), as a possible foundation for software industrialization, and the authors introduce the concept of Software Process Lines as complimentary foundation for software industrialization. The chapter discusses a number of questions: What are the Software Process Lines? What are the justifications and benefits of Software Process Lines? What are the steps for implementing Software Process Lines? How can Software Process Lines enable and facilitate the establishment of a continuous Software Process Improvement environment?

# Chapter 2

Requirements Engineering (RE) is a key discipline in software development, and several standards and models are available to help assess and improve RE processes. However, different standards and models can also help achieve different improvement goals. Thus, organizations are challenged to select these standards and models to best suit their specific context and available resources. This chapter presents a review of selected RE-specific and generic process improvement models that are available in the public domain. The review aims to provide preliminary information that might be needed by organizations in selecting these models. The chapter begins with analyses of how RE maturity is addressed in the Capability Maturity Model Integration (CMMI) for Development. Then, it describes the principal characteristics of, and the assessment and improvement framework applied in four RE-specific process assessment and improvement models: the Requirements Engineering Good Practice Guide (REGPG), the Requirements Engineering Process Maturity(REPM), the Requirements Capability Maturity Model (R-CMM), and the Market-Driven Requirements Engineering Process Model (MDREPM). This chapter also examines the utility and lesson learned of these models.

Chapter 3

Claude Y. Laporte, École de Technologie Supérieure, Canada
Edgardo Palza Vargas, École de Technologie Supérieure, Canada

Industry recognizes that Very Small Enterprises (VSEs) that develop software are very important to the economy. VSEs are organizations with up to 25 employees. Failure to deliver a quality product on time and within budget threatens the competitiveness of VSEs and impacts their customers. One way to mitigate these risks is to put in place proven software engineering practices. Many international standards and models, like ISO/IEC 12207 or CMMI®, have been developed to capture proven engineering practices. However, these documents were not designed for VSEs and are often difficult to apply in such settings. This chapter presents a description of the development of international process improvement standards (IS) targeting VSEs developing software as a standalone product or software as a component of a system. The documents used by ISO/IEC JTC1/SC7 Working Group 24 (WG24) and the approach that led to the development, balloting of the ISs, and TRs (Technical Reports) for VSEs are also presented. The chapter focuses on the ISO/IEC 29110 Standard, the development of means to help VSEs improve their processes, and the description of a few pilot projects conducted to implement the processes of 29110 standard.

Chapter 4

Edgardo Palza Vargas, University of Ottawa, Canada

The author aims to improve quality in software engineering projects by introducing Verification and Validation (V&V) best practices in terms of process, artifacts, and quality performance indicators. The chapter presents a Quality Measurement Management Tool (QMT) in order to support quality activities and process. This tool is based on a measurement meta-model repository for collecting, storing, analyzing and reporting measurement data. It is important to note that the proposed QMT supports the IEEE Standard 1012 for Software Verification and Validation (management, acquisition, supply, development, operation, and maintenance), as well as measurement information needs to Capability Maturity Model Integration (CMMI) processes and products requirements. The repository is generic, flexible, and integrated, supporting a dynamic measurement system. It was originally designed to support Ericsson Research Canada's business information needs.

Software process assessments have become commonplace in the software industry because the software industry usually does not recognize the level of their software process. From the time software is developed, a phenomenon called software crisis exists subsuming wrong schedules and cost estimates, low productivity of people, as well as low productivity. A promising approach out of this crisis is now growing up in the software engineering community. One of the approaches is Software Process Assessment. The authors present their experience in implementing internal software process assessment at one of the mid-size Information Technology (IT) company by using the customized SPA method. The customized model is basically based on Standard CMMI Appraisal Method for Process Improvement (SCAMPI).

# Chapter 6

Several companies have been carrying out software processes improvement projects. However, some of them give up before the project ends, and others take much longer than expected to get it accomplished. This way, identifying the resistance factors that influence the implementation of such projects might serve as a reference to professionals in this area on the one hand, and help to manage future projects on the other, through the use of preventive actions that either lessen or eliminate the resistance factors' consequences. For this matter, this chapter presents a survey with 36 professionals involved in initiatives of software processes improvement in 18 companies in the state of Rio Grande do Sul, Brazil.

The Personal Software Process (PSP) is a structured software development framework that includes defined operations, measurements, and analysis techniques designed to help software engineers understand and build on their personal skills and improve their performance. The PSP provides a defined personal process, guides software engineers in collecting and recording data, and defines ways to analyse data and make process improvements. This chapter reviews the previous literature on the implementation of the PSP in academic settings. Lessons learned from PSP implementations are then highlighted. The authors found that there were mixed outcomes due to several issues that later become a barrier to the adoption of the PSP. Several tools have been developed to overcome these barriers and constitute a helping hand for both students and engineers in adopting the PSP.

Chapter 8

Salmiza Saul Hamid, Two Sigma Technologies, Malaysia & University of Malaya, Malaysia
Mohd Hairul Nizam Md Nasir, University of Malaya, Malaysia
Shamsul Sahibuddin, Universiti Teknologi Malaysia, Malaysia
Mustaffa Kamal Mohd Nor, University of Malaya, Malaysia

Despite the widespread use of sound project management practices and process improvement models over the last several years, the failure of software projects remains a challenge to organisations. As part of the attempt to address software industry challenges, several models, frameworks, and methods have been developed that are intended to improve software processes to produce quality software on time, under budget, and in accordance with previously stipulated functionalities. One of the most widely practised methods is the Team Software Process (TSP). The TSP was designed to provide an operational framework for establishing an effective team environment and guiding engineering teams in their work. This chapter provides an overview of the TSP and its associated structures and processes. It also highlights how the TSP operational framework can assist project manager and software development team to deliver successful projects by controlling and minimizing the most common software failure factors. Comparative analysis between the TSP and conventional project management has also been presented. Additionally, the results of TSP implementation in industrial settings are highlighted with particular reference to scheduling, quality, and productivity. The last section indicates additional advantages of TSP and comments on the future of TSP in the global software development project.

Chapter 9

Mohammad Zarour, King Abdulaziz City for Science and Technology, Saudi Arabia
Alain Abran, École de Technologie Supérieure, Canada
Jean-Marc Desharnais, Boğaziçi University, Turkey

Software organizations have been struggling for decades to improve the quality of their products by improving their software development processes. Designing an improvement program for a software development process is a demanding and complex task. This task consists of two main processes: the assessment process and the improvement process. A successful improvement process requires first a successful assessment; failing to assess the organization's software development process could create unsatisfactory results. Although very small enterprises (VSEs) have several interesting characteristics such as flexibility and ease of communications, initiating an assessment and improvement process based on well-known Software Process Improvement (SPI) models such as Capability Maturity Model Integration (CMMI) and ISO 15504 or Software Process Improvement and Capability Determination (SPICE) is more challenging in such VSEs. Accordingly, researchers and practitioners have designed a few assessment methods to meet the needs of VSEs organizations to initiate an SPI process. This chapter discusses the assessment and improvement process in VSEs; the authors first examine VSEs characteristics and problems. Next, the chapter discusses the different assessment methods and standards designed to fit the needs of such organizations and how to compare them. Finally, the authors present future research work perceived in this context.

Chapter 10

Ho-Jin Choi, Korea Advanced Institute of Science and Technology, South Korea
Sang-Hun Lee, Korea Advanced Institute of Science and Technology, South Korea
Syed Ahsan Fahmi, Korea Advanced Institute of Science and Technology, South Korea
Ahmad Ibrahim, Korea Advanced Institute of Science and Technology, South Korea
Hyun-Il Shin, Korea Advanced Institute of Science and Technology, South Korea
Young-Kyu Park, Korea Advanced Institute of Science and Technology, South Korea

Personal Software Process (PSP) and Team Software Process (TSP) have been developed and used to help individual developers and teams make high-quality products through improving their personal and team software development processes. For the PSP and TSP practices, data collection and analysis of software metrics need to be done at fine-grained levels. These tasks are not trivial, requiring tool support. This chapter aims to discuss issues to building such a tool, and introduce an on-going endeavor towards an integrated PSP and TSP supporting tool. In particular, features of sensor-based automated data collection for PSP, utilization of Six Sigma techniques into PSP and TSP activities, and incorporation of electronic process guide will be paid attention.

Chapter 11

Maged Abdullah, University of Malaya, Malaysia
Rodina Ahmad, University of Malaya, Malaysia
Lee Sai Peck, University of Malaya, Malaysia
Zarinah Mohd Kasirun, University of Malaya, Malaysia
Fahad Alshammari, University of Malaya, Malaysia

Software Process Improvement (SPI) has become the survival key of numerous software development organizations who want to deliver their products cheaper, faster, and better. A software process ultimately describes the way that organizations develop their software products and supporting services; meanwhile, SPI on the other hand, is the act of changing the software process and maintenance activities. This chapter purposefully describes the benefits of software process improvement. The Capability Maturity Model (CMM) and the Capability Maturity Model Integration (CMMI) are briefly surveyed and extensively discussed. Prior literature on the benefits and impacts of CMM and CMMI-based software process improvement is also highlighted.

Preface

While editing this book in the year 2011, we realized that the concept of software engineering was forty-three years old. The term "software engineering" was coined at the first NATO Software Engineering Conference in Germany in 1968 amid widespread consensus that problems were emerging with software development and maintenance. These problems were later widely discussed, and the term "software crisis" emerged to describe the software industry's inability to provide customers with high-quality products within schedule and under budget. Hardware costs were dropping, while software costs were rapidly rising. Major computer system projects arrived years late, and the resulting software was unreliable, hard to maintain, and performed poorly. Today, the situation is not much changed. Software development projects are notorious for being completed far over budget and behind schedule. A survey conducted by the Standish Group in the United States (US) in 2008 examined data from several thousand information technology (IT) projects and revealed a software project success rate of only 32%. Twenty-four percent of projects failed, whereas the remaining 44% had cost overruns, time overruns, and impaired functionalities.

The processes of large-scale software development can be vast and complex, involving many software engineers, programmers, and designers. As a result, they are often hard to define, difficult to understand, and even harder to establish. For these reasons, software process improvement (SPI) models were developed. The use of SPI is based on the premise that mature and capable processes generate quality software products. Over the decades, several models for improving software quality through management of the software process have become significant in the software industry. The importance of the software process concept is indicated by the widespread popularity of the software process and software process improvement approaches in software development organizations around the world. To this end, various efforts, initiatives, models, methodologies, and standards have been developed in the last few years, and exhaustive lists of models are available. As members of the software engineering community, we realized that we must continue to promote the education of software engineers to develop and expand knowledge in this area. We believe that the implementation and proper management of software process improvement will lead to the production of high-quality software products.

Software process improvement and management is now such an enormous discipline that is impossible to cover the whole area of knowledge in one book. Therefore, this book gathers the latest advances in various topics in software process improvement and reports on ways that organizations and companies can gain a competitive advantage by applying various emergent methodologies and techniques to real-world scenarios. We focus on emerging key topics, including software process lines, requirement engineering process improvement, process standards and improvement for very small enterprises, software process improvement, software process assessment, process tools and automated support, and software process improvement benefits. With 11 chapters written by 29 international experts in the area of software process improvement and management, this book is intended to serve as a standard reference.

The software industry has come a long way since its early days as a cottage industry. In its short history, it has passed through a number of profound changes and waves of changes, moving it firmly toward its status as a discipline, mirroring what happened to manufacturing during the Industrial Revolution. The **first chapter** of this book positions the concept of Software Product Lines as a possible foundation for software industrialization, and the authors introduce the concept of Software Process Lines as a complementary foundation for software industrialization. The authors believe that an era of software industrialization is coming in spite of the difficulties facing software development efforts. In this chapter, the authors discuss the justifications and benefits of Software Process Lines. They describe the steps for implementing Software Process Lines and explain how Software Process Lines can enable and facilitate the establishment of a continuous Software Process Improvement environment. Because the idea of Software Process Lines is very new, the authors suggest that further research is needed to move the concept forward.

Chapter 2 focuses on Requirement Engineering (RE) process improvement models. It presents a review of selected requirement engineering-specific and generic process improvement models available in the public domain. The review aims to provide preliminary information that might be needed by organizations when selecting these models. The chapter begins with an analysis of the way RE maturity is addressed in the Capability Maturity Model Integration (CMMI) for Development. It then describes both the principal characteristics of and the assessment and improvement framework applied in four RE-specific process assessment and improvement models: the Requirements Engineering Good Practice Guide (REGPG), the Requirements Engineering Process Maturity (REPM), the Requirements Capability Maturity Model (R-CMM), and the Market-Driven Requirements Engineering Process Model (MDREPM). It also examines the utility of, and lessons learned from, these models.

Most software engineering centers, such as the Software Engineering Institute (SEI), dedicate a large portion of their resources to large organizations. Although there seems to be an awareness of the needs of Very Small Enterprises (VSEs), published software engineering practices are still, for the most part, unusable by organizations with less than 25 people. Only a few centers around the world are focusing their Software Process Improvement (SPI) activities on small enterprises and VSEs. Many international standards and models, such as ISO/IEC 12207 or CMMI, have been developed to capture proven engineering practices. However, these documents were not designed for VSEs and are often difficult to apply in such settings. **Chapter 3** presents a description of the development of international process improvement standards (ISs) targeting VSEs developing software as a standalone product or software as a component of a system. The documents used by the ISO/IEC JTC1/SC7 Working Group 24 (WG24) and the approaches that led to the development, and balloting of the ISs and Technical Reports (TRs) for VSEs are also presented. The chapter also focuses on the ISO/IEC 29110 Standard, the development of means of helping VSEs improve their processes and the description of a few pilot projects conducted to implement the processes of the 29110 standard.

Chapter 4 aims to improve quality in software engineering projects by introducing Verification and Validation (V&V): best practices in terms of process, artifacts, and quality performance indicators. It presents a Quality Measurement Management Tool (QMT) to support quality activities and processes. This tool is based on a measurement meta-model repository for collecting, storing, analyzing, and reporting measurement data. It is important to note that the proposed QMT supports the IEEE Standard 1012 for Software Verification and Validation (management, acquisition, supply, development, operation, and maintenance) as well as the measurement information needs for Capability Maturity Model Integration (CMMI) processes and products requirements. The proposed repository is generic, flexible, and integrated, supporting a dynamic measurement system. It was originally designed to support Ericsson Research Canada's business information needs.

Software process assessments have become commonplace in the software industry, because the software industry usually does not recognize the level of their software processes. As long as software has existed, the phenomenon of the software crisis has existed, subsuming faulty schedules, inaccurate cost estimates, low productivity of software engineers, and low productivity in general. Promising approaches to the path out of this crisis are developing in the software engineering community. One of the approaches utilizes Software Process Assessment (SPA). **Chapter 5** presents the authors' experiences implementing internal software process assessment at a mid-size Information Technology (IT) company using a customized SPA method. The customized model is based on the Standard CMMI Appraisal Method for Process Improvement (SCAMPI). Software process assessment can be extremely beneficial to an organization with respect to various standards because a smart organization can use the assessment as a framework to evaluate how projects are completed by conscious analysis rather than slavish adherence; thus, an organization can plan and take steps to improve its operations. However, the authors are concerned that the focus of existing assessment processes, at least in the way that many people apply them, tends to over-value technique at the expense of the goal.

Several companies have implemented software process improvement projects. However, some of them give up before the project ends, and others take much longer than expected to complete the project. Therefore, identifying the resistance factors that influence the implementation of such projects might serve, on the one hand, as a reference for professionals in the area and, on the other hand, help manage future projects through the use of preventive actions that either lessen or eliminate the consequences of the resistance factors. To this end, **Chapter 6** presents a survey of 36 professionals involved in software processes improvement initiatives in 18 companies in the state of Rio Grande do Sul, Brazil. The author expected that the results of this survey would contribute to the planning of future software processes improvement projects, in which preventive actions could be designed to lessen or eliminate the consequences of the resistance factors that impede implementation of these projects. In any case, an initial analysis of the risk of these factors is of paramount importance, as is their impact and the probability that associated risks may occur vary across organizations.

Chapter 7 provides reviews of previous literature on the implementation of the Personal Software Process (PSP) in academic settings. The PSP is a structured software development framework that includes defined operations, measurements, and analysis techniques designed to help software engineers understand and build on their personal skills and improve their performance. The PSP provides a specific personal process, guides software engineers in collecting and recording data, and defines ways of analyzing data and making process improvements. Lessons learned from PSP implementations are then highlighted. The authors encountered mixed outcomes due to several issues that later become barriers to the adoption of the PSP. Several tools have been developed to overcome these barriers and to provide a helping hand to students and engineers adopting the PSP.

Software engineering is progressively becoming a collaborative activity, relying on the knowledge, expertise, and experience of a sizable and frequently varied group of individuals. Although individuals can develop some software products, it is no longer practical for one person to do most software development jobs because the scale and the complexity of the systems have increased, and the demand for short time to delivery is high. System development is a team activity, and the quality of software products is largely determined by the effectiveness of the team coordination. Thus, **Chapter 8** brings the readers from the individual-focused level of PSP to the team-focused level of the Team Software Process (TSP). The TSP was designed to provide an operational framework for establishing an effective team environment and guiding engineering teams in their work. This chapter provides an overview of the TSP and its associated structures and processes. It also highlights the ways that the TSP operational framework can help project managers and software development teams to deliver successful projects by controlling and minimizing the most common software failure factors. A comparative analysis of the TSP and conventional project management strategies is also presented. Additionally, the results of TSP implementation in industrial settings are highlighted with particular reference to scheduling, quality, and productivity. The last section indicates the additional advantages of TSP and comments on the future of TSP in global software development projects.

From team-focused level TSP, we bring the readers to software process improvement at the organizational-focus level, targeting small and very small enterprises. Although Very Small Enterprises (VSEs) have several beneficial characteristics, such as flexibility and ease of communications, initiating an assessment and improvement process based on well-known Software Process Improvement (SPI) models, such as Capability Maturity Model Integration (CMMI) and ISO 15504 or Software Process Improvement and Capability Determination (SPICE), is more challenging in VSEs. Accordingly, researchers and practitioners have designed a few assessment methods to meet VSEs' needs as they attempt to initiate an SPI process. **Chapter 9** discusses the assessment and improvement process in the context of VSEs after first examining VSEs' particular characteristics and problems. Next, it reviews and considers ways to compare the different assessment methods and standards designed to fit the needs of such organizations. Finally, it presents future research plans on the topic.

In the PSP and TSP practices, data collection and analysis of software metrics need to be performed at fine-grained levels. These tasks are not trivial and require tool support. **Chapter 10** discusses automated tool support for PSP and TSP. The chapter focuses on the issues involved in building such a tool and introduces the authors' ongoing endeavors to develop an integrated tool to support PSP and TSP. Particular attention is given to the features of sensor-based automated data collection for PSP, the utilization of Six Sigma techniques in PSP and TSP activities, and the incorporation of electronic process guides.

The **final chapter (Chapter 11)** of the book describes the benefits of the software process improvement. The Capability Maturity Model (CMM) and the Capability Maturity Model Integration (CMMI) are briefly surveyed and extensively discussed. Prior literature on the benefits and impact of CMM- and CMMI-based software process improvement is highlighted. Much has been learned about the effect and benefits of CMM- and CMMI-based software process improvement from the literature reviewed in this final chapter. There is substantial evidence that software process improvement based on CMM and CMMI can result in considerable improvements in cost, schedule, return on investment (ROI), product quality, and other performance measures.

The primary target audience for this book includes academicians, researchers, scholars, and students who are interested in software process improvement research and related issues. It will also be useful for professionals who are involved in software development and software process improvement, such as project managers, process champions, quality specialists, software engineers, et cetera. There are no prerequisites necessary to understand the content of this book. It has been organized into self-contained chapters to provide the greatest reading flexibility.

Shukor Sanim Mohd Fauzi
Universiti Teknologi Mara, Malaysia

Mohd Hairul Nizam Md Nasir
University of Malaya, Malaysia

Nuraminah Ramli
Universiti Pendidikan Sultan Idris, Malaysia

Shamsul Sahibuddin
Universiti Teknologi Malaysia, Malaysia

Chapter 1
Software Process Lines:
A Step towards Software Industrialization

Mahmood Niazi
Keele University, UK & King Fahd University of Petroleum and Minerals, Saudi Arabia

Sami Zahran
Process Improvement Consultant, UK

ABSTRACT

The industrial revolution transformed the cottage industry into mass production. In this chapter, the authors trace the recent advancement of the software industry and establish that it is following a similar route followed by the manufacturing industry towards industrialization. The chapter positions the concept of Software Product Lines (http://www.sei.cmu.edu/productlines/), as a possible foundation for software industrialization, and the authors introduce the concept of Software Process Lines as complimentary foundation for software industrialization. The chapter discusses a number of questions: What are the Software Process Lines? What are the justifications and benefits of Software Process Lines? What are the steps for implementing Software Process Lines? How can Software Process Lines enable and facilitate the establishment of a continuous Software Process Improvement environment?

INTRODUCTION AND JUSTIFICATION

Mega Waves in the Software Industry

The software industry has moved a long way since the early times of it being a cottage industry. In its short history it has passed through a number of mega changes and waves of changes moving

firmly towards a discipline similar to what happened to manufacturing through the industrial revolution. The authors believe that the era of software industrialization is coming, in spite of some difficulties facing software development efforts. The first wave of the software industry started with the structured methods in the 1970's, which were developed to cater for the increasing demands and complexity of software. The efforts to adopt structured methods were assisted by

DOI: 10.4018/978-1-61350-141-2.ch001

automated tools, and this was the beginning of transforming the software industry from a 'cottage industry' towards a disciplined production culture. The second wave of the software industry came with the rise of the object-oriented technology and its associated reuse, combined with the emergence of the focus of the software process maturity and improvement started by Watts Humphrey (Humphrey, 1989) and championed by the Software Engineering Institute (SEI). The software process movement had great promises towards injecting discipline and continuous improvement into the software industry. However this was not enough to move the software industry into the state of industrialization.

Research and industry survey show that the effort put into Software Process Improvement (SPI) models and frameworks can assist in producing high quality software, reducing cost and time, and increasing productivity and employee satisfaction (Ashrafi, 2003; Butler, 1995; Jiang, Klein, Hwang, Huang, & Hung, 2004; Niazi, Wilson, & Zowghi, 2006b; Pitterman, 2000; Yamamura, 1999; Zahran, 1998). However, only a small proportion of the software developing organisations' population has adopted SPI models and framework. This is depicted in the SEI CMMI appraisal report in which only 3113 CMMI appraisals were reported to the SEI (SEI, 2008). Research also shows that a large majority of software development organisations appear to be unwilling to follow SPI initiatives based on process capability maturity models like CMMI (Staples et al., 2007). This may be due to the fact that an SPI programme is quite an expensive undertaking as organisations need to commit significant resources over a long time period (Coleman & O'Connor, 2008). Even organisations who are willing to commit the resources and time do not always achieve their desired results from their SPI initiatives (Florence, 2001; Kautz & Nielsen, 2000). Hence, the significant investment required and limited success are considered two of the main reasons why many organisations are reluctant to embark on a long path of systematic

process improvement (Staples et al., 2007). In the case of small and medium size organisations, there are more concerns about the relevance and applicability of SPI models like CMM or CMMI (Brodman & Johnson, 1994; Staples et al., 2007).

Due to complex nature of SPI initiatives it has been proven to be hard for companies to successfully design and implement software process improvement. A typical approach to SPI in general has three stages: process appraisal, process definition/redesign and process implementation and deployment. The process appraisal phase consumes a larger percent of the budget and resources; process definition requires model knowledge, process design knowledge and skills and knowledge of the organisation/company; and often process implementation and deployment is not only across multi-project, but also across multi-site and multi-customer type. The whole SPI initiative is a long-term approach and it takes time to fully implement a SPI initiative. This is one of the reasons that many organisations are reluctant to embark on a long path of systematic process improvement.

Extensive literature review revealed that many standards and models exist for SPI but little attention has been paid to their effective adoption and implementation of these models. The chaotic implementation process is the most common cause of SPI implementation failure (Zahran, 1998). Attention to a defined SPI implementation process is essential for the success of any SPI initiative. In order to address the SPI implementation issues a Software Process Lines approach has been proposed in this chapter. The objective of the Software Process Lines is to reuse the artefacts in SPI initiatives which are costly to develop from scratch. This will not only help organisations to save their time for process definition/ deployment but will also assist them in quickly moving from lower maturity level to higher maturity levels. We believe that the concept of Software Process Lines, introduced in this chapter, in association with the concept of Software Product Line, championed by the SEI (http://www.softwareproductlines.com/), has the potential to instil process discipline and continuous improvement into software development. We believe that are witnessing the early stage of moving towards an era of software industrialization.

Need to Address both the Software Product and the Software Process

In our view, the move towards Software Industrialization requires parallel progress on two fronts: the first is the software product development and the second is the software process maturity and improvement. There are some serious progress and promising results on the front of software product development as reported by the Software Engineering Institute's (SEI) program on Software Product Lines (http://www.sei.cmu.edu/productlines/index.cfm). There should be a similar progress on the front of software development process.

For the last decade there have been many advances in standards and models to improve the software development process. Research shows that the effort put into these SPI models and standards can assist in producing high quality software, reducing cost and time, and increasing productivity (Ashrafi, 2003; Butler, 1995; Pitterman, 2000; Yamamura, 1999). However, these advances have not been matched by equal advances in the adoption of these standards and models in software development (Leung, 1999) which has resulted in limited success for many SPI efforts. Studies show that 67% of SPI managers want guidance on 'how' to implement SPI activities, rather than 'what' SPI activities to actually implement (Herbsleb & Goldenson, 1996). Despite the importance of the SPI implementation process, little empirical research has been carried out on developing ways in which to effectively implement SPI programmes. This suggests that the current problem with SPI is not due to a lack of a standard or model, but rather a lack of effec-

tive strategies to successfully implement these standards or models.

Software quality has received much attention in both academia and industry. This is due to the role software plays in modern-day business and, to some extent, modern-day living. Attempts to improve software quality have been going on for several decades. Software organisations have been struggling with a questionable quality image for their products for a long time (Zahran, 1998). Customer satisfaction has also become the motto of many software organisations in order to survive with quality software (Paulk, Weber, Curtis, & Chrissis, 1994). Software quality has become more critical as software pervades our day-to-day lives (Pitterman, 2000; Yamamura, 1999). We believe that Software Industrialization will provide a way to deliver quality software within budget and schedule, something that currently eludes most software organisations (Ashrafi, 2003; Jiang et al., 2004; Paulk et al., 1994; Standish-Group, 2003). In order to effectively address the software quality issues different approaches have been developed, of which software process improvement (SPI) is the one most widely used (SEI, 2004).

TOWARDS SOFTWARE INDUSTRIALIZATION

We believe that the Software Industry has made big steps over the past five decades towards achieving moving the software industry away from being a "cottage industry" towards achieving a level of process discipline, automation and mass production similar to those achieved in the manufacturing industry as a result of the industrial revolution.

Achieving the status of Industrialization, there is a need to make progress at two parallel fronts: one on the Product Development front, and the other on the Process and Tools front. Figure 1 highlights a number of major milestones of the software industry's progress along the route

Figure 1. The route towards software industrialization (Northrop, 2008; Zahran, 2008)

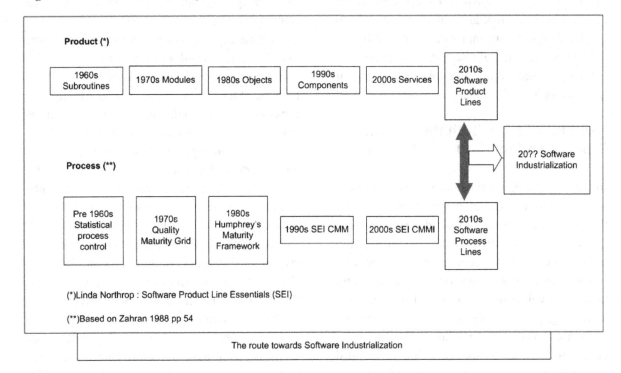

The route towards Software Industrialization

towards Software Industrialization on the two fronts of Product and Process.

Software Product Lines need to be supported by corresponding Software Process Lines in order to achieve the qualitative shift towards the industrialization of software product development. Successful implementation of Software Product Lines will not be possible in the absence of mature disciplined processes that are continuously optimised and improving. In the case of the manufacturing industry, there was no way for it to achieve its current advanced status without well defined and mostly automated processes. The concept of Software Product Lines is well developed and is now pioneered by a number of product domains in diverse areas including: mobile phones, satellite ground station systems, command and control ship systems, mass storage systems, billing systems, printers and medical devices). Leading organisations who piloted the Software Product Lines and achieved gains and benefits include: Boeing, ERICSSON, NOKIA, HP, ABB, and GM. (Northrop, 2008).

The concept of Software Process Lines, which we developed and describe in this chapter, is still in the early stages of development. Figure 2 illustrates how Product Lines and Process Lines may interact with each other. As illustrated, the Software Process Lines are used to tailor generic processes to generate specific processes to be followed to develop specific products using the generic assets in the Software Product Lines. That means that the Process Lines provide guidance on how to customise and use the core component assets in the Product Lines to develop specific products. In the other direction, there should be feedback from the Product Lines to the Process Lines on the process performance and any need to upgrade or modify the processes in the Process Lines. That feedback should include all the lessons learned resulting from the tailoring of the product lines and any additions to the product lines.

Figure 2. Interaction between process lines and product line

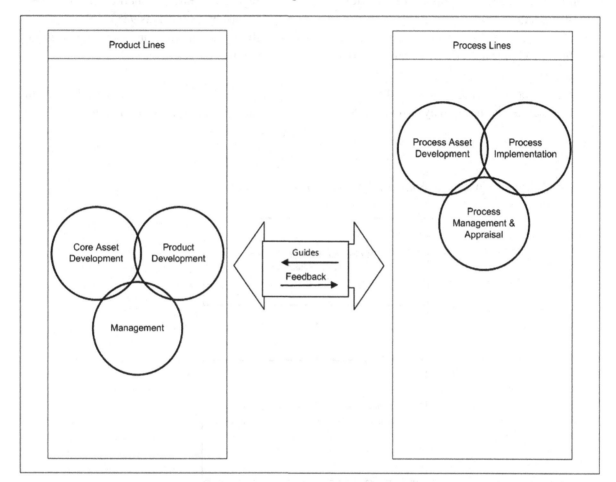

OVERVIEW OF SOFTWARE PRODUCT LINES

Software product lines are emerging as a new and important software development paradigm. A software product line is "a set of software-intensive systems sharing a common set of features that satisfy the specific needs of a particular market segment or mission" (Clements & Northrop, 1999)

The rationale behind software product lines is that "the practice of building sets of related systems from common assets can yield remarkable quantitative improvements in productivity, time to market, product quality, and customer satisfaction" (Clements & Northrop, 1999) in contrast to being developed one at a time in separate efforts.

Using common sets, a new product is formed by taking applicable components from the asset base, tailoring them as necessary through pre-planned variation mechanisms such as parameterisation, adding new components that may be necessary, and assembling the collection under the umbrella of a common, product line-wide architecture (Clements & Northrop, 1999). Building a new product becomes more a matter of generation than creation; the predominant activity is integration rather than programming.

According to the SEI (http://www.sei.cmu.edu/productlines/), organisations of all types and sizes have discovered that a product line strategy, when skilfully implemented, can produce many benefits—and ultimately give the organisations a competitive edge. Example organisational benefits include:

- Improved productivity by as much as 10x
- Increased quality by as much as 10x
- Decreased cost by as much as 60%
- Decreased labour needs by as much as 87%

- Decreased time to market (to field, to launch) by as much as 98%
- Ability to move into new markets in months, not years

Figure 3 illustrates the main activity flow in a software product line environment.

Figure 3. Main activity flow in Software Product Lines environment

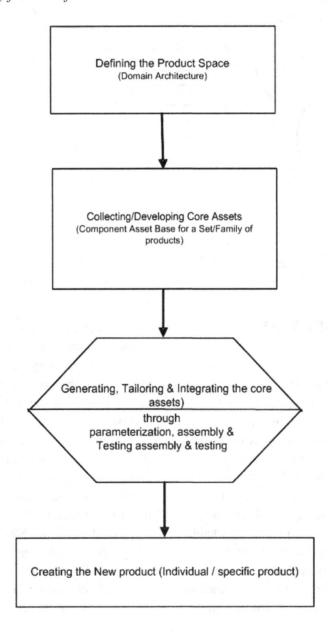

Generally, adopting a software product line approach involves two classes of activities: Core asset development or acquisition, and Product development or acquisition using core assets. The activities involved are:

- Defining the product space
- Producing the core assets

- Requirements for the specific product
- Developing the production plan

A number of practice areas relevant to each of these activities are suggested by the SEI Product Lines Program in a framework for software product line practice (www.sei.cmu.edu/productlines/ frame_report/PL.essential.act.htm)

Figure 4. Main activity flow in software process lines environment

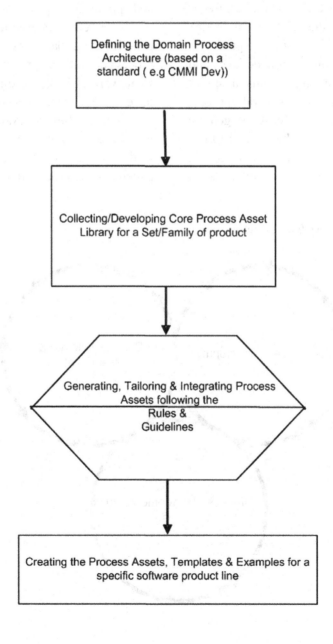

SOFTWARE PROCESS LINES

Our suggested Software Process lines approach is based on the concept of software product line approach (Northrop, 2002). As mentioned above, "A software product line is a set of software-intensive systems that share a common, managed feature set satisfying a particular market segment's specific needs or mission and that are developed from a common set of core assets in a prescribed way" (Northrop, 2002). One of the important characteristics of a software product line is Strategic Reuse of a set of reusable product components which has a significant impact on cost of the product.

We have noticed through our experience and working in academia and industry that a similar approach can be adapted for a software process lines which encourages the reuse of generic process assets, thus avoiding the costly effort of developing the process artefacts from scratch. Software Process Line can be defined as "a set of core processes that share a common feature set to satisfy the needs and requirements for process implementation strategies". These core processes form the basis for the software process lines (Figure 4).

Like the essential product line activities described in (Northrop, 2002), we have proposed three essential activities in software process line as shown in Figure 5. Software Process line involves "core process development", "process implementation" and "process management and appraisal".

In the "core process development" activity, generic process patterns will be developed, using process definitions, process patterns, styles and frameworks, which can be adapted by the product development team to their process needs and requirements. Several examples of process patterns are already available (Forster, 2006; Telesko & Ferber, 2007; Zahran, 2008). Reuse of these patterns in the process development should save

Figure 5. Software process lines activities

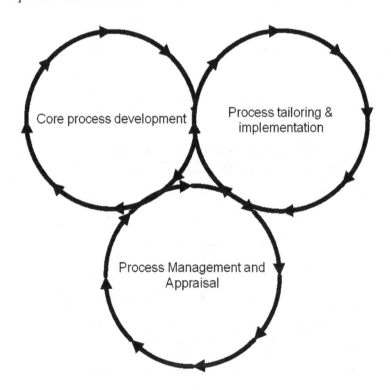

the organisation effort and time in the core process development.

In the "core process implementation" activity, generic process implementation strategies will be developed, using change management methods and process improvement implementation theories, practices and frameworks, which can be adapted by organisations in their SPI implementation initiatives in order to save organisations time for designing new SPI implementation strategies.

The objective of "process management and appraisal" activity is to provide technical and organisational support to other two activities of the software process line in order to successfully implement the software process line initiative.

Core Process Development

The objective of core process development is to develop core generic process patterns which can easily be adapted by organisations to their SPI needs and requirements as shown in Figure 6. This will not only help organisations to save their time for process definition and development

but will also assist them in quickly moving from lower maturity level to higher maturity levels. Research shows that organisations are spending a lot of time in moving from lower maturity level to higher maturity levels which is depicted in the Software Engineering Institute report (SEI, 2004):

• Maturity level 1 to 2 is 22 months
• Maturity level 2 to 3 is 19 months
• Maturity level 3 to 4 is 25 months
• Maturity level 4 to 5 is 13 months

The basic reason for this delay is that in any SPI initiative organisations develop processes from scratch because there are little benchmark processes and process patterns available which might be used to develop these new processes quickly. Despite the importance of this issue, little research has been carried out on software process implementation strategies in general and designing of benchmark process or process patterns in particular. As mentioned earlier only recently some pioneering work on software process pat-

Figure 6. Core process line development

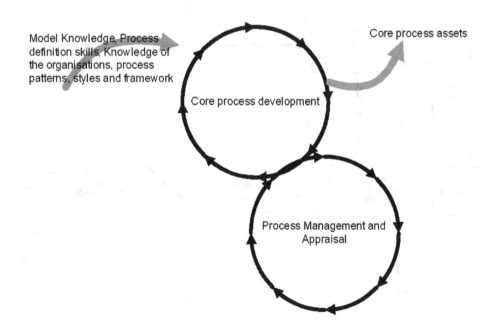

terns has taken place (Forster, 2006; Telesko & Ferber, 2007; Zahran, 2008).

In our previous research (Niazi, Hickman, Ahmad, & Babar, 2008) we have taken initiatives to start work in this missing area of SPI. The objective was, as a pilot project, to design a process pattern for CMMI Level 2 specific practice–"manage requirements changes" as shown in Figure 7. We have proposed a pattern in the form of a model for requirements change management and also discussed initial validation of that model in (Niazi et al., 2008). That model was based on both an empirical study that we have carried out and our extensive literature review of SPI and requirements engineering. For data collection we have interviewed SPI experts from reputed organisations. Further work included analysing research articles, published experience reports and case studies. Our model is based

on five core elements: request, validate, implement, verify and update. Within each of these elements we have identified specific activities that need to take place during requirements change management process.

The initial stage is the change "Request". The main sources of requests may be either internal or external. The internal requests come from the project management or software maintenance teams within the company. The external requests come from the customers. These internal and external requests are then fed to a requirements change pool. The requirements change pool contains a description of the change, the reasons behind the changes and who has requested the change.

The next stage is to "Validate" the change request. The first activity in the validate stage is to understand the change request (i.e. what needs

Figure 7. An example of a process pattern for core process line

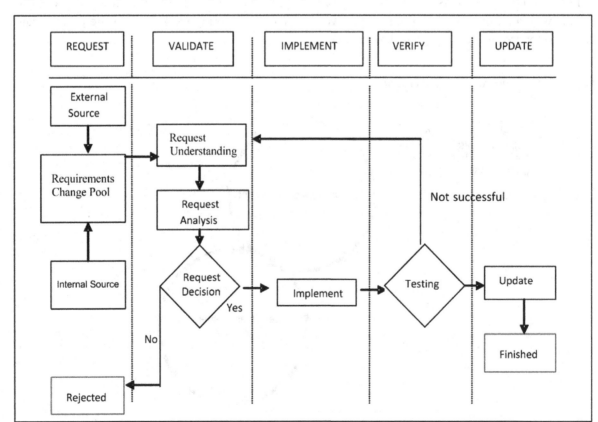

to be done–fix, an enhancement or removal). Request analysis is the activity to look at the different ways in which the request can be met, i.e. how much effort is needed to make this change, how much effort is needed to implement this change, the impact of the change, the risk of change and the priority of each change request.

The final activity of the validation process is to make decision if the change request should be accepted, rejected or reanalysed with new evidence. The third stage is to "Implement" the changes. In this stage all the accepted changes are consolidated and are implemented in the form of end product or software.

The fourth stage is to "Verify" changes where it is ascertained that the software conforms to its specification. In this stage the new product/ software is tested in the form of regression testing, field trials or user acceptance. The testing method will depend on the characteristics of the request and the environment of the product/software. If the verification stage is not successful the change request is sent back to the "Validate" stage for further understanding and analysis of the change request.

The final stage is "Update". Documentation on the software is updated with the changes made. The customers and the project team are all informed about these update so that everyone is working on the current up to date version. The finished step is when the product/software is released with the new requirements included.

The initial evaluation of the model was performed via an expert review process. The initial evaluation of the model showed that the requirements change management model is clear, easy to use and can effectively manage the requirements change process. However, more case studies are needed to evaluate this model in order to further evaluate its effectiveness in the domain of the requirements process.

After successfully developing the pattern for one specific practice we are now planning to develop patterns for all of the specific practices

of CMMI. However, we encourage other people to conduct more studies to develop new process patterns which can satisfy CMMI specific and generic practices.

Process Implementation

The objective of process implementation activity is to develop process implementation strategies which can easily be adapted by organisations in their software process implementation and process implementation initiatives as shown in Figure 8 This will also help organisations to save time and effort in designing new process implementation and process improvement strategies.

A number of researchers have tried to address some of the issues of SPI implementation by exploring SPI implementation success factors, barriers, motivators and de-motivators (Baddoo & Hall, 2002, 2003; El-Emam, Fusaro, & Smith, 1999; Goldenson & Herbsleb, 1995; Niazi & Babar, 2008, 2007a, 2007b; Niazi & Staples, 2005; Niazi, Wilson, & Zowghi, 2004, 2006a). These studies indeed contribute towards SPI implementation where SPI managers can use their lessons and concepts as motivators in their SPI implementation strategies. In addition the SPI managers can also design some strategies to cope with and overcome any barriers and or de-motivators to software process improvements in their organisations. However, more work is needed to assist SPI managers in the form of models and frameworks that could help in successfully implementing SPI initiatives. More work is also needed to develop generic implementation strategies which can easily be adapted by organisations in their SPI implementation initiatives to save their time for designing new SPI implementation strategies.

Process Management and Appraisal

The objective of process management and appraisal activity is to provide technical and or-

Figure 8. Process implementation

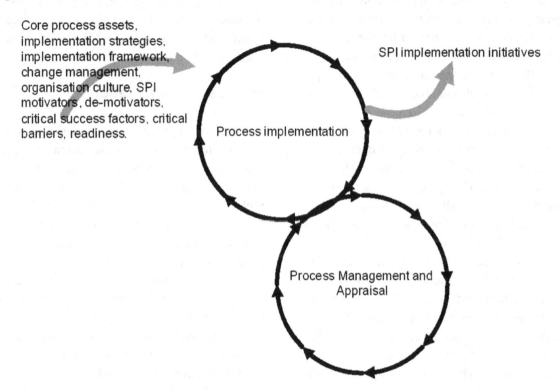

ganisational support to other two activities of process line SPI in order to successfully develop the whole process line SPI initiative as shown in Figure 9. In addition, different appraisals are performed to assess the core process development and process implementation activities. The technical management oversees the core process development and process implementation, ensuring that the stakeholders involved in building processes and patterns engage in the right activities and collect sufficient data to perform these activities. The organisational support ensures that the SPI teams receive the right and enough resources (i.e. experienced people, training, and budget) for SPI activities. In the organisational support the management assist SPI teams to address any barriers or risks that threaten Software Process Line activities. Finally, someone should be designated as the process line manager to lead all the Software Process Line activities.

In order to perform process appraisals, there are three classes available of CMMI SCAMPI appraisals Class A, B, and C (Ahern et al., 2005; CMMI-Product-Team, 2001). Class A appraisals are very costly, time-consuming, and resource-intensive, but provide the highest levels of assurance about their findings. Class B appraisals are less costly, time-consuming and resource-intensive as they use fewer appraisers, appraise fewer projects, and rely on fewer forms of evidence. Class C appraisals are the cheapest and easiest to perform, and can approach the simplicity of a structured questionnaire. All appraisals result in a report of findings about an organisation's capability, but only Class A appraisals can result in a publicly-reportable "rating" of the organisation's CMMI level.

Conducting research on SPI implementation has convinced us to conduct some research on appraisal of organisations readiness for SPI

Figure 9. Process management and appraisal

implementation. It is very important to measure organisations readiness for SPI implementation as the failure rate for SPI programmes has been reported up to 70% in a report from the Software Engineering Institute (SEI) (Ngwenyama & Nielsen, 2003; SEI, 2002). This shows that many organisations go for SPI implementation prior to testing their readiness for SPI activities. We have focused on these issues and developed a SPI readiness model (as shown in Figure 10) in order to assess the SPI implementation readiness of the organisations (Niazi et al., 2005). The

Figure 10. SPI implementation readiness model (Niazi, Wilson, & Zowghi, 2005)

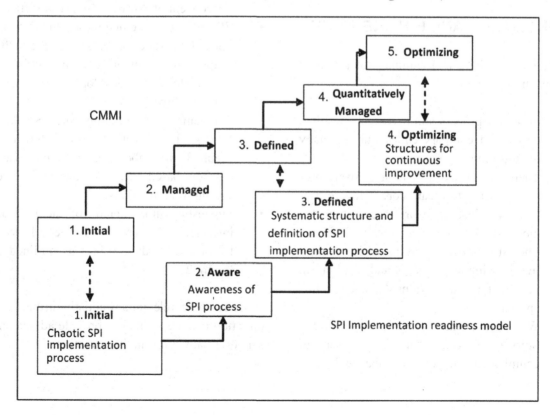

CMMI perspective (Chrissis, Konrad, & Shrum, 2006) and the findings from our previous empirical study (Niazi, Wilson, & Zowghi, 2003; Niazi et al., 2004) were used in the design of the SPI readiness model. The SPI readiness model has four SPI implementation readiness levels abstracted from CMMI. These readiness levels contain different critical success factors (Niazi et al., 2006a) and critical barriers (Niazi et al., 2004) identified through the literature and interviews. Under each factor, different practices have been designed that guide how to assess and implement each factor. We have evaluated this model with three large sized and two medium sized organisations. The evaluation results showed that this model can be used effectively to identify SPI implementation issues with a goal of increasing SPI implementation readiness. All the case study participants agreed that this model is clear, easy to use and specifically geared to assess the organisations' SPI implementation readiness.

CONCLUSION AND FUTURE WORK

In conclusion, here is a summary of the main points in this chapter:

- Software process improvement is still a costly and complex endeavour for many organisations.
- There is a lack of re-use of software process patterns to create core software processes and instil software process improvement practices in the organisation's fabric.
- The SEI Software Product Lines initiative is achieving success and resulting in benefits for organisations that adopted this approach.
- We believe that an effort to develop Software Process Lines is necessary to complement, support and enhance the val-

ue of adopting the Software Product Lines approach.
- In this chapter we have introduced our approach to Software Process Lines, which we believe together with the Software Product Lines can provide a good springboard to moving towards the Software Industrialization

We suggest that further work is still needed in progressing our concepts forward, especially in the following areas which we recommend them for students and researchers:

- Prototyping our approach to Software Process Lines in order to prove the concepts viability in commercial and business environment
- Piloting the combined implementation of the Software Product Lines and the Software Process Lines (in a software factory-like environment) to order to prove the concept of Software Industrialization
- Elaborating of the definitions and descriptions of the basic concepts described in this chapter and formulating them in coherent methodology for developing and using Software Process Lines
- Practicing and piloting the Software Process Lines activity flow shown in Figure 3, and elaborating the activities and the flow based on the lessons learned resulting from the pilots.
- Suggesting more details of the possible interface and interaction between Process Lines and Products Lines as outlined in Figure 2.

The authors welcome any initiative in the above direction and are willing to provide advice and support to any effort in this direction.

REFERENCES

Ahern, D. M., Armstrong, J., Clouse, A., Ferguson, J. R., Hayes, W., & Nidiffer, K. E. (2005). *CMMI SCAMPI distilled: Appraisals for process improvement*. Addison-Wesley Professional.

Ashrafi, N. (2003). The impact of software process improvement on quality: In theory and practice. *Information & Management, 40*(7), 677–690. doi:10.1016/S0378-7206(02)00096-4

Baddoo, N., & Hall, T. (2002). Motivators of software process improvement: An analysis of practitioner's views. *Journal of Systems and Software*, (62): 85–96. doi:10.1016/S0164-1212(01)00125-X

Baddoo, N., & Hall, T. (2003). De-motivators of software process improvement: An analysis of practitioner's views. *Journal of Systems and Software, 66*(1), 23–33.

Brodman, J. G., & Johnson, D. L. (1994). What small businesses and small organizations say about the CMMI. In *Proceedings of 16th International Conference on Software Engineering* (pp. 331-340). IEEE Computer Society Press.

Butler, K. (1995). The economics benefits of software process improvement. *CrossTalk. The Journal of Defense Software Engineering, 8*(7).

Chrissis, M. B., Konrad, M., & Shrum, S. (2006). *CMMI guidelines for process integration and product improvement*. Addison Wesley.

Clements, P., & Northrop, L. (1999). *A framework for software product line practice*. Retrieved Dec 2009, from http://www.sei.cmu.edu/library/abstracts/news-at-sei/backgroundsep99pdf.cfm

CMMI-Product-Team. (2001). *Appraisal requirements for CMMI, version 1.1*. Technical Report CMU/SEI-2001-TR-034, Carnegie Mellon University Software Engineering Institute.

Coleman, G., & O'Connor, R. (2008). Investigating software process in practice: A grounded theory perspective. *Journal of Systems and Software, 81*, 772–784. doi:10.1016/j.jss.2007.07.027

El-Emam, K., Fusaro, P., & Smith, B. (1999). Success factors and barriers for software process improvement. In Messnarz, R., & Tully, C. (Eds.), *Better software practice for business benefit: Principles and experience* (pp. 355–371). Los Alamitos, CA: IEEE Computer Society.

Florence, A. (2001). Lessons learned in attempting to achieve software CMM Level 4. *CrossTalk, The Journal of Defense Software Engineering*, 29-30.

Forster, F. (2006). *Business process improvement patterns*. Doctoral dissertation, Queensland University of Technology & Technische Universitat, Munich.

Goldenson, D. R., & Herbsleb, J. D. (1995). *After the appraisal: A systematic survey of process improvement, its benefits, and factors that influence success* (No. CMU/SEI-95-TR-009, Software Engineering Institute, USA): SEI.

Herbsleb, J. D., & Goldenson, D. R. (1996). *A systematic survey of CMM experience and results*. Paper presented at the 18th International Conference on Software Engineering (ICSE-18), Berlin, Germany.

Humphrey, W. (1989). *Managing the software process*. Addison-Wesley.

Jiang, J., Klein, G., Hwang, H., Huang, J., & Hung, S. (2004). An exploration of the relationship between software development process maturity and project performance. *Information & Management, 41*, 279–288. doi:10.1016/S0378-7206(03)00052-1

Kautz, K., & Nielsen, P. A. (2000). *Implementing software process improvement: Two cases of technology transfer*. Paper presented at the 33rd Hawaii Conference on System Sciences, Maui, USA.

Leung, H. (1999). Slow change of information system development practice. *Software Quality Journal, 8*(3), 197–210. doi:10.1023/A:1008915509865

Ngwenyama, O., & Nielsen, P., A. (2003). Competing values in software process improvement: An assumption analysis of CMM from an organizational culture perspective. *IEEE Transactions on Engineering Management, 50*(1), 100–112. doi:10.1109/TEM.2002.808267

Niazi, M., & Babar, M. A. (2007a). *De-motivators for software process improvement: An analysis of Vietnamese practitioners' views.* Paper presented at the International Conference on Product Focused Software Process Improvement PROFES 2007, LNCS 4589.

Niazi, M., & Babar, M. A. (2007b). *Motivators of software process improvement: An analysis of vietnamese practitioners' views.* Paper presented at the International Conference on Evaluation and Assessment in Software Engineering (EASE 2007).

Niazi, M., & Babar, M. A. (2008). Demotivators for software process improvement: An empirical investigation. *Software Process Improvement and Practice Journal (Perspectives on Global Software Development: Special Issue on PROFES 2007), 13*(3), 249-264.

Niazi, M., Hickman, C., Ahmad, R., & Babar, M. A. (2008). *A model for requirements change management: Implementation of CMMI level 2 specific practice.* Paper presented at the International Conference on Product Focused Software Process Improvement PROFES 2008, Italy, LNCS 5089.

Niazi, M., & Staples, M. (2005). *Systematic review of organizational motivations for adopting CMM-based SPI.* Technical Report (No. National ICT Australia, PA005957).

Niazi, M., Wilson, D., & Zowghi, D. (2003). *Critical success factors and critical barriers for software process improvement: An analysis of literature.* Paper presented at the Australasian Conference on Information Systems (ACIS03), Perth, Australia.

Niazi, M., Wilson, D., & Zowghi, D. (2004). *Critical barriers for SPI implementation: An empirical study.* Paper presented at the IASTED International Conference on Software Engineering (SE 2004), Austria.

Niazi, M., Wilson, D., & Zowghi, D. (2005). A maturity model for the implementation of software process improvement: An empirical study. *Journal of Systems and Software, 74*(2), 155–172. doi:10.1016/j.jss.2003.10.017

Niazi, M., Wilson, D., & Zowghi, D. (2006a). Critical success factors for software process improvement: An empirical study. *Software Process Improvement and Practice Journal, 11*(2), 193–211. doi:10.1002/spip.261

Niazi, M., Wilson, D., & Zowghi, D. (2006b). *Implementing software process improvement initiatives: An empirical study.* Paper presented at the The 7th International Conference on Product Focused Software Process Improvement, LNCS.

Northrop, L. (2002). SEI's software product line tenets. *IEEE Software, 19*(4), 32–40. doi:10.1109/MS.2002.1020285

Northrop, L. (2008). Software product line essential. Retrieved Dec 2009, from http://www.sei.cmu.edu/library/assets/spl-essentials.pdf

Paulk, M., Weber, C., Curtis, B., & Chrissis, M. (1994). *A high maturity example: Space shuttle onboard software, in the capability maturity model: Guidelines for improving software process.* California, US: Addison-Wesley.

Pitterman, B. (2000). Telcordia Technologies: The journey to high maturity. *IEEE Software*, *17*(4), 89–96. doi:10.1109/52.854074

SEI. (2002). *Process maturity profile of the software community*. Software Engineering Institute Carnegie Mellon University.

SEI. (2004). *Process maturity profile*. Software Engineering Institute Carnegie Mellon University.

SEI. (2008). *Process maturity profile*. Software Engineering Institute Carnegie Mellon University. Retrieved Oct 2008, from http://www.sei.cmu.edu/appraisal-program/profile/pdf/CMMI/2008MarCMMI.pdf

Standish-Group. (2003). *Chaos - The state of the software industry*.

Staples, M., Niazi, M., Jeffery, R., Abrahams, A., Byatt, P., & Murphy, R. (2007). An exploratory study of why organizations do not adopt CMMI. *Journal of Systems and Software*, *80*(6), 883–895. doi:10.1016/j.jss.2006.09.008

Telesko, R., & Ferber, S. (2007). *Applying design patterns on processes*. Paper presented at the SEI SEPG European Conference.

Yamamura, G. (1999). Software process satisfied employees. *IEEE Software*, (September/October): 83–85. doi:10.1109/52.795105

Zahran, S. (1998). *Software process improvement - Practical guidelines for business success*. Addison-Wesley.

Zahran, S. (2008). *Patterns for the enterprise process architecture*. Paper presented at the SEI SEPG European Conference.

Chapter 2
Requirements Engineering Process Improvement and Related Models

Badariah Solemon
Universiti Tenaga Nasional, Malaysia

Shamsul Sahibuddin
Universiti Teknologi Malaysia, Malaysia

Abdul Azim Abd Ghani
Universiti Putra Malaysia, Malaysia

ABSTRACT

Requirements Engineering (RE) is a key discipline in software development, and several standards and models are available to help assess and improve RE processes. However, different standards and models can also help achieve different improvement goals. Thus, organizations are challenged to select these standards and models to best suit their specific context and available resources. This chapter presents a review of selected RE-specific and generic process improvement models that are available in the public domain. The review aims to provide preliminary information that might be needed by organizations in selecting these models. The chapter begins with analyses of how RE maturity is addressed in the Capability Maturity Model Integration (CMMI) for Development. Then, it describes the principal characteristics of, and the assessment and improvement framework applied in four RE-specific process assessment and improvement models: the Requirements Engineering Good Practice Guide (REGPG), the Requirements Engineering Process Maturity(REPM), the Requirements Capability Maturity Model (R-CMM), and the Market-Driven Requirements Engineering Process Model (MDREPM). This chapter also examines the utility and lesson learned of these models.

DOI: 10.4018/978-1-61350-141-2.ch002

INTRODUCTION

Requirements Engineering (RE) is an important part of software development, which covers all aspects of the discovery, documentation, and maintenance of requirements throughout the software development life cycle (Sommerville & Sawyer, 1997). There exist RE standards that describe general principles as well as detailed guidelines for performing the RE process. Such standards include the IEEE Recommended Practice for Software Requirements Specifications (IEEE, 1998a), and the IEEE Guide for Developing System Requirements Specifications (IEEE, 1998b). However, these standards do not provide support to organization particularly in selecting appropriate methods or in designing an optimized RE process (Sawyer, 2004). In a survey conducted by Beecham, Hall, Britton, Cottee, and Rainer (2005), an expert panel consists of both practitioners and academics agreed that RE process remains the most problematic of all software engineering activities. Findings of other surveys conducted involving UK and Australian software companies (Beecham, Hall, & Rainer, 2003b; Niazi & Shastry, 2003) confirmed that these companies still considered requirements engineering problems very significant.

Consequently, many organizations seek to improve RE process by adopting the Software Process Improvement (SPI) approach (Napier, Mathiassen, & Johnson, 2009). However, according to Sawyer (2004), a European survey involving organizations who took part in SPI programs during the 1980s confirmed that the then available SPI models do not alleviate their problems in handling requirements. This is despite the fact that the SPI brought them several significant benefits. These scenarios have led to the development of a number of RE process improvement models such as the Requirements Engineering Good Practice Guide (REGPG) (Sommerville & Sawyer, 1997); the Requirements Capability Maturity Model (R-CMM) (Beecham, Hall, & Rainer, 2003a, 2005);

the Requirements Engineering Process Maturity Model (REPM) (Gorschek & Tejle, 2002), and the Market-Driven Requirements Engineering Process Model (MDREPM) (Gomes & Petters-son, 2007). Sources of requirements engineering process improvement advice are available in the literature. For example, books written by Young (2001) and Wiegers (2003) are focusing at RE practice recommendations and advices on what organizations can do to improve their RE processes. However, these recommendations and advices for improving RE practices are not presented in a process maturity model.

Many business success stories often advice organizations to begin their process improvement journey by first applying a standard or model. Applying a standard or model is often perceived to provide a great tool and a good guide to achieve process improvement goals. However, different standards and models can also help achieve different goals. Thus, organizations are challenged to select different types of assessment and improvement standards and models to best suit their specific context and available resources (Nielsen & Pries-Heje, 2002; Sanders & Richardson, 2007).

This chapter aims to provide initial information for organizations to get to know some of the process improvement models, and perhaps later choose the appropriate models that can help achieve their desired goal. We begin with an overview of two RE-related process areas of the Capability Maturity Model Integration for Development (CMMI-DEV) developed by the Software Engineering Institute (SEI). Even though software engineering has witnessed the development of several other generic SPI standards and models such as ISO 9001 standard for quality management system (Weissfelner, 1999), BOOTSTRAP (Stienen, 1999), and ISO/IEC 15504 (Drouin, 1999), we limit our review to the CMMI-DEV only for several reasons. The main reason is easy availability of CMMI-DEV as a free download from the SEI website while other standards/models like ISO/IEC 15504 must be purchased from the

ISO. In this chapter, we also present reviews of the four RE process assessment and improvement models available in the literature: the REGPG, the REPM, the R-CMM, and the MDREPM in their respective sub-sections.

Requirements Engineering Maturity in the CMMI for Development

The SEI's Capability Maturity Model Integration (CMMI) is a combination of several models, including CMM for Software Engineering (SW_ CMM), CMM for Systems Engineering (EIA 731 SECM), and CMM for Integrated Product Development (IPD_CMM), into a single improvement framework (Chrissis, Konrad, & Shrum, 2007). This was intended for use by organization in their pursuit of enterprise-wide process improvement. To apply to multiple areas of interest, the framework groups best practices into "constellations" where a constellation is a collection of CMMI components that are used to build models, training materials, and appraisal documents (Chrissis et al., 2007). The three constellations of CMMI are CMMI for Services (CMMI-SVC), CMMI for Acquisition (CMMI-ACQ), and CMMI for Development (CMMI-DEV). This review is based on CMMI-DEV version 1.2, which was released in August 2006.

The CMMI-DEV is a reference model that covers the development and maintenance activities applied to both products and services. The CMMI-DEV builds on and extends the best practices of the CMM. Also, new process areas were added, modern best practices were added, and a generic goal was added that applies to each process area of the model. CMMI-DEV enables companies to approach process improvement and assessment (appraisal) using either one or both the two different representations: staged presentation (that provides a sequence of improvements), and continuous representation (that allows selection of individual Process Areas (PAs). Specific to the RE domain, CMMI-DEV has a new process area

known as Requirements Development (RD) added. This is an additional to the existing Requirements Management (REQM) PA. Both the REQM and RD PAs consist of categories (or taxonomy) of RE activities (i.e., manage requirements, develop customer requirements, develops product requirements, and analyzes and validates requirements). Maturity of the two PAs are measured based on the chosen type of representation of the model. In the staged representation, all PAs are defined at one of four maturity levels (2–5). In this representation, REQM is placed at maturity level 2 and RD at maturity level 3. In the continuous representation, each PA is assigned one of six capability levels (0–5).

Despite the many perceived potential benefits of CMM-based SPI programs reported in the literature (e.g., Hansen, Rose, & Tjornehoj, 2004), several challenges lie ahead of the model. Specific to the RE domain, the attempt of CMMI-DEV to define RE maturity is deficient and has raised several issues. These issues include the following:

1. The CMMI-DEV does not define RE maturity the way it should be defined based on industry standard and practices as elaborated in Linscomb (2003). Linscomb explains that placing the RE phases into two PAs in two separate maturity levels (with the order REQM PA first then RD PA) can create an issue. For example, if an organization does not have an institutionalized way of eliciting requirements (at maturity level 3), by right the organization would not have any requirements to be managed at lower maturity level 2. In another example, there might be a case where an organization with a high capability for REQM (for example, 5) has a low capability level (for example, 0) for RD. As contended by Linscomb, the order of RE implementation and institutionalizations in this model is not always logical.

2. Like ISO 9000, CMMI-DEV does not tell specifically how to actually do the REQM

and RD work as stated by Humphrey in Chrissis et al. (2007). Thus, to create a comprehensive software process improvement approach that would satisfy the demanding CMMI assessors, organizations are forced to depend highly on paid consultants or CMMI training and/or experiences of their team members or reference books, causing the cost associated with the model to be very high.

3. There are now cases where high-maturity ratings do not correlate with high-maturity practices. An example case can be seen in our own survey discussed in Badariah, Sahibuddin, and Azim (2009). According to Humphrey in Chrissis et al. (2007) "… with increasing marketplace pressure, organization often focuses on maturity levels rather than process capability… we now see cases where high-maturity ratings do not indicate effective, high-maturity practices. It is not that they appraisal process is faulty or that organizations are dishonest, merely that the maturity framework does not look deeply enough into all organizational practices". As pointed out by Moore in Chrissis et al. (2007) many 'good' practices were omitted from the CMMI because they could not be generalized to the broad audience of the model. In the case of RE process, omissions can especially be seen in components of RD PA (i.e., develop customer and product requirements, analyze and validate requirements) versus RE components commonly found in the literature (i.e., management, elicitation, analysis, specification, validation).

4. The CMMI-DEV process maturity profile, published in September 2009 and accessible from the SEI website, shows that the numbers of organizations adopting the model in most countries are still low (58% countries only have 10 or fewer appraisals) (SEI, 2009). The primary reason of not-adopting is high cost associated with the model (Staples et

al., 2006; Khurshid, Bannerman, & Staples, 2009). Other reasons include organizations were too small, organizations had no time, organizations were unsure of the SPI benefits, organizations had other priorities, and organizations were using another SPI approach (Staples et al., 2006; Khurshid et al., 2009).

RE Process Assessment and Improvements Models

The rest of this chapter reviews the four RE process improvement models: the REGPG introduced by Sommerville and Sawyer (1997), the REPM developed by Gorschek and Tejle (2002), the R-CMM by Beecham et al. (2003a; 2005), and the MDREPM by Gomes and Pettersson (2007). Each model is reviewed in terms of its principal characteristics and structure, and assessment and improvement framework applied. The chapter also reviews the use and evaluation or validation undergone by each model, which then reveals strengths, drawbacks and utility of each model.

The Requirements Engineering Good Practice (REGPG)

The Requirements Engineering Good Practice Guide (REGPG), or also known as the Requirements Engineering Process Maturity Model (Sommerville & Ransom, 2005), is probably the first public-domain process improvement and assessment model for RE. The REGPG is designed with three levels of Requirements Engineering process maturity that mirrors the first three levels (Initial, Repeatable, and Defined) in the SEI's Capability Maturity Model (CMM) for Software. The REGPG is purposely developed to complements the CMM, which does not cover RE processes. Only three levels were chosen because their initial work in formulating the model suggested that there were so few companies with defined RE processes that including the higher CMM levels (Sommerville & Ransom, 2005)

The three levels of REGPG are:

- **Level 1–Initial.** Organizations mature at this level do not have a defined RE process and often suffer from RE-related problems such as late delivery of products, budget over-runs, and poor requirements management.
- **Level 2–Repeatable.** Organizations mature at this level have explicit standards for requirements documents and have introduced policies and procedures for requirements management. Their Requirements Engineering processes may use some advanced tools and techniques.
- **Level 3–Managed.** At this level, the Requirements Engineering process for both management and engineering are documented, standardized and integrated into a standard process. They have an active process improvement program in place and can make objective assessments of the value of new methods and techniques.

The REGPG has 66 practices (called guidelines or also known as key practices in CMM) that were abstracted from existing standards, reports of requirements practices, and the experience of REAIMS partners (Sommerville & Ransom, 2005). The level of process maturity in the model reflects the extent that requirements practices are used and standardized in an organization. These practices are classified into *Basic*, *Immediate*, and *Advanced* practices. The REGPG presents the practices in the form of guidelines with each guideline detailing benefits, implementation, and problems of the practice. Furthermore, each guideline states cost of introduction and cost of application allowing organizations to make a cost/benefit analysis (Sommerville & Sawyer, 1997).

The 66 REGPG practices are also organized according to eight RE process activities, which are described in detail in Sommerville and Sawyer (1997). The process areas include: *the Requirement Document, Eliciting Requirements, Requirements Analysis and Negotiation, Describing Requirements, System Modeling, Requirements Validation, Requirements Management, and Critical System Requirements.* Unlike CMM, the process activities are not associated to a single maturity level. The REGPG uses a continuous representation rather than a staged one, which resembles the one used in CMMI. This allows organizations to achieve improvement by adopting practices across a range of process deliverables or activities.

RE Process Maturity Assessment of the REGPG

The method for the RE maturity assessment of this model includes a cyclical process (described in Sommerville & Ransom, 2005), which is an extension to the original method introduced in 1997:

1. Assess the RE process maturity of the organization.
2. Identify the most cost-effective improvements that can be introduced.
3. Implement the recommended improvements and re-assess the maturity level.

To assess process maturity, RE processes in an organization are examined against a checklist of the 66 REGPG guidelines. Against each guideline, the company practice is assessed and allocated a weighted score as being *Standardized - used throughout the company in a standardized way* (Score = 3), *Normal – used by many teams but in different way* (Score = 2), *Discretionary – used at the discretion of* individuals (Score = 1) or *Never Used* (Score = 0) (Sommerville & Ransom, 2005). The maturity level is calculated by summing the weighted scores for all implemented practices based on threshold levels in the model as summarized in Table 1. This assessment is able to tell companies about particular areas of weaknesses.

Table 1. REGPG process maturity levels (Sommerville & Ransom, 2005)

Level	Criteria
Initial	Score of above 54 in Basic Guidelines
Repeatable	Score of above 54 in Basic Guidelines and below 40 in (Intermediate + Advanced) Guidelines
Defined	Score of above 54 in Basic Guidelines and above 39 in (intermediate + Advanced) Guidelines

To help organizations who want to know what improvements could be introduced in the time available, the developed IMPRESSION tool (Sommerville & Ransom, 2005) would be used to recommend possible improvements.

Validation of the REGPG

Sawyer (2004) claims that the REGPG is considered as the longest-established and most widely-disseminated model that has undergone extensive validation with over 10,000 copies of the REGPG has been sold. Initially, the model has been validated and improved especially through a project called IMPRESSION (Sawyer, 2004; Sommerville & Ransom, 2005). In IMPRESSION project, the REGPG validation process involves nine companies in Greek from variety of domains. None had previous experience of formalized software process improvement. The validation results indicate that the RE maturity model is useful in supporting maturity assessment and in identifying process improvement. Also there is some evidence to suggest that process improvement leads to business benefits. Another validation of the REGPG was done through implementation of the model in four Finnish organizations (Kaupinnen, Aaltio, & Kujala, 2002).

These validations results include strengths and weaknesses of the REGPG. The validations performed not only demonstrated that it is a useful basis for supporting RE process improvement but

also confirm their hypothesis that improving RE process maturity could improve organizational business performance. The REGPG was originally developed for the safety-critical domain. Since the model was not the entirely generic (Sawyer, 2004), adaptation to the different domain is necessary but is currently lacking (Sommerville & Ransom, 2005). Furthermore, the classification of the good practices in the model with eight-level of cost of introduction of guidelines was perceived as far too complex.

The Requirements Engineering Process Maturity (REPM)

The Requirements Engineering Process Maturity (REPM) is developed by Gorschek and Tejle (2002) based on the REGPG, CMM and other studies on RE process improvement. However, unlike REGPG and R-CMM, the REPM was designed only for evaluating the RE process maturity of a project and not for the whole of an organization. Results of a project evolution are then expected to give 'idea' on what can be done to improve the RE process of the evaluated project. The REPM is developed with five maturity levels based on the CMM framework. These maturity levels (explained in detail in Gorschek & Tejle, 2002) include the following:

- **REPM 1–Initial (Wood).** At this level, the Requirements Engineering process is very poor and not necessarily repeatable. Organizations at this level typically do not provide a stable development environment where projects typically abandon planned procedures; revert to coding and testing, and no validation of requirements.
- **REPM 2–Basic (Bronze).** At this level, the Requirements Engineering process is more structured and complete. To ensure repeatability, organizations at this level have policies of standardized requirements specifications and documentations, and

stakeholders are identified. Organizations may denote separate resources for Requirements Engineering process but may not take notice on the system environment such as application domain or business processes.

- **REPM 3–Formulated (Silver).** At this level, application domain and business processes are studied and taken into consideration, and all stakeholders are consulted. The requirements are prioritized and re-prioritized in case of new requirements, and the dependencies, interactions and conflicts between requirements are taken into consideration too. In addition, risk assessment is conducted on selected requirements.
- **REPM 4–Developed (Gold).** At this level, human domain and business domain are taken into consideration. In addition, advanced risk assessment and traceability are performed. A well scrutinized and standardized Requirements Engineering process is present but not planned and systematic requirements and systematic requirements reuse structure.
- **REPM 5–Advanced (Platinum).** At this level, requirements reuse is performed whenever possible and rejected requirements are documented. In addition, architectural models are created, system model paraphrasing is used to validate requirements, and advanced requirements re-prioritization is performed.

The REPM model is organized into a logical and expandable tree-structure. At the top of the structure are three main areas of Requirements Engineering activities (*Requirements Elicitation, Requirements Analysis and Negotiation, and Requirements Management)*, called *Main Process Areas (MPAs)* (Gorschek & Tejle, 2002). MPAs are also known as process areas in CMM and REGPG. However, MPAs are different to process

areas in the REGPG where it is not obligatory to implement practices for each process activity in order to achieve a maturity level (Sawyer, 2004). Under each MPAs are typically several *Sub Process Areas (SPAs)* and at the bottom of the structure are several *Actions* (analogous to CMM key practices or REGPG practices). Actions denote an activity and/or something that should present in the project. Actions are general in nature and mapped to the five maturity levels of REPM. The model was structured in such a way to enable its content to be arranged in a way that does not hinder further development of the model (Gorschek & Tejle, 2002). Strangely, although these levels could denote RE process maturity of a project, organizations are not required or recommended to get all their projects to reside on the highest maturity level.

RE Process Maturity Assessment of the REPM

Like the REGPG, a checklist (known as *Project Evaluation Checklist*) of 60 Actions is used when assessing RE process maturity of projects. An Action can be evaluated as in three states: *completed, not completed,* and *satisfied-explained.* Action is given satisfied-explained state, which carry the same weight as completed state, if it is not completed or partially completed but not applicable to the RE process of the organization evaluating the project. When REPM assessment checklist is completed, the results are added up according to REPM level. A project needs to have *completed* or *satisfied*-explained all of the Actions associated with a certain REPM level to achieve a maturity level (Gorschek & Tejle, 2002).

Validation of the REPM

The validation performed to the REPM involves two parts. The first part was done by interviewing a senior project manager with more than 10 years experience in software development outside his/

her own company and the company has at least 10 years experience in the field of Software Engineering. The interview results indicate that the REPM model was a good initiative and could be helpful in improving the Requirements Engineering process (Gorschek & Tejle, 2002). The second part of validation was performed through evaluating four different projects conducted by four different companies. These were Small Medium Enterprises (SMEs) of the size for which REPM was designed. The dual purpose of the project evaluation was to use the model in industry to validate its contents and structure, and to validate the REPM evaluation checklist developed by using it. The results indicate that its lightweight assessment method yields useful results and the model appears to show promise as an assessment tool for SMEs. However, focus of the evaluation is more to the validation of the model's generality rather than the model's applicability (Sawyer, 2004).

The Requirements Capability Maturity Model (R-CMM)

The Requirements Capability Maturity Model (R-CMM) (Beecham et al., 2003a) is also known as the University of Hertfordshire Model (Sawyer, 2004). This model provides guidelines for practitioners, to understand their own RE process and go through the many stages involved in RE process improvement. The R-CMM is a direct adaptation of the newer version of the CMM i.e. Software Capability Maturity Model (SW_CMM). The R-CMM uses the five SW_CMM maturity levels to classify RE processes. This model uses a Goal Question Process Metric (GQM) approach to guide organization to look at their current practices and set realistic goals when planning for requirements engineering process improvement. The five R-CMM levels, explained in detail in Beecham et al. (2003a; 2005b), are:

- **R-CMM Level 1:** The goal of this level is to raise awareness of the requirements

process, and an organization at this level has ad-hoc requirements processes and requirements problems are common. Organizations at this level are working towards developing a disciplined process.

- **R-CMM Level 2:** The goal of this level is to implement a repeatable requirements process. A company at this level has repeatable requirements processes, focus on establishing project level standards, and standard requirements processes are documented and instituted within similar projects. Organizations at this level are working towards a standard consistent process.

- **R-CMM Level 3:** The goal of this level is to implement a defined requirements process. A level 3 organization has company-wide communication and standardization of requirements processes instituted across all projects. Organizations at this level are working towards a predictable process.

- **R-CMM Level 4:** The goal of this level is to implement a managed requirements process. A level 4 organization has requirements processes that are measured to control the processes and assess where improvements are needed. Organizations at this level are working towards a continuously improving the process.

- **R-CMM Level 5:** The goal of this level is to implement an optimizing requirements process. A level 5 organization has improved requirements methods/tools that are instituted within a stable and predictable environment. Organizations at this level are working towards a continuous process improvement.

The goal of each level is then decomposed into 5 requirements related questions that are used to recognized requirements process stages (called phases). The phases are *requirements management, elicitation, analysis and negotiation, documentation,* and *verification and validation*. Like

REPM MPAs, each phase in the R-CMM defines a set of processes (also called key processes in Beecham et al. (2003b) at each maturity level. This model recognizes a total of 68 processes from three main sources: SW_CMM, empirical research (including Hall, Beecham, & Rainer, 2002), and literature. To aid interpretation and correct implementation, a more detailed guideline for each process was planned. The detailed guideline retains the Goal Question Process Metric framework and each guideline of a process prescribes lower level processes (also called sub-processes) needed to achieve improvement goals. However, at the time of writing, only detailed guidelines of level 2 had been completed and tested while guidelines of levels 3 to 5 remain exist in draft form.

RE Process Maturity Assessment of the R-CMM

Process assessment of R-CMM is carried out by allocating a score (outstanding=10, qualified=8, marginally qualified=6, fair=4, weak=2, and poor=0) to each process against three assessment criteria (approach, deployment, and results). These assessment criteria are adopted from the assessment method used in Motorola as explained in Daskalantonakis (1994). The average of the score for approach, deployment and results are recorded for each process. Then the scores are summed for each phase and the sum of all five phases yields an overall/ capability score that highlights where their requirements process weakness. The overall/ capability score and its maturity level are as the following:

- 0->2: Level 1,
- 3->4: Level 2,
- 5->6: Level 3,
- 7->8: Level 4, and
- 9->10: Level 5.

The authors claimed that only after performing this assessment, which could help organizations understand their current processes and problems areas, an organization can set and work on realistic RE process improvement goals.

Validation of the R-CMM

Validation of the R-CMM was performed involving a group of SPI and RE experts. Beecham and colleagues (2005) define an expert as "a person who has either (a) published widely in recognized journals in the field of RE and/or SPI; or (b) has practical experience of RE and/or SPI–working in the field for several years and holding positions of responsibility". Twenty experts participated in the validation process by examining the model components and completing a detailed questionnaire.

The R-CMM was tested against 7 success criteria: *adherence to CMM characteristics, limited scope, consistency, understandable, ease of use, tailorable, and verifiable*. The experts viewed the R-CMM as an independent from the SW_CMM and strongly support the question of "it would be helpful to provide guidelines for all processes listed in the level 2 models" (Beecham et al., 2005) suggests strength of the model. The questionnaire responses also highlight some weaknesses of the R-CMM such as the model is unlikely to appeal to all practitioners and researchers, the model cannot relate to all kinds of RE development processes, and the model presentation does not reflect the on-going, cyclical nature of RE process. Furthermore, the model may remain partially-completed until the subsequent development can complete levels 3 to 5.

The Market-Driven Requirements Engineering Process Model (MDREPM)

The Market-Driven Requirements Engineering Process Model (MDREPM) is developed specifically to be used by organizations developing software to a market rather than a specific customer (also known as a market-driven environment) (Gomes & Pettersson, 2007). The MDREM consists of a collection of practices and an assessment model. Furthermore, it provides software organizations with a step by step process improvement path towards a better requirements engineering process. They achieve this by organizing the good practices in 5 different maturity levels (spanning from Level 1 to Level 5), and also indicating dependencies between practices that should be considered when deciding to implement them (i.e., recommended pre-requisite practices and related practices).

The architecture of the MDREPM consists of elements such as *process areas, sub-process areas, practices and maturity levels* (similar to REPM MPAs and SPAs). This model recognizes a total of 76 practices organized in 5 process areas (similar to the PAs of the CMMI-DEV). The process areas in the model include *Organizational Support, Release Planning, Requirements Management, Requirements Elicitation, and Requirements Analysis.* The MDREPM enables assessment and improvement using two representations: *Practices by Process Areas* and *Practices by (maturity) Levels.* Table 2 lists process areas and sub-process areas applied in the model. Elaboration of practices for each process area in the model is available in the Gomes and Pettersson (2007).

In the Practices by Level representation, the maturity levels of the MDREPM include the following:

- Level 1–organizations at this level are expected to implement basic practices related to process areas *Organizational Support, Requirements Management, and Requirements Elicitation*.
- Level 2–organizations at this level are expected to gain better understanding of their own strengths and weaknesses. Basic practices of *Release Planning* and *Requirements Analysis* process areas and advanced practices of the other process areas should be implemented at this level.
- Level 3–organizations at this level are expected to implement strategies to guide release planning, basic practices for requirements prioritization, and practices of Requirements Management that could produce requirements, which are understandable for different audiences and usable for different purposes.
- Level 4–advanced practices of *Prioritization* sub-process area and a practice for product portfolio management are expected to be performed by organization at this level.
- Level 5–organizations at this level are expected to perform advanced practices in Release *Planning* and *Requirements Elicitation*.

Table 2. The MDREPM process areas and sub-process areas

Process Area	Sub-process Area
Organizational Support	Strategic Marketing
Release Planning	Prioritization
Requirements Management	Configuration Management Requirements Traceability Requirements Specification
Requirements Elicitation	Techniques Practices
Requirements Analysis	None

RE Process Maturity Assessment of the MDREPM

The MDREPM uses questionnaires approach to evaluate each practice of all process areas in the model, which is very similar to the assessment checklist used in REGPG and REPM. The questions are asked in the same order as practices are presented in the Practices *by Process Area* representation of the model. Three answer options are provided: *yes, no,* or *satisfied/explained*. The *satisfied/explained* concept is similar with action state of the REPM since the authors borrowed the concept from the REPM. This concept is expected to help measure *model lag* (Gomes & Pettersson, 2007) which indicate usefulness of the model to the industry. A high lag exists when several practices are assessed as satisfied/explained, which means these practices are not applicable to an organization. A graph is used to represent series of the maximum number of practices that can be fulfilled in each maturity level, series of *fulfilled* practices, and series of satisfied/explained practices. The model lag is viewed as the area between the fulfilled and satisfied/explained series where the lower the area, i.e. the model lags, the higher the model, and vice versa.

Validation of the MDREPM

Like the REPM, validation performed to the MDREPM involves two stages known as static and dynamic validations. The static validation was intended to analyze the model completeness, effectiveness and usefulness prior to performing the dynamic validation which was to evaluate the model usefulness and applicability in industry. The static validation involved review with checklist and semi-structured interviews with two researchers who have a different background on market-driven requirements engineering in addition to their own research specialization. Based on results of the static validation, significant changes were incorporated to the model structure. The

dynamic validation stage of the model involved performing case studies with three organizations. In all cases, the model was acknowledged to be useful which was shown by the low model lag. However, the large model size could pose an issue to its usability in the industry.

SUMMARY AND CONCLUSION

This chapter presents a review of selected RE-specific and generic process improvement standards and models that exist in the literature and are publicly available. Preliminary information presented in this chapter is hoped to help organizations in selecting these different types of improvement standards and models, which best suit their specific context and available resources. We explained how the CMMI-DEV v1.2 addresses RE maturity in the model. We also discussed several issues of the model related to RE (e.g., the order of RE implementation and institutionalization in the CMMI-DEV is not always logical, the low rate of adoption in most countries due to high cost associated with the model, and etc). Then, we described the principal characteristics of four RE process assessment and improvement models: the REGPG, the REPM, the R-CMM, and the MDREPM. We also reviewed the structure, assessment and improvement framework applied in these models as well as the validation undergone by each model.

In general, all the RE-specific process improvement models reviewed were developed either directly or indirectly based on the retired CMM or SW_CMM. The REGPG was entirely based on the CMM. The REPM inherits, though not entirely, characteristics of the CMM and the REGPG. Unlike the first two models, the R-CMM was developed based on the newer version of the CMM (i.e., SW_CMM) and is the only one that applied the GQM approach in defining the RE practices of its maturity level. The MDREPM borrowed heavily the REPM's characteristic but focuses at the market-driven RE. These models use either a three-level or five-level maturity model. Each maturity level of the models is defined with a set of RE practices and each practice is classified according to RE process areas or activities (called phases in R-CMM). Although they are referring to the same thing, the terms used to refer to the RE practices are different in different model: in REGPG–good practice guideline; in REPM–actions; in R-CMM–processes; and in MDREPM – practices. Unlike CMM and SW_CMM KPAs, the RE process areas of all the models are not associated with a single maturity level. Additionally, the REPM MPAs and MDREPM process areas are also different to the process areas of the CMM, SW_CMM, REGPG and R-CMM where it is not

obligatory to implement practices of each RE process area to achieve a given maturity level.

Each RE practice of the different models is supplemented with different levels of details. For example, the REGPG provides each practice with detailed descriptions of benefits, implementation, and cost and problems in implementing the practice. Whereas, contrast to the REGPG practices, each action in the REPM is only described using a one-sentence statement about the action. This is probably caused by the different structures used by each of these models as described earlier. The model sizes (i.e., number of practices defined) of the REGPG, REPM and R-CMM range from 60 to 68. However, the number is slightly higher for the MDREPM (i.e. 76 practices), which may pose an issue to the model usability in the targeted industry.

Table 3. Summary of the RE process improvement model

	REGPG	REPM	R-CMM	MDREPM
Maturity levels	• 3	• 5	• 5	• 5
Theoretical base to develop the model	• CMM for Software	• CMM for Software • REGPG	• SW_CMM • Goal-Question-Process-Metric (GQM)	• REPM • CMMI
CMM key process area analogues	• 8 Process Areas	• 3 Process areas	• 5 Phases	• 5 Process Areas
CMM key practice analogues	• 66 good practice guide-lines Categorised into Basic, Immediate, Advanced	• 60 Actions	• 68 Key Processes	• 76 market-driven good RE practices
Applicability of assessment/im-provement	• Organisation	• Project	• Organisation	• Organisation
Validation	• IMPRESSION project – Nine companies in Greek • Four Finnish organisa-tions	• Part 1: One project managers • Part 2: Four projects in 4 different companies	• Twenty experts panel	• Static validation: Two other researchers focus-ing at market-driven RE • Dynamic validation: Three organizations
Method used in validation process	• Implementation of model in industry	• Part 1: Interview project managers • Part 2: assess projects in industry	• Review model com-ponent and complete questionnaire	• Static validation: model review via a checklist and interview • Dynamic validation: assess market-driven RE practices in the organiza-tions

continued on following page

Table 3. continued

Process maturity assessment mechanism	• Assessment checklist of the guidelines 　　Score of each guideline: 　　Standardise =3 　　Normal use=2 　　Discretionary=1 　　Never=0.	• Assessment checklist of projects' action 　　States of each action: 　　Completed 　　Not completed 　　Satisfied-explained • Determine model lag	• Assessment checklist of processes 　　Score of each process: 　　Outstanding=10 　　Qualified=8 　　Marginally qualified=6 　　Fair=4 　　Weak=2 　　Poor=0 　　Criteria: approach, deployment, results	• Assessment questionnaire sheet 　　Answer options of each practice: 　　Yes (Fulfilled) 　　No (Not Fulfilled) 　　Satisfied-explained
Process maturity determination	• Points scored map into maturity levels:	• To achieve a maturity level, all actions in the level and all actions from lower levels (if any) have to be completed or satisfied-explained.	• Average of criteria score/ process summed/phase; sum of all phases determine maturity level.	• Used the similar REPM concept to determine process maturity and model lag
Model strengths	• Identify areas of weaknesses and allow organisations to select practical options for improvement • Suitable for organizations to begin an RE process improvement program	• A promising lightweight assessment tool for SMEs	• Controls, prioritise and measures RE processes • Guides practitioners to relate process improvement activities to goals • Provide detailed guidance for each RE process	• A reference model specific to market-driven RE
Main limitations	• Classification of good guidelines too complex. • Model is not entirely generic since it was initially developed specific for the safety-critical application domain. Hence, adaptation to different domain is necessary but currently lacking. • Implicit dependencies between practices were sometimes wrong	• Focus at projects evaluation and not the whole of an organization • Focus at process assessment only (for process improvement need to use other model) • Model acts as a checklist of what RE practices to be implemented in a project)	• Model is not completely developed since its Level 3 to 5 only exist in draft form • Model cannot relate to all types of RE process model • Model structure too rigid • Model presentation does not reflect iterative RE process	• Applicability limited to market-driven RE • Focus at providing fast process assessment only (to easily identify problem areas in the RE) • Large model size may pose an issue to its usability in industry

Similar validations were performed to the REPM and MDREPM. Preliminary validation of the models involves model review by different experts (i.e., an experienced project manager for REGPG, and two market-driven RE researchers for the MDREPM). Additionally, both models were validated by assessing projects and RE practices in several related organizations in the industry. The R-CMM, whereas, only rely on review of model components and questionnaire, which involved twenty SPI and RE experts in the academia and industry. Of all the four models, the REGPG is the only one that has been implemented in the industry and it is also continuously validated and improved by the model authors.

Despite the earlier mentioned differences, there are three process areas commonly defined by the models, which include requirements elicitation, requirements analysis and negotiation, and requirements management. On top of these three process areas, the R-CMM is defined with two others (i.e., documentation, and verification and validation). The REGPG, with the most process areas defined in it; in addition to the R-CMM process areas also include describing requirements, system modeling, and critical system requirements. These additional process areas are included since the model was originally developed for a safety-critical domain. However, this has caused the REGPG to be less generic and adaptation to the different domain is necessary but is currently lacking. Additionally, although RE process maturity is determined in each model using different formulas and approaches, all the models use a similar assessment checklist of RE practices when assessing RE process maturity of projects or organizations. Table 3 summarizes several characteristics of each model, which include a list of strengths and limitations of the models.

Although deficient, attempts by all the reviewed RE-specific and generic process improvement models to define levels of maturity for RE processes are admirable. We appreciate that these standards and models are not perfect models of RE process assessment and improvement, but as Paulk, Weber, Curtis, and Chrissis (1995) admit, "all models are wrong; some are useful". Despite their deficiencies, models such as the REGPG and CMMI are still widely used. Sawyer (2004), for instance, claims that over 10,000 copies of the REGPG have been sold. Also, the process maturity profile, from 2002 through June 2009, published by SEI (SEI, 2009) states that 25, 013 projects worldwide have been appraised with the SCAMPI Appraisals using CMMI v 1.1 or v1.2. Perhaps, future research may be required to enhance, complement or eliminate the deficiencies of these models, which in turn would improve the applicability and useful of the models in the system or software development industry.

REFERENCES

Badariah, S., Sahibuddin, S., & Azim, A. A. A. (2009). Requirements engineering problems and practices in software companies: An industrial survey. In *Proceedings of International Conference on Advanced Software Engineering and Its Application, ASEA 2009 Held as Part of the Future Generation Information Technology, FGIT 2009* (pp. 70-77). Jeju Island, Korea.

Beecham, S., Hall, T., Britton, C., Cottee, M., & Rainer, A. (2005). Using an expert panel to validate a requirements process improvement model. *Journal of Systems and Software, 76*, 251–275. doi:10.1016/j.jss.2004.06.004

Beecham, S., Hall, T., & Rainer, A. (2003a). *Defining a requirements process improvement model* (Technical Report No. 379). University of Hertfordshire, Hatfield.

Beecham, S., Hall, T., & Rainer, A. (2003b). Software process improvement problems in twelve software companies: An empirical analysis. *Empirical Software Engineering, 8*(1), 7–42. doi:10.1023/A:1021764731148

Beecham, S., Hall, T., & Rainer, A. (2005). Defining a requirements process improvement model. *Software Quality Journal, 13*(3), 247–279. doi:10.1007/s11219-005-1752-9

Chrissis, M. B., Konrad, M., & Shrum, S. (2007). *CMMI: Guidelines for process integration and product improvement* (2nd ed.). Upper Saddle River, NJ: Addison Wesley.

Daskalantonakis, M. K. (1994). Achieving higher SEI levels. *IEEE Software, 11*(4), 17–24. doi:10.1109/52.300079

Drouin, J. (1999). The SPICE project. In Emam, K. E., & Madhavji, N. H. (Eds.), *Elements of software process assessment and improvement* (pp. 45–56). California: IEEE Computer Society.

Gomes, A., & Pettersson, A. (2007). *Market-driven requirements engineering process model – MDREPM* (Master's thesis). Blekinge Institute of Technology, Sweden.

Gorschek, T., & Tejle, K. (2002). *A method for assessing requirements engineering process maturity in software projects* (Master's thesis). Blekinge Institute of Technology, Sweden.

Hall, T., Beecham, S., & Rainer, A. (2002). Requirements problems in twelve software companies: An empirical analysis. *IEEE Proceedings of Software*, *149*(5), 153–160. doi:10.1049/ip-sen:20020694

Hansen, B., Rose, J., & Tjørnehøj, G. (2004). Prescription, description, reflection: The shape of the software process improvement field. *International Journal of Information Management*, *24*(6), 457–472. doi:10.1016/j.ijinfomgt.2004.08.007

Kauppinen, M., Aaltio, T., & Kujala, S. (2002). Lessons learned from applying the requirements engineering good practice guide for process improvement. In *Proceedings of Seventh European Conference on Software Quality (QC2002)* (pp. 73-81). Helsinki, Finland.

Khurshid, N., Bannerman, P. L., & Staples, M. (2009). Overcoming the first hurdle: Why organizations do not adopt CMMI. In *Proceedings of the International Conference on Software Process* (pp. 38-49). Vancouver, Canada.

Linscomb, D. (2003). Requirements engineering maturity in the CMMI. *The Journal of Defense Software Engineering.* Retrieved October 11, 2009, from http://www.stsc.hill.af.mil./crosstalk/2003/12/ 0312linscomb.html

Napier, N. P., Mathiassen, L., & Johnson, R. (2009). Combining perceptions and prescriptions in requirements engineering process assessment: An industrial case study. *IEEE Transactions on Software Engineering*, *35*(5), 593–606. doi:10.1109/TSE.2009.33

Niazi, M., & Shastry, S. (2003). Role of requirements engineering in software development process: An empirical study. In. *Proceedings of IEEE INMIC*, *2003*, 402–407.

Nielsen, P. A., & Pries-Heje, J. (2002). A framework for selecting an assessment strategy. In Mathiassen, L., Pries-Heje, J., & Ngwenyama, O. (Eds.), *Improving software organizations: From principles to practice.* New Jersey: Addison-Wesley.

Paulk, M. C., Weber, C. V., Curtis, B., & Chrissis, M. B. (1995). The capability maturity model: Guidelines for improving the software process. In Institute, C. M. U. S. E. (Ed.), *The SEI Series in Software Engineering.* Reading, MA: Addison Wesley Longman Inc.

Sanders, M., & Richardson, I. (2007). Research into long-term improvements in small- to medium-sized organizations using SPICE as a framework for standards. *Software Process Improvement and Practice*, *12*, 351–359. doi:10.1002/spip.319

Sawyer, P. (2004). Maturing requirements engineering process maturity models. In Maté, J., & Silva, A. (Eds.), *Requirements engineering for socio-technical systems* (pp. 84–99). Hershey, PA: Idea Group Inc.doi:10.4018/978-1-59140-506-1.ch006

Software Engineering Institute. (2009). *Process maturity profiles.* Retrieved November 25, 2009, from http://www.sei.cmu.edu/cmmi/casestudies/profiles/pdfs/upload/2009SeptCMMI.pdf

Sommerville, I., & Ransom, J. (2005). An empirical study of industrial requirements engineering process assessment and improvement. *ACM Transactions on Software Engineering and Methodology*, *14*(1), 85–117. doi:10.1145/1044834.1044837

Sommerville, I., & Sawyer, P. (1997). *Requirements engineering: A good practice guide.* Chichester, UK: John Wiley and Sons.

Staples, M., Niazi, M., Jeffery, R., Abrahams, A., Byatt, P., & Murphy, R. (2006). An exploratory study why organizations do not adopt CMMI. *The Journal of Systems and Software, 80*(2007), 883-895.

Std, I. E. E. E. (1998a). *IEEE guide for developing system requirements specifications* (pp. 1233–1998). New York: The Institute of Electrical and Electronics Engineers, Inc.

Std, I. E. E. E. (1998b). *IEEE recommended practice for software requirements specifications* (pp. 830–1998). New York: The Institute of Electrical and Electronics Engineers, Inc.

Steinen, H. (1999). Software process assessment and improvement: Five years of experiences with BOOTSTRAP. In Emam, K. E., & Madhavji, N. H. (Eds.), *Elements of software process assessment and improvement* (pp. 57–76). California: IEEE Computer Society.

Weissfelner, S. (1999). ISO 9001 for software organizations. In Emam, K. E., & Madhavji, N. H. (Eds.), *Elements of software process assessment and improvement* (pp. 77–100). California: IEEE Computer Society.

Wiegers, K. (2003). *Software requirements* (2nd ed.). Redmond, CA: Microsoft Press.

Young, R. R. (2001). *Effective requirements practices*. Boston, MA: Addison-Wesley.

Chapter 3
The Development of International Standards to Facilitate Process Improvements for Very Small Entities

Claude Y. Laporte
École de Technologie Supérieure, Canada

Edgardo Palza Vargas
École de Technologie Supérieure, Canada

ABSTRACT

Industry recognizes that Very Small Entities (VSEs) that develop software are very important to the economy. A Very Small Entity (VSE) is an entity (enterprise, organization, department or project) with up to 25 people..Failure to deliver a quality product on time and within budget threatens the competitiveness of VSEs and impacts their customers. One way to mitigate these risks is to put in place proven software engineering practices. Many international standards and models, like ISO/IEC 12207 or CMMI®1, have been developed to capture proven engineering practices. However, these documents were not designed for VSEs and are often difficult to apply in such settings. This chapter presents a description of the development of process improvement international standards (IS) targeting VSEs developing or maintaining software as a standalone product or software as a component of a system. The documents used by ISO/IEC JTC1/SC72 Working Group 24 (WG24), mandated to develop a set of standards and guides, and the approach that led to the development, balloting of the ISs, and TRs (Technical Reports) for VSEs are also presented. The chapter focuses on the ISO/IEC 29110 Standard3, the development of means to help VSEs improve their processes, and the description of a few pilot projects conducted to implement the processes of ISO/IEC 29110 standard.

DOI: 10.4018/978-1-61350-141-2.ch003

INTRODUCTION

Most software engineering centers, such as the Software Engineering Institute (SEI), dedicate a large portion of their resources to large organizations. Even though there seems to be an awareness of the needs of Very Small Entities (VSEs), a VSE is an entity (enterprise, organization, department or project) with up to 25 people, published software engineering practices are still for the most part difficult to use by organizations with up to 25 people. A few centers around the world are focusing their Software Process Improvement (SPI) activities on small enterprises and VSEs. Some centers and initiatives and their accomplishments in helping VSEs are discussed in (Laporte, Alexandre, & O'Connor, 2008; Laporte, Alexandre, & Renault, 2008; Oktaba et al., 2007; Laporte, April, & Renault, 2005; Habra, Alexandre, Desharnais, Laporte, & Renault, 2008).

Since a standard from the International Organization for Standardization (ISO) dedicated to software life cycle processes was already available, i.e. ISO/IEC 12207 (ISO/IEC 12207, 2008), WG24 decided to use the concept of the ISO Standardized Profile (SP) to develop the new standards for VSEs. A profile is defined as "a set of one or more base standards and/or SPs, and, where applicable, the identification of chosen classes, conforming subsets, options and parameters of those base standards, or SPs necessary to accomplish a particular function" (ISO/IEC TR 10000-1, 1998). From a practical point of view, a profile is a matrix that identifies the elements that are taken from existing standards from those that are not to produce a Standardized Profile. The overall approach followed by WG24 to develop this standard for VSEs consisted of six steps:

- Select, from existing standards, process subsets applicable to VSEs;
- Develop a roadmap to help VSE grow their capabilities;
- Tailor the subset to fit VSE needs;

- Develop International Standard (ISs) and Technical Report (TRs);
- Produce guides which are easy to understand, affordable, and usable by VSEs;
- Develop means to accelerate the adoption and implementation of the ISs and TRs.

In the next section, the standards that have been used by WG24 to develop the ISs and TRs for VSEs are described.

STANDARDS USED TO DEVELOP STANDARDS FOR VSES

ISO/IEC 12207–Software Life Cycle Processes[4]

ISO/IEC 12207 establishes a framework for software life cycle processes and terminology: "It applies to the acquisition of systems and software products and services, to the supply, development, operation, maintenance, and disposal of software products and the software portion of a system, whether performed internally or externally to an organization" (ISO/IEC 12207, 2008). This standard defines two sets of processes (see Figure 1): in one of these, called Software Specific Processes, the final product is a standalone software product or service, and in another, called System Context Processes, the software is part of a larger system. Since most modern systems are controlled by software, this standard has been updated in 2008 to 'interface' with the equivalent standard at the systems engineering level: ISO/IEC 15288:2008 Systems engineering – Systems life cycle processes (ISO/IEC 15288, 2008).

Each ISO 12207 process is described in terms of the following attributes, as defined in ISO TR 24774 (ISO/IEC TR 24774, 2010):

- A title, which conveys the scope of the process as a whole. The title of a process is a

Figure 1. Life cycle process groups (adapted from (ISO/IEC 12207, 2008))

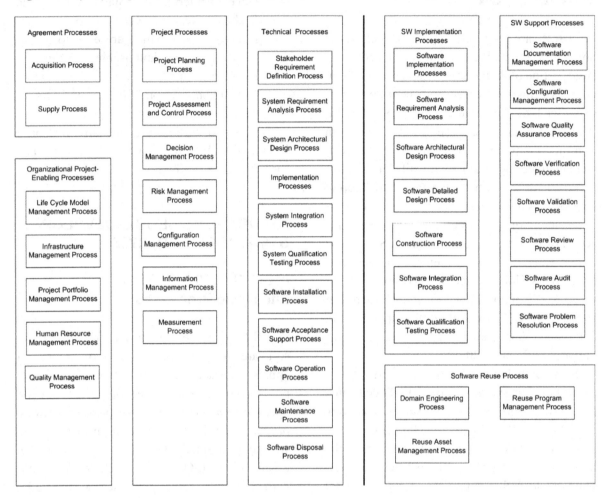

short noun phrase intended to summarize the scope of the process.

- A purpose, which describes the goals of the process.
- A set of outcomes, which expresses what is expected from the execution of the process. An outcome is an observable result of the successful achievement of the process purpose.
- A set of activities, which is a list of actions that may be used to achieve the outcomes. Each activity may be further elaborated as a grouping of related lower-level actions (e.g. a task)
- A set of tasks, which is a list of specific actions that may be performed to achieve

an activity. Multiple related tasks are often grouped within an activity.

To illustrate the structure and content of the ISO 12207 standard, the software configuration management process is used as an example (see Figure 2).

As has been explained previously, such a high-level description of a ISO 12207 process is almost useless to most VSEs, since these organizations do not have the expertise, the budget to hire an external consultant or the time to transform the processes of ISO 12207 into a set of usable processes.

Figure 2. Software configuration management process (adapted from (ISO/IEC 12207, 2008))

Purpose

The purpose of the Software Configuration Management Process is to establish and maintain the integrity of the software items of a process or project, and make them available to concerned parties.

Outcomes

As a result of the successful implementation of the Software Configuration Management Process:

- a software configuration management strategy is developed;
- items generated by the process or project are identified, defined, and baselined;
- modifications and releases of the items are controlled;
- modifications and releases are made available to affected parties;
- the status of the items and modifications is recorded and reported;
- the completeness and consistency of the items is ensured; and
- the storage, handling, and delivery of the items are controlled.

Activities and Tasks

The project shall implement the following activities in accordance with applicable organization policies and procedures with respect to the Software Configuration Management Process:

Process Implementation. This activity consists of the following task:

A software configuration management plan shall be developed. The plan shall describe: the configuration management activities; procedures and schedule for performing these activities; the organization(s) responsible for performing these activities; and their relationship with other organizations, such as software development or maintenance. The plan shall be documented and implemented.

NOTE: The plan may be a part of the System Configuration Management Plan.

Configuration Identification. This activity consists of the following task:

A scheme shall be established for identification of software items and their versions to be controlled for the project. For each software item and its versions, the following shall be identified: the documentation that establishes the baseline; the version references; and other identification details.

Configuration Control. This activity consists of the following tasks:

Change requests shall be identified and recorded; the changes shall be analyzed and evaluated; the request shall be approved or not; and the modified software item shall be implemented, verified, and released. An audit trail shall exist, whereby each modification, the reason for the modification, and authorization of the modification can be traced. Control and audit of all accesses to the controlled software items that handle safety- or security-critical functions shall be performed.

NOTE: The Software Problem Resolution Management Process could provide support for this activity.

Configuration Status Accounting. This activity consists of the following task:

Management records and status reports that show the status and history of controlled software items including baseline shall be prepared. Status reports should include the number of changes for a project, the latest software item versions, release identifiers, the number of releases, and comparisons of releases.

Configuration Evaluation. This activity consists of the following task:

The functional completeness of the software items against their requirements and the physical completeness of the software items (whether or not their design and code reflect an up-to-date technical description) shall be determined and ensured.

Release Management and Delivery. This activity consists of the following tasks:

The release and delivery of software products and documentation shall be formally controlled. Master copies of code and documentation shall be maintained for the life of the software product. The code and documentation that contain safety- or security-critical functions shall be handled, stored, packaged, and delivered in accordance with the policies of the organizations involved.

ISO/IEC 15289–Content of Systems and Software Life Cycle Process Information Products (Documentation)[5]

This standard is a companion standard to ISO 12207. It is used to identify and plan the information items to be produced during a project. It describes the information content of different types of documents, such as a record or a plan. Table 1 lists the different types of documents described in the ISO 15289 standard (ISO/IEC 15289, 2006).

Since most VSEs are not prone to documenting their project activities, and since most practitioners do not like to produce documentation, we can hardly expect them to develop a set of templates which describes the content and format of documents produced during a project.

In a section below, we will describe a new type of document, called Deployment Package (DP), designed to help VSEs implement some ISO 12207 processes and produce useful project documentation.

A Mexican National Standard, MoProSoft

A Mexican standard has been developed with three levels of decisions in mind, as illustrated in Figure 3: the decisions made by top-level management, those made by middle management, and those made by the people who develop projects.

Processes are grouped into three categories: Top Management, Middle management, and Operations (adapted from (NMX-059-NYCE, 2005)):

Table 1. Life cycle product types (adapted from (ISO/IEC 15289, 2006)

Type	Purpose	Sample of recommended output information types
Record	Characterized the data retained by an organizational entity	Configuration record Problem record
Description	Represents a planned or actual function, design, or item	High level software design description
Plan	Define when how, and by whom specific activities or tasks, including tools needed	Project management plan
Procedure	Define in detail when and how to perform certain activities or tasks, including tools needed	Problem resolution procedure
Report	Describe the results of activities such as investigations, assessment, and tests	Problem report Validation report
Request	Record information needed to solicit a response	Change request
Specification	Specify a required function, performance or process (such as, requirements specification, standard, policy)	Software requirement specification

Figure 3. MoProSoft's process categories (Oktaba et al., 2007)

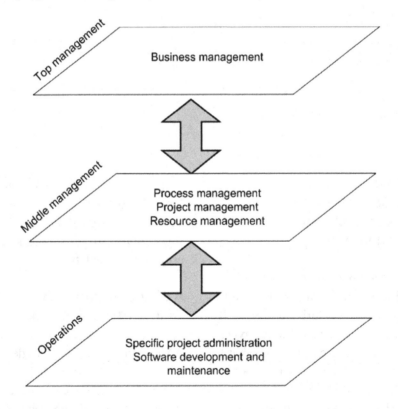

- **Top management.** Members in this category are concerned with business-management practices, and receive and direct reports from middle management.

- **Middle management.** Members in this category deal with process-, project-, and resource management practices in line with top management's business goals. They provide elements for the performance of operations processes receive and evaluate the information those processes generate, and inform top management of the results. The resource management process includes three sub processes: human resources and work environment; goods, services, and infrastructure; and knowledge of the organization.

- **Operations.** Members in this category address the practices of software-development and -maintenance projects. They perform activities using elements provided by management, and deliver reports and the software products generated.

The approach used by WG24 to develop a set of international standards and technical reports is described in the next section.

THE APPROACH USED BY WG24

Since WG24 wanted to prepare an initial set of standards as quickly as possible, WG24 analyzed international reference standards and models that could help subset ISO 12207 for VSEs. To create these initial products quickly, WG24 began a search for existing standards or models that could be tailored or adapted to the needs of VSEs. The MoProSoft standard (NMX-059-NYCE, 2005), developed to assist small and medium-sized enterprises (SMEs), was selected to achieve this objective.

WG24 decided to use the notion of the profile to develop standards to meet the needs of VSEs. A profile is a grouping of one or more base standards to accomplish a particular function. The notion of the profile was selected for the following reasons (adapted from (ISO/IEC 29110-2, 2011))

- Standards generally target large enterprises, making initial compliance difficult for VSEs;

- Preparing profiles with progressive capability levels enables a stepwise approach to full compliance;
- SE Standards are generally large, and specify many elements that are not necessarily applicable to VSEs;
- Preparing profiles that subset the base standards facilitates the match between the standards and the targeted VSEs;
- Since the ISO standards do not necessarily cover all the topics needed, profiles can be used to integrate required elements not yet in the ISO standards catalog.

To assemble profiles, WG24 used two types of standards:

- Process standards, such as ISO 12207, which define the activities required to achieve identified objectives or outcomes;
- Product standards, such as ISO 15289, which define the structure and content of artifacts produced by the processes.

WG24 defined the scope of the life cycle processes described in the set of ISs and TRs as follows (adapted from (ISO/IEC 29110-2, 2011): they were not intended to preclude or discourage their use by organizations larger than VSEs. Certain issues faced by larger organizations may not be covered by this set of ISs. The life cycle processes can be used by VSEs when acquiring and using, as well as when creating and supplying, a software system. They can be applied at any level in a software system's structure and at any stage in the life cycle. The processes described were not intended to preclude or discourage the use of additional processes that VSEs find useful. ISO/IEC 29110 standard is not intended to preclude the use of different lifecycles such as: waterfall, iterative, incremental, evolutionary or agile.

Figure 4. Elements of the composition columns (ISO/IEC 29110-2, 2011)

a) **Profile Document ID**
The unique identifier assigned to the profile (required).
b) **Profile Conformity Level**
Each row in the specification table identifies a requirement. The conformity level identifies whether this requirement is mandatory (MAN) or optional (OPT) (required).
c) **Profile Capability Level**
For process-related element types, this column identifies the required capability level (1, 2, 3, 4, 5), as defined in ISO/IEC 15504:2003. This column is required for this type of elements, and is not used for the other types.
d) **Profile Element1 Type**
The nature of the element of the profile (process, task, objective, outcome, work product, etc.) (required).
e) **Profile Element1 ID**
The unique identifier assigned to the profile element. In the absence of a unique identifier, a clause number in the definition or specification document can be used (required).
f) **Profile Element1 Name**
The name assigned to the profile element (required).

Specification of a Standardized Profile

A standardized profile (SP) includes the following (adapted from (ISO/IEC 29110-2, 2011)):

- The profile element identification and composition part, which identifies elements in the profile, as listed in Figure 4.

- The profile element relationship specification tables: when a profile contains the specification for a relationship between two elements; for instance, if activity A produces work product W, this relationship is specified by the identification of each element, as described above, separated by a relationship type.
- Profile Relationship Type: the relationship is expressed by a meaningful abbreviation; for instance, INP for uses as input.

- The source document reference table identifies which elements in the source documents have been selected to be part of the profile. These tables are created by adding the columns to the tables specified in the two previous clauses, as described in Figure 5.

When a profile has selected both informative and normative elements from the source documents, then these must be clearly identified to facilitate conformance evaluation and assessment. An example of the application of these specifications is provided in a later section.

Conformance to a Standardized Profile

The purpose of a standardized profile (SP) is to specify the use of sets of specifications to provide clearly defined functionality. Hence, conformance to an ISO 29110 SP always implies conformance

Figure 5. Elements of the part columns (ISO/IEC 29110-2, 2011)

a) **Source Document ID**
The unique identifier assigned to the source document (required).
b) **Source Conformity Type**
The conformity type of the source requirement. The conformity level identifies whether this requirement is mandatory (MAN) or optional (OPT) (required).
c) **Source Element1 Type**
The nature of the element of the source document (process, task, objective, outcome, work product, etc.) (required).
d) **Source Element1 ID**
The unique identifier assigned to the source element. In the absence of a unique identifier, a clause number in the source document can be used (required).
e) **Source Element1 Name**
The name assigned to the source element (optional, for readability purposes).
f) **Source Element1 Property(ies)**
The selected value of the selected property applicable to the selected element (required if applicable).
g) **Source Element1 Mapping Notes**
Explanatory text on the selection and the correspondence (optional).

to the referenced base standards specifications, if it is referenced in its entirety in the profile. Conformance is specified within each SP published as a separate document, called Part 4. SPs are pre-tailored packages of related software engineering standards, therefore:

- Tailoring of ISO/IEC 29110 profiles is not needed nor allowed;
- Partial compliance is not allowed (except in one case);
- There are no levels of conformance.

It is acceptable for an implementation to incorporate functionality beyond what is defined in the specification of the profile. This is called an extension. If a profile allows extensions, each implementation shall fully support all the required functionality of the profile specification exactly as specified, and the extensions shall neither contradict the functionality defined in the profile specification, nor cause its non-conformance.

Generic Profile Group

WG24 decided to develop an initial profile group, titled Generic Profile Group (GPG). A profile group (PG) is defined as a collection of profiles related either by composition of processes (i.e. activities, tasks), or by capability level, or both. A GPG contains profiles which are applicable to a vast majority of VSEs that do not develop critical software and which are characterized by typical situational factors. Critical software is defined as software whose failure could have an impact on safety, or could cause major financial or social losses (IEEE Std 610.12, 1990). Membership in this PG does not imply any specific application domain; however, it is envisaged that new domain-specific profiles, such as the medical domain, may be developed in the future (Laporte, 2009)

WG24 decided to develop a set of four profiles for the GPG to provide VSEs with a roadmap to improve their processes and their capabilities. The following profiles have been defined: Entry, Basic, Intermediate, and Advanced. In the next section, the Basic Profile, which was developed first, is presented. The Entry profile, which has been developed using the Basic profile, is presented in a subsequent section.

OVERVIEW OF THE BASIC PROFILE AND ITS DEVELOPMENT[6]

The purpose of the Basic Profile is to define software implementation and project management elements for a subset of processes and outcomes of ISO12207 and ISO15289 products, appropriate for a set of common VSE characteristics. The main reason to include project management is that the core business of VSEs is software development, and their financial success depends on successful project completion within schedule and on budget, as well as on making a profit. The Basic Profile describes the development of a single software application by a single project team with no special risk or situational factors. The project may be to fulfill an external or internal contract. This profile drew on sections from the following standards:

- ISO/IEC 12207:2008–Information Technology–Software life cycle processes.
- ISO/IEC 15289:2006–Software Engineering–Software life cycle processes–Guidelines for the content of software life cycle process information products (Documentation).

The preparation of the Basic Profile followed these five steps, as illustrated in Figure 6:

- The recognition of VSE characteristics related to: finance, resources, customer interface, internal business processes, learning, and growth.

Figure 6. Basic VSE profile preparation steps (ISO/IEC 29110-4-1, 2011)

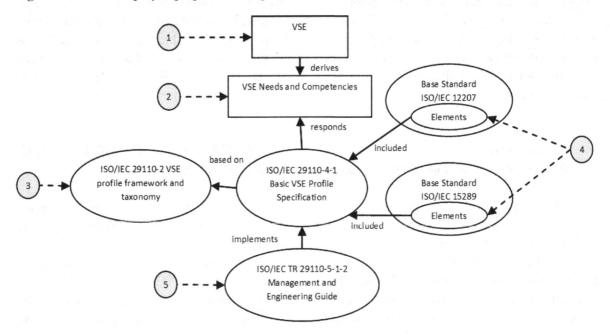

- The identification of VSE needs and suggested competencies that derive from those characteristics.
- The specification of the Basic Profile elements proper to respond to the VSE needs and suggested competencies, according to the ISO/IEC 29110-2 Lifecycle profiles for Very Small Entities (VSEs): Framework and Taxonomy (described below).
- The selection and link of the subset of the Basic Profile elements that map to the ISO/IEC 12207 processes and outcomes elements and ISO/IEC 15289 product elements related to the Basic VSE Profile elements.
- The definition of the Basic Profile Guide ISO/IEC TR 29110-5-1-2 Management and Engineering Guide for the Implementation of the Basic Profile (described below).

The diagram is to be interpreted as follows: the rectangle represents the VSE elements; the ellipse represents standards or subsets of its elements;

solid arrow is a labelled relation; and circle with a dashed arrow is a number of the preparation step.

In the next section, the authors describe the set of ISO/IEC 29110 documents developed for the GPG and the Basic Profile. Then, a detailed description of the Basic Profile is presented.

DESCRIPTION OF THE SET OF ISO/IEC 29110 DOCUMENTS TARGETED BY AUDIENCE[7]

A set of documents, targeted by audience, has been developed to improve product, service quality, and process performance (see Table 2).

If a new profile is needed, ISO/IEC 29110-4 and ISO/IEC 29110-5 can be developed without impacting existing documents, becoming ISO/IEC 29110-4-m and ISO/IEC 29110-5-m-n respectively through the ISO/IEC process. Figure 7 describes the ISO/IEC 29110 series and positions the parts within the framework of reference. Overviews and guides are published as Technical

Table 2. ISO/IEC 29110 target audience (ISO/IEC 29110-5-1-2, 2011)

ISO / IEC 29110	Title	Target audience
Part 1	Overview	VSEs
Part 2	Framework and taxonomy	Standards producers, tool vendors and methodology vendors. Not intended for VSEs
Part 3	Assessment guide	Assessors and VSEs
Part 4	Profile specifications	Standards producers, tool vendors and methodology vendors. Not intended for VSEs
Part 5	Management and engineering guide	VSEs

Reports (TRs), and profiles are published as International Standards (ISs).

Request to Make the ISO/IEC 29110 Technical Reports Freely Available

One of the requirements collected from the international survey was as follow: the guides should be available free of charge on the Web. In 2009, the Editor of WG24 made such a request to ISO. The request was approved at the ISO Joint Technical Committee 1 Plenary meeting in Israel and forwarded to ISO for final approval. The request has since been approved. By making the most useful documents to VSEs freely available, it means that not only the VSEs will have a free access

Figure 7. Set of ISO/IEC 29110 documents targeted by audience (ISO/IEC TR 29110-5-1-2, 2011)

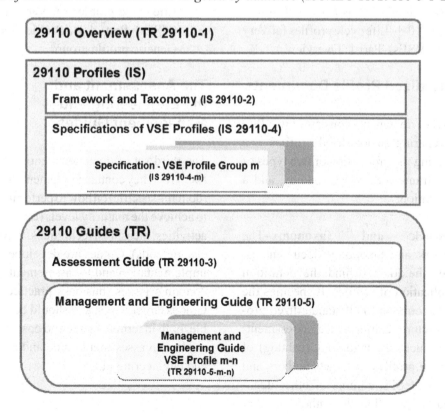

to these documents but people from academia too. Academia will have access to documents to allow them to prepare teaching material and use them in class. The ISO/IEC 29110 technical reports are available at no cost from ISO at: http://standards.iso.org/ittf/PubliclyAvailableStandards/index.html

The Overview Document

The first document, titled Overview, is an ISO TR. It introduces the major concepts required to understand and use the suite of documents. It introduces the business aspects, characteristics, and requirements of VSEs, and clarifies the rationale for VSE-specific profiles, documents, standards, and guides. It also introduces life cycle concepts, improvement, capability and assessment concepts, standardization concepts, and the ISO 29110 set of documents. It targets both a general audience interested in the set of documents and, more specifically, users of the set of documents. The Overview is identified as a TR as follows: ISO/IEC TR 29110-1–Life cycle profiles for Very Small Entities (VSEs)–Part 1: Overview.

The Standardized Profile Documents

The second set of documents consists of two ISO standards. Preparing standardized profiles is a process involving the production of two types of documents, a framework and taxonomy, and a profile specification:

- **Framework and Taxonomy**–The Framework and taxonomy document establishes the logic behind the definition and application of profiles. It specifies the elements common to all standardized profiles (structure, conformance, assessment) and introduces the taxonomy (catalog) of ISO 29110 profiles. It targets authors and reviewers of SPs, authors of other document parts, as well as the authors of other

VSE-targeted profiles. The Framework and Taxonomy is applicable to all profiles and is identified as follows: ISO/IEC 29110-2 Software engineering–Life cycle profiles for Very Small Entities (VSEs)–Part 2: Framework and taxonomy.

- **Profile Specifications**–There is a profile specification document for each profile. Its purpose is to provide the definitive composition of a profile, provide normative links to the normative subset of standards (e.g. ISO/IEC 12207) used in the profile, and provide informative links (references) to input documents. It targets the authors/providers of guides and the authors/providers of tools and other support material. There is one profile specification document for each profile, identified as ISO 29110-4-m, where m is the number assigned to the profile. The profile specification for the Basic Profile is identified as follows: ISO/IEC 29110-4-1 Software engineering–Life cycle profiles for Very Small Entities (VSEs)–Part 4-1: Profile specifications: Generic profile group.

The Assessment and the Engineering and Management Guides

The third set of documents entitled Guides, are ISO TRs. They contain implementation guidelines (domain-specific) on how to perform the processes to achieve the maturity levels (e.g. recommended activities, measures, techniques, templates, models, methods). Guides are developed for process implementation and for assessment based on the domain's issues, business practices, and risks. Guides target VSEs, and should be VSE-accessible, both in terms of style and cost. There are two guides, an assessment guide and a management and engineering guide:

- **Assessment Guide**–This guide describes the process to follow to perform an assessment to determine process capabilities and organizational process maturity, that is, when an organization wants an assessment carried out in order to obtain a process capability profile of the processes implemented, as well as an organizational process maturity level assigned to it. It is also applicable to the situation where a customer asks for a third-party assessment in order to obtain a capability level profile of the process implemented by the software development and maintenance provider. It is also suitable for self-assessment. The Assessment Guide is applicable to all profiles and is identified as follows: ISO/IEC TR 29110-3–Software engineering - Life cycle profiles for Very Small Entities (VSEs)–Part 3: Assessment Guide.

- **Management and Engineering Guide**–The management and engineering guides provide guidance on process implementation and the use of a profile. It targets VSEs (management and technical staff), VSE-related organizations (technology transfer centers, government industry ministries, national standards, consortia and associations, academic use for training, authors of derived products (software, courseware, and acquirers and suppliers. There is one management and engineering guide document for each profile, identified as ISO 29110-5.X, where x is the number assigned to the profile. This number matches the number assigned to the profile specification. The management and engineering guide for the Basic Profile is identified as follows: ISO/IEC TR 29110-5-1-2 Software engineering–Life cycle profiles for Very Small Entities (VSEs)–Part 5-1-2: Management and Engineering Guide: Generic profile group: Basic Profile.

The final step of the approach consisted of developing guidelines explaining the processes defined in the profile in more detail. At the Moscow meeting, the authors proposed the development of a series of deployment packages as additional guidelines. A deployment package (DP) is a set of artifacts developed to facilitate the adoption and implementation of a set of practices of the selected framework in a VSE. The table of contents of a DP is illustrated in Figure 8.

Table 3 shows the list of DPs developed to date for the Basic Profile and the developing partners. These DPs are freely available, as Microsoft Word documents, on the Internet8 (Laporte, 2010).

Implementation Guides

In addition to the DPs, a set of "Implementation Guides" have been developed. The guides explain, step-by-step, how to help implement a specific process supported by a specific tool. The guides are also freely available from (Laporte, 2010). The following implementation guides have been developed:

- Version Control with CVS or with SVN
- Project Management with GForge

Table 3. Deployment packages to support the basic profile (ISO/IEC 29110-5-1-2, 2011)

Deployment Package Title	Developed by
Requirement Analysis	Belgium, Canada
Architecture and Detailed Design	Canada
Construction and Unit Testing	Mexico
Integration and Test	Columbia
Verification and Validation	Canada
Version Control	Thailand
Project Management	Ireland
Product Delivery	Canada, Thailand
Self- Assessment	Finland

Figure 8. Table of contents of a deployment package (ISO/IEC TR 29110-5-1-2, 2011)

1. Introduction
   Purpose of this document
   Key definitions

2. Why this topic is important

3. Overview of the main tasks
   3.1 Tasks
   3.2 Roles and artefacts
   3.3 Activity life cycle and examples of lifecycles

Appendix A Templates

Appendix B Checklists

Appendix C Coverage Matrices (ISO 12207, ISO 9001, CMMI)

Appendix D Tools

Appendix E Training Material

Appendix F Deployment Package Evaluation Form

- Issue tracking with GForge
- Software Process Improvement with OpenOffice Calc

DETAILED DESCRIPTION OF THE BASIC PROFILE[9]

VSEs are subject to a number of characteristics, needs, and desirable competencies that affect the content, nature, and extent of their activities. The Basic Profile addresses the VSEs that are described through the following characteristics, needs, and desirable competencies, classified into four categories: Finance and Resources, Customer Interface, Internal Business Processes, and Learning and Growth. The four categories and their needs and desirable competencies are as follows (ISO/IEC 29110-4-1, 2011):

Finance and Resources characteristics

- Small number of engineers (e.g. the cost of a payroll up to 25 people)
- Potential for short-term cash flow problems
- Low-budget projects, which last a few months and involve only a few people developing small products
- Dependent on successful project completion within schedule and budget
- Preference for separate projects to perform corrective post delivery maintenance
- Limited internal resources to perform management support and organizational processes like: risk management, training, quality management, process improvement, and reuse.

Needs and desirable competencies of the Finance and Resources characteristics:

- Projects carried out within budget and the product delivered on schedule

- Close communication maintained with the customer to manage risks

Customer Interface characteristics:

- Usually one customer per project at a time
- Customer satisfaction dependent on:
- Fulfillment of specific requirements that may change during the project;
- Information received in a timely fashion during product development;
- Delivery on schedule;
- Low-level of defects found post-delivery; and
- Close communication and prompt response to any changes.
- Quantitative quality requirements not usually defined by customers
- A VSE usually not in charge of the management of the system, or of software integration, installation, or operation

Needs and desirable competencies for the customer interface characteristics:

- Fulfillment of customer requirements
- Management of changes to customer requirements during the project
- Provision of close communication and timely update information to the customer during product development
- Delivery of the product with a low level of defects

Internal Business Process characteristics

- The main process is designed to develop custom software systems written in-house on contract.
- The software product is elaborated progressively and has to be consistent with customer requirements.
- Products are developed or maintained through projects with a single line of communication between implementation group and customer.
- There are a small number of engineers (e.g. up to 25 people) in the organization, and therefore most of the communication, decision making, and problem resolution can be performed promptly, face-to-face.
- VSEs have lean project management budgets and conduct focused software implementation activities.
- The Infrastructure Management, Project Portfolio Management, and Human Resources Management Processes are performed through informal, face-to-face mechanisms.
- Products generated in projects are software items which may have more than one version and have to be saved and controlled.

Needs and desirable competencies for the Internal Business characteristics:

- Version control and storage of the products generated during a project
- Progressive elaboration of the software product, achieving consistency with customer requirements

Learning and Growth characteristics:

- Awareness of the importance of standards
- Lack of human resources to engage in standardization
- Lack of information of ISO/IEC standards
- Lack of knowledge of software process improvement and process evaluation

Needs and desirable competencies for the Learning and Growth characteristics:

- Guidelines which are flexible and easy to use for beginners on the adoption of practices of international standards focused on

Figure 9. Needs and suggested competencies derived from finance and resources characteristics (ISO/IEC 29110-4-1, 2011)

Perform the projects within budget and deliver the product on schedule. To respond to this need and suggested competencies, Basic VSE Profile processes, objectives, and work products are the following:

Project Management Process
- **PM.O1.** The Project Plan for the execution of the project is developed according to the Statement of Work and validated with the Customer. The tasks and resources necessary to complete the work are sized and estimated.
- **PM.O2.** Progress of the project is monitored against the Project Plan and recorded in the Progress Status Record. Corrections to remedy problems and deviations from the plan are undertaken when project targets are not achieved. Appropriate treatment is applied to correct or avoid the impact of risk. Closure of the project is performed to obtain Customer acceptance, which is documented in the Acceptance Record.

Software Implementation Process
- **SI.O1.** Tasks of the activities are performed through the accomplishment of the current Project Plan.

Work Products: Statement of Work, Progress Status Record, Project Plan, Correction Register, and Acceptance Record.

Maintain close communication with the customer to manage risks. To respond to this need and suggested Competencies, the Basic VSE Profile processes, objectives, and work products are the following:

Project Management Process
- **PM.O5.** Risks are identified as they develop and during the conduct of the project.

Work Product: Project Plan.

Figure 10. Project management objectives (ISO/IEC 29110-4-1, 2011)

- **PM.O1.** The Project Plan for the execution of the project is developed according to the Statement of Work and validated with the Customer. The tasks and resources necessary to complete the work are sized and estimated.
- **PM.O2.** Progress of the project is monitored against the Project Plan and recorded in the Progress Status Record. Corrections to remedy problems and deviations from the plan are undertaken when project targets are not achieved. Appropriate treatment is applied to correct or avoid the impact of risk. Closure of the project is performed to obtain Customer acceptance documented in the Acceptance Record.
- **PM.O3.** Change Requests are addressed through their reception and analysis. Changes to the software requirements are evaluated for cost, schedule, and technical impact.
- **PM.O4.** Review meetings with the Work Team and the Customer are held. Agreements are registered and tracked.
- **PM.O5.** Risks are identified as they develop and during the project.
- **PM.O6.** A software Version Control Strategy is developed. Items of Software Configuration are identified, defined, and baselined. Modifications and releases of the items are controlled and made available to the Customer and Work Team, including the storage, handling, and delivery of the items.
- **PM.O7.** Software Quality Assurance is performed to provide assurance that work products and processes comply with the Project Plan and Requirements Specification.

processes to support their software development projects needs

To use the Basic VSE Profile, it is assumed that the VSE fulfills the following entry conditions:

- Project contract or agreement with a statement of work

- Cost, technical, and schedule feasibility assessments performed before the start of the project
- Project work team, including project manager, assigned and trained
- Goods and infrastructure services available

Now that the characteristics of the Basic Profile have been defined, the next step consists of identifying the process elements, from the base standards, that will be used to define the Basic Profile specifications. To illustrate this step, Figure 9 lists the needs and suggested competencies derived from the finance and resources characteristics. In this figure, the acronym PM stands for project management and the acronym SI stands for software implementation.

Similar lists have been developed for the other characteristics, e.g. customer interface characteristics. The final list of the Basic Profile elements is composed of PM and SI processes with their corresponding objectives (identified as PM.O1, PM.O2, etc.; and SI.O1, SI.O2, etc.), and

Figure 11. Project management work products (ISO/IEC 29110-4-1, 2011)

- Statement of Work,
- Progress Status Record,
- Project Plan,
- Change Requests,
- Meeting Record,
- Correction Register,
- Verification Results,
- Validation Results Project Repository,
- Project Repository Backup
- Acceptance Record.

Figure 12. Software implementation objectives (ISO/IEC 29110-4-1, 2011)

- **SI.O1.** Tasks of the activities are performed through the accomplishment of the current Project Plan.
- **SI.O2.** Software requirements are defined, analyzed for correctness and testability, approved by the Customer, baselined, and communicated.
- **SI.O3.** Software architectural and detailed design are developed and baselined. Their software items and internal and external interfaces are described. Consistency and traceability to software requirements are established.
- **SI.O4.** Software components defined by the design are produced. Unit tests are defined and performed to verify their consistency with requirements and the design. Traceability to the requirements and design are established.
- **SI.O5.** Software is produced integrating software components and verified using Test Cases and Test Procedures. Results are recorded on the Test Report. Defects are corrected and consistency and traceability to Software Design are established.
- **SI.O6.** A Software Configuration that meets the Requirements Specifications as agreed with the Customer, which includes user, operation, and maintenance documentation, is integrated, baselined, and stored in the Project Repository. The need for change to the Software Configuration is detected and related Change Requests are initiated.
- **SI.O7.** Verification and Validation tasks of all required work products are performed using the defined criteria to achieve consistency among output and input products in each activity. Defects are identified and corrected; records are stored in Verification/Validation Results.

Figure 13. Software implementation work products (ISO/IEC 29110-4-1, 2011)

- Requirements Specification,
- Components,
- Test Report,
- Maintenance Documentation,
- Product Operation Guide, Software,
- Software Configuration,
- Software Design,
- Software User Documentation,
- Test Cases and Test Procedures,
- Traceability Record,
- Verification Results and Validation Results.

the work products are listed below. The Project Management Objectives are listed in Figure 10.

The Project management Work Products are listed in Figure 11.

The Software Implementation Objectives are listed in Figure 12.

The Software Implementation Work Products are listed in Figure 13.

Basic Profile Specifications[10]

The Basic Profile specifications are a set of tables containing the information. The following tables are defined in clause 7 of ISO/IEC 29110 Part 4-1:

- A table for Process Specifications containing the following information:
  - Process definition and composition specification:
  - All processes are mandatory.
  - All activities are mandatory.
  - All tasks are optional.

For illustration purposes, a subset of the table listing the Project Management Tasks is reproduced in Table 4.

- A table for Objective Specifications containing the following information:
  - Process objective specifications:
  - All objectives are required.
- A table for Work Product Specifications containing the following information:
  - Work product specifications:
  - All work products are required.
- A table for Input/Output Specifications containing the following information:
  - Activity input and output specifications:
  - All outputs are required.
  - All inputs are optional.

Table 4. Subset of the table listing the project management tasks (ISO/IEC 29110-4-1, 2011)

Profile Process Identification and Composition						
Prof. Conf. Lev	Profile Element 2 Type	Profile Element2 ID	Profile Element2 Name	Profile Element3 Type	Profile Element3 ID	Profile Element3 Name
MAN	Activity	PM.1	Project Planning,			
OPT	"	"	"	Task	PM.1.01	Review the Statement of Work
OPT	"	"	"	Task	PM.1.02	Define the customer Delivery Instruction of each one of the deliverables specified in the Statement of Work
OPT	"	"	"	Task	PM.1.03	Identify the specific tasks to be performed in order to produce the deliverables and their software components identified in the Statement of Work

Table 5. Source elements from ISO/IEC 12207 for the project management activities

Source Element from ISO 12207	Project Management Activities	
6.3.1	Project Planning	
6.3.2	Project Assessment and Control	
6.3.2	Project Assessment and Control	
6.3.4	Risk Management	
6.3.7	Measurement	
6.4.8	Software Acceptance Support	
7.1.2	Software Requirement Analysis	
7.2.2	Software Configuration Management	
7.2.3	Software Quality Assurance	
7.2.6	Software Review	

Basic Profile Base Document References

The last step in the specification of a profile is the development of a set of tables referencing the base standard selected for the Basic Profile, the ISO/IEC 12207 and ISO/IEC 15289 standards. Table 5 lists the source elements from ISO 12207 which have been used as project management activities for this profile.

For illustration purposes, one table of ISO/IEC 29110 Part 4-1, for Project Management activities, is presented in Table 6.

Description of Processes Documented in ISO/IEC 29110 Part 5

ISO/IEC TR 29110 Part 5-1-2, the Engineering and Management Guide for the Basic Profile (ISO/IEC TR 29110-5-1-2, 2011), provides Project Management (PM) and Software Implementation (SI) processes at a level of detail that should allow a VSE to be able to translate this information into usable processes. ISO/IEC 29110 standard is not intended to preclude the use of different lifecycles such as: waterfall, iterative, incremental, evolutionary or agile. The high-level relationship between the SI process and the PM process is illustrated in Figure 14.

The PM process uses the customer's statement of work to elaborate the project plan. The PM project assessment and control tasks compare the project progress against the project plan, and action is taken to eliminate deviations from the project plan, or incorporate changes into it. The PM project closure activity delivers the software configuration, produced by SI, and obtains the customer's acceptance to formalize the end of the project. A project repository is established to save the work products and to control its versions during the project.

The execution of the SI process is driven by the project plan. The SI process starts with an initiation activity of the project plan review. The project plan will guide the execution of the software requirements analysis, software architectural

Table 6. References for the project management activities (ISO/IEC 29110-4-1, 2011)

Profile Process Identification and Composition			Process Source Document Reference							
Profile Element2 Type	Profile Element2 ID	Profile Element2 Name	Source Conf, Level	Source Doc. ID	Source Element1 Type	Source Element1 ID	Source Element1 Name	Source Element2 Type	Source Element2 ID	Source Element2 Name
Activity	PM.1	Project Planning,	OPT	ISO/IEC 12207: 2008	Process	6.3.1	Project Planning	Activity	6.3.1.3.2	Project Planning

Figure 14. Basic profile process relationship (ISO/IEC TR 29110-5-1-2, 2011)

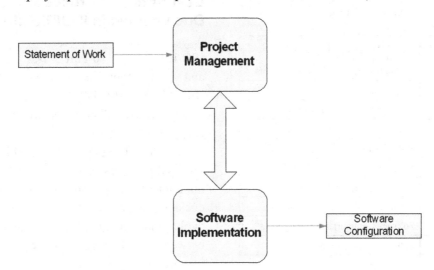

Table 7. Software requirements analysis tasks (ISO/IEC TR 29110-5-1-2, 2011)

Identification of Task	Description of Tasks
SI.2.1	Assign tasks to the work team members in accordance with their role, based on the current Project Plan
SI.2.2	Document or Update in the Requirement Specifications
SI.2.3	Verify the Requirements Specifications
SI.2.4	Validate the Requirements Specifications
SI.2.5	Document the preliminary version of the of the Software User Documentation or update the present manual
SI.2.6	Verify the Software User Documentation
SI.2. 7	Incorporate the Requirements Specifications and Software User Documentation into the Software Configuration in the baseline

and detailed design, software construction, and software integration and test, and product delivery activities. To remove a product's defects, verification, validation, and test tasks are included in the activities workflow.

The customer provides a statement of work as an input to PM process and receives a software configuration as a result of SI process execution.

Description of the Project Management Process

The purpose of the Project Management process is to establish and carry out the tasks of the software

implementation project in a systematic way, which allows compliance with the project's objectives in terms of expected quality, time, and costs (see Figure 15).

Description of the Software Implementation Process

The purpose of the Software Implementation process is to achieve systematic performance of the analysis, design, construction, integration, and test activities for new or modified software products according to the specified requirements (see Figure 16).

Figure 15. Project management process diagram (ISO/IEC TR 29110-5-1-2, 2011)

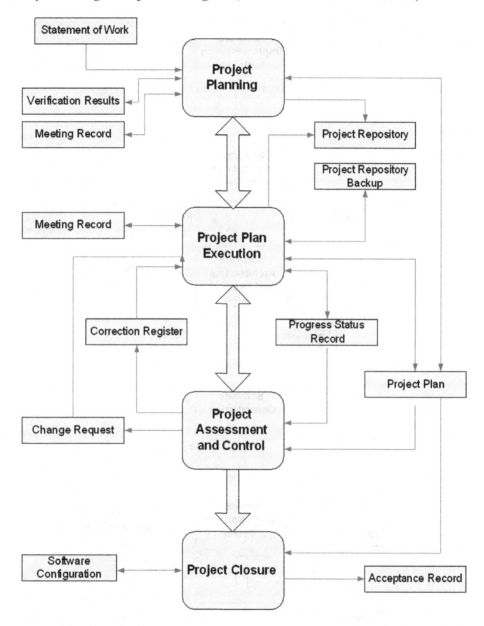

For illustration purposes, the tasks of the software requirements analysis activity are listed in Table 7.

The description of the Analyst's role is presented in Table 8.

Table 9 illustrates the definition of a work product: the Change Request.

DESCRIPTION OF THE DRAFT ENTRY PROFILE[11]

At the Berlin meeting, the delegates from Belgium and Canada proposed the elaboration of a profile targeting start-up VSEs and short-intensity projects of about 6 person-months of effort. At the Mexico meeting, the delegate from Canada

Figure 16. Software implementation process diagram (ISO/IEC TR 29110-5-1-2, 2011)

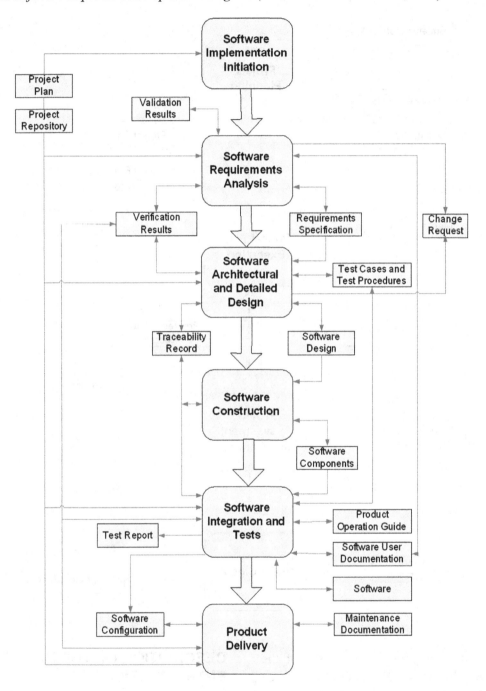

presented a set of practices that could be embedded in this future profile. After discussion, the members of the working group agreed to the practices listed in Figure 17.

Although a consensus on the practices targeting VSEs was reached during the interim meeting in Lima (Peru), the working group had to formally define characteristics, needs, and desirable competencies, as it was done for the Basic Profile.

Table 8. Description of the analyst's role (ISO/IEC TR 29110-5-1-2, 2011)

Role	Abbreviation	Competency
1. Analyst	AN	Knowledge and experience in eliciting, specifying, and analyzing the requirements Knowledge in designing user interfaces and ergonomic criteria Knowledge of revision techniques and experience in software development and maintenance Knowledge of editing techniques and experience in software development and maintenance

Table 9. Description of the change request work product (ISO/IEC TR 29110-5-1-2, 2011)

Name	Description	Source
Change Request	It may have the following characteristics: Identifies the purpose of the change Identifies the request status (new, accepted, rejected) Identifies the requestor's contact information Identifies the impacted system(s) Impact on operations of existing system(s) defined Impact of associated documentation defined Critically of the request, deadline The applicable statuses are: initiated, evaluated, and accepted	Software Implementation Customer Project Management

At the May 2010 meeting in Niigata (Japan), the working group agreed on a set of characteristics, objectives for the project management and software implementation processes. The following paragraphs describe these elements.

Characteristics of the Targeted VSEs:

- Primarily involved in the design and/or coding of minor software package
- Do not have significant experience with large software development projects, and so do not attract contract jobs from larger software firms
- Personnel often relatively inexperienced

Figure 17. Proposed practices for the entry profile (ISO/IEC PDTR 29110-5-1-1, 2011)

Project Planning and Monitoring
Develop an agreement with customer
  Develop a plan
    1. Determine phases, tasks, milestones, deliverables
    2. Assess available resources, estimate effort
    3. Monitor project status and perform reviews (e.g. retrospective)
      4. Collect data (e.g. effort spent on tasks)
Software Development
Requirement Analysis and Design
    1. Identify the set of requirements to implement,
    2. Plan interactions with customer
    3. Design the software
Software Code and Test
    1. Code and debug
    2. Perform unit and system testing

- Often lack discipline in product development tasks: focus mostly in coding activities
- Lack of tangible process assets
- Limited access to investments and loans
- May lack credibility and need for a reference (e.g. from a previous customer)
- Customers may impose a software development process

Objectives of the Entry Profile

- The Entry Profile should provide a foundation for a migration to the Basic Profile Processes.
- The Entry Profile could be used by VSEs to help them implement a start-up management-and-implementation process.

Project Management and Software Implementation Objectives of the Entry Profile

Since the Entry Profile has been developed using the Basic Profile (see Figures 18 and 19), to illustrate was has been added or deleted/modified the following convention is used:

- Information added or modified to the Basic Profile is shown in Underline while information deleted is shown like this: strike out.

The objectives of the Project Management (PM) Process of the Entry profile, listed in the draft ISO/IEC PDTR 29110 Part 5-1-1, are:

The objectives of the Software Implementation (SI) Process of the Entry profile, listed in the draft ISO/IEC PDTR 29110, Part 5-1-1 are:

Figure 18. PM objectives for Entry Profile developed using the Basic Profile (ISO/IEC PDTR 29110-5-1-1, 2011)

Objectives ID	Objectives
PM.01	The *Project Plan* for the execution of the project is developed according to *the Statement of Work* and reviewed and accepted by the Customer. The tasks and resources necessary to complete the work are sized and estimated.
PM.02	Progress of the project monitored against the *Project Plan* ~~and recorded in the Progress Status Record. Corrections to remediate problems and deviations from the plan are taken when project targets are not achieved.~~ Closure of the project is performed to get the Customer acceptance documented in *the Acceptance Record*.
PM.03	The *Changes Requests* are addressed ~~through their reception and analysis.~~ Changes to **the** software requirements are evaluated for ~~cost, schedule and technical impact.~~ **Impact.**
PM.04	Review meetings with the Work Team and the Customer are held. Agreements are registered and tracked.
PM.05	~~*Risks* are identified as they develop and during the conduct of the project.~~
PM.06	~~A software *Version Control Strategy* is developed. Items of *Software Configuration* are identified, defined and baseline. Modifications and releases of the items are controlled and made available to the Customer and Work Team. The storage, handling and delivery of the items are controlled.~~ **Items of Software Configuration are identified and controlled.**
PM.07	~~Software Quality Assurance is performed to provide assurance that work products and processes comply with the *Project Plan* and *Requirements Specification*.~~

Figure 19. SI objectives for Entry Profile developed using the Basic Profile (ISO/IEC PDTR 29110-5-1-1, 2011)

Objectives ID	Objectives
SI.01	Tasks of the activities are performed through the accomplishment of the current *Project Plan*.
SI.02	Software requirements are defined, analyzed for correctness and testability, approved by the Customer, ~~baseline~~ and communicated.
SI.03	**Software components are identified**. ~~Software architectural and detailed design is developed and baseline. It describes the software components and internal and external interfaces of them. Consistency and traceability to software requirements are established.~~
SI.04	Software **components** ~~defined by the design~~ are produced. Unit test are ~~defined and~~ performed to verify the consistency with **software** requirements. ~~And the design. Traceability to the requirements and design are established.~~
SI.05	**Software is integrated and tested, and defects are corrected**. ~~*Software* is produced performing integration of software components and verified using *Test Cases and Test Procedures*. Results are recorded at the *Test Report*. Defects are corrected and consistency and traceability to *Software Design* are established.~~
SI.06	**Software configuration is prepared for delivery**. ~~A *Software Configuration*, that meets the *Requirements Specification* as agreed to with the Customer, which includes user, operation and maintenance documentations is integrated, baselined and stored at the *Project Repository*. Needs for changes to the *Software Configuration* are detected and related *Change Requests* are initiated.~~
SI.07	~~Verification and Validation tasks of all required work products are performed using the defined criteria to achieve consistency among output and input products in each activity. Defects are identified, and corrected; records are stored in the *Verification/Validation*~~

The delegates from Thailand prepared a first draft of the engineering and management guide, i.e. Part 5, for review for the Fall 2010 meeting in Washington. Two deployment packages, a project management DP and a software implementation DP, have been developed to experiment with the draft Entry Profile.

Conducting Pilot Projects and Developing Additional Support Tools

Further research should be related to the study of SPI success in VSEs. We advocate the use of pilot projects as a mean to accelerate the adoption and utilization of SPI initiatives by VSEs. Pilot projects, which could also be used as case studies to promote the adoption of the ISO/IEC 29110 standard, are an important mean of reducing risks and learning more about the organizational and technical issues associated with the deployment of new software engineering practices (Palza, Levano, & Mamani, 2010). A successful pilot project is also an effective means of building adoption of new practices by members of a VSE. In particular, with pilot project we would be able to collect, as a minimum, the following data:

- Effort and time to deploy by the VSE
- Usefulness for the VSE
- Verification of the understanding of the VSE
- Self-assessments data - A self-assessment at the beginning of the pilot and at the end of the pilot project

The feasibility study of a pilot project should be also evaluated and documented. Some elements to be considered about how conducting and implementing pilot projects could be the followings:

- Assess the opportunity,
- Plan and Execution of activities,
- Evaluate the results
- Document all results

The members of WG24 requested a set of guidelines such that pilot projects are conducted similarly around the world. Canada agreed to provide a DP to describe a process to conduct pilot projects. The purpose of this DP is to provide tailorable and usable guidelines and materials in order to select and conduct pilot projects in VSEs. The high-level tasks of this DP are:

- Assess the opportunity to conduct a pilot project,
- Plan the pilot project,
- Conduct the pilot project, and
- Evaluate the results of the pilot project.

Some initiatives about how to implement performance indicators in projects (pilots projects) for organizations (small and others) is found in (Palza, Abran, & Fuhrman, 2003), (Palza, Sanchez, Abran, & Mamani, 2010), (Palza, 2005).

Others initiatives regarding templates and activities using OpenUP and EPFC (Eclipse Process Framework Composer) for VSEs are underway. OpenUP is an open source software development process developed as part of the Eclipse Process Framework Project. A group of students at Universidad Peruana Union (UpeU)12 has been developing "Plug-ins" based on OpenUP and EPFC Composer (Palza & UpeU, 2010) for the standard ISO 29110. Other "Plug-ins" are being developed, by graduate students of École de technologie supérieure, to support the set of DPs of the draft Entry Profile and the Basic Profile (Laporte, 2010). As an example, pilot projects are being conducted to develop and implement software processes used by graduate students of a telecommunication research laboratory and of a medical imagery research laboratory. Finally, senior undergraduate software engineering students are experimenting with the draft Entry Profile by developing processes for two start-up VSEs.

FUTURE WORK

Even if the ISO/IEC 29110 Set of Documents for the Basic Profile has been published, there is still much work yet to be done. The main remaining work item is to finalise the development of the three other profiles of the Generic Profile Group: (a) the Entry Profile; (b) the Intermediate Profile–with additional practices for the management of more than one project and (c) the Advanced Profile–with additional practices for business management and portfolio management. In addition the development of additional Profile Groups for other domains such as profiles for the medical domain.

Some means to accelerate the adoption and implementation of standards by VSEs have been described. A target audience, and an often forgotten one in the area of software engineering standards comprise undergraduate and graduate students studying software engineering, computer engineering or computer science. At the Hyderabad meeting (India), the delegate from Canada proposed the establishment of an informal interest group about education. The main objective of this interest group is to develop a set of courses for software undergraduate and graduate students such that students learn and apply the ISO standards for VSEs before they graduate. To date, four of the six proposed courses, at the Hyderabad meeting, have been developed and are freely available on Internet. Finally, work is underway on the development of self-learning course modules to support the ISO/IEC 29110 ISs, TRs and DPs.

CONCLUSION

The documents used by WG24 and the approach that led to the development of the International Standards and Technical Reports for VSEs were presented. The approach taken by WG24 corresponds to the mixed economy approach, where the intent is to help VSEs succeed in business by providing them with a set of software engineering practices tailored to their needs, in the form of international standards, technical reports and deployment packages.

It is expected that some VSEs will use the technology developed on their own, other VSEs will get some help from government organizations, such as training or coaching, and some large organizations will impose the ISO/IEC 29110 standards on the VSEs that supply components for their products. A few countries have opted for the 'survival of the fittest' strategy for their VSEs, i.e. an approach where a government does not intervene in the marketplace and lets the market decide which VSEs will survive. At the same time, a number of government agencies, universities, research centers and associations are working to determine how to help VSEs. They share some of the following assumptions about the needs of VSEs:

- VSEs require low-cost solutions;
- VSEs require readily usable processes supported by guides, templates, examples and tools;
- VSEs require additional effort in communications and in standardizing vocabulary;
- VSEs require a staged approach to help them grow their capabilities;
- VSEs require ways to identify potential quick wins;
- VSEs require guidance in the selection and implementation of software practices.

REFERENCES

April, A.Laporte, Laporte, C.Y., Renault, A., Alexandre, S., Applying ISO/IEC Software Engineering Standards in Very Small Enterprises. In *Software Process Improvement for Small and Medium Enterprises: Techniques and Case Studies*. Hershey: Idea Group Inc.

Habra, N., Alexandre, S., Desharnais, J., Laporte, C. Y., & Renault, A. (2008). Initiating software process improvement in very small enterprises experience with a light assessment tool. *Information and Software Technology, 50*(7-8), 763–771. doi:10.1016/j.infsof.2007.08.004

ISO/IEC 12207. (2008). Systems and software engineering - Software life cycle processes. Geneva, Switzerland: International Organization for Standardization (ISO).

ISO/IEC 15288. (2008). Systems engineering - Systems life cycle processes. Geneva, Switzerland: International Organization for Standardization (ISO).

ISO/IEC 15289. (2006). Systems and software engineering - Content of systems and software life cycle process information products. Geneva, Switzerland: International Organization for Standardization (ISO).

ISO/IEC 24765. (2010). Systems and software engineering–Vocabulary, Geneva, Switzerland: International Organization for Standardization (ISO).

ISO/IEC 29110-2. (2011). Software engineering - Lifecycle profiles for Very Small Entities (VSEs) -- Part 2: Framework and taxonomy. Geneva, Switzerland: International Organization for Standardization (ISO).

ISO/IEC 29110-4-1. (2011). Software engineering - Lifecycle profiles for Very Small Entities (VSEs) -- Part 4-1: Profile specifications: Generic profile group. Geneva, Switzerland: International Organization for Standardization (ISO).

ISO/IEC PDTR 29110-5-1-1. (2011). Software engineering - Lifecycle profiles for Very Small Entities (VSEs) -- Part 5-1-1: Management and engineering guide: Generic profile group: Entry profile. Geneva, Switzerland: International Organization for Standardization (ISO).

ISO/IEC TR 10000-1. (1998). Information technology – Framework and taxonomy of international standardized profiles – Part 1: General principles and documentation framework. Geneva, Switzerland: International Organization for Standardization (ISO).

ISO/IEC TR 24774. (2010). Software and systems engineering — Life cycle management- Guidelines for process description. Geneva, Switzerland: International Organization for Standardization (ISO).

ISO/IEC TR 29110-5-1-2. (2011). Software engineering - Lifecycle profiles for Very Small Entities (VSEs) -- Part 5-1-2: Management and engineering guide: Generic profile group: Basic profile. Geneva, Switzerland: International Organization for Standardization (ISO).

Laporte, C. Y. (2009). Contributions to software engineering and the development and deployment of international software engineering standards for very small entities (Doctoral dissertation, Université de Bretagne Occidentale, Brest).

Laporte, C. Y. (2010). Deployment Packages repository. Retrieved from http://profs.logti.etsmtl.ca/claporte/English/VSE/index.html

Laporte, C. Y., Alexandre, S., & O'Connor, R. A Software Engineering Lifecycle Standard for Very Small Enterprises, in R. V. O'Connor et al. (Eds.): EuroSPI 2008, CCIS 16, pp. 129–141

Laporte, C. Y., Alexandre, S., & O'Connor, R. V. (2008). A software engineering lifecycle standard for very small enterprises. In O'Connor, R. V., Baddoo, N., Smolander, K., & Messnarz, R. (Eds.), *Software process improvement (Vol. 16*, pp. 129–141). Berlin, Germany: Springer. doi:10.1007/978-3-540-85936-9_12

Laporte, C. Y., Alexandre, S., & Renault, A. (2008). The application of international software engineering standards in very small enterprises. *Software Quality Professional, ASQ, 10*(3), 4–11.

Laporte, C. Y., Alexandre, S., & Renault, A. (2008, June). The Application of International Software Engineering Standards in Very Small Enterprises. *Software Quality Professional Journal, ASQ, 10*(3), 4–11.

NMX-059-NYCE. (2005). Information technology-Software-models of processes and assessment for software development and maintenance. Part 01: Definition of concepts and products; Part 02: Process requirements (MoProSoft). Part 03: Guidelines for process implementation; Part 04: Guidelines for process assessment (EvalProSoft).

Oktaba, H., Felix, G., Mario, P., Francisco, R., Francisco, P., & Claudia, A. (2007). Software process improvement: The Competisoft project. IEEE Computer, 40(10).

Palza, E. (2005). *Facilitating measurement indicators in software improvements projects. Systems & Software Engineering Review*. Lima, Peru: Faculty of Systems & Computer Engineering, San Marcos University.

Palza, E., Abran, A., & Fuhrman, C. (2003). *Establishing a generic and multidimensional measurement repository in CMMI context.* Paper presented at the 28th Annual IEEE/NASA Software Engineering Workshop, Greenbelt, MD, USA.

Palza, E., Levano, D., & Mamani, G. (2010). *Creating a model for software project management in the context of small and medium enterprises (SMEs)*. Paper presented at the Software Engineering Process Group Conference SEPG 2010.

Palza, E., Sanchez, J., Abran, A., & Mamani, G. (2010). *Implementing KPI with open source BI software in an academic department*. Paper presented at the Computer Professional Conference /Software Maintenance and Evolution.

Palza, E., & Upe, U. (2010). OpenUP - EPFC plugin for ISO 29110. Retrieved from http://investigacion.upeu.edu.pe/index.php/Portada#

ENDNOTES

[1] SEI CMMI (Capability Maturity Model Integration). http://www.sei.cmu.edu/cmmi/

[2] ISO/IEC JTC 1/SC7 stands for the International Organization for Standardization/ International Electrotechnical Commission Joint Technical Committee 1/Sub Committee 7, which is in charge of the development and maintenance of software and systems engineering standards.

[3] To be published in 2011.

[4] Adapted from: ISO/IEC 12207:2008 Systems and software engineering—Software life cycle processes (ISO 2008d).

[5] Adapted from ISO/IEC 15289:2006, Systems and Software Engineering—Content of systems and software life cycle process information products (Documentation)

[6] Adapted from ISO 29110 Part 1, ISO 2009d and ISO 29110 Part 5.

[7] Adapted from ISO 29110 Part 4.

[8] http://profs.etsmtl.ca/claporte/English/VSE/index.html

[9] This section is adapted from (ISO 29110 Part 5)

[10] Adapted from ISO 29110 Part 4.

[11] This profile was discussed at the meetings in Lima (Peru) in November 2009, in Niigata (Japan) in May 2010 and in Paris (France) in May 2011

[12] www.upeu.edu.pe

Chapter 4
Quality, Improvement and Measurements in High Risk Software

Edgardo Palza Vargas
University of Ottawa, Canada

ABSTRACT

We aim to improve quality in software engineering projects by introducing Verification and Validation (V&V) best practices in terms of process, artifacts, and quality performance indicators. We present a Quality Measurement Management Tool (QMT) in order to support quality activities and process. This tool is based on a measurement meta-model repository for collecting, storing, analyzing and reporting measurement data. It is important to note that the proposed QMT supports the IEEE Standard 1012 for Software Verification and Validation (management, acquisition, supply, development, operation, and maintenance), as well as measurement information needs to Capability Maturity Model Integration (CMMI) processes and products requirements. Our repository is generic, flexible, and integrated, supporting a dynamic measurement system. It was originally designed to support Ericsson Research Canada's business information needs.

INTRODUCTION

Since software has become an important component of critical systems (e.g., in aeronautics/aerospace, power plants, medical devices, chemical plants, automobiles, military weapons, etc.)

the impact of software on systems safety has been demanding greater attention in organizations dedicated to the production of this high critical software. In the same vein today's software is becoming increasingly more complex: heterogeneous composition on a diversity of platforms, distributed execution, complexity in calculation

DOI: 10.4018/978-1-61350-141-2.ch004

algorithms, multiplicity of contractors with diverse development methodologies, etc. The result of such complexity is increased risk and higher costs in software projects.

The type of software that, directly or indirectly, ensures the safety of human life or significant financial investments is referred to as high risk Software or safety-critical software. This type of software is required to meet very high levels of safety and reliability and to meet demanding quality standards. Therefore, the related development process must be tightly managed, because of the very high level of quality required. Indeed, many accidents caused by deficient quality of critical software have been reported in the software engineering literature (Levenson, 1993), Ariane 5 (Lions, 1996), etc.

In this chapter we propose a Quality Measurement Management (QMT) in order to support quality activities and process. This tool is based on a measurement meta-model repository (Abran & Palza, 2003; Palza, 2010; Palza, Abran, & Fuhrman, 2003). It is important to note that the proposed QMT supports the IEEE Standard for Software Verification and Validation (IEEE Std 1012, 2004), as well as CMMI best practices (CMMI Product Team, 2006). The software processes described in IEEE Std. 1012 include: management, acquisition, supply, development, operation, and maintenance. This IEEE standard is also recommended for use in software-intensive projects: for instance, the NASA IV&V Facility's "Program Manager Handbook" (NASA Software IV&V Facility, 2000) makes clear the usefulness of the IEEE Std 1012 and (IEEE Std 1059, 1993) for the planning and execution of V&V activities in their projects.

The effectiveness of V&V depends on the timeliness of the development processes and on the quality of the deliverables. In this proposal, we discuss how the QMT can help to support measurements activities for Management V&V processes in organizations. Our approach is described in terms of activities, processes and

tasks recommended in IEEE 1012, section 5.1. This should facilitate measurements in terms of:

- Software Verification and Validation Plan (SVVP).
- Baseline change assessment.
- Management Review of V&V.
- Management and Technical Review Support.
- Interface with Organizational and Supporting Process.

Moreover, this chapter also reports how QMR tool supports a dynamic measurement system with CMMI requirements in a changing and dynamic environment, such as that of Ericsson Research Canada. The QMR tool was expected to meet further criteria and constraints for a better fit to the Ericsson context:

- Improvements to the quality of the software engineering measures.
- Design of a coherent and consistent model of enterprise performance evaluation.
- An integrated and generic multidimensional measurement platform.
- Individual and team performance measures aligned with organizational goals.
- Ability to allow managers to extract value from the vast amounts of data and information in the organization.

Quality in High Risk Software

Software V&V is a set of activities aimed at attaining software quality during the development life cycle. Although there are several approaches (or models) to planning the life cycle for software development, there are clearly certain disciplines that exist in phases within any life cycle. These disciplines include requirements engineering, analysis, design, implementation and testing. At each step along the development life cycle, mistakes can be made, which in turn can affect the quality of the final software product.

Verification strives to detect and correct mistakes made within each step of the software life cycle to determine whether the products of a life-cycle activity satisfy the requirements of that activity. These verification activities are not sufficient, however, to assure that the final software product fulfills its intended purpose and meets its users' needs. Therefore, validation determines if the software meets the needs for its intended use. Software V&V is a set of activities whose goal is to foster software quality during the development life cycle. In general, V&V is a process that helps to ensure that software products in a given phase of software development correspond to the specified requirements defined to be implemented into it.

V&V can represent up to fifty percent of the budget in software/system critical projects (Kit, 1995). For safety-critical software, risk mitigation is very important (Wallace & Fujii, 1989). Many software projects, for instance within NASA and elsewhere, involve software V&V activities to mitigate certain software development risks.

For safety-critical software, risk mitigation must be taken very seriously. Many software projects, within NASA and elsewhere, require software V&V activities to mitigate certain software development risks. Some NASA projects may even require independent V&V (IV&V) activities, in which an organization independent from the one developing the software performs the V&V activities during the lifecycle.

The IEEE Standard for Software Verification and Validation is a process standard that addresses V&V processes with respect to the life cycle processes for software. This standard was designed to be applicable to all life-cycle models, even though not all of these models include the processes contained in the standard. IEEE 1012 has been used by several private and government organizations to structure the V&V activities performed on various projects; for instance, NASA's Independent Verification and Validation Facility (IV&V) uses the IEEE 1012 for the its software IV&V plans.

Figure 1 shows how the IEEE 1012 defines a V&V framework at three levels: processes, activities and tasks. A top-level *process*, such as Development V&V, is comprised of *activities*, such as Concept V&V, Requirements V&V, etc. These are, in turn, comprised of *tasks*, such as Traceability Analysis, Software Design Evaluation, etc. These tasks provide the highest level of detail, including the specific nature of the V&V work to be performed, the required inputs and the required outputs.

A key artifact of the IEEE 1012 is the Software V&V Plan (SVVP), which includes a mandatory section to describe the roles and responsibilities for organizational elements or individuals involved with the software V&V. IEEE 1012 was designed to integrate with the IEEE/EIA 12207.0 (ISO/IEC 12207, 2008) a broader standard providing a framework for managing and developing software (IEEE, 1998). Such integration is described in an appendix of IEEE 1012, to facilitate conformance between both IEEE 1012 and IEEE/EIA 12207.0 in development projects where both standards must be used. The goal of this integration is to avoid unnecessary duplication of documentation or processes resulting from the application of distinct standards.

Quality Performance and Continous Improvement

Quality Performance Indicators are designed and developed to improve understanding, planning and control of productivity, effectiveness and timeliness of projects and deliverables. They must be based on shared views of the project and must include a performance measurement repository that organizes and stores historical measurement data to be used for trend analysis and monitoring, to improve both quality products and processes.

Today, organizations are competing in complex and dynamic environments. Static measurement

Figure 1. V&V framework (IEEE Std 1012, 2004)

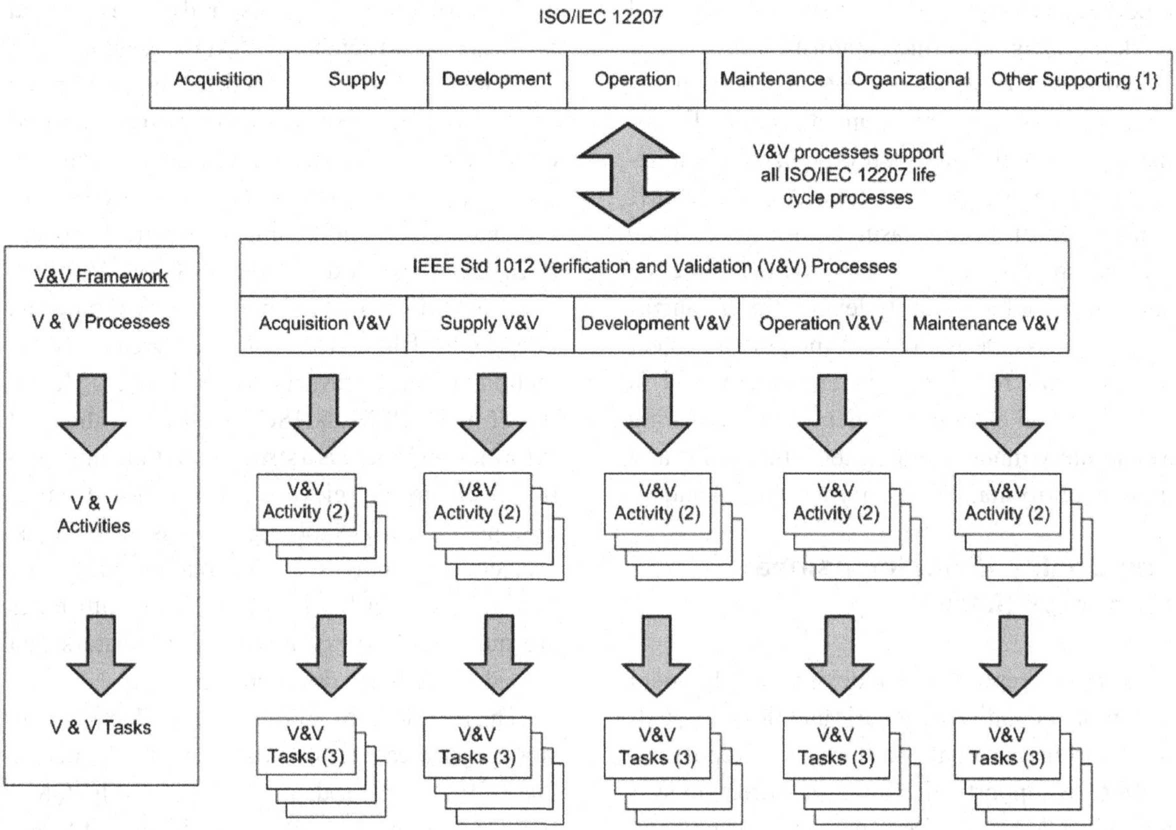

ISO/IEC 12207

Acquisition	Supply	Development	Operation	Maintenance	Organizational	Other Supporting {1}

V&V processes support all ISO/IEC 12207 life cycle processes

V&V Framework

V & V Processes

IEEE Std 1012 Verification and Validation (V&V) Processes

Acquisition V&V	Supply V&V	Development V&V	Operation V&V	Maintenance V&V

V & V Activities

V&V Activity (2)	V&V Activity (2)	V&V Activity (2)	V&V Activity (2)	V&V Activity (2)

V & V Tasks

V&V Tasks (3)	V&V Tasks (3)	V&V Tasks (3)	V&V Tasks (3)	V&V Tasks (3)

models are inadequate for estimation and performance management in dynamic and rapidly changing business environments. What is required is a system measurement model with a flexible and integrated process to allow managers to handle continuously changing business conditions (Harrison, 2000).

Frequent re-engineering of business units and product lines often renders obsolete a significant amount of critical historical data stored in predominantly static measurement systems. In today's ever changing technical and business environments, there is now a critical need for the re-design of measurement systems to give them the flexibility to be reconfigured continuously, while preserving the value of historical data initially organized along outdated organizational structures.

Quality Performance and Improvement According to CMMI

It is obvious that in an environment of continuous improvement, the measurement of the software processes and products is essential. The commonsense rule of "what you cannot measure, you cannot manage" in a context of software process improvement will be understood like "what we cannot measure we cannot improve" (McGarry et al., 2002).

In the CMMI context, measurement has a clearly defined purpose, which is expressed in specific goals (SG), generics goals (GG), specific practices (SP) and generic practices (GP) as well as in particular work products into given processes areas. Our intention in this chapter is to present a tool to facilitate the establishment of the measurement collection, storage, analysis and reporting, according to CMMI specific goals and work products, in defined maturity levels.

The CMMI establishes several requirements about process and product quantification. Establishing and maintaining an organization's measurement repository is referenced in the CMMI maturity level 2 (in Measurement and Analysis process area), established as a specific practice and referenced in maturity level 3 (in Organizational Process Definition and Integrated Project Management for IPPD process areas), and is considered an essential element for establishing a quantitative understanding about the quality and process performance in maturity levels 4 and 5.

The Quality Multidimensional repository (QMR)

This section reports on the design, development and implementation of generic and flexible Quality Multidimensional Measurement Repository (QMR) to support a dynamic measurement system with CMMI requirements in a changing and dynamic environment.

The core of the QMR tool contains a database structure that does not presuppose any particular measures or relationship between them; the measures themselves are treated as data. We call this characteristic metadata—data that represent measurement data of products and processes for different maturity levels in CMMI context.

The QMR tool only store base measures. Derived measures—those involving one or more measures and a computation process to calculate their value—will be handled by the Analytical Engine, that is, the OLAP services. The QMR tool was constructed, as ISO 15939 requires, following the principle that the Software measurement process is flexible, tailorable and adaptable to the needs of particular users.

The QMR tool is based on the definition of characteristics of CMMI Measurement Analysis process area. The QMR tool allows specifying and

tracking measures based on base measures and derived measures. This is inspired by the Practical Software Measurement—PSM (McGarry, 2001) and ISO 15939 (ISO/IEC Std 15939, 2007). The data collection and storage mechanisms are based on a database system. The data analysis and reporting indicators are based on Structured Query Language (SQL) and Online Analytical Process (OLAP) cubes (Codd, Codd, & Salley, 1993).

The QMR tool is designed to facilitate the integration of the concepts of a Measurement Information Model and a Measurement Process Model. According to PSM and ISO 15939 a Measurement Information Model is a structure linking information needs to the relevant entities and attributes of concern. Entities include processes, products, projects and resources. The Measurement Information Model describes how the relevant attributes are quantified and converted to indicators that provide a basis for decision-making.

The QMR tool allows the collection and storage of measurement data directly related to the information needs of the project. The QMR tool set these measurement data in a flexible and tailorable hierarchy. This hierarchy is composed of an association's levels to facilitate the ever-changing information needs of the organization. The PSM states that a Measurement Process Model describes a set of related measurement activities that are generally applicable in all circumstances, regardless of the specific information needs of any particular situation. The QMR tool is composed of a set of Measurement Process activities that are inspired from Software Process Measurement Standard (ISO 15939) and PSM.

ISO 15939 standard explains that the Process Measurement consists of four iterative measurement activities: establish, plan, perform and evaluate measurement and each activity is related to specific tasks that contribute towards achieving the purpose and outcomes of the software measurement process. This standard supports the management and improvement of software processes and products. It is important to note that our QMR tool facilitates the implementation of the software measurement of processes and products. In Figure 2 we described how the QMR tool supports different activities and tasks of the ISO 15939 standard.

QMR AND ISO 1012

V&V Measurement Management

The QMR provides support to management of V&V activities described in IEEE 1012. This support is expressed in terms of the facilitation of the following tasks: (1) monitor the execution of the SVVP, (2) analyze problems discovered during the execution of the SVVP, (3) report progress of the process, (4) ensure products satisfy requirements, (5) assess evaluation results, (6) determine whether a task is complete and check the results for completeness.

Figure 2 shows how the QMR interacts with processes, activities and tasks established in IEEE 1012. The management of V&V activities monitoring and evaluate all the V&V outputs. Through the QMR we can identify trend data and potential risks in the management of V&V.

In the following paragraphs we present some characteristics of the QMR that are directly related to implementation of an efficient V&V management in safety-critical software.

V&V Measurement Quality and Effectiveness

The QMR provides a quantitative understanding of the effectiveness of V&V in terms of the quality, reliability and maintenance of software projects. The QMR facilitates evaluation of quality performance of the processes, activities and tasks, through the establishment of the relevant measures. The QMR facilitates the monitoring of the identified milestones established in the SVVP according to IEEE 1012 (5.1.1 task 1).

Examples of measures in process performance that the QMR could implement are as follows: effectiveness of process activities, percentage of defects removed by product verification activities, percentage of rework time, mean time between

Figure 2. Support of QMR to IEEE 1012

Process Acquisition (5.2)	Process Supply (5.3)	Process Development (5.4)	Process Operation (5.5)	Process Maintenance (5.6)

Activity: Acquisition Support V&V (5.2.1)	Activity: Planning V&V (5.3.1)	Activity: Concept V&V (5.4.1)	Activity: Requirements V&V (5.4.2)	Activity: Design V&V (5.4.3)	Activity: Implementation V&V (5.4.4)	Activity: Test V&V (5.4.5)	Activity: Installation and Checkout V&V (5.4.6)	Activity: Operation V&V (5.5.1)	Activity: Maintenance V&V (5.6.1)

Activity : Management of V&V (5.1.1)

V&V Inputs	V&V Tasks	V&V Outputs
(1) All V&V inputs (2) All V&V Outputs	(1) SVVP Generation (2) Proposed-Baseline Change Assessment (3) Management Review of the V&V Effort (4) Management and Technical Review Support (5) Interface With Organizational and Supporting Processes (6) Identify Improvement Opportunities in the Conduct of V&V	(1) SVVP Updates (2) Task Reports (3) Anomaly Reports

failures, number and severity of defects in the released product, etc.

Measurement V&V Baseline

The QMR allows the collection and storage of measurement data directly related to the information needs of V&V tasks (IEEE 1012, 5.1.1 task 2). The QMR set these measurement data in a flexible and tailorable hierarchy. This hierarchy is composed of an association's levels to facilitate the evaluation of software changes for V&V tasks (e.g., anomaly corrections and requirements changes). It is important to note that the QMR has been built according to a set of related measures that are generally applicable in several circumstances, regardless of the specific information needs of any particular situation.

The QMR collects measurement data from several V&V tasks and allows analyzing them to establish a process performance baseline for quality and process performance in the project. The QMR offers the possibility of establishing estimations based on historical measurement V&V data, as well as providing an understanding of the nature and extent of variation experienced in process performance.

V&V Measurement Improvement

The QMR can facilitate summarization of the V&V effort to define changes to V&V tasks or redirect V&V effort (IEEE 1012, 5.1.1 task 3). The QMR can contribute to establish measures to determine the value of each process improvement with respect to the organization's quality and process-performance objectives. Examples of pertinent measurement include: the ratio of the number of software modules verified and validated to the total number of modules, the ratio of the number of defects identified by V&V to the number of defect missed, etc. The QMT facilitates the measurement of actual V&V cost vs. planned V&V cost, V&V effort on tasks, and schedule for

deploying V&V on each processes and products. Additionally, it is possibly establish a measure of the progress toward achieving the organization's quality and process-performance objectives, as well as the number and severity of customer complaints concerning the provided service.

Measurement V&V Indicators

The QMT incorporates the possibility to establish indicators based on hierarchical measurement data stored in the meta-model database system. The tool is designed to accept a customized definition of the parameters, e.g., the definition of a trigger alerts when a maximum value is reached.

The repository tool can quantitatively determine the status of the processes; it can monitor and detect changes in the performance and then decision-makers can implement corrective actions as necessary. The QMT offers the possibility of verifying the timely delivery according to the approved schedule of all software products (IEEE 1012, 5.1.1 task 4 and 6). The QMT offers the option of establishing both process measurements (e.g., efforts, cycle time, and defect removal effectiveness) and product measurements (e.g., reliability, defect density).

Interface with Organizational and Supporting Process

The QMT offers the possibility of exporting the V&V data in different file formats to facilitate the exchange with other processes implemented in the organization (IEEE 1012, 5.1.1 task 5).

QMR and CMMI

In the next sections we will show some comprehension about how QMR tool could facilitate the implementation of different CMMI maturity levels in an organization.

QMR Tool and Maturity Level 2

It is important to note that Measurement and Analysis (MA) is one of principal process areas that have direct impact of all process areas in the CMMI. The purpose of MA is directly related to information needs. The CMMI states that the purpose of MA is to develop and sustain a measurement capability that is used to support management information needs. It means that the measurement capability is expressed in terms of the support of information needs. The QMR tool was designed to help decision makers evaluate objectively the evolution of the products and processes related to defined information needs in software organizations and projects.

MA recommends storing project-specific data and results in a repository. The CMMI states that when the data of this repository is shared more widely across projects, the data may reside in the Organization's Measurement Repository. This repository is used to make available data on processes and work products, particularly as they relate to the Organization's Set of Standard Process (OSSP). The repository contains or references actual measurement data and relates information needed to understand and analyze the measurement data. This is the principle that we adopted to develop our QMR tool: the capability of the repository to store different types of related measurement data in the context of an integrated environment.

In the CMMI, the MA SP 1.1 indicates that measures should be related to organizational needs and objectives. Measures should have a clear purpose and not be employed only to accumulate data. The data should answer the questions about processes and products.

QMR Tool and Maturity Level 3

In Maturity level 3 of the CMMI, the implementation of a Measurement Repository is used to establish and maintain a usable set of organizational process assets (MA SP 1.4). The repository in this context contains product and process measures that are related to the OSSP. Additionally it contains or refers to the information needed to understand and interpret the measures and assess them for reasonableness or applicability.

An OSSP contains definitions of the processes that guide all activities in an organization. These process descriptions cover the fundamental process elements that must be incorporated into the defined processes that are implemented in projects across the organization. At this stage the QMR tool can be integrated across the organization and tailored to particular contexts in projects.

Furthermore, it can facilitate the storing, retrieving and analyzing of measurements across the organization. Additionally the QMR tool provides measurement data about the typical work products, such a set of product and process for the OSSP, etc. The commonly used measurements provided by the QMR tool are as follows: estimations of effort and cost, peer review coverage, test coverage, number of defects found, severity of defects, etc.

One of the principal characteristics of the QMR tool is the flexibility to change the measure's definition and implementation, as the organization's needs change. This characteristic is cover by the definition of a meta-model structure of the measurement data. This property allows, for example, the addition and retirement of measures at any time without affecting the integrity of the measurement data.

The QMR tool incorporates the capability of monitoring and controlling the organizational processes against the plan for performing the processes, to allow decision makers to take the appropriate corrective action (MA GP 2.8). This characteristic is implemented in the QMR tool, for example, by measuring the process elements of the OSSP or by measuring the percentage of projects using the process architectures and process elements of the OSSP.

The QMR tool facilitates the institutionalization of the CMMI generic practice Collect

Improvement Information (MA GP 3.2). The QMR tool allows the collection of measures, the measurements results and derived information (indicators) about the planning and executed processes.

The Integrated Project Management for IPPD process area of the CMMI establishes the use of a measurement repository for estimating and planning the projects activities (SP 1.2). The QMR tool allows using the historical measurement data for estimating the project's planning parameters, by finding similarities and differences between the current project and past projects, and then building custom indicators based on, for example, application domain, operational environment, experience of the people, etc. Of course it is possible to take measurements of effort by phase, effort by project, cost (actual vs. planned), schedule (actual vs. planned), staffing, etc.

QMR Tool and Maturity Level 4

Maturity level 4 is composed of two process areas: Organizational Process Performance and Quantitative Project Management. These process areas are strongly based on process measurements. In this stage the QMR tool has a capital role to success of the CMMI implementation.

Organizational Process Performance (OPP) process area establishes and maintains a quantitative understanding of the performance of the OSSP in support of the of quality and process-performance objectives, and provides the process performance data, baselines, and models to quantitatively manage the organization's projects (CMMI Product Team, 2006).

The QMR tool collects measurement data from several projects and allows analyzing them to establish a process performance baseline for quality and process performance in the organization. The QMR tool facilitates the understanding of the divergence between the organization's performance and the performance required for an ever-changing market. The QMR tool can quan-

titatively determine the status of the processes; it can monitor and detect changes in the performance and then decision-makers can implement corrective actions as necessary. The QMR tool offers the option of establishing both process measurements (e.g., efforts, cycle time, defect removal effectiveness) and product measurements (e.g., reliability, defect density).

The purpose of Quantitative Project Management (QPM) PA is to quantitatively manage the project's defined process to achieve the project's established quality and process-performance objectives (CMMI Product Team, 2006). With the QMR tool we have the option, for instance, of measuring the performance of actual results achieved by following a process. It is possible to establish a minimum set of measures for processes and products in the organization. The QMR tool offers the possibility of establishing estimations based on historical measurement data, as well as providing an understanding of the nature and extent of variation experienced in process performance.

The QMR tool can measure quality attributes such as mean time between failures, number and severity of defects in the released product, number and severity of customer complaints concerning the provided service. Examples of measures in process performance that the QMR tool could implement are as follows: percentage of defect removed by product verification activities, percentage of rework time, and severity of defects by product. The QMR tool offers the possibility of exporting the data in different file formats for statistical analysis, if a more specific evaluation is required.

QMR Tool and Maturity Level 5

Maturity level 5 contains two process areas: Organizational Innovation and Deployment (OID) and Causal Analysis and Resolution (CAR). The purpose of the OID is to select and deploy incremental and innovative improvements that measurably improve the organization's process and technologies. The improvements support the organization's quality and process-performance objectives as derived from the organization's business objectives (CMMI Product Team, 2006). The QMR tool provides a quantitative understanding of organization's quality performance and facilitates, by the establishment of the pertinent measures, the estimation of the improvement in quality and process performance resulting from deploying the process and technology improvements. Examples of pertinent measurement are: effectiveness of process activities, customer satisfaction, etc.

OID SG 2 states that measurable improvement to the organization's process and technologies are continually and systematically deployed. The QMR tool can contribute to establish measures to determining the value of each process and technology improvement with respect to the organization's quality and process-performance objectives. OID SP 2.3 refers to measure the effects of the deployed process and technology improvements. QMR tool facilitate the measures of actual cost, effort, and schedule for deploying each process and technology improvement. Additionally, it is possibly establish a measure of the progress toward achieving the organization's quality and process-performance objectives.

CAR process area refers to identify causes of defects and other problems and take action to prevent them from occurring in the future (CMMI Product Team, 2006). A measurement process based on the QMR tool can be used for gather relevant defect data, for example: defects reported by customer, defects found in peer reviews, defects found in testing, etc. In SP 2.2, Measures of performance and performance change are establishes as typical work products. QMR can provide measures, for example, to relate to peer review before and after the improvement has been made.

QMR TOOL DESIGN: OVERVIEW

To meet the constraints of a dynamic business environment, the QMR tool must have a generic database repository with a high level of flexibility. This requires then that the definitions of the measures, and of their and relationships, be stored in the repository in a metadata entity. The metadata are a level of abstraction of the measurements rather than the measurements themselves. The metadata entity can then provide the flexibility required by the ever-changing needs of the organization.

The set of relationships among entities are defined and stored as another entity in the repository to support both hierarchical and multidimensional views of data. This allows taking advantage of the OLAP (On Line Analytical Process) services such a drill-down/drill-up, for the measurements associated with a lower-/upper-level entity, and from an aggregated value to its atomic components. Analytic and drill-down facilitates provide the users with the possibility of making data analysis at different levels of granularity.

The OLAP services play an important role in the QMR tool. In particular, OLAP pulls together data from multiple sources in the organization and stores that data in a form convenient for further analysis and decisions support (Kimball & Ross, 2002). These services allow creating, querying and maintaining OLAP cubes, which are materialized views of the information. This is a way of pre-computing summaries of data, so that requests can be answered quickly (Train & Jacobson, 2000).

To provide the multidimensional feature, the OLAP pivoting cubes approach was selected to dynamically display and rearrange multiple dimensions of data. To provide data collection, communication and diffusion of Performance Measurement, according to CMMI requirements (MA SP 2.4), a portal approach was selected for the QMR. The portal provides a dual perspective of overall quality performance information (Ferguson, 2002).

Of course, a security mechanism according to a level of responsibility and authority (MA GP 2.4 AB 3) has to be designed and implemented in the QMR tool. This mechanism prevents unauthorized access to, accidental modification or destruction of data. It also provides audit mechanisms and for quality assurance purposes (MA GP 2.9 VE 1 and 2.10 VE 2).

Measurement Collection

According to Measurement and Analysis Process Area of the CMMI (SP 1.3), the QMR tool design provides for two modes of collecting measurement data:

Automated via an Extraction, Transformation and Loading (ETL) tool for high volume-high periodic measurements, such as those collected through the time reporting system or the trouble reporting system. Manual via a data-entry, web-based form, for low frequency–low volume data such as turnover rates and hourly rates.

Information Needs Indicator

The repository facilitates the mapping of the information needs of the organization to the indicators proposed to satisfy those Information Needs (MA SG 1 and SP 1.1 and 1.2). The business indicators initially proposed by Ericsson were as follows:

- **Effectiveness & Efficiency:** Are we delivering the right products at the right time at the promised cost?
- **Financial:** What is the cost of our operations? Are expenditures growing or declining? Are we meeting the goals of the efficiency program?
- **Quality:** Are our products satisfying our customers? Does (the tool) provide support for TL 9000 (QuEST Forum, 2007) certification?
- **Strategic goals:** Can we monitor the specific goals set for the month/quarter/year?

QMR ARCHITECTURE

This section presents the architecture selected for the deployment of the functionalities of the QMR tool. The Indicators and Trending capabilities, for Management needs, present the information based on predefined reports and charts navigable in a web page style to facilitate the implementation of the Measurement and Analysis process area, SP 1.4 and 2.2. A home page will display the names of the different reports available using an indented structure from which it will be possible to jump into the selected report.

The Analytic and drill-down/drill-up capabilities are designed to support Middle Managers and Operations Development personnel with dynamic reports, Excel export capabilities and drill-down/drill-up functionality similar to that provided in on-line analytical applications.

The administration and quality control interface allows the person designated as administrator to define new measures, grant privileges and audit the quality and timeliness of the data entered into the system (MA SP 3.1).

The analytical engine (OLAP technology) provides the capability to compute derived measures and aggregate them across multiple dimensions. The Measurement Repository itself provides, of course, permanent storage for the measurements taken and the metadata necessary to administer them (MA SP 2.3).

The design of the data model for the QMR tool is, of course, critical. The design of the Repository tool incorporates an object-oriented measurement meta-model (Walkerden, 1995) The object-oriented data model with all the class diagrams and associations for the Repository tool is illustrated in Figure 3 and Table 1. Table 1 presents a brief description of the entities involved in the object-oriented data model. Detailed information of all of the entities considered in the model is presented in (Abran & Palza, 2003).

Measurement Management and Trends

We have developed a web interface for collecting data manually from managers in the Ericsson Intranet environment. Data are collected directly to OLAP dimension tables, each one representing a dimension of interest, such as unit, project, product, etc.

OLAP technology provides graphical representation of multidimensional measures in the QMT. This is an important functionality to determine why certain trends or patterns are occurring. The next figure shows the visualization of cubes (Earn

Figure 3. Depicts the entities and the relationships of the repository

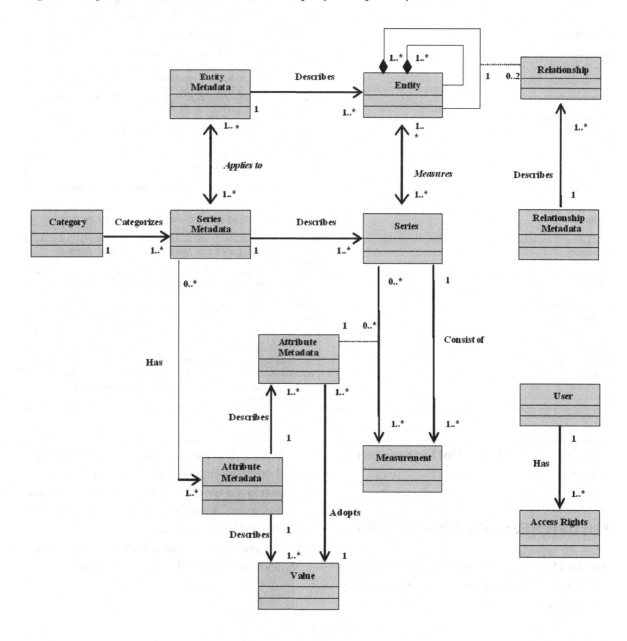

Table 1. List of the measurement classes

Class	Description
Entity Metadata	Instances of the class store all common data associated with given entity type, i.e Organization, Unit, Product, Project, Version
Entity	Instances of this class Entity store all data associated with a specific Unit, Product, Project, or any other entity type defined by entity metadata
Relationship	This associative class is used to model arbitrary relationship between two entities. The nature of the relationship is given by the relationship metadata
Relationship Metadata	Instances of this class store the nature of the relationship
Series	Instances of this class are a chronologically ordered collection of measurements representing the value of measure over time
Measures	This non-relationship links a specific series to the object or objects being measures by it
Measurement	Each instance of this class captures the value of measurement, as well as the date on which it was taken
Series Metadata	This class describes the attributes that classify the measurement by the series
Attributes	This associative class qualifies the measurement according to difference attributes. For example of the 5 TR's (Trouble Reports) recorded on Oct 7 2002, three could be of severity "A", one of the severity "B", and another "C"
Attribute Metadata	This class describes the attributes that classify the measurement in the series
Value	Instance of this class store the admissible values for the given attribute
Category	Describe the categories, ex. Quality, Cost, which measures are categorized
Applies To	This non-relationship defines the applicable set of measures for each object type
User	This class captures the user ids of those authorized to access the repository. Access to this table is restricted to the database administrator
Access Rights	Indicates the specific object and relationship instances to which a given user has access and what he or she can do with them, i.e. Create, Change, Delete. Access to this table is restricted to the database adminstrator

Value and Failures) in the QMT at Ericsson (see Figure 4).

FUTURE RESEARCH DIRECTIONS

The QMT was developed and implemented as a prototype and some important improvements should be considered:

Data collection for QMT is currently still predominantly manual. A Web Interface should be developed for collecting data from an Intranet environment. Actually data is collected directly to OLAP dimension tables.

An interface for client/server databases and legacy systems is still being investigated.

Figure 4. CPI/SPI chart and downtime failures chart cubes

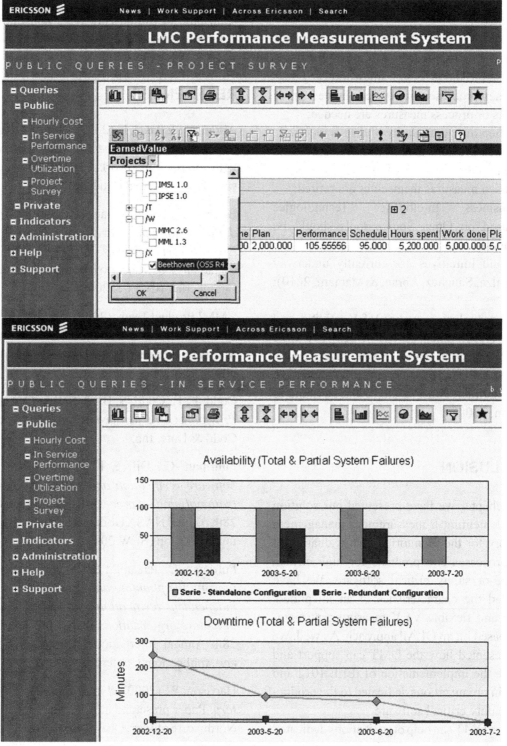

In a dynamically changing business environment, the measures themselves will need to be revisited

- When new processes improvement are added to the process framework;
- When processes are revised and new products or process measures are needed;
- When finer granularity of data is required;
- When greater visibility into the process is required;
- When measures themselves are retired;
- Business Intelligence Technologies based on Open Source tools should be investigated.
- Some initiatives are currently underway (Palza, Sanchez, Abran, & Mamani, 2010);

Further analysis regarding V&V activities and Iterative Development as RUP / OpenUP /CMMI should be accomplished. Some investigation has been achieved (Fuhrman, Djlive, & Palza, 2003; Fuhrman, Palza, & Do, 2004; Bertrand & Fuhrman, 2008).

CONCLUSION

In this chapter we have presented our solution for implementing a measurement management repository for the monitoring and evaluation of V&V processes and products for high critical software or safety critical software. We have illustrated the characteristics of an integrated, generic and flexible V&V measurement meta-model based on an OLAP approach. As well, we have presented how the QMT can support and facilitate the implementation of IEEE 1012 and CMMI in organizations dedicated to the production of safety critical software.

Such a QMT can help organizations dedicated to the production of software, in particular critical software to improve monitoring and to control trend indicators in safety and reliability of their products as well as quality and coverage of V&V tasks. Thus, the use of our proposed QMT could contribute to minimizing risks and optimizing investments in software quality and improvement.

REFERENCES

Abran, A., & Palza, E. (2003). *Design of a generic performance measurement repository in industry.* 13th International Workshop on Software Measurement, Montréal (Québec).

Bertrand, C., & Fuhrman, C. P. (2008). *Towards defining software development processes in DO-178B with openup.* Paper presented at the Canadian Conference on Electrical and Computer Engineering (CCECE 2008).

CMMI Product Team. (2006). *CMMI® for development*, version 1.2.Carnegie Mellon University, Software Engineering Institute. Retrieved from http://www.sei.cmu.edu

Codd, E. F., Codd, S. B., & Salley, C. T. (1993). *Providing OLAP to user-analysts: An IT mandate.* Codd & Date, Inc.

Fuhrman, C., Djlive, F., & Palza, E. (2003). *Software verification and validation within the (rational) unified process.* Paper presented at the 28th Annual NASA Goddard Software Engineering Workshop (SEW 2003).

Fuhrman, C., Palza, E., & Do, K. L. (2004). *Optimizing the planning and executing of software independent verification and validation (IV&V) in mature organizations.* Paper presented at the 28th Annual International Computer Software and Applications Conference (COMPSAC 2004).

Harrison, W. (2000). *A universal metrics repository.* Paper presented at the 18th Annual Pacific Northwest Software Quality Conference, Portland, Oregon.

IEEE. (1998). *IEEE/EIA 12207.0-1996 industry implementation of international standard ISO/IEC 12207: 1995 (ISO/IEC 12207) Standard for information technology software life cycle processes. IEEE/EIA 12207.0-1996* (pp. i-75).

ISO/IEC 12207. (2008). *Systems and software engineering - Software life cycle processes.* ISO/IEC 12207:2008.

ISO/IEC Std 15939. (2007). *Information Technology - Software engineering - Software measurement process.* Geneva, Switzerland: International Organization for Standardization.

Kit, E. (Ed.). (1995). *Software testing in the real world: Improving the process.* Addison-Wesley.

Levenson, N., & Turner, C. (1993). An investigation of the Therac-25 accidents. *IEEE Computer, 26*(7), 18–41.

Lions, P. (1996). *Ariane 5: Flight 501 failure - Report by the inquiry board.* Retrieved from http://sunnyday.mit.edu/accidents/Ariane5accidentreport.html

McGarry, J. (Ed.). (2001). *PSM - Practical software measurement: Objective information for decision makers.* Addison-Wesley.

McGarry, J., Card, D., Jones, C., Layman, B., Clark, E., & Dean, J. (2002). *Practical software measurement: Objective information for decision makers.* Boston, MA: Addison-Wesley.

NASA Software IV&V Facility. (2000, 31 August 2000). Software independent verification and validation. In *Program manager handbook.* Retrieved Jan 30, 2003, from http://www.ivv.nasa.gov/about/tutorial/PM_Handbook_v1.pdf

Palza, E. (2010). *Process and datamarts for V&V in critical projects.* Éditions Universitaires Européennes: Südwestdeutscher Verlag für Hochschulschriften Aktiengesellschaft & Co. KG.

Palza, E., Abran, A., & Fuhrman, C. (2003). *Establishing a generic and multidimensional measurement repository in CMMI context.* Paper presented at the 28th Annual IEEE/NASA Software Engineering Workshop, Greenbelt, MD, USA.

Palza, E., Sanchez, J., Abran, A., & Mamani, G. (2010). *Implementing KPI with open source BI software in an academic department.* Paper presented at the Computer Professional Conference /Software Maintenance and Evolution.

QuEST Forum. (2007). *TL 9000 quality system requirements: Measurements handbook* (Release 4). Kimball, R., & Ross, M. (Ed.). (2002). *The data warehouse toolkit: The complete guide to dimensional modeling.* John Wiley & Sons. Ferguson, R. (Ed.). (2002). *Special edition using Microsoft SharePoint portal server.* Indianapolis, IN: Que.

IEEE Std 1059. (1993). *IEEE guide for software verification and validation plans.*

IEEE Std 1012. (2004). IEEE standard for software verificiation and validation. *IEEE Std 1012-2004 (Revision of IEEE Std 1012-1998)*, 0_1-110.

Train, O., & Jacobson, R. (Eds.). (2000). *Microsoft(r) SQL Server(tm) 2000 analysis services step by step.* Microsoft Press.

Walkerden, F. (1995). *A design for a software metrics repository (CAESAR Technical Report).* Sydney, Australia: Centre for Advanced Empirical Software Research, School of Information Systems, University of New South Wales.

Wallace, D. R., & Fujii, R. U. (1989). Software verification and validation: An overview. *IEEE Software, 6*(3), 10. doi:10.1109/52.28119

Chapter 5

Implementing Internal Software Process Assessment:
An Experience at a Mid–Size IT Company

Shukor Sanim Mohd Fauzi
Universiti Teknologi Mara, Malaysia

Nuraminah Ramli
Universiti Pendidikan Sultan Idris, Malaysia

Mustafa Kamal Mohd Noor
University of Malaya, Malaysia

ABSTRACT

Software process assessments have become commonplace in the software industry because the software industry usually does not recognize the level of their software process. From the time software is developed, a phenomenon called software crisis exists subsuming wrong schedules and cost estimates, low productivity of people, as well as low productivity. A promising approach out of this crisis is now growing up in the software engineering community. One of the approaches is Software Process Assessment. We present our experience in implementing internal software process assessment at one of the mid-size Information Technology (IT) company by using the customized SPA method. The customized model is basically based on Standard CMMI Appraisal Method for Process Improvement (SCAMPI).

INTRODUCTION

Software engineering body of knowledge (SWe-BOK) has identified ten areas that is fall under software engineering field (Abran et al., 2004). It includes software requirements, software design, software construction, software testing, software maintenance, software configuration management, software engineering management, software engineering tools and methods and software quality. Other area includes software engineering process. Software engineering process can be alienated into two categories. The first category encompasses the technical and managerial activities; whereas the second category is refer to meta-level. Meta-level category concerned with

DOI: 10.4018/978-1-61350-141-2.ch005

the definition, implementation, assessment, measurement, management, change and improvement of the software life cycle. Next paragraph will discuss more on meta-level category, focusing on software process assessment (SPA) and software process improvement (SPI).

Software engineering process can be interpreted as a set of process involved to accomplish certain activities in software development (Singh, 1996). Another researcher define software engineering process itself as a process or a set of processes used by an organization or project to plan, manage, execute, monitor, control and improve its software related activities (Zahran, 1998). It is usually understood as a combination of activities like system and software requirement analysis, software design, software implementation, testing and maintenance. Software process improvement means the action taken to change an organization's business needs and achieve its business goals more effectively. The objective of SPI is to improve an organization's capability to produce better products. In order to improve software processes, an organization needs to know what the current state of processes is. This is where SPA plays a part. SPA is a disciplined evaluation of an organization's software processes against an process model (Zahran, 1998). One of the main objectives of SPA includes identifying the maturity level of the processes in an organization and also to identify the highest priority areas for improvement and to provide guidance on how to make the improvements. Other main objectives of SPA as mentioned by (Zahran, 1998) are as follows:

- To understand and determine the organization's current software engineering practices, and to learn how the whole organization works.
- To identify strengths, major weaknesses and key areas for software process improvement.

- To facilitate the initiation of process improvement activities and enroll opinion leaders in the change process.
- To provide a framework for process improvement actions.
- To help obtain sponsorship and support for action through following a participative approach to the assessment.

SPA also helps software organizations improve themselves by identifying their critical problems and establishing improvement priorities (Humphrey, Kitson, & Kasse, 1989). It is conducted to find out which processed need to be changed as it provides a baseline of the current status of the prevailing software practices in the organization. SPA will leads to capability determination, which uses a set of criteria in order to identify, analyze and quantify strengths, weaknesses and particularly risks. Software process capability determination is used in the selection of suppliers but also can be used internally within the organization (Dorling, 1993).

Software process assessment and improvement is recognized as an important part of the software development life cycle (Figure 1). Several contemporary models have been developed to assist organizations evaluate and improve their software development processes and capabilities.

Interoperability between them are necessary because the outcome can lead to the identification and selection of key activities for improvement and the continuous application of improvements to match the business needs of the organization. These can be integrated into the process focus, by an institutionalization of procedures, policies, standards and organizational structure (McGuire & Randall, 1998).

SPA is normally carried out at project level by looking at the processes used on past or current projects in order to capture actual practice. The capability to perform the next project is based on the process maturity distribution of current projects. Large projects will have a lifecycle

Figure 1. Relationship between software process assessment, software process improvement and capability determination (Jung & Hunter, 2001)

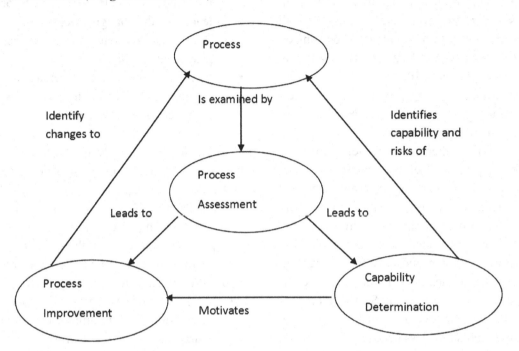

and processes defined specifically to meet the needs of the project. Different types of product or different development modes may result in significantly different process profiles. Hence an effective assessment scheme needs flexibility to handle the variations.

The main intention of this chapter is to discuss on the experience in implementing SPA at one of mid-size IT company. The next section of this chapter will explain about several SPA models which have been used widely by most of the organizations, followed by the discussion of our experience in conducting SPA. Finally, lessons learned, future works and conclusion is presented.

EXISTING SOFTWARE PROCESS ASSESSMENT MODEL

This section will discuss on the SPA models which includes Standard CMMI Appraisal Method for Process Improvement (SCAMPI), Software Pro-

cess Improvement and Capability Determination (SPICE) or ISO/IEC 15504 and BOOTSTRAP.

Standard CMMI Appraisal Method for Process Improvement (SCAMPI)

The Standard CMMI Appraisal Method for Process Improvement (SCAMPI) is designed to provide benchmark quality ratings (Barbour et al., 2002)() relative to Capability Maturity Model Integration (CMMI) models (CMMI Product Team, 2001). SCAMPI consists of three (3) phases and eleven (11) essential processes, as is shown in Table 1.

Next paragraph will only discuss on the important component that exist in SCAMPI. This includes objective evidence, practice implementation indicator (PII) and also characterizing practices.

SCAMPI identified several tools for the collection of data from the organization or project. SCAMPI refer tools for data collection as objective evidence. Table 2 shows type of objective evidence used in SCAMPI.

Table 1. SCAMPI methodology (Barbour et al., 2002)

Phase		Process
1: Plan and Prepare for Appraisal	1. 1	Analyze Requirements
	1. 2	Develop Appraisal Plan
	1. 3	Select and Prepare Team
	1. 4	Obtain and Analyze Initial Objective
		Evidence
	1. 5	Prepare for Collection of Objective Evidence
2: Conduct Appraisal	2. 1	Examine Objective Evidence
	2. 2	Verify and Validate Objective Evidence
	2. 3	Document Objective Evidence
	2. 4	Generate Appraisal Results
3: Report Results	3. 1	Deliver Appraisal Results
	3. 2	Package and Archive Appraisal Assets

Table 2. Tools used as described in SCAMPI (Barbour et al., 2002)

Objective Evidence	Description
Instruments	Written information relative to the organizational unit's implementation of CMMI model practices. It includes questionnaires, surveys, or an organizational mapping of CMMI model practices to its corresponding processes.
Presentations	Information prepared by the organization and delivered visually or verbally to the appraisal team to describe organizational processes and implementation of CMMI model practices. This includes overview briefings, and demonstrations of tools or capabilities.
Documents	Artifacts reflecting the implementation of one or more model practices. It includes organizational policies, procedures, and implementation-level artifacts which is available in hardcopy or softcopy, or may be accessible via hyperlinks in a web-based environment.
Interviews	Face-to-face interaction with the practitioner. Interviews are conducted with various groups or individuals, such as project leaders, managers, and practitioners. A combination of formal and informal interviews may be held, using interview scripts or exploratory questions developed to elicit the information needed.

In SCAMPI, Practice Implementation Indicators (PII) is the necessary consequence of implementing CMMI model practices. The fundamental idea of Practice Implementation Indicators (PIIs) is that the conduct of an activity or the implementation of a practice results in footprints; evidence that provides a basis for verification of the activity or practice. Characterization of PII is described in Table 3.

The input or data gathered by the appraisal team then will be characterized by using 'characterizing practices'. The characterization practices are used to summarize the appraisal's team judgment on each practices assessed. This will give an in-depth idea on the implementation level in their organization or project. Table 4 shows the characterization practices used in SCAMPI.

The Software Process Improvement and Capability Determination (SPICE)

SPICE stands for Software Process Improvement and Capability Determination. It is an international

Table 3. Practice implementation indicator as described in SCAMPI (Barbour et al., 2002)

Indicator Type	Description	Examples
Direct artifacts	Outputs resulting directly from implementation of a specific or generic practice.	Typical work products listed in CMMI model practices Target products of an Establish and Maintain specific practice Documents, deliverable products, training materials and others.
Indirect artifacts	Artifacts that are a consequence of performing a certain practice. This indicator type is especially useful when there may be doubts about whether the intent of the practice has been met.	Typical work products listed in CMMI model practices Meeting minutes, review results, status reports Performance measures.
Affirmations	Oral or written statements confirming or supporting implementation of a specific or generic practice. These are usually provided by the implementers of the practice	Questionnaire responses Interviews Presentations.

Table 4. Characterizing practices in SCAMPI (Barbour et al., 2002)

Label	Description
Fully Implemented (FI)	The direct artifact is present and judged to be appropriate. At least one indirect artifact and/or affirmation exists to confirm the implementation. No substantial weaknesses were noted.
Largely Implemented (LI)	The direct artifact is present and judged to be appropriate. At least one indirect artifact and/or affirmation exist to confirm the implementation. One or more weaknesses were noted.
Partially Implemented (PI)	The direct artifact is absent or judged to be inadequate. Artifacts or affirmations suggest that some aspects of the practice are implemented. Weaknesses have been documented.
Not Implemented (NI)	Any situation not covered above.

initiative to develop a Standard for Software Process Assessment. The objective is to assist the software industry to make significant gains in productivity and quality, while at the same time helping purchasers to get better value for money and reduce the risk associated with large software projects and purchases. The standard (ISO 15504) being prepared under supervision of ISO/IEC JTC1/SC7 WG10 deals with software processes such as development, management, customer support and quality (Dorling, 1993). SPICE is comprised of nine (9) parts. This section describes each of the parts and its role within the Standard. Table 5 shows the parts in SPICE.

The context of a process assessment in SPICE is summarized in Figure 2. The formal entry to the assessment processes occurs with the compilation of several components such as:

- **Process assessment input**
  - Purpose
  - Scope
  - Constraints
  - Responsibilities
  - Additional information to be collected
- **Assessment activities**
  - Planning
  - Data collection
  - Data validation
  - Process rating
  - Reporting
- **Indicator set**
  - Process performance indicators
  - Process capability indicators
- **Reference model**
  - Process purpose
  - Process attributes

Table 5. Description for each part in international standard (Dorling, 1993)

Parts	Description
Part 1	It describes how the parts of the suite fit together, and provides guidance for their selection and use. It explains the requirements contained within the Standard and their applicability to the conduct of an assessment, to the construction and selection of supporting tools, and to the construction of extended processes.
Part 2	It describes the fundamental activities that are essential to software engineering, structured according to increasing levels of process capability. These baseline practices may be extended, through the generation of application or sector specific practice guides, to take account of specific industry, sector or other requirements.
Part 3	Defines a framework for conducting an assessment, and sets out the basis for rating, scoring and profiling process capabilities.
Part 4	Provides guidance on the conduct of team-based software process assessments. This guidance is generic enough to be applicable across all organizations, and also for performing assessments using a variety of different methods and techniques, and supported by a range of tools.
Part 5	Defines the framework elements required to construct an instrument to assist an assessor in the performance of an assessment.
Part 6	Describes the competence, education, training and experience of assessors that are relevant to conducting process assessments.
Part 7	Describes how to define the inputs to and use the results of an assessment for the purposes of process improvement.
Part 8	Describes how to define the inputs to and use the results of an assessment for the purpose of process capability determination.
Part 9	Consolidated vocabulary of all terms specifically defined for the purposes of this International Standard.

Figure 2. Context of process assessment (Dorling, 1993)

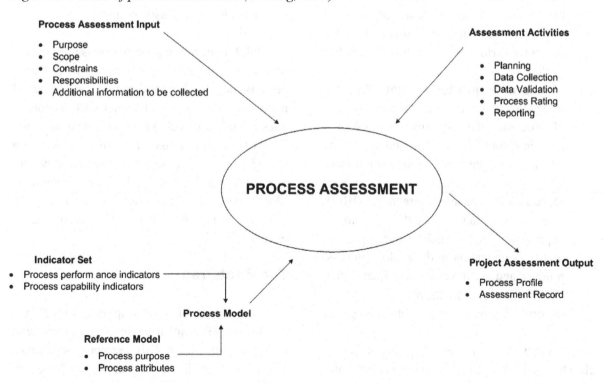

- **Process assessment output**
  ○ Process profile
  ○ Assessment record

The assessment framework depends upon an assessment architecture that defines the practices and processes that should be implemented. The process categories covered in the SPICE architecture address five (5) general areas of activity:

1. **Customer-supplier process category (CUS).** The customer-supplier process category consists of processes that directly impact the customer, support development and transition of the software to the customer, and provide for its correct operation and use of the software product and/or service.
2. **Engineering process category (ENG).** The engineering process category consists of processes that directly specify, implement or maintain the software products, its relation to the system and its customer documentation.
3. **Support process category (SUP).** The support process category consists of processes that may be employed by any of the other processes (including other supporting processes) at various points in the software life cycle.
4. **Management process category (MAN).** The management process category consists of processes that contain practices of a generic nature that may be used by anyone who manages any type of project or process within a software life cycle.
5. **Organization process category (ORG).** The organization process category consists of processes that establish the business goals of the organization and develop process, product and resource assets which, when used by the projects in the organization, help the organization achieve its business goals.

The practices are addressed by capability levels. The capability levels defined within SPICE are:

1. **Incomplete process (0):** The process is not implemented, or fails to achieve its defined process outcomes.
2. **Performed process (1):** The implemented process achieves is defined process outcomes.
3. **Managed process (2):** The previously defined performed process now delivers work products that fulfill expressed quality requirements within defined timescales and resource needs.
4. **Established process (3):** The previously defined managed processes are performs using a defined process that is based upon good software engineering principles and is capable of achieving its defined process outcomes.
5. **Predictable process (4):** The previously defined established process now performs consistently within defined limits to achieve its defined process outcomes.
6. **Optimizing process (5):** The previously defined predictable process now dynamically changes and adapts to effectively meet current future business goals.

SPICE does not require an assessment instrument to take any particular form or format. It may be constructed to be, for example, a paper-based instrument containing elements such as forms, questionnaires or checklists, or it may take the form of a computer-based instrument such as a spreadsheet, a data base system, an expert system or an integrated CASE tool. The assessment in SPICE consists of the eight (8) stages shown in Figure 3. Detail explanation for each stage is described in Table 6.

The Bootstrap

The main goal of Bootstrap is to develop a method for SPA, quantitative measurement, and improvement. Bootstrap is a project done as part of the European Strategic Program for Research

Figure 3. Assessment stages (Dorling, 1993)

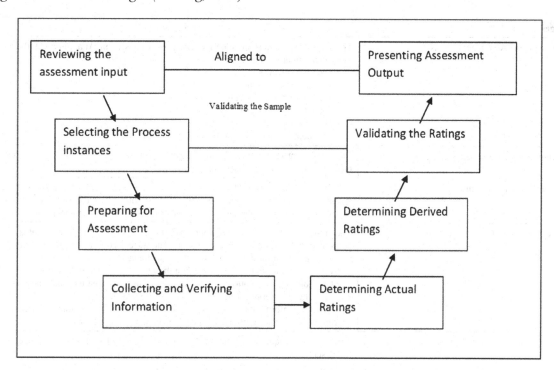

in Information Technology. Bootstrap is customized based on the Software Engineering Institute's process assessment method. This is to ensure that the model can fulfill and can be applied to the variety of European companies. (Haase, Messnarz, Koch, Kugler, & Decrinis, 2002).

The Bootstrap method assesses both the SPU and its projects, thus providing answers to two (2) important questions: Is the SPU providing all the necessary resources to do the projects, and are the projects using the resources efficiently. Bootstraps's process assessment and improvement methodology includes:

1. Description to guide the assessment.
2. Questionnaires and an algorithm to determine maturity and capability.
3. Guidelines for process improvement (standards for generating an action plan).
4. Guidelines for establishing an assessor training program and licensing policy.

5. A database of European companies that supports consultancy activities and the comparison of maturity and capability levels of the assessed companies.

COMPANY BACKGROUND

IT companies must now move to the new era of software development by considering the quality aspect in their software process. It can be done by employing several certifications such as CMMI, ISO and any other model in place. In sequence to move for a formal certification, the IT companies should make an effort to carry out their own SPA to ensure they are well prepared before a formal assessment set on. Formal assessment for some certification such as CMMI involves a lot amount of money.

In short coming years in Malaysia, we assume that all the bidders for the government tender for information technology infrastructure should

Table 6. Description for ISO/IEC 15504 Assessment Guidance Stages (Dorling, 1993)

Stages	Description
Reviewing the Assessment Inputs	The assessment input shall be defined prior to an assessment. At a minimum, the assessment input shall define: • The assessment purpose. • The assessment scope. • The assessment constraint. • The identity of qualified assessor. • The definition of extended process. • The identification of any information.
Selecting the Process Instances	The assessment scoping activity should specify which organizational unit and what process instances will be assessed.
Preparing for Assessment	The first stage in preparing for the assessment is the selection and preparation of the assessment team. At this stage, the organization should choose the assessment team size, define the roles of the assessment team and prepare the assessment team.
Collecting and Verifying Information	The fourth assessment stage defined in ISO/IEC 15504 Guide for Assessment is concerned with fact gathering and analysis. The stage is concerned with collecting and verifying the information. It has three (3) main tasks: • Collecting information – It depend on the assessment instrument used. • Categorizing information – The categories of information that should be collected during an assessment include the degree of adequacy. • Verifying information – Support documentation and records should be used as appropriate to verify the information collected during an assessment.
Determining Actual Rating	Base practice adequacy shall be rated using the following base practice adequacy rating scale: • Not Adequate (N) – The base practice either not implemented or does not to any degree contribute to satisfying the process purpose. • Partially Adequate (P) – The implemented base practice does little to contribute to satisfying the process purpose. • Largely Adequate (L) – The implemented base practice largely contributes to satisfying the process purpose. • Fully Adequate (F) – The implemented base practice fully contributes to satisfying the process purpose. Base practice existence shall be rated using the following base practice existence rating scale: • Non-existent (N) – The base practice is either not implemented or does not produce any identifiable work products. • Existent (Y) – The implemented base practice produces identifiable work products.
Determining Derived Ratings	The ISO/IEC 15504 guideline for these steps is that Equal weighting shall be applied to each practice adequacy rating when aggregating or deriving ratings. The following notes should be observed by the assessment team while determining derived ratings: • From the actual ratings, derived ratings may be determined which can help to gain further insight into the processes within the organizational unit as a whole. • The assessment team should decide which of the following derived ratings are useful in helping to ensure that the assessment purpose can best fulfill. • Since any derived ratings are based on an aggregation of actual ratings for process instances, the assessment team has to ensure that traceability is provided from the derived ratings to the actual ratings.
Validating the Rating	The ratings should be validated to ensure that they are an accurate representation of the processes assessed. The validation should include assessing whether the sample size is chosen is representative of the processes assessed and that it is capable of fulfilling the assessment purpose.
Presenting Assessment Output	The assessor shall ensure that all of the information required in the assessment output is recorded in a suitable format to fulfill the assessment purpose and that it meets the requirements of International Standard. The assessment output will normally be used as a basis for developing an agreed improvement plan.

be recognized with the software process certification. It is to ensure the companies have well established practices that can be applied to the undertaking projects.

In this day and age, reported in the *ZDNET* on March 2005, government through its Multimedia Super Corridor (MSC) backbone company; Multimedia Development Corporation Sdn Bhd (MDeC) has launched its Quality Excellence for Software and Technology SMEs (Quests) programme, which it said would help local small and medium software company to get international recognition from Software Engineering Institute (SEI). It is believed from the subsequent of that programme momentum, the government will come out with a policy to grant a project only to the company, which has a certification from SEI (Lee, 2005).

SPA is important to one of the mid-size IT company (called ABC after this for confidentiality reason) to provide structured framework for software development. Apart of that, it also can help ABC Company to standardize, stabilize and increase quality and repeatability within software development area. Next, from the implementation of the project implementation, it can help the ABC Company to:

- Be well prepared and equipped with improvement strategies for the technology changes to curtail workloads.
- Create an effective working environment with a consistency improvement.
- Improve product quality and reduce cost.
- Increase work efficiency and improve software maintainability.

ABC Company has involved in most of the government's big project. Most of their projects involve the development of the system. They also provide other services such supplying hardware, software and providing networking services across the country and also continents. In order to perform the SPA, one pilot project has been selected. The project comprises of 40 staffs including Head of Project, Project Manager, Project Leader, System Analyst, Programmer, Business Analyst and other personnel. Besides, two different modules have been selected for the assessment.

THE ESTABLISHMENT OF INTERNAL ASSESSMENT METHOD

An assessment method constitutes the activities that must be performed in order to conduct an assessment. There are many methods that are used in practice and most of them are tailored to the needs of the assessed organizations. For instance—ISO/IEC 15504, BOOTSTRAP, AMI and TRILLIUM. Perhaps one of the best-known methods is the SEI's SCAMPI. All of the method can be applied to small and medium size software companies or software departments within large organization. All of these assessment methods are based on an underlying model of good software practice as well as a model of the improvement process itself. Some assessments that are performed with small organizations may last only a single day, whereas assessments in larger, high maturity organizations can take over two (2) weeks of interviews, document reviews, and consolidation of findings.

We had established an internal assessment method, which was based on Standard CMMI Appraisal Method for Process Improvement (SCAMPI), which had been developed by Software Engineering Institute (SEI). A typical weeklong assessment, which had been organized as is shown in Table 7 and Table 8.

Two plausible reasons why we choose CMMI SCAMPI are 1) to make sure that the internal assessment done was parallel with the CMMI formal assessment which will be done next year. 2) we would like to make sure that all the staffs in selected project had experienced in the assessment. Besides, SCAMPI also contained number of elements:

Table 7. Detail schedule for ABC internal assessment

Activity	Process
Plan and Prepare for Assessment	Analyze Requirements
	Develop Assessment Plan
	Select and Prepare Team
	Obtain and Analyze Objective Evidence
	Prepare for Collection of Objective Evidence
Conduct Assessment	Examine Objective Evidence
	Verify and Validate Objective Evidence
	Document Objective Evidence
	Generate Assessment Results
Report Result	Deliver Assessment Results
	Package and Archive Assessment Assets

Table 8. Schedule for the on-site activities

Day 1	Day 2	Day 3	Day 4
Review Questionnaires	Conduct Interviews	Conduct Interviews	Conduct Interviews
Document Review	Conduct Interviews	Conduct Interviews	Conduct Interviews
Document Review	Conduct Interviews	Conduct Interviews	Conduct Interviews
Consolidate Information	Consolidate Information	Consolidate Information	Prepare Findings

- A diagnostic tool or instrument to enable the maturity of software processes to be measured and maturity level or profile to be drawn up.
- Underlying generic process maturity model on which to base the assessment and to derive the priorities for improvement.
- A set of best practices or norms for comparison, either explicitly, or implicitly in the assignment of levels or profiles.
- Supporting best practice guidelines to support the improvement planning process.
- A clear mechanism for presenting results.

We had presented the SCAMPI method in one of the internal meeting to the ABC Company's Engineering Process Group (EPG). We had to explain all the phases in SCAMPI to the group to make sure that the EPG had a clear understanding

in SCAMPI methodology. SCAMPI typically had three (3) phases, which is plan and prepare for assessment, conduct assessment and also report the result for assessment. In each phase, it had been alienated into several processes and in that process it had been divided into several activities. We had to estimate the effort spent on each of the following:

- Preparing the assessment input.
- Briefing the sponsor and project staff about the methodology to be used.
- Collecting evidence such as reviewing documentation, interviewing project staff and management.
- Producing and verifying ratings for process areas assessed.
- Preparing the assessment results.
- Presenting the results to management.

The method established was used to assess eighteen (18) process areas, which had been established in ABC Company's repository. The eighteen (18) process areas, which had been established, were:

- Requirements Development
- Project Planning
- Project Monitoring and Control
- Risk Management
- Requirements Management
- Process and Product Quality Assurance
- Decision Analysis and Resolution
- Technical Solution
- Configuration Management
- Integrated Project Management
- Organizational Process Focus
- Organizational Process Definition
- Organizational Training
- Product Integration
- Supplier Agreement Management
- Validation
- Verification
- Measurement and Analysis

PREPARING FOR INTERNAL ASSESSMENT

Next section will discuss in-depth about the implementation of internal assessment at ABC Company.

Criteria for Selecting the Pilot Project

Several criteria were considered during the process of selecting a project for software assessment. While it is impossible to formulate rules that apply in every case, these guidelines can be helpful in making reasonable selection decisions. There were:

- **Special attention:** The project had software of sufficient significance to warrant special attention.
- **Top management cooperation:** The senior site manager or the head of the project agreed to personally participate by being present for the opening on-site assessment briefing and the on-site review of final findings and recommendations; the manager or the head of project also agreed to develop appropriate action plans in response to the assessment recommendations.

Selecting Team Members

The assessment team consists of a team leader, organizational unit coordinator, facilitator, timekeeper, process area mini team and observer. We believe that, larger team can be hard to manage and generally less productive. The description for each role is described below:

- **Team Leader:** The person is should ensure that the assessment is conducted in a proper and productive manner. Team leader also should most of the discussions during the assessment, makes the formal presentations (e.g., introductory management presentation and the assessment findings presentation to the ABC Company).
- **Organizational Unit Coordinator (OUC):** Handle on-site logistics and provides technical, administrative, and logistical support to the assessment team leader. This usually includes activities such as coordinating schedules, notifying participants, arranging adequate facilities and resources and obtaining requested documentation. OUC also is responsible for tracking time and schedule constraints during interviews and other activities.
- **Process Area Mini-Teams:** Mini teams take the lead for data collection in assigned process areas. They ensure that informa-

tion collected during a data gathering session covers each process areas.

- **Facilitator:** The facilitator conducts interviews, asking questions of interview participants.
- **Observer:** Observer is the integral part of the assessment team. They will perform an observation to the project activities.

The assessment team had been given training related to internal assessment. Such training includes:

- **Site Overview:** It is important for the assessment team to understand the mission and function of the site to be assessed. This session was devoted to a discussion of the organization which will be assessed.
- **Assessment Introduction and Guidelines:** This training session was spent in an overview of the assessment process. The guideline for assessment was discussed, use of the assessment instrument was explained, the role of supporting materials was discussed, and assessment evaluation was explained.
- **Assessment Questionnaire Review:** The assessment is based on responses to the assessment instrument. Therefore, it is important for all assessment team members to fully understand the spirit and intent of all questions. Thus, this session was devoted to a detailed review of each question. A simulated assessment was conducted based on previous experiences of team members.
- **Supporting Materials Discussion:** It is important to be able to verify the accuracy of the responses to the questionnaire. This is achieved through the requests for supporting materials which serve to validate responses to the questionnaire. During this session, the process for identifying areas for further investigation was reviewed and

particular questions were identified based on assessment responses.

- **Assessment Evaluation and Findings:** This session was used to discuss on the techniques to be used to evaluate the findings.
- **Planning for Site Visit:** Details of the plan for the site visit was discussed. The plan for the on-site assessment itself included the identification of the specific projects to be examined, the people to be interviewed, and the facilities required. Since the people and facilities in the project was heavily committed, significant advance notice is generally required. Daily agendas of the visit should be discussed and agreed upon.

Preparing the Assessment Instruments

We then continue the assessment preparation by preparing several instruments such as questionnaires, process areas checklist and also interview question. The use of instruments to gather written or unwritten information from the project provides a relatively low-cost data collection technique. The questionnaires were used to gather additional information regarding the software process in ABC Company. The questionnaires developed were based on the practices governed by the Software Engineering Institute (SEI). It had been alienated into three (3) categories. There were Project Management, Engineering and Support categories. The interview questions were developed as a preparation for the interview session. It was the main instruments in the assessment because the assessment team could gather all the information regarding the software process face-to-face. The last instrument used was a checklist. We had proposed the checklist to list up all the information gathered from questionnaires, interview question and also document review session. The checklist had been prepared based on process areas specific practices.

CONDUCTING THE INTERNAL ASSESSMENT

Assessment Briefing

After all the preparations, the assessment team then went to ABC Company project site for an introductory session or briefing related to internal assessment. The session was held at 9 am and ended at 1 pm. In that briefing, we had explained the main purpose of the internal assessment. It includes—the assessment process, assessment principles and the detailed period for the assessment period, outlining the purpose, location, time and length of each meeting along with identifying who should attend the on site assessment. The assessment team then had distributed the questionnaires to the project's representative. Besides, the assessment team also had discussed with the project's representative on the suitable date for the on site assessment session. The whole four (4) hours had been used by the assessment team to educate the staffs.

Conducting the Onsite Assessment

The purpose for this second visit was to conduct an interview, review the project documentation and as well collect the questionnaires. The assessment team had interviewed all the staffs at the project site to gain a better understanding of the project's software development practices and the project managers' perceptions of strengths and weaknesses in the process. To meet these objectives, the interview session contained the following five (5) categories of questions:

- Background of the interviewees.
- Description of a specific software development project.
- Critical events and problems in the project.
- Practices, problems, and suggestions for improvement within specific software process.

- Other strengths and weaknesses in the project's software development process.

Apart of that, the interview session itself was developed in two (2) stages. A first version with a list of cues and topics for the interviewers was developed before the first interview. The second version of the session contained more explicitly phrased questions, but the interviewers could still choose to phrase questions suited for the interview. The final version of the guide also included an introductory section, explaining the framework and purpose of the interview, and a final section about the interviewee's impression of the interview as well as comments and suggestions within areas not covered by the interview.

Other than the interview session, the assessment team also had reviewed the project's deliverables. A substantial portion of data used by the assessment team was derived from the documents reviewed. Document review was an effective means to gain detailed insight about the practices in use in the project. We had classified the documents into three (3) different levels. There were organization, project and implementation. All the documentation from early phase until the end of software process had been reviewed. There were:

- Standard Operating Procedure (SOP)
- Technical Solution Document (TSD)
- Project Plan
- Project Management Guide
- Quality Management Plan
- Change Request Log
- Project Control File which contain minutes of meeting, memo, e-mail and other supporting document.
- Business Area Requirement Analysis (BARA) which contain context diagram, decomposition diagram, business area elementary process, business area elementary requirement, business area entity relationship diagram
- Testing Review

- Test Result, Test Incident and Test Verification
- Unit Testing Design Documentation
- Integration Testing Design
- System Testing Design
- User Acceptance Testing Design
- Training Approach document

All the information in documentation had been gathered and filled up in the checklist prepared. We found the project involve in the internal assessment had prepared all the documentation as guided in CMMI reference model. But there was other documentation, which had not been prepared by the project. There were configuration management plan, risk list and also requirement traceability matrix.

Formulate the Internal Assessment Findings

The on-site assessment gave the assessment team detailed information about the project's software process and many suggestions from the project managers and the staffs about how to improve the process. Therefore, we need to systematize all the problems, issues, and opportunities rose during the interviews. The assessment team discussed the lessons learned from the interviews on two (2) occasions: after the first interview and after the last interview. Immediately after the first interview, a discussion took place in the group. First each interviewer or observer in turn stated what they saw as the important lessons. Then these lessons were discussed, categorized, and documented in Assessment Preliminary Findings Template.

After the last interview, the assessment team sought to reach a common understanding of what were the major lessons from each interview. Before the meeting, each member of the group had gone through the summaries of the interviews and had collected a list of lessons to be learned from each interview. Each interview was then analyzed through the discussion of these lessons. There

were different opinions of what would constitute a major lesson, but for each interview there was a certain sense of consolidation of the views held by the individual members of the assessment team. After going through all the interviews in this way, a conclusion spanning all interviews was discussed. No common conclusion was reached and the task of compiling the analysis in an assessment findings template was assigned to the author.

The findings represent the assessment team's view of the software process currently faces the organization. The findings were based on the questionnaires responses, discussion with the assessment participants in the interview session and discussions among the assessment team members. All the information from the assessment instruments had been listed in the checklist prepared by the author. From the checklist the assessment team might have the idea on which practices was not really followed by the project. The mapping process was quite difficult for the reason that there was a lot of information that should be covered. The findings represent the starting point for formulating recommendations. The assessment team should have achieved a team consensus for the assessment findings and completed the preliminary findings presentation.

Presenting the Assessment Findings

We then presented the assessment findings to the head of the project, project managers and also project leader. The presentation session also served the purpose of getting the project managers' commitment to undertake specific improvement initiatives as part of their next software development project. The presentation session had the following format:

The purpose of the validation of the assessment finding was fulfilled in the sense that the head of project, project managers and project leader could recognize what they believed to be important and relevant problems. Some items were particularly useful, for example, project conclusion. Other items were relevant but not significant, for example, descriptive process model. For one item, technical solution, they did not see the problem and they believed the technology to be too immature to get any benefit from such an improvement initiative.

By the end of the presentation, considerable commitment had been established among the head of project, project managers and project leaders. All but one project manager were committed to

undertake process improvement integrated with their current or next software development project.

Results from the Software Process Assessment

Table 9 shows some of the result achieved from the assessment. This is to give a clear overview on how we classified and mapped the results. We only focus the results from three process areas which has involved in the SPA; Risk Manage-

Table 9. Mapping result

Risk Management	
CMMI Goals	SPA Result
Prepare for Risk Management	-Risk Management Approach was stated in the Project Plan, where it explained the procedure to control and monitor the risk. -There was no tool, hierarchy, categorization, classes and attributes. -Minutes of meeting was used to list up the risk
Identify and Analyze Risks	-The risks in the Risk List had not been listed and identified -There was no Risk Contingency Plan -The risk identified would be discussed in the meeting
Mitigate Risks	-There was no Risk Mitigation Plan -There was no proper documentation to update the risk. The project only used minutes of meeting to update the risk
Project Monitoring & Control	
CMMI Goals	SPA Result
Monitor Project Against Plan	-ABC company had monitored the actual performance and progresses of the project. The progress report will be used to monitor the actual project performance against the plan. The entire actual project's performances were stored in Project Control File. -To handle the service request, the ABC company in-charged staff had established Service Request Control Register.
Manage Corrective Action to Closure	-The corrective actions were managed to closure when the project's performance or results deviate significantly from the plan. ABC company had recorded the activities in the minutes of meeting
Project Planning	
CMMI Goals	SPA Result
Establish Estimates	-There were several sections in Project Plan, which indicate High Level Work Plan, Related Projects High Level Budget, and Cost Benefit Analysis. ABC company had used 'expert judgment' to estimate on size, cost and schedule
Develop a Project Plan	-For Project Planning Process Area, ABC company generally had a Project Plan, which consists of several sections such as Project Scope, Project Management Approach, Project Organization, High Level Work Plan, Related Projects High Level Budget, and Cost Benefit Analysis. -However, there was an area, which has not been covered by ABC company. ABC company should identify, list and monitor the risks in the Risk List. ABC company also should come up with Risk Mitigation and Risk Contingency Plan
Obtain Commitment to the Plan	-The Project Manager, Quality and Technical Reviewers and also Project Sponsor had properly signed off the Project Plan. In term of work breakdown structure, it had been prepared at the early stage of development. -There was no staffing requirement included in the Project Plan

ment, Project Planning and Project monitoring and Control.

From the mapping process in Table 9, we have used the formal characterization from SCAMPI. The intent of this characterization is very effective in order to summarize the assessment team's judgment. Table 10 shows the characterization for the process areas assessed.

Recommendation Formulation

After the findings presentation, the head of the project and the assessment team leader hold an executive meeting to discuss next steps. The purpose of the meeting was to confirm the time for the recommendations presentation and final report, discussed the importance of forming the action plan team and developing action plan, and address any questions or concerns of management.

After the findings presentation and the senior management meeting, there was one more on site session; the initial formulation of the recommendations to address the findings. The purpose of the meeting was to obtain a team consensus on the recommendations to be documented in the final report. Some guidelines were used by the team for formulating the recommendations to ensure the formulated recommendations are reachable. It includes limit the number of recommendations, make the recommendations specific, prioritize the recommendations.

In forming recommendations, the team had been really sensitive to the impact on the project

Table 10. Formal characterization result for each process areas

Process Area	Characterization
Project Planning	Largely Implemented
Project Monitoring & Control	Largely Implemented
Risk Management	Partially Implemented

resources. The project cannot handle too much high priority issues at a time. For example, working on 20 high priority recommendations at once was unrealistic. So, that was the reason why the team had only recommended 7 main recommendations to the project. The main areas for recommendations for the project were:

- **Configuration Management**
  - The project should assign one staff responsible as a 'configuration manager'. The CM will manage all the items in term of documentation, coding and others
  - The project has to develop configuration management plan which identify all the items
- **Risk Management**
  - Project should identify and documented the risk in Risk List
  - Risk Mitigation Plan also should be develop and well documented
  - The risk management approach and risk contingency plan also should be clearly discuss
- **Process and Product Quality Assurance**
  - The project should employ external reviewer or entities to review the document
  - Another possible way is to establish 'Quality Unit' as an external entity. This unit will take external reviewer responsibility
- **Requirements Development**
  - The Project should establish proper agreement which indicate that the stakeholders have agreed to resolution of "conflicts" that surfaced during the gathering and consolidation of their needs, expectations, constraints and possible operational concepts

-     ◦ Requirement traceability matrix should be one of the activity to map the requirements
- **Requirements Management**
  - ◦ The project should employ external reviewer or entities to review the document
  - ◦ Another possible way is to establish 'Quality Unit' as an external entity. This unit will take external reviewer responsibility
- **Project Planning**
  - ◦ Estimation guideline should be established in the project

Assessment Final Report

Following that, the assessment team had prepared a final report of the assessment findings and recommendations. The purpose of the final report was to document the assessment, describe the key findings, and make specific recommendations to the project based on the findings. Besides, the assessment report also consists of the characterization for each process areas assessed. We had used the formal characterization in SCAMPI such as Fully Implemented (FI), Largely Implemented (LI), Partially Implemented (PI) and Not Implemented (NI). The formal characterization helps the assessed project knew the achievement for each process areas. The intent of this characterization also was effective to summarize the assessment team's judgment and to prioritize process areas where further investigation or corroboration might be necessary.

A carefully written final report was vital since it is the only permanent record of the assessment. It was also used as a reference for the action plan formulation and execution, and for future reassessments.

Post-Assessment Follow-Up

Although the goal of an assessment is to accurately characterize the current state of the software process that is practiced in the project and identify the key software issues, the ultimate intent is to be catalyst for software process improvement in the assessed project.

Following the recommendations, the assessed project prepares an action plan that specifies how, when and by whom each recommendations to be implemented. Each action that addresses a recommendation was called an action task. The purpose of the action plan was to identify and plan the work effort for each action task, identify responsibility and resources, and provide a mechanism for tracking and reporting on task status.

An action plan sufficiently detailed to provide a clear guide for execution. It had specifies the following:

- What recommendations will be implemented (action tasks).
- What recommendations will not be implemented, and why.
- How each action task will be implemented.
- Resources required to implement each action task.
- The person or people responsible for each action task.
- Action task schedules, with appropriate management review checkpoints.

For action tasks that require major changes, the following incremental approach to change was recommended:

- Implement the action task on the project.
- Evaluate the result of the change.
- Revise the action task implementation plan based on feedback from the project.
- Implement the action task on a broader basis.

The gradual approach to major change efforts reduces the risk of failure, and smaller early successes can pave the way for larger successes as the effort builds momentum via acceptance and participation throughout the project. After the action plan was formulated, it had been reviewed in order to:

- Improve the quality of the action plan.
- Provide opportunities for participation in the action plan formulation by practitioners and senior management, and help enroll them into the change process.
- Provide a mechanism to build consensus to the action plan.
- Help to build and confirm the commitment of senior management to the action plan, as well as the resources necessary to implement it.

Two (2) reviews had been done:

- **Peer Review** –The review give opportunity for technical professionals to provide the expertise and suggestions for improving the action plan.
- **Senior Management Review** – senior management reviewed the action plan by examined from above perspectives:
  ○ Does the plan balance the need for software process improvements with the economic necessity of simultaneous producing software products?
  ○ Does the plan identify the appropriate level of resources to implement the proposed plan? Is the time for implementing the plan realistic?
  ○ Are the action task checkpoints concisely identified and clearly stated?

If the action plan addresses these and other questions specific to the assessed project, senior management gives approval to proceed with action plan implementation. If not, the plan is revised to address senior management concerns. In any case, senior management signifies its approval to proceed with implementation by committing the needed resources and personnel to the software process improvement effort.

Lessons Learned from the Internal Assessment

The lessons learned about the internal assessment performed are summarized in the following.

- **Lesson 1:** Software process assessment has the following advantages:
  ○ It is easy to understand and plan.
  ○ It focuses attention on perceived problems.
  ○ It is efficient as well as effective.
  ○ Actors are involved and commitment is created.
- **Lesson 2:** Software process assessment has the following disadvantages:
  ○ Interviewers must have a firm background in software engineering and software process improvement.
  ○ The approach is only sufficiently efficient if carefully planned in terms of writing notes and summaries, and having a manageable number of interviewees.
  ○ It is inefficient to interview all organizational actors who need to be involved in discussions and decisions.
  ○ Software process assessment is not an easy or straightforward approach. It should be seen as part of a general Software Process Improvement initiative and be planned and implemented according to the priorities and goals of that approach.
- **Lesson 3:** Software process assessment requires the following conditions:

- ○ Interviewers skilled in interviewing.
- ○ A well-structured interview guide.
- ○ Plans and commitment for processing and interpreting interview data Assessment team are involved in interviews as well as interpretation and decision-making. As part of an organization's general Software Process Improvement initiative, Software process assessment should be planned and performed by the assessment team. This presupposes, however, that the members of this team receive the necessary training in planning, conducting, and analyzing guide-based interviews.
- ○ Supporting materials for conducting the assessment such as questionnaires, checklist and interview question.
- **Lesson 4:** To reduce cost – In order to reduce cost, the assessment team can use pre-scripted questions and also conducting the interview session simultaneously.
- **Lesson 5:** Maintain assessment accuracy by emphasis on direct evidence – From the interview session, the assessment team simply can confirm the evidence is 'real'.
- **Lesson 6:** Most assessment time is spent mapping evidence to CMMI practices.
- **Lesson 7:** The assessment team should use a self-assessment tool to organize the mapping. It can be fully automated tool such as Appraisal Wizard or manual tools such as checklist.
- **Lesson 8:** Creating findings - Projects simply want to know which practices they do not comply with.

FUTURE WORKS

Further research is needed in order to make sure software process assessment technique generally powerful tools. Among the relevant research questions are the following:

- Does software process assessment create sufficient commitment for software process improvement program?

Software process assessment has created commitment towards software process improvement program. Further studies are needed to determine whether this commitment is strong enough to sustain and anchor process improvement in the long run.

- Does software process assessment uncover an organization's significant software problems?

For example, software process assessment has identified a number of software process related problems in the project. To determine whether these are the significant or most important problems, further studies and comparisons with other approaches to software process assessment are required.

- Can software process assessment cope with conflicts and organizational politics?

Software process assessment is designed to formulate an improvement strategy based on the views and perceptions of assessment team members. It remains to be seen whether this makes the approach vulnerable to manipulation by powerful organizational actors, or a valuable way to reveal and make explicit the social and political dimensions of software process improvement.

CONCLUSION

We have presented our experience in implementing the internal software process assessment at one of the mid-size IT company. The best part of software process assessment with respect to various standards is that a smart organization can use the assessment as a framework to evaluate how projects are done and by conscious analysis rather than slavish adherence; the organization can plan and take steps that will improve its operation. We concerned that the focus of existence processes, at least in the way that many people apply the assessments tends to over-value the technique at the expense of the goal.

Software process assessment in other word is the process of evaluating an organization or project against a model for continuous improvement, in order to highlight what has been achieved and what needs improving. The success of software process assessment is dependent on many variables but from our experience this important process would indicate that there are three (3) main elements:

Software Process Assessment = Model + Measurement + Management

A model used as a framework for evaluating the organization or project's progress in software development process. A means of measuring how well the organization or project is performing against each element of the model. This provides tangible output to assist with the evaluation of the results achieved and the identification of priorities for future improvement. A way of managing the whole software process assessment, from selecting the model, identifying the scope, preparing the groundwork and governing the assessment plan, to conducting the assessment and reporting the results. It is also essential that the senior management be committed to the assessment process including acting on the results in a positive way rather than seeking to apportion blame for any lack of progress.

REFERENCES

Abran, A., Bourque, P., Dupuis, R., Moore, J. W., Tripp, L. L., Abran, A., et al. (2004). *Guide to the software engineering body of knowledge - SWEBOK* (2004 version ed.). Piscataway, NJ: IEEE Press.

Barbour, R., Benhoff, M., Gallagher, B., Eslinger, S., Bernard, T., Ming, L., et al. (2002). *Handbook CMU/SEI-2002-HB-002.*

CMMI Product Team. (2001). *Capability maturity model® integration (CMMI SM), version 1.1 (No. CMU/SEI-2002-TR-001).* Pittsburgh, PA: Carnegie Mellon University.

Dorling, A. (1993). SPICE: Software process improvement and capability determination. *Software Quality Journal, 2*(4), 209–224. doi:10.1007/BF00403764

Haase, V., Messnarz, R., Koch, G., Kugler, H., & Decrinis, P. (2002). Bootstrap: Fine-tuning process assessment. *Software, IEEE, 11*(4), 25–35. doi:10.1109/52.300080

Humphrey, W. S., Kitson, D. H., & Kasse, T. C. (1989). The state of software engineering practice. *ICSE '89: Proceedings of the 11th International Conference on Software Engineering,* Pittsburgh, Pennsylvania, United States (pp. 277-285).

Jung, H. W., & Hunter, R. (2001). The relationship between ISO/IEC 15504 process capability levels, ISO 9001 certification and organization size: An empirical study. *Journal of Systems and Software, 59*(1), 43–55. doi:10.1016/S0164-1212(01)00047-4

Lee, C. (2005). Malaysia helps local developers deliver quality software. *ZDNET Software.* Retrieved March 4, 2011, from http://www.zdnetasia.com/malaysia-helps-local-developers-deliver-quality-software-39220761.htm

McGuire, E. G., & Randall, K. A. (1998). Process improvement competencies for IS professionals: A survey of perceived needs. *Proceedings of the 1998 ACM SIGCPR Conference on Computer Personnel Research,* (pp. 1-8).

Singh, R. (1996). International Standard ISO/IEC 12207 software life cycle processes. *Software Process Improvement and Practice, 2*(1), 35–50. doi:10.1002/(SICI)1099-1670(199603)2:1<35::AID-SPIP29>3.0.CO;2-3

Zahran, S. (1998). *Software process improvement: Practical guidelines for business success.* Reading, MA: Addison-Wesley.

Chapter 6

Resistance Factors in Software Processes Improvement:
A Study of the Brazilian Industry

Josiane Brietzke Porto
La Salle University, Brazil

ABSTRACT

Several companies have been carrying out software processes improvement projects. However, some of them give up before the project ends, and others take much longer than expected to get it accomplished. This way, identifying the resistance factors that influence the implementation of such projects might serve as a reference to professionals in this area on the one hand, and help to manage future projects on the other, through the use of preventive actions that either lessen or eliminate the resistance factors' consequences. For this matter, this chapter presents a survey with 36 professionals involved in initiatives of software processes improvement in 18 companies in the state of Rio Grande do Sul, Brazil.

INTRODUCTION

The quality of software products is highly related to the quality of the software process (Rocha, Maldonado, Weber, & Kival, 2001). As a consequence of this and the demands of the software market, the companies are establishing software processes improvement projects in order to better

the quality of their software products, have a competitive differential in relation to their competitors, enable their entrance in the international market, reduce costs and meet deadlines. However, there may be many resistance factors influencing the course of a software process improvement project, mainly if these projects are performed in small companies with scant resources. Moreover, some companies begin but not conclude the project, and others take much longer than expected to

DOI: 10.4018/978-1-61350-141-2.ch006

Table 1. Summary of national and international standards

Standard	Objective	How
ISO/IEC 15504	Perform software processes assessments, aiming at processes improvement and determining the processes capabilities of an organization.	Through the implantation of processes related to software engineering and a measurement model, which allows the assessment of a certain process' capability.
CMMI - Staged Representation	Providing a guide to improve processes and empower the organization to manage the development, acquisition and maintenance of products or services.	By serving process areas structured in 5 sequential maturity levels that allow the definition of an organization's profile as a whole.
CMMI -Continuous Representation	Providing a guide to improve processes and empower the organization to manage the development, acquisition and maintenance of products or services.	Through the refinement of each process area. These process area are grouped in categories and in 6 levels of capability that allow the definition of the organization's profile in each process area.
NBR ISO/IEC 12207	Help defining the processes that involve the software's life cycle.	Through the implantation of processes of the software's life cycle, which must be adapted to the organization's or to the projects' characteristics.
MR-MPS	Offering the Brazilian market a cheaper qualification alternative.	By serving area process in 7 maturity levels that allow reaching short-term results.
NBR ISO 9001/2000	Meet the clients' needs, understand their current and future needs and exceed their expectations.	By setting up an effective Quality Management System.

get it accomplished. In this context, this study aims at identifying resistance factors in software processes improvement projects by means of a survey comprising companies in the state of Rio Grande do Sul, Brazil.

The relevance of such a research project relies on the following reasons: it can contribute significantly to the management and control of the resistance factors in future in software processes improvement projects through the implementation of preventive actions; the data found here may serve as reference to professionals involved in projects alike and to researchers in the area of Software Engineering as well. There is little work in the field of software quality sharing this very objective, or either, based on companies' empirical experience.

This chapter is organized in sections: section 2 introduces a general overview of software process improvement standards; section 3 presents a collection of published experiences concerning resistance factors in software processes improvement; section 4 describes the methodology ad-

opted in this study and it presents the consolidation of research; section 5 analyzes results and the last sections presents future researches and final considerations.

Software Processes Improvement

It is believed that, by improving a software process, one can enhance product quality because, according to Sommerville (2003), the quality of the process exerts a significant influence on the software quality. In this section some widely adopted national and international standards will be described, with the main objective of highlighting their focus of action. Except for CMMI model, it is observed that the standards presented in this section do not exclude one another, that is, they are complementary. This evidence is confirmed by MR-MPS (SOFTEX, 2005), which developmental basis consists of the union of ISO/IEC 12207 (ABNT, 1998), ISO/IEC 15504 (ISO/SPICE, 2003) regulations and the CMMI-DEV (CMMI, 2006).

Section 3 approaches resistance factors in software processes improvement projects that usually use the standards presented in this section as reference.

RESISTANCE FACTORS IN SOFTWARE PROCESSES IMPROVEMENT PROJECTS

This section presents a set of hypotheses concerning resistance factors found in software processes improvement projects, which were identified in accounts of professionals and in previous publications and are classified according to Beecham, Hall, and Rainer (2003) research.

Organizational Factors

These are related to problems within the scope of the organization and are usually under senior managers' responsibility (Abrahamsson, 2001; Andrade, Albuquerque, Campos, & Rocha, 2004; Basili, McGarry, Pajerski, & Zelkowitz, 2002; Beecham et al., 2003; Conradi & Fuggeta, 2002; Iversen, Nielsen, & Norbjerg, 1998; Wheeler & Duggins, 1998; Wiegers, 1996).

Human

This is the most frequently mentioned factor by the authors that report experiences in software processes improvement projects (Abrahamsson, 2001; Andrade et al., 2004; Basili et al., 2002; Beecham et al., 2003; Conradi & Fuggeta, 2002; Iversen et al., 1998; Wheeler & Duggins, 1998; Wiegers, 1996). According to Abrahamssom (2001), the concept of commitment (to the improvement of processes across all levels of the organization) has been one of the most important factors determining whether a well planned improvement process project will succeed. Although the commitment and support of all management levels are required, the adhesion of the technical

staff as a whole is also necessary (Beecham et al., 2003).

In a research carried out in Brazil, the aspects "lack of support from the board of directors" and "lack of coordination and leadership in the implementation activities" were also perceived as critical by the participants (Andrade et al., 2004).

Political

By setting up organizational policies, directors make their intentions clear regarding a software processes improvement project and obtain an active and consistent commitment in all managerial levels (Wheeler & Duggins, 1998) and (Wiegers, 1996). According to Wiegers (1996), this can be a way to deal with problems related to project leaders/project managers, for they can manage the urgency in delivering a current product through the reduction of effort, which could point to the improvement of the organization's processes capabilities. Wheeler and Duggins (1998) also consider the political factor important to the construction of a department to software quality assurance. He states that the commitment of senior managers and leadership are the first step to be taken, followed by the establishment of a quality policy. This policy describes the organizational goals and the objectives related to the quality.

Cultural

Although some reference models worry about the creation of a quality culture, this factor requires a lot of skill, because a software processes improvement project will demand cultural changes. One of Conradi and Fuggeta (2002) assumptions concerning this factor is that the accomplishment of such changes implies expertise in social sciences. He complements such idea by saying that Engineering, including Software Engineering, mixes both technical and social aspects.

Goals

A software processes improvement project must be associated with the organization's strategic goals and objectives (Basili et al., 2002; Conradi & Fuggeta, 2002; Wiegers, 1996). One of the traps to undermine a software processes improvement project are the management's unrealistic expectations, since the excessive enthusiasm on the part of ambitious managers can also be risky to the improvement program. If the goals, deadlines and expected results are unrealistic, the efforts toward processes improvement may fail (Wiegers, 1996). Managers, particularly the little experienced ones, may not appreciate the time and effort involved in software processes improvement. They may focus on issues of pressing importance to them that are not realistic outcomes of processes improvement effort (Wiegers, 1996).

Change Management

Change management must be aligned with the organization's business objectives. For this reason, it is suggested that an initial analysis be made to identify whether the company really needs this sort of project, and whether it matches the organization's interests. Wiegers (1996) also posits that the software processes improvement project's team be used to actively facilitate the efforts toward changes on the part of the project teams rather than simply check the situation of the ongoing process in order to report a long and depressing list of findings (non-conformity).

Project Factors

These factors relate to problems regarding the software process improvement project: planning, activities, resources and, among others (Beecham et al., 2003; Wiegers, 1996).

Budget and Estimates

This factor is crucial to the majority of software processes improvement projects, because these projects need financial investment (personnel and equipment) that will return to the organization only on a long-term basis. Wiegers (1996) adds that the lack of progress in improvement plans is frustrating to those who really want to achieve progress, and this belittles the importance of the time and money investments made in the process evaluation.

Documentation

In the case of software processes improvement projects, it will be necessary to create an infrastructure to the documentation, since many mandatory practices in the reference models must be documented and formalized in order to objective evidence and dissemination throughout the organization. According to Beecham et al. (2003) research, the documentation is also gaining importance in the list of problems associated to software processes improvement. It includes data measurement, proceedings register, coordination and management of the documentation, data collecting methods and others.

Regarding the documentation factor, Wiegers (1996) raises another associated issue: the fact of a small organization loosing the CMM spirit (or any other process model) while trying to apply it to the letter, introducing excessive documentation and formality.

Tools and Technology

The problems associated to tools and technology are the second most frequently mentioned concerns on the part of developers and project managers (Beecham et al., 2003). This refers to the implementation of new technologies and tools, amount of work and pressures that hinder the use of new tools. In the case of the software processes improvement project, the orientation is to implement the use of tools and technology in a second stage of the process.

Quality

This factor refers to the person in charge of the quality or to the quality assurance group in an organization (SQA, PPQA, etc). Most of the times, the main duty of this person or group is to guarantee the institutionalization of the improvement of processes and, because of that, they feel directly the resistance in the implementation of improvements. According to Pires, Marinho, Tellas, and Belchior (2004), at first the project teams were reluctant to adopt the new processes and assessments carried out by the SQA group. This problem was solved by involving the senior managers in the process, who motivated their teams by means of lectures and workshops. Furthermore, the SQA group directed its activities more strongly towards supporting the execution of the new process activities.

Some Considerations

The professionals responsible for future software processes improvement projects may include in their planning, more specifically in their risk management, some preventive actions to the factors presented in this section. Paragraph following shows a set of hypotheses concerning resistance factors that are believed to be crucial to software processes improvement, taking the study performed so far as a reference.

Organizational Factors

- **Human**
  - Lack of commitment in all levels of the organization;
  - Little adhesion and participation;
  - Professionals short of experience and skill;

  - Lack of leadership and backup by the senior management;
  - Lack of adequate training.
- **Political**
  - Lack of the establishment of organizational policies;
  - Lack of establishment of the Quality policy.
- **Cultural**
  - Lack of expertise in implementing cultural changes.
- **Goals**
  - Lack of consistency between the software processes improvement project and the organization's strategic objectives;
  - Absence of focus on the organization's most urgent needs;
  - Unrealistic expectations towards the software processes improvement project.
- **Change Management**
  - Insufficient and ineffective assessment of the current software process;
  - Existence of a software processes improvement project team not focused on orientation and technical support;
  - Simultaneous focus on many improvement areas.

Project Factors

- **Budget and Estimates**
  - Current budget exceeds planning;
  - Lack of understanding, on the part of senior management, that the software processes improvement project is a long-term return on investment process;
  - Lack of visibility about the ongoing software processes improvement project activities.
- **Documentation**

- ◦ Excessive documentation and formality;
- ◦ Lack of infrastructure and of a documentation management;
- ◦ Little flexibility in the use of the documentation in projects of different types and sizes.

- **Quality**
  - ◦ Lack of involvement of senior management in the relationship between the project teams and the person or group of quality assurance;
  - ◦ Lack of treatment to guarantee process conformity in instances of hiring and/or dismissal of skilled professionals.

- **Tools and Technology**
  - ◦ Automatization of not well defined processes;
  - ◦ Lack of training on the support tools and technologies;
  - ◦ Pressure and absence of planning concerning the adaptation period.

Taking this set of assumptions concerning resistance factors as a starting point, we have developed a research project to find out whether they are present in some companies in the state of Rio Grande do Sul - Brazil, through a survey whose methodology is described in section 4.

METHODOLOGY AND CONSOLIDATION OF RESEARCH

In this section the some aspects of the methodology adopted will be described, drawing on Farias (2002), Andrade et al. (2004) and Nogueira and Rocha (2003). It describes the sample profile and consolidation of the data obtained too. The present research project aims primarily at identifying resistance factors in software processes improvement projects through professionals acting in

enterprises in Rio Grande do Sul, Brazil. It is of a quantitative nature and a descriptive character. The research method comprises two phases, the first one corresponding to a review on prior literature and the second one to a survey.

The element is the professional involved in software processes improvement initiatives. The universe consists of 36 professionals of small, medium and large sized companies located in Porto Alegre, its adjacent areas and also in Vale do Sinos in Rio Grande do Sul. The sample is non-probabilistic and intentional. Therefore, the results of this research project are valid only to the group of companies taking part in the study. The research instrument consists of a questionnaire based on a theoretical referential, applied to respondents either personally or via e-mail. In the data analysis, the professionals are characterized according to the attribution of weight to their answers, so that the final results take into consideration the professional's experience. The calculation for assigning weight to a participant and the scoring tables used in this calculation are detailed in Brietzke and Abraham (2006).

Sample Profile

On the whole, 94 companies were contacted and 25,53% of the contacted companies fit the intended profile, that is, posses a software development department based either in Porto Alegre, its adjacencies or in the Vale do Sinos and have already implemented – or are on the way to implement – any software processes improvement project (analyzed in section 2). It is observed that 36,17% of the companies do not meet all the requirements of the profile desired to this research, that is, they do not possess the characteristics mentioned above. Moreover, it evidences a little significant adoption of initiatives of quality of software in the scene where if it finds the sample of this research inserted. Some of the contacts made were not successful (e-mails and messages were not replied, could not contact person in charge, etc) and, as a consequence, it is not known whether the contacted company fits the desired profile or not. Thus, 38,30% of the contacted companies fall into this category. Anyway, 18 out of the 24 companies with the desired profile (25,53%) belong to the sample of this research, what accounts for a sample with 75% of representation. The professionals in the sample are characterized according to the following criteria: working area in the software industry and at University; academic background; working time in the software development area; number of projects; working time and experience level in the area of software processes improvement. We shall now partly characterize the 36 professionals in the sample according to the criteria aforementioned. The participants work in diverse areas and many of them develop more than one function within the company, as shown in Table 2. Such result mirrors the reality of many Brazilian companies, which lack resources to keep specialized professionals to each working area.

In Figure 1, it is observed that there is a higher concentration of experienced participants in a smaller number of software processes improvement projects.

These results evidence the dificulty on the part of the companies to allocate resources to projects

Table 2. Number of participants per working area

Working Area	Number of participants
Businessperson	8
Technology manager	1
Quality manager	7
Project manager	9
Software Development Manager	5
Systems Analyst	11
SW Quality Analyst	2
TI Consultant	3
Programmer	2
Others	3

Notes: 1. Multiple choice question; 2. The functions of Executive Manager, SQA and Software Development Director were mentioned in the Others category.

in this area; moreover, in some cases, such projects are not formalized as projects (resources, costs, estimates, etc), being considered as initiatives or improvement programs. It is evident in Figure 2 a certain homogeneity among participants regarding intervals of working time in the area of software processes improvement. These results allow us to conclude that the software processes improvement projects last long, and that invest-

Figure 1. Participants per number of software processes improvement projects

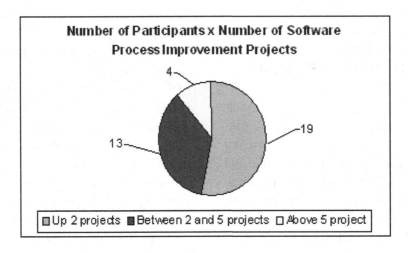

Figure 2. Participants per working time in software processes improvement

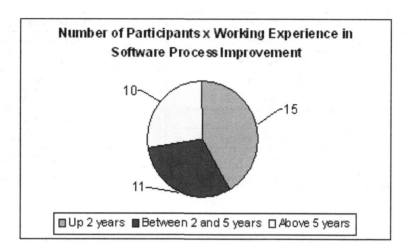

Figure 3. Participants per level experience in software processes improvement

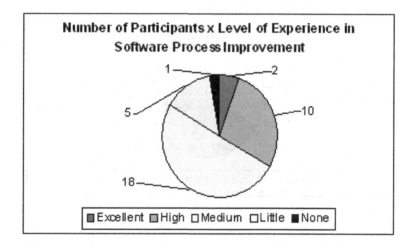

ments in this area of software engeneering cannot be assumed as something recent.

In Figure 3, it can also be noted that the participants in the sample possess a rather satisfactory level of experience in software processes improvrement.

The companies in the sample are characterized according to the criteria of size, location, activities concerning software treatment, domains, kinds of software application developed and quality standards used as referential to the software processes improvement projects. Following, part of

the characterization of the 18 companies in the sample is introduced, according to the criteria mentioned above. Figure 4 depicts the distribution of the companies in the sample according to the size criterium and confirms the predominance of small companies in the sample.

To define de size of the companies, this study relies on the criterion per number of employees to the Commerce/Services industry defined by SEBRAE/RS (2004), as shown in Table 3.

As shown in Figure 5, the highest concentration of participant companies is located in Porto

Table 3. Ranking of company size per number of employees

Size	Sector	Number of employees
Micro	Industry	Up to 19 employees
	Commerce/Services	Up to 9 employees
Small	Industry	20 to 99 employees
	Commerce/Services	10 to 49 employees
Medium	Industry	100 to 499 employees
	Commerce/Services	50 to 249 employees
Large	Industry	above 499 employees
	Commerce/Services	above 250 employees

Figure 4. Company size per number of employees

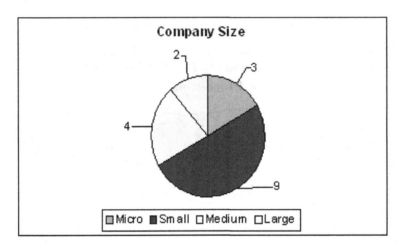

Table 4. Standards of software processes improvement used as reference by the companies

Standard	Nunber of companies	%
CMM (SW-CMM)	13	38,24
ISO/IEC 15504	1	2,94
CMMI (Staged Representation)	5	14,71
CMMI (Continuous Representation)	2	5,88
NBR ISO/IEC 12207	2	5,88
MR-MPS	1	2,94
NBR ISO 9001:2000	3	8,82
Others	7	20,59
Base (Sample)	18	100,00

Notes: 1. Multiple choice question; 2.The following standards were mentioned in the other category: Rational Unified Process (RUP), Own Methodology, PMI/PMBOK, Six Sigma, ISO 90003:2004 and Microsoft Solution Framework (MSF).

Figure 5. Companies per region

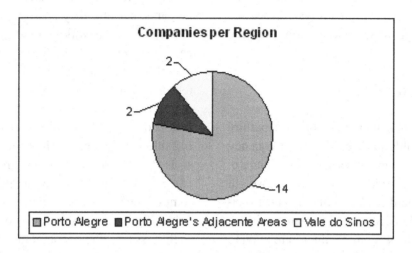

Alegre and, in second place, with the same number of companies, the regions surrounding Porto Alegre and Vale do Sinos.

It is observed in Table 4 a higher predominance of the CMM (SW-CMM) model adopted as a reference by the majority of the companies in the software processes improvement projects. Such a result must be linked to the fact that this model is an older one, and because it is more widely spread in the market. Furthermore, there are many reports published concerning its implementation (Beecham et al., 2003; Conradi & Fuggeta, 2002; Marczak, Audy, & Sá, 2005; Scheible & Bastos,

2005), as well as actions and projects performed by support entities (ESICENTER, 2003) and (SOFTSUL, 2001). Anyway, this situation is likely to change by the end of 2005, since SEI will suspend assessments based on this model and operate only with the CMMI model. Most likely, the companies in the sample that are adopting the CMMI model will soon be making the final adjustments to follow this shift (14, 71% in Staged Representation and 5, 88% in Continuous Representation). It can also be seen in Table 4 that other non-studied standards have also been used as reference by the companies (20, 59%).

Figure 6. Frequency distribution of weight

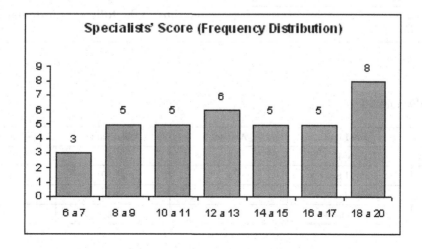

And, what is more, the adoption of more than one standard as reference in software processes improvement projects is common practice across companies.

Consolidation

Taking each participant's weight as a departure point, it is possible to determine the frequency distribution in the sample, as shown in Figure 6.

Besides, this sample shows an average weight of 13,33, a standard deviation of 4,08 and a variable ratio of 30,61%. Since the standard deviation determines the dispersion of values in relation to the average (Nazareth, 1998), a high dispersion of the values is confirmed. Moreover, the value of the variable ratio allows us to consider this distribution as an heterogeneous one. In Figure 6, it can be noted that the participants of the frequency intervals 6 to 7 and 18 to 20 correspond to the participants with lower and higher experience in the area of software processes improvement, respectively. This differentiation is based

on the characteristics of the last interval's participants, because they possess a higher number of projects, more working time and more experience in the area of software processes improvement than the participants of the first interval. For this reason, it is necessary to assess the participant's opinion in relation to his experience, so that this factor does not influence the results of the research. In Table 5, the sample can be divided into quartiles so as to obtain score limits and group the specialists in classes. By this, we can quite increase the sample's degree of homogeneity and diminish the value of the standard deviation of the weights in each class (the dispersion of the values observed is diminished). Besides, the possible distortions resulting from the individual comparison among each specialist's weight would be eliminated (Nogueira & Rocha, 2003); it would also be possible to consider as non-significant the differences of weight among each one of the components (Andrade et al., 2004).

Therefore, in Table 6, it is possible to visualize the specialists grouped in classes (A, B, C and D), as well as the average and the standard deviation of the weights for those belonging to the same class.

The objective of this division into classes is to attribute a single weight to the answers belonging to the same class, according to Table 7 below. To calculate the weight of each class, the first class is used as a reference (Class A); it is weighed 1,0 and the weight of the others is calculated according to the following formula:

Table 5. Quartiles

Quartiles	Score
Minimum Value– Q0	6
1st Quartile Limit – Q1	10
2nd Quartile Limit – Q2	13
3rd Quartile Limit – Q3	16
4th Quartile Limit – Q4	20

Table 6. Specialist classes

Class	Score Limit	Amount	Mean Value	Standard Deviation
A	Up to 10	10	8,40	1,35
B	From 11 to 13	9	11,89	0,93
C	From 14 to 16	8	15,13	0,83
D	Higher than 16	9	18,67	1,12

Table 7. Weight per class of specialist

Class	Weight Calculation	Weight
A	1	1,00
B	11,89/8,40	1,42
C	15,13/8,40	1,80
D	18,67/8,40	2,22

$$P(j) = \frac{\overline{X}(j)}{\overline{X}(A)}$$

P (j) is the weight attributed to class j;

X (j) is the average weight of class j;

X (A) is the average weight of class A.

Formula 1. Participant's weight

In which:

As one can observe in the table above, the other classes have their weight calculated as a function of the percentage distance of the average

Figure 7. Most critical resistance factors

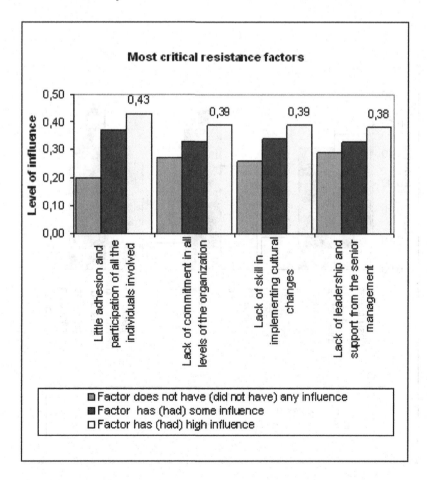

weight of the professionals of the class in relation to the average weight of the professionals in class A. Therefore, the weight of class B is calculated as a function of the number of professionals in class A necessary to equal the weight of a single professional in class B. Likewise, the weight of class C is determined as a function of the number of professionals in class A necessary to equal the weight of a single professional in class C and so on.

RESULTS ANALYSIS

The present section shows the consolidation and the analysis of results obtained in the survey performed from March 21st to May 6th, 2005 with the sample described in section 4.1. In order to consolidate the data obtained, each vote was calculated according to the weight of the class it belonged to, and a normalization was applied to the total of votes of each factor, so that they could be presented in Figures 7 and 8. These figures present the partial result of the resistance factors in software processes improvement projects, that is, the 3 most and least voted factors, which will be analyzed as follows.

In Figure 7, it is possible to see that the factor considered as the most critical by the participants in a software processes improvement project is "Little adhesion and participation of all the individuals involved". This results corroborates the great influence of the human factor in such an

Figure 8. Least critical resistance factors

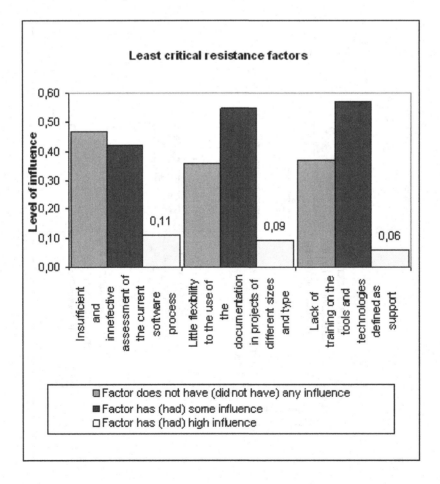

initiative and is in accordance with the results obtained in the literature (presented in section 3). According to participants, the second most important factors were "Lack of commitment in all levels of the organization" and "Lack of skill in implementing cultural changes". Regarding this second position, the participants also show some concern with the human factor, although they report some concern with the organization's culture and it is in accordance with the gotten one of literature in section 3. These two factors fall into a broader classification, the organizational factor. At this point, the importance of the organization's capability to operate and adapt to changes is noted. Besides, the factor "Lack of skill in implementing cultural changes" is directly influenced by the resources the company possesses to implement the necessary changes. This factor helps to stress the issue of the size of the company, because the larger the size of a company, the more resources it will be able to allocate to operate the cultural change demanded by such a project. The third most critical factor was "Lack of leadership and support from the senior management". This factor highlights the importance given by the respondents to the senior management support and leadership in the implementation of improvements and it is in accordance with the results gotten in the research of Andrade et al. (2004).

Figure 8 shows that the factors considered least influent in a software processes improvement project are, respectively: "Lack of training on the tools and technologies defined as support", "Little flexibility to the use of the documentation in projects of different sizes and types" and "Insufficient and ineffective assessment of the current software process". These factors might have been considered least influential by the participants due to the easiness of executing actions to deal with them. The factors "Lack of training on the tools and technologies defined as support" and "Little flexibility to the use of the documentation in projects of different sizes and types" fall

into the classification of project factor, having a smaller scope and being more easily dealt with, that is, they do not involve organizational factors whose treatment is more complex. From any form, the factor "Lack of Training on the tools and technologies defined as support" to be pointed with lesser influence differs from the results of the research of Beecham et al. (2003). The factor "Insufficient and ineffective assessment of the current software process" might have been considered less risky because such assessments are usually accomplished by specialists who make use of well-known process assessment methods. However, this result differs from the concern and the risk pointed for Wiegers (1996) with respect to this factor.

From the results obtained, it is observed that the final set of factors equals the initial one, since none of the factors added achieved a total of votes higher than half of the maximum value of votes to one of the factors. The repetition of this research with another sample of enterprises (situated in other regions of Rio Grande do Sul, in other states of Brazil, or countries for example) could allow a comparative analysis of the results obtained in this sample. This is due to the absence of related studies, which could serve as a basis to this comparison and to the verification of results.

FUTURE RESEARCH DIRECTIONS

In further studies, this research could be performed in other regions, states in the country and/or countries, what would allow a comparative analysis of the results obtained and a verification of the influence exerted by the cultural factor. Another suggestion to further studies would be the one of preventive actions to cope with some factors and the implementation of such actions in some organizations, in order to check whether the results would be positive or not.

CONCLUSION

This chapter presents a set of resistance factors identified in software processes improvement projects, that is, it presents the factors of influence in the transition phase from the current software process to the improved one within the companies. It is concluded from this study that a software processes improvement project may use more than a standard as reference, since they can be complementary due to the differentiation in focus of action and of the roles involved. This evidence is confirmed by the analysis of Table 1 which used a multiple choice question and were given more than one standard by the participants. One of the limitations of this research project is that since it adopted a questionnaire as a data collection instrument, it is not always possible to trust the veracity of the information provided, thus diminishing the degree of reliability of the answers given. Another limitation lies on the size of the sample that could be increased and applied to other places within the state, were the deadlines more stretched. On the other hand, this methodology presents an advantage that is its high degree of flexibility, since it can be applied in other research projects with qualitative data and in other fields of science as well, provided that both the criteria and the scoring tables be adapted (because they characterize a participant). With respect to the data collection stage, we can point out another limitation to this research project: most of the times the gathering occurred via e-mail, thus hindering a closer approach to the filling out of the questionnaire; it was also impossible to learn about the implementation strategy of software processes improvement. As a main contribution, we expect that the results shown in this research project may serve as reference to the professionals involved in software processes improvement projects and to researchers in the field of Software Engineering. It is also expected that these results may contribute to the planning of future software processes improvement projects, in which preventive actions can be designed to lessen or eliminate their consequences. Anyway, an initial analysis on the risk of these factors is of paramount importance, for the impact and the probability of an associated risk occur may vary across organizations.

REFERENCES

ABNT. (1998). *Associação Brasileira de Normas Técnicas.* Retrieved March 24, 2006, from http://www.abnt.org.br

Abrahamsson, P. (2001). Commitment development in software process improvement: Critical misconceptions. *Paper presented at the 23rd International Conference on Software Engineering.* Los Alamitos, CA: IEEE Computer Society.

Andrade, J. M., Albuquerque, A. B., Campos, F. B., & Rocha, A. R. C. (2004). *Conseqüências e características de um processo de desenvolvimento de software de qualidade e aspectos que o influenciam: Uma avaliação de especialistas.* Paper presented at the 3rd Brazilian Symposium on Software Quality, Brasilia, Brazil.

Basili, V. R., McGarry, F. E., Pajerski, R., & Zelkowitz, M. V. (2002). *Lessons learned from 25 years of process improvement: The rise and fall the NASA Software Engineering Laboratory.* Paper presented at the Proceedings of the 24th International Conference on Software Engineering. Orlando, Florida: ACM.

Beecham, S., Hall, T., & Rainer, A. (2003). Software process improvement problems in twelve software companies: An empirical analysis. *Empirical Software Engineering, 8*(1), 7–42. doi:10.1023/A:1021764731148

Brietzke, J., & Abraham. R. (2006). Resistance factors in software process improvement. *Clei Electronic Journal, 9*(1).

CMMI Product Team. (2006). *Capability maturity model integration*. Retrieved March 24, 2006, from http://www.sei.cmu.edu/cmmi

Conradi, R., & Fuggeta, A. (2002). Improving software process improvement. *IEEE Software, 19*(4), 92–99. doi:10.1109/MS.2002.1020295

ESICENTER. (2003). *ESICenter UNISINOS*. Retrieved March 24, 2006, from http://www.esicenter.unisinos.br

Farias, L. D. L. (2002). *Planejamento de riscos em ambientes de desenvolvimento de software orientados à organização* (Unpublished master's dissertation). Instituto Alberto Luiz Coimbra de Pós-graduação e Pesquisa de Engenharia, Brazil.

ISO/SPICE. (2003). *ISO/SPICE*. Retrieved March 24, 2006, from http://www.isospice.com

Iversen, J., Nielsen, P. A., & Norbjerg, J. (1998). *Problem diagnosis software process improvement*. Paper presented at the IFIP on Information systems: Current Issues and Future Changes. Retrieved March 24, 2006, from http://citeseer.ist.psu.edu/cache/papers/cs/12921/http:zSzzSzis.lse.ac.ukzSzhelsinkizSziversen.pdf/ive rsen-98problem.pdf

Marczak, S., Audy, J., & Sá, L. (2005). *Proposta e aplicação de um instrumento de acompanhamento da implantação do SW-CMM Nível 2*. Paper presented at the 4th Symposium on Software Quality, Porto Alegre, Brazil.

Nazareth, H. R. D. S. (1998). *Curso básico de estatística*. São Paulo, Brasil: Ática.

Nogueira, M. O., & Rocha, A. R. C. (2003). *Práticas relevantes em engenharia de software: Uma avaliação de especialistas*. Paper presented at the 2nd Symposium on Software Quality, Salvador, Brazil.

Pires, C. G., Marinho, F., Tellas, G., & Belchior, A. (2004). *A experiência de melhoria do processo do Instituto Atlântico baseado no SW-CMM nível 2*. Paper presented at the 3rd Symposium on Quality of Software, Brasilia, Brazil.

Rocha, A. R. C., Maldonado, J. C., & Weber, K. C. (2001). *Qualidade de software teoria e prática*. São Paulo, Brazil: Prentice Hall.

Scheible, A., & Bastos, A. V. (2005). *CMM e comprometimento: Um estudo de caso na implantação do nível 2*. Paper presented at the 4th Symposium on Software Quality, Porto Alegre, Brazil.

SEBRAE. (2004). *Serviço de apoio às micro e pequenas empresas do Rio Grande do Sul*. Retrieved March 24, 2006, from http://www.sebrae-rs.com.br

SOFTEX. (2005). *Associação para Promoção da Excelência do Software Brasileiro*. Retrieved March 24, 2006, from http://www.softex.br/mpsbr

SOFTSUL. (2001). *Sociedade Sul-riograndense de Apoio ao Desenvolvimento de Software*. Retrieved March 24, 2006, from http://www.softsul.org.br

Sommerville, I. (2003). *Engenharia de software*. São Paulo, Brazil: Addison-Wesley.

Wheeler, S., & Duggins, S. (1998). Improving software quality. *Paper presented at the Proceedings of the 36th Annual Southeast Regional Conference*, ACM.

Wiegers, K. E. (1996). Software process improvement: Ten traps to avoid. *Software Development, 4*, 51–58.

ADDITIONAL READING

Albertuni, I., & Brietzke, J. (2008). *Avaliação e Melhoria do Processo Organizacional Alinhada ao MPS.BR e PGQP*. Retrieved January, 06, 2010, from http://www.devmedia.com.br/articles/viewcomp.asp?comp=9873

Brietzke, J., López, P. D. P., Albertuni, I., & Richter, L. (2007). *A Conquista do MPS.BR Nível F na Qualità Informática: Um Caso de Sucesso*. SBQS'2007: 4th Symposium on Quality of Software, Porto de Galinhas, Brazil

FNQ. (2010). Fundação Nacional da Qualidade: Publicaçõess. Retrieved January 06, 2010, from http://www.fnq.org.br/site/689/default.aspx

iMPS (2008). Melhoria de Processo do Software Brasileiro: Resultados de Desempenho. Retrieved January 06, 2010, from http://www.softex.br/mpsbr/_livros/imps/imps.pdf

MPS.BR. (2004). Melhoria de Processo do Software Brasileiro: Artigos. Retrieved January 06, 2010, from http://www.softex.br/mpsbr/_artigos/default.asp

MPS.BR. (2008). Melhoria de Processo do Software Brasileiro: Lições Aprendidas. Retrieved January 06, 2010, from http://www.softex.br/mpsbr/_livros/licoes/mpsbr_en.pdf

MPS.BR. (2009). Melhoria de Processo do Software Brasileiro: Guias. Retrieved January 06, 2010, from http://www.softex.br/mpsbr/_guias/default.asp

Porto, J. B., et al. (2007). A Experiência de Avaliação MPS.BR Nível F na Qualità. Retrieved January 06, 2010, from http://www.softex.br/portal/softexweb/uploadDocuments/_mpsbr/T2-Qualita-WE.pdf

KEY TERMS AND DEFINITIONS

Preventive Action: Action to prevent or minimize the impact caused by a particular incident or event.

Quality of Software: Knowledge area of software engineering that aims to ensure the quality of software through activities and development processes well defined, managed, and continuous improvement.

Resistance Factors: Problems or issues that may be risks and critical to the success of software process improvement.

Risk: Probability of occurrence of an event whose impact can generate an opportunity or a threat.

Software Engineering: Knowledge area that covers the specification, development, maintenance, operation and discontinuation of software systems using a set of methods, techniques and tools.

Software Process Improvement: Assessment of software processes from their results, identifying their strengths and weaknesses, implementing the improvements identified and accompanied them to the institutionalization of the organization.

Software Processes Improvement Project: Temporary initiative with clear and well-defined purpose of software process improvement, sponsor, resource allocation, and planning and monitoring their implementation.

Chapter 7
Implementation of the Personal Software Process in Academic Settings and Current Support Tools

Mohd Hairul Nizam Md Nasir
University of Malaya, Malaysia

Nur Aalyaa Alias
Two Sigma Technologies, Malaysia

Shukor Sanim Mohd Fauzi
Universiti Teknologi Mara, Malaysia

Mohd Hashim Massatu
Two Sigma Technologies, Malaysia

ABSTRACT

The Personal Software Process (PSP) is a structured software development framework that includes defined operations, measurements, and analysis techniques designed to help software engineers understand and build on their personal skills and improve their performance. The PSP provides a defined personal process, guides software engineers in collecting and recording data, and defines ways to analyse data and make process improvements. This chapter reviews the previous literature on the implementation of the PSP in academic settings. Lessons learned from PSP implementations are then highlighted. We found that there were mixed outcomes due to several issues that later become a barrier to the adoption of the PSP. Several tools have been developed to overcome these barriers and constitute a helping hand for both students and engineers in adopting the PSP.

DOI: 10.4018/978-1-61350-141-2.ch007

BACKGROUND

The Personal Software Process (PSP) is a self-improvement process that helps software engineers develop high-quality and predictable software. The PSP is intended to control, manage, and improve the way engineers work. Additionally, the PSP helps to improve software quality during the development process because engineers can systematically track and plan their work accordingly and manage any defects they encounter in completing the project. These features ultimately facilitate the production of high-quality software and also help to assure product delivery within time constraints.

The PSP was developed by Watts Humphrey in April 1989. Despite the circumstances, he managed to develop a total of 62 programs and 15 distinct versions of PSP implementations in three years. Humphrey utilised approximately 25,000 lines of code (LOC) in the Pascal, Object Pascal and C++ programming languages during PSP development. Before Humphrey developed the PSP framework, he led the initial development of the Software Engineering Institute's Capability Maturity Model (CMM) and applied CMM to many software development projects. However, many questions remained, such as how to apply CMM principles to small organisations or to the work of a small software team, because the CMM principles focused more on assuring that the management system provided full support and assistance to the development engineers. Initially, Humphrey intended to apply CMM principles to write a small program. However, in a small group setting, Humphrey conceded that is not generally possible to have dedicated process specialists; hence, every engineer must participate at least part-time in process improvement.

Engineers can certainly benefit from a more detailed process, and it is thus required to deal overtly with actual practices in software development and to show engineers precisely how to apply the CMM process principles. As a result, the PSP was invented to convince software engineers that improvement requires change, and changing the behaviour of software engineers is a nontrivial problem. Humphrey also asserted that the PSP design is based on the principles of consensus planning and quality, providing an internal reference point for software quality before its public release.

One of the principles also espoused by Humphrey is that every engineer is different; therefore, engineers must plan their work based on their own personal data. Occasionally, an engineer may be *a doubting Thomas*; i.c., one who is sceptical about changes to their work habits. Although engineers may be willing to make a few minor changes, engineers generally hold fairly closely to what has worked for them in the past, unless they can be convinced that a new method is more effective. The second principle implied in the PSP is that engineers should use well-defined and measured processes to consistently improve their own performance. Altogether, engineers need to understand their personal performance, measures of the time they spend on each job step, defect injection and removal as well as the size of the product they produce. Subsequently, engineers are required to produce quality products and, to do this, they must plan, measure, and track product quality; the overall message is to focus on quality from the outset of the project. Additionally, engineers need to find and fix defects earlier during the process rather than later, as the latter tends to increase project expenses. In other words, prevention is better than cure; hence, defects are more effectively prevented and fixed earlier rather than later, when the project is nearly ready for release for public use. Equally important, the results of each job should be analysed for future reference, as any findings may be helpful in improving their personal processes, bearing in mind that the right way to complete the project is to find the fastest and cheapest way to do the job.

Figure 1. Diagram of planning processes involved in the PSP

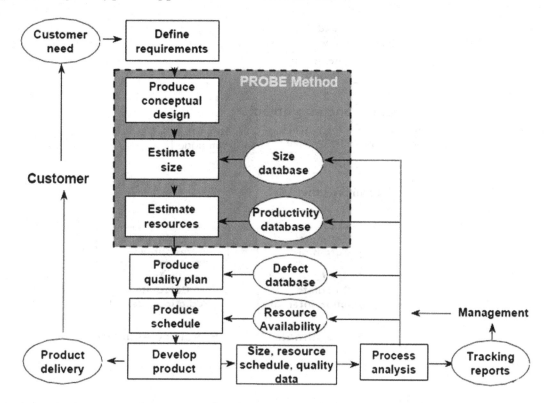

Structures and Processes

The first step in the PSP is planning, which consists of a planning script that is used to guide work and also a plan summary which records planning data. After gathering and analysing all the requirements for the project, engineers follow each step in the planning script and perform time recording and defect logging. In the planning phase, the overall plan is created with a gross estimate, wherein the engineer uses process scripts in defining each step required for each part of the process. Using this structure, engineers are able to quantify their work (Figure 1).

Initially, engineers should know about the work to be done; thus, they should plan their tasks based on their own historical time, size and defect data. They should define their work in detail because this will provide more accurate estimates. After-

wards, as all the products may seem to be vague and indistinguishable, engineers may transfer all the details and ideas into a conceptual design, which is a rough outline for the outcome because it relies on historical data, which is the main reference, as well as on data from the previous project. Subsequently, the resource and size estimations are made using the PROBE method. Theoretically, engineers estimate the product size and, based on this estimation, later determine the approximate amount of time required for the project to be completed. Figure 2 illustrates the PROBE method in detail.

PROBE uses historical relationships between estimated object LOCs and actual resources to estimate resource requirements. For example, engineers may refer to historical data on the size of similar projects they have previously developed and use linear regression to estimate the overall

Figure 2. Diagram of the PROBE method

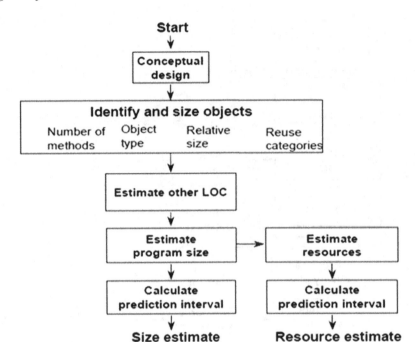

size of the finished product, estimate a total plan for the code to be developed, and estimate the development resources needed. Using the percentage estimates for guidance, every phase in the development process (design, design review, coding, code review, compiling, unit testing, and postmortem phases) may also be estimated accordingly. This estimation serves as an assurance that the predicted project time is congruent with the actual time and also helps to correct defects during the development phase.

Engineers may log time and defect data in the process as they perform their tasks. This is to ensure that the quality plan should first be determined to yield a quality product. After the estimation (which is part of the quality plan) is verified with the PROBE method, the schedule is conveyed, and the task time is laid out to achieve the planning target. This is the way to drive the activities required to achieve the desired outcome within the time constraints. Subsequently, as engineers work to develop the products, they start

the actual process earlier planned in detail, and these new data may be reused for future projects. Thereafter, the engineers perform an evaluation and a postmortem analysis to summarise the time and defects recorded in the actual logging data. Finally, they measure the program size and enter the actual data in a plan summary form. As they review all the analysis of the logs, they update the historical size and productivity in the database. Defects found are also reviewed during compilation, where they undergo testing and are fixed for future reference.

The PSP is based on several methods consisting of a series of seven process versions (Figure 3). These seven process levels progressively introduce data and analysis techniques (W. S. Humphrey, 1994). The methods are labelled PSP0 to PSP3. Each of these versions consists of sets of logs, forms, scripts and standards. Below, the details of the seven process levels of the PSP are listed, from PSP0 to PSP3.

Figure 3. Seven process levels in the PSP

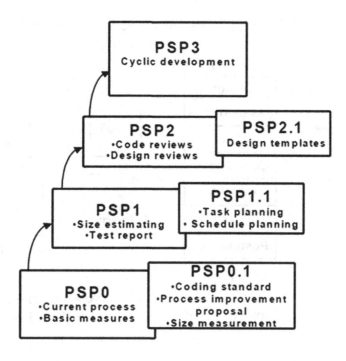

• PSP0

In the first level, engineers essentially follow their current practices, learning some basic PSP techniques (Figure 4). These current processes are enhanced with time and defect tracking instruments. In PSP0, engineers establish a baseline against which to measure progress and identify the bases for improvement. This process level provides a convenient structure for doing small-scale tasks, a framework for measuring these tasks and a foundation for process improvement. Thus, at this process level, there are several tasks that must be completed by the engineers before completing a PSP0 plan summary. Each task requires them to define the current process in detail with the use of scripts. Each script guides their plans in detail. Next, they implement a time recording log. The log is used to clock the time spent in each subprocess of the PSP. The objective is to determine that engineers spend the bulk of their time efficiently. Engineers record data on each defect found and corrected in a defect recording

log, with the same objectives as the time recording log. Additionally, the defect type standard is the next task to be considered, and engineers can apply several of the defect type standards such as documentation, syntax, assignment, and interface. When the current process, time and defect recording and the defect type standard have been carefully determined, engineers can summarise all the planning and properly log PSP0 time and defect data scripts in the Plan Summary form. However, engineers should bear in mind that the Project Plan summary contains not only estimated data but also the actual data recorded during the development process.

• PSP0.1

PSP0 was enhanced to PSP0.1 by adding size measurements in terms of LOC and the process improvement proposal, noting any issues and brainstorming ideas for their resolution. (Börstler et al., 2002) stated that at this level, the personal baseline process is extended to include a systema-

Figure 4. The processes in the PSP0 summarised in a diagram (Watts S. Humphrey, 2000b)

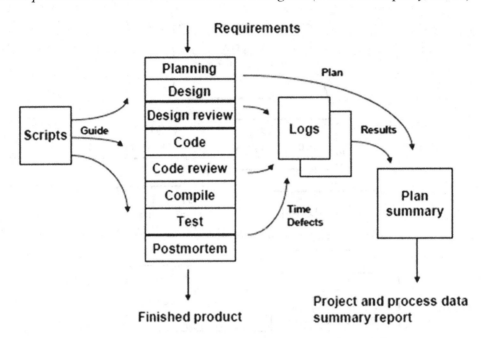

tised coding standard, software size measurement in terms of logical LOC and a personal process improvement proposal mechanism. The coding standards are also developed at this level; each standard should include definitions with examples. Moreover, the standards also include estimate of job size as a function of LOC and additionally, standards are developed that deal with LOC count alterations made in the project. Furthermore, items such as problems encountered on the project, proposals for process improvement, overall comments about the project and much more data are also recorded.

• PSP1

This level introduces software size and resource estimation and PSP test reporting. In principle, size estimates of a project are made by determining the planned project size based on previous projects undertaken within the organisation. In PSP1, engineers can establish an orderly and repeatable procedure for developing software using size,

resource and schedule estimations. Additionally, the estimating process may become progressively more accurate as more data is gathered from various projects completed by an organisation. In estimating project size, engineers should have the actual size data for a number of previously developed projects to establish baseline initial estimates. The test report is also used to maintain a record of the tests run and the results obtained. To ensure that the same tests and results are captured again in future projects, the results should be recorded in detail. Finally, throughout this level, the PROBE method is also introduced to the engineer, which uses historical data to estimate size and determine the accuracy of the estimate. PROBE is a regression-based size-estimation method that was developed specifically for the PSP.

• PSP1.1

Additionally, this level enhances PSP1 to augment it with task and schedule planning and also adds earned-value tracking. Engineers often have trouble tracking their work because they tend to perform tasks other than those they have planned. Hence, in PSP1.1, task planning helps them to estimate the development time and completion data for each project task. Furthermore, it also provides a basis for tracking schedule progress. Additionally, schedule planning is used in this level to record the number of actual hours expanded in a calendar period, and this data is used to relate planned tasks to the calendar schedule. Normally, when scheduling a project, the schedule is made on a weekly basis; however, this depends on the size of the project itself. Small projects are preferably tracked daily. Furthermore, earned-value tracking allows engineers to weight the relative importance of each task and to judge their progress as they finish some tasks early and others late.

- PSP2

This level introduces design and code review with quality measurement and evaluation. This may help to improve the quality of software and subsequently improve personal quality management more than any other single change made to the personal software process (Xiaohong, Percy, Huiming, & Yaohang, 2008); this idea is supported by (Shen, Hsueh, & Chu, 2006). When using defect data from their earlier exercises, engineers also develop personal design and code review checklists. A technical review is performed to assure that the quality of the program was improved, and this is done by examining part or all of the software system and its associated documentation. Nonetheless, the main objective of the technical review (or program inspection) is to identify defects (code anomalies, logical errors or noncompliance with standards). This review procedure has several advantages compared with dynamic testing, such as not requiring the program to be run and providing a direct measure of defects or quality attributes, and it is considered more effective. In conjunction with the technical review, a code review helps to ensure that the code complies with the coding

standards. Design review is done to certify that the requirements, specifications and high-level design are completely satisfied. Additionally, design review ensures that the product complies with all applicable design standards.

- PSP2.1

Throughout this level, engineers learn to use design specification templates or techniques that provide an orderly framework and format to record designs properly. Additionally, engineers are also provided with ways of preventing defects. Templates consists of operational scenario templates containing descriptions of likely operational scenarios to be followed in using the program such as scenario steps, likely user objectives, sources of scenario action and lists of significant comments. The next template is the functional specification template, which is used to describe functions and procedures for functional design or objects for object-oriented design. Finally, the logic specification template specifies pseudo-code logic for each function or program unit and contains lists of any new or unusual included features that are required by the functions, noting all unusual or special types or prototypes, and documents any auxiliary information required, the number or level of each significant logic statement and lastly documents the program logic.

- PSP3

This level covers design verification techniques and methods for adapting the PSP to the engineers' working environment. The tasks include all of the PSP2 and PSP2.1 tasks plus cyclic development (see Figure 5). Cyclic development is useful in tracking data regarding program size, time spent in each development phase, defects detected and defects removed. Its objective is to extend PSP or to scale up the process to large program development such as industrial-sized projects and to cover team project work. This strategy focuses on structuring product development into increments suitable for cyclic development.

PSP3 addresses this scalability with the cyclic development strategy, in which large programs are decomposed into parts for development and then integrated (Hayes & Over, 1997). To scale up PSP2 to a larger project, the personal process of developing a larger program is subdivided into PSP2-sized pieces. Subsequently, the design is developed in incremental steps in PSP3. The first build is the kernel, and it is enhanced in iterative cycles. At each iteration, PSP2 is used, including design, coding, compiling and testing. Each enhancement is built on the previously completed increment up to a size of several thousand LOC. This helps engineers concentrate on verifying the quality of the latest increment without worrying about defects in the earlier cycles.

Figure 5. A diagram of cyclic development (W. S. Humphrey, 1994)

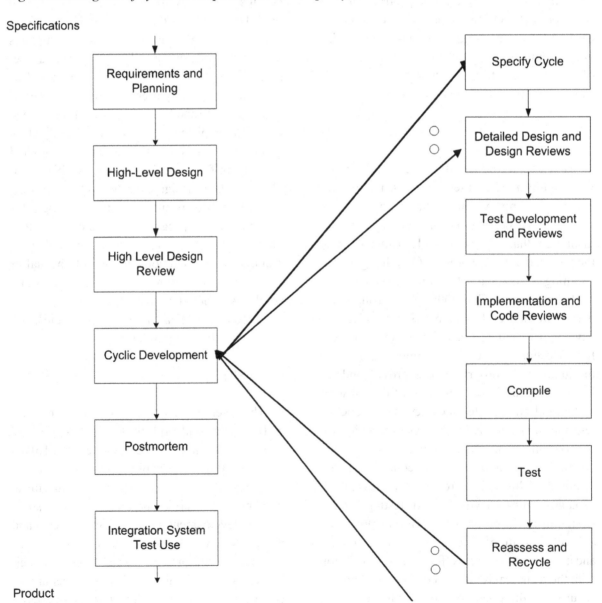

PSP Implementation in Academic Settings

This section reports on implementation of the PSP in academic settings based on the previous literature. The cited reports centre on two criteria: (1) the course environment and method and (2) coverage level and support tools. Initially, the course environment setting is determined by deciding on criteria for the target audience, herein classified by the grade level of the students in the participating institutions. Several universities have implemented the PSP in their undergraduate classes, enrolling freshmen (either in CS1 or CS2), sophomores, juniors, or seniors. There also several universities applying PSP to their graduate programs, and in both cases, the gender and age of the target audience are not mentioned. We thus concluded that studies of the implementation of PSP in these universities was not intended to measure its significance based on the demographic data of the target audience (except in the study conducted by (Prechelt & Unger, 2001), where the student body consisted only of male Computer Science students). The students' backgrounds in these studies were mostly determined to be computer-based (either Computer Science students, Software Engineering students or Electrical Engineering students), although undoubtedly, several universities noted that some students with noncomputer backgrounds were studying this subject; however, the authors later eliminated the data collected from these students.

The studies found that the material covered was basically from Humphrey's books: *Introduction to the Personal Software Process* and *A Discipline for Software Engineering*. Some universities altered the contents of the book to suit time constraints; in particular, a modified version of *Introduction to the Personal Software Process* called "PSP-lite" was deemed to be appropriate and comprehensible for undergraduate students, especially freshmen. Most of the course curricula complied with Humphrey's standards, from PSP0

to PSP3, whereas some only complied up to PSP2. Universities even embedded PSP in their existing courses or introduced a new PSP course to their students to provide PSP benefits. In determining the support tool used, most of the universities chose to develop their own local support tools to collect PSP data or to collect the data manually using spreadsheets or paper-based methods based on Humphrey's sample PSP template included in the book. However, there are many automated tools that exist today, as discussed later in this chapter.

Course Environment and Method

To ensure that PSP implementation is worth undertaking, many universities sought to create a suitable environment in which a PSP course would be taught. This environment was also created to ensure that the outcomes were apt to their satisfaction and that students could understand the material. The universities tested PSP application at each grade level to see which students had the most positive outcomes. The reasons behind their decisions are stated clearly with supporting evidence in their reports.

Target Audience

Freshmen

Some universities implemented PSP at the freshmen level, reasoning that adoption in the early years may influence students to use the PSP. Afterwards, PSP may be chosen as a method when dealing with any tasks given by an instructor, and later, they may apply PSP when working in industry. This is supported by (Hou & Tomayko, 1998), as they realised that there is great potential in teaching some aspects of the PSP to college freshmen. Humphrey allowed that PSP concepts are within the intellectual grasp of most college freshmen (Watts S. Humphrey, 1996) and later prepared a book with consideration given to undergraduates. Some universities have applied the

PSP to freshmen within their existing programs such as computer science, software engineering, information systems, electrical engineering, and software management. The University of Utah, for example, integrated the PSP into a two-semester sequence (CS1 and CS2). The PSP coverage in the syllabus differs in each semester; in CS1 it more involves covering and handling defects, whereas the focus in CS2 diverges to resource estimation and tracking. Nevertheless, defect covering and handling is also covered in CS2. At Lund University, the implementation of the PSP for freshmen is aimed at measuring PSP effectiveness. Three goals were determined: knowledge, skills and attitude. There are approximately 31 students taking the course, and they used Java as the main programming language. This allows for ease of use, as Java has listed packages to support program development and other assigned tasks. Based on 16 analyses surveyed, only two universities implemented the PSP for freshmen.

Sophomores

There are three universities that implemented the PSP in the sophomore year. This decision was made not randomly but for concrete reasons with supporting proof. This is consistent with (Börstler et al., 2002), who reported that sophomores were chosen as the subjects of a PSP experiment, as they had already taken several courses to develop their computer literacy. The University of Utah, for example, moved its implementation of the PSP from senior students in software engineering to sophomores to measure the effectiveness of the PSP. Purdue University also incorporated PSP material into the introductory programming courses in the first course only (CS1) and also across a two-semester sequence (CS1 and CS2) for sophomore students in Computer Information Systems. To assist and ensure that students adopt the PSP effectively, instructors check PSP data occasionally and later complete brief questionnaires at the end of the course to rate student attitudes

towards the PSP. This is also done in the Milwaukee School of Engineering, where the software process is also introduced to sophomore students. The introduction of Humphrey's PSP courses is intended to equip students with good software practices early in the curriculum. Students are taught to plan, track and measure product quality while in progress throughout the curriculum. Here, Software Engineering Process (SE280) is the course that provides an introduction to the PSP and the management of software projects based on Humphrey's book. This course consists of three or four credit hours and has no final exam. Additionally, at Umea University, the PSP is integrated into two courses, the C++ course and Software Engineering, intended for sophomore students. It is introduced in two extra 45-minute lectures and used throughout all the exercises in the C++ course. For the Software Engineering course, lectures and assignments (theory track) are also provided, and students are required to develop a tool in the tasks given to them.

Juniors

At Montana Tech of the University of Montana, the PSP is taught at the junior level and implemented in a single semester course (CS1). Students taking this course have completed two courses in data structures and algorithms and are assumed to have obtained a high-level programming competency. In this university, the PSP course is taught to students three days per week. At the Curtin University of Technology, the PSP is implemented in one of the subjects during the students' third year. There were 155 students taking this course, but seven were excluded from the analysis due to the diversity of their academic backgrounds. Most of the students were bachelor's students in Software Engineering, Computer Science and Information Technology. The PSP was used in this study to measure the actual time spent by students working on a major assignment in a Software Engineering subject. Umea University implemented the PSP not only in the sophomore-level classes but also in the third-year Software Engineering course. The students were required to develop tools to support data collection and analysis for the PSP. Moreover, the students were required to attend lectures on the PSP, and assignments were given to track the grasp of the theory that had been taught. Only these three universities applied the PSP in the courses taken by their junior undergraduate students.

Seniors

Among the studies across the 16 universities, the students in their fourth year or higher were considered the senior students. Several universities did apply the PSP for their senior students because they were already taking programming courses. Additionally, it was believed that most of their programming skills were already sharpened during their years in the university. At the University of Oulu, for example, student instruction was divided into three 10 week periods (nine weekly 2–4 hour lectures, 7 programming exercises, 2 reporting (mid-term and final) assignments and an examination). In total, the course includes 160 direct hours, and 68% of the students work in software organisations, either part-time or full-time. The programming languages used by the students are Java and C++, and each assignment must be completed within six calendar days. Initially, the University of Utah implemented the PSP for senior students in a Software Engineering course, and it was necessary for them to do the assigned tasks in pairs. Even though the PSP is more likely to be done individually to measure the progress of work done by engineers or students, Williams (2001), for example, made changes to the PSP to leverage the power of two programmers working together, thereby formulating the Collaborative Software Process (CSP). However, the university later converted the implementation for sophomore students. Additionally, the Copenhagen Business School implemented the PSP for their senior students and obtained quite positive outcomes.

Unspecified

Several universities in the studies did not state at which student level they implemented the PSP but confirmed that the implementation was done with undergraduate students. For example, McGill University performed an experiment with undergraduate students using the PSP as a subject, and class assignments were given to students in the form of programming assignments. These were later taken into account to measure the effectiveness of the PSP; they additionally were expected to complete 8 projects, one per week. Data were collected for approximately 53 students, all taking the Personal Software Engineering course. The main programming language used was C++. The experiment performed by this university basically measured the critical factors affecting the PSP. Like McGill University, the University of Queensland did not state which undergraduate level was supplemented with PSP, but it was incorporated into the 2nd programming course (CS2). The class size consisted of 360 undergraduate students, which is quite a large sample size. The implementation took place in the School of Computer Science and Electrical Engineering and was taught within a segment of CS2, consisting of four lectures and a set of Java programming assignments. Similarly, Auburn University did not report the undergraduate level taking their PSP course, but there were approximately 110 undergraduate students in either Computer Science or Software Engineering completing the PSP course. This university applied the "Warren Buffet Approach" in the second offering of the course (CS2) so as to endorse a software development process. Students completed weekly assignments and used their own personal metrics for academic assignments laced with simulated data. Likewise, the University of Memphis implemented the PSP into its undergraduate course, and students were required to verify their own programming background and experience. The software engineering course claimed to deviate from the traditional model by introducing the PSP to cover process models, process improvement, estimation and metrics. Only a small number of students had one or two years of industry experience, and at the end of the term, students were asked to complete a questionnaire to evaluate the PSP implementation.

Graduate

Drexel University was one of the universities that implemented the PSP for their graduate students in Information Systems and Software Engineering, offering a PSP course once or twice annually. Graduate students here have a wide range of experience and programming ability. These differences are because the students come from different backgrounds, some having minimal classroom programming experience. If students happened to come from industry, previously they were likely to be software developers involved with many projects, and this extensive experience helped them to achieve programming expertise. Some of the students had also been managers and had not performed any programming projects in many years. However, this was not a determining factor, as experience and programming ability was not measured with relation to the adoption of the PSP by the students. Instead of implementing PSP for freshmen, Lund University also offered a PSP course to the graduate students in the Electrical Engineering Master's Program and the Computer Science and Engineering Master's Program. However, this course was optional in their 4th year of study. The total number of students taking this course was 131, and at first, they used C as the mandatory programming language to provide a coding and counting standard. Later, students were free to choose their own programming language and also developed their own coding and counting standards during project completion. Feng Chia University also implemented the PSP for their

graduate students, and they were taught in a one-semester PSP course modified in certain ways to improve quality in their PSP data. In one experimental treatment, paper forms were filled out by students with the PSP dataset and collected and submitted to the instructor after each assignment. Any errors found were corrected, and the students were required to resubmit the corrected work. The class consisted of 16 students, and their data were assembled in a report and a secondary analysis of the students' aggregate form was performed. In the PSP training, students in this university were enabled with statistical methods, providing a means to analyse their personal data and thus gain the benefits of using the PSP. Auburn University had approximately 202 graduate students majoring in Software Engineering, with a minimum of 4 years of working experience, take a PSP course. Similarly to their undergraduate program, the PSP course taught here also applied a "Warren Buffet Approach", with weekly assignments, and the students also used their own personal metrics.

Experiments measuring PSP training were performed involving 48 participants, consisting of all male Computer Science Master Students (Prechelt & Unger, 2001). They were divided into two groups, P and N, where P indicates the PSP group, consisting of 29 participants, and N is the non-PSP group, consisting of 19 participants. The P group had previously participated in a 15-week graduate lab course that introduced PSP methodology. They were required to complete 10 small programming tasks, with five process improvement assignments. All students, except for 8 participants in the N group who came from other lab courses of similar content, participated in a six-week graduate compact lab course on component software in Java (KOJAK) and had to complete five larger programming assignments. During the course, 8 participants dropped out, leaving 40 participants for the evaluation. These 8 participants were ignored in the subsequent data analysis. In this experiment, the task given to participants revolved on the *phoneword*. A few graduate students at the University of Memphis had already taken part in an undergraduate PSP course. Thus, as they continued to use PSP, the baseline process was more mature and more focused on team-oriented issues. Each student worked in a group consisting of 3–5 students, and the background of each individual varied; they were either experienced industrial software developers or less experienced graduate students. The instructors split individuals working together in previous projects in other courses into different teams. The instructors kept records to document each team member's contribution, consisting of recorded faults and amount of effort in each phase. The Middle East Technical University taught a PSP course during the spring semester of 2002, where it was included in the Software Management Program. The students were graduate students in the Software Management Program of the Informatics Institute and professionals from the software industry. PSP concepts were introduced here up to PSP2, and students completed six out of ten assignments (from assignments listed in the textbook). The programming languages used by most of the students were Java, C++ and Delphi, and students were required to complete the assignments in one week; if an incorrect or incomplete submission was made, they were given one extra week to rework the assignment and resubmit it to the instructor to facilitate the collection of quality PSP data.

Coverage Level and Support Tools

Humphrey's books on the PSP have become a useful course books in some of the universities for teaching it to their students. However, universities tend to use either only *Introduction to the Personal Software Process* or *A Discipline for Software Engineering* in the teaching process, and only Montana Tech used both books to teach the PSP. Montana Tech used *A Discipline for Software Engineering* when selecting a series of exercises to occupy their students, as did Lund

University, Auburn University, Milwaukee School of Engineering, the University of Memphis, Oulu University, McGill University and Copenhagen Business School. The differences among these institutions lie in the methods and ways of teaching the PSP to their students, e.g., how instructors determine the number of tasks or exercises to be done by the students to ensure that the benefits of the PSP are fully obtained. For example, Auburn University required their students to perform weekly programming assignments to illustrate various elements of the PSP; similarly, at Oulu University 7 programming exercises were assigned, and mid-term and final reports were submitted. Additionally, McGill University, Drexel University and Middle East University required their students to submit 8, 7 and 6 assignments each, respectively.

Most of the universities also embedded PSP methods based on Humphrey's book in their existing courses; for example, at the Milwaukee School of Engineering in an existing SE280 course, the software engineering process is introduced along with the management of software projects, based on Humphrey's *A Discipline of Software Engineering*. Similarly, at the Curtin University of Technology, the PSP became a method for generating a software-based gas-warning and evacuation system controller. These studies showed that the PSP can be embedded within existing courses as well as any new courses, even non-computer-science-related courses, as long as the students understood the reasons for applying the PSP and obtained the benefits from it.

Furthermore, the University of Queensland, the University of Utah, Umea University, and Purdue University used simplified or modified PSP curricula, called "PSP-lite", based on Humphrey's book *An Introduction to Personal Software Process*. They decided to use PSP-lite because it is shorter, easier to read, and specifically intended for teaching first-year students the basic principles of using disciplined software processes to produce high-quality software (Börstler et al.,

2002). Similar to the Curtin University of Technology and the Milwaukee School of Engineering, Purdue University implemented PSP into existing courses by covering half of the book in each of two courses. However, even at universities using the same methods to teach the PSP, the effectiveness of its implementation necessarily determines the results, as all of the PSP implementations were neither completely successful nor total failures (Table 1). Most universities in the cited studies used manual data recording such as spreadsheets to reduce overhead issues; the use of only electronic documents reduced the workload involving paper forms.

Additional Lessons Learned

Adoption by Graduate and Undergraduate Students

Among the lessons learned at the various universities, it was found that graduate students tended to perform well when implementing the PSP in their assignments and tasks given by the instructor. This can be seen in the studies from Drexel University and the University of Memphis, where the overall results of PSP implementation were excellent and students were eager to implement the PSP in their working environments later. The results from (Shen et al., 2006) were also encouraging in that improvement in several areas was observed (i.e., size and effort estimation accuracy, product quality, process quality and personal productivity). However, students decided not to implement the PSP in future development work, even though they realised the benefits and thought that size measurement, effort logging and postmortem were important in software development. In contrast with the experimental results, PSP implementation at Auburn University and the Middle East University seemed to show negative results. However, this likely happened because most graduate students came from industrial backgrounds, with several years of experience in project development; hence,

they tended to adopt their own personal habits when developing projects, as this was less burdensome for them. Adopting a new method was seen as time consuming and, furthermore, did not guarantee any effectiveness in project completion. Additionally, Middle East University encountered problems with the developed tool that may have somehow contributed to the ineffectiveness and affected the reliability of collected data.

Undergraduate students, in contrast, seemed to report results which were vague and undetermined. A pessimistic adoption of the PSP was observed in sophomores at Umea and Purdue University, where it was seen as unbearable, with an excessive workload, and they not interested in the PSP disciplinary process because they found it too fussy. Surprisingly, adoption by freshmen (at the University of Utah and Montana Tech of the University of Montana) was better than expected, as freshman at both universities received the PSP well, although they felt resistant and burdened by the workload at first. Initial resistance to adoption due to the burdensome nature of data collection and recording was perhaps due to the fact that the students were just starting their first semester at the university. Additionally, the freshmen students spent significantly more time to fulfil the tasks than the graduate students (Runeson, 2003). Hence, their assignments were simpler; even so, they tended to delay delivery time (Runeson, 2003). Additionally, fourth-year students from the University of Oulu also encountered similar problems, even though they were in their senior year. This may due to the fact that students faced difficulties in keeping up with the rigorous tracking practices.

McGill University tended to show a positive impact of PSP implementation. Students at McGill presumed the PSP to be a black box tool in their personal process improvements. Likewise, at Montana Tech, University of Montana and the Milwaukee School of Engineering, students claimed that the PSP course taught them effective ways of becoming better programmers. Students

Table 1. Lessons learned in universities

University	Lesson Learned (Results)
Umeå University (Börstler et al., 2002)	Adoption failed due to an excessively strict PSP process that did not pay off and was assumed to be ineffective. However, in the future, the optional use of PSP was advised, and team projects to develop the PSP were considered to be a good learning experience.
University of Utah (Börstler et al., 2002)	Adoption was a success and was well received by the students. This is because the knowledge gained learning the PSP greatly aided the students. Additionally, students in pair outperformed student working individually.
Purdue University (Börstler et al., 2002)	Adoption failed due to several factors, including: • The PSP was viewed as extra work. • Students did not appreciate the PSP. Students were busy learning other programming languages. • No feedback was given by the instructor after submission. • No actual examples of data were provided by the instructor. However, the university planned to teach the PSP at the graduate or upper undergraduate levels.
Montana Tech of the University of Montana (Börstler et al., 2002)	Adoption was a success, and the results were excellent. Students were resistant at the beginning, but fortunately, the course happened to produce excellent programmers. Students become aware of any failures and the performance of each student was measured in a senior exit interview.
Drexel University (Börstler et al., 2002)	Adoption was a success, and the results were excellent because students were able to manage labour-intensive coursework. Additionally, effective teaching material for the course also contributed to the success of the implementation. Even though students were resistant at the beginning, it did not prevent them from achieving more, and this was a good learning experience for the students. Moreover, some students implemented the PSP in their working environment.
University of Oulu, Finland (Pekka Abrahamsson & Kautz, 2006)	Adoption was a failure. Students criticised the problem to be solved because it was too mathematical, consisting of a huge amount of paperwork and a lack of automated tools. It did not improve student productivity or their ability to estimate program size and their effort. Additionally, the concept of defect was vague, and defect tracking results were inconsistent. However, students initially appreciated the use of the PSP in explaining how effort is distributed over different software development phases and their diversity in basic programming. Moreover, they were able to produce global-level program designs. Implementation in industrial practice is suggested to emphasise what was taught in the PSP method.
Lund University (Runeson, 2001)	Adoption was a failure for undergraduates but a success for graduates. The reasons were: • Freshmen wrote smaller programs in a majority of the tasks. • Freshmen spent more time on programming tasks. • There was no significance difference in the number of defects between freshmen and graduates. • Task delivery for graduates was better than task delivery of freshmen. • Freshmen encountered data accuracy problems (incomplete data) more than graduates. • Freshmen had issues with programming. The overall results were that the freshmen's number of defects was the only factor to decrease, but graduates showed significance improvements in estimation accuracy and productivity. Later, the university will implement the PSP for sophomore students
McGill University (Zhong, Madhavji, & Emam, 2000)	PSP implementation was encouraging. The PSP is somewhat of a "black box" tool for personal software improvement. However, students were unable to identify the detailed factors underlying personal processes and effects on product quality and productivity
Feng Chia University (Shen et al., 2006)	Implementation of the PSP was a success, and students improved their capabilities in size estimation accuracy, effort estimation accuracy, product quality and process quality. PSP topics were understandable by the students, and a PSP log (which consisted of PSP topics covered in class) was completed. Students realised the benefits and importance of the PSP in size measurement, effort logging and postmortem, and PSP will likely be continued in future semesters due to the majority of favourable comments from the students who worked with and realised the benefits of the PSP. However, the PSP required better quality design to reduce test defects and also to make significant improvements in the productivity area.

continued on following page

Table 1. Continued

University	Lesson Learned (Results)
Curtin University of Technology(Konsky, Ivins, & Robey, 2005)	Adoption of the PSP was a success. Students managed their time well, and time was spent considerably on assignments and activities. Students also thought they achieved the defined learning outcome and realise the benefits of faithfully logged PSP data.
University of Queensland (Carrington, McEniery, & Johnston, 2001)	PSP adoption was a partial success. The extra tasks of time logging and defect recording led to cognitive overload, and the rapid iterations increased record-keeping overhead. Additionally, PSP practices interfered with students well-established habits, resulting in imbalanced reward and workload. This was not a major area of interest for the students. Results varied with master's students, who performed significantly better with the same material and lecturers as the undergraduates. To be fully successful, future improvement is required.
Auburn University (Umphress & John A. Hamilton, 2002)	PSP implementation was a failure. Students were unable to acquire change processes in accepting new information and faced difficulty in some PSP activities. Furthermore, student data were not suitable for use as personal historical data for reference in later projects. The implementation produced unnecessary paperwork in promoting the notion of processes, and students claimed that the PSP is a burden, as no one volunteered to use it in the future. However, exposure to handling processes helped to improve students' software development skills.
Experiment (Prechelt & Unger, 2001)	The adoption was a failure. The P group performed better error checking, was able to handle unexpected situations, reduced inconsistency in team performance, had more accurate time average defect-fixing estimation, developed more reliable programs, wrote more comments on each program and had better productivity estimation than the N group; however, the N group had a better total effort estimate and a shorter time to completion. The authors concluded from the experiment that the PSP is preferable for use in larger tasks rather than small ones. Additionally, it is believed that a working environment that actively encourages PSP usage is a key ingredient for PSP success, and the PSP needs to be better understood before making people use the methods.
University of Memphis (Maletic, Marcus, & Howald, 2001)	The adoption was a success for both undergraduate and graduate students. For the undergraduates, the experienced students first understood the benefits of the PSP and were interested in perfecting their skills to achieve goals. They believed the learning part was easy but faced difficulty in applying the PSP. They kept good records. However, the undergraduates did not notice PSP contributions to software process improvements and had a tendency to record defects inaccurately. The university found that the introduction of the PSP concepts in CS1/CS2 seemed premature. As for the graduates, they were positive regarding PSP concepts, but the inexperienced students thought that the efforts were unnecessary. Luckily, they acknowledged the ability of the PSP to make better estimates. However, the PSP will not be taught in the future because too many issues need to be covered in detail within the limited time constraints.
Middle East Technical University, (Karagöz & Grubu, 2004)	The adoption was a failure. Students viewed the PSP as monolithic rather than modular, and they were unable to acknowledge the benefits of defect recording because sceptical students recorded defects that were corrected (data accuracy problem). However, the university planned to improve PSP structures, as the PSP was believed to be necessary for establishing effective software organisations that develop quality software.
Milwaukee School of Engineering (Suri & Sebern, 2004)	The PSP was successfully adopted by the students even though the program complexity was increased. Students spent more time recording and analysing data, which enhanced their overall productivity and helped to improve program quality, and students were able to estimate their effort accurately. Furthermore, as the assignments increased in difficulty, the students likewise became better programmers.
Copenhagen Business School (P. Abrahamsson & Kautz, 2002)	PSP adoption was a success. Students improved in effort estimation skills, and the total defect density was reduced (product quality increased). Instructors checked assignments carefully and gave feedback via email to the students to ensure the validity of the collected data. Furthermore, students realised the benefits of tracking time and effort distribution, identifying targets for improvement, and were able to provide various solutions in solving problems. The authors concluded that the software industry should implement the PSP and explore it to experience its benefits. Additionally, other universities and institutions should consider an embedded PSP method in the course curriculum (focusing on a personal level) to monitor improvement. However, several difficulties in the PSP were also encountered due to lack of student programming skill, and students did not improve in estimating project size.

at the Curtin University of Technology and the University of Queensland were able to assimilate PSP benefits and realised the importance of noting the amount of time spent on unproductive activity. However, at University of Queensland, the students felt that they only achieved partial success and needed future improvement to realise the benefits that the PSP brings in improving their project development process. They also assimilated the benefits of PSP implementation in their curriculum. More experienced students adopted it faster due to the maturity level and greater programming skills. However, this demographic variation did not have a great impact on the experiment, and additionally, a simplified version of the PSP may be more helpful in acquiring good results. However, PSP should not hinder project flow, as it actually introduces changes in engineers' habits as they train themselves to be more disciplined in handling projects. The diverse output from students may be due to the fact that the courses were not properly structured for student assimilation; for example, the course structure was too hard and complex or was applied to the freshmen who did not yet have strong programming skills. Other than that, some of the undergraduates felt that it was too much for their workload and the benefits were undetermined; this may make it more feasible to apply the PSP course to graduate students, as they are more able to think out of the box and are able to relate and see other perspectives regardless of whether the PSP implementation brings the desired benefits or not. The PSP process could be taught in an upper division elective programming course (where presumably the students are more interested in programming) (Lisack, 2000) or at the graduate level (Maletic et al., 2001), because the introduction of PSP concepts at the CS1/CS2 level (normally freshmen and sophomore students) seems to be premature.

Feedback and Motivation from Instructor

To ensure PSP implementation is fully effective, engineers need the support of a disciplined and efficient environment (Watts S. Humphrey, 1996). This is applicable to an academic setting, as students are able to train themselves starting in their earlier career; after being introduced to the PSP and later applying it in industry, it improves the quality of their software projects. However, it is also important to provide them with an efficient learning environment, consisting of instructors that teach students the correct ways of PSP adoption. The PSP is effectively taught and delivered to students where there is an adequate support and feedback mechanism to transmit the influence of the instructor. Based on the lessons learned at Purdue University, late review and feedback from instructors contributes to poor PSP adoption by students. One of the factors in performing corrective actions in the initiation phase is the instructor's ability to maintain student motivation (Macke et al., 1996). Thus, instructors also play an important part in determining students' compatibility with the PSP learning process. Additionally, the availability of the instructor and continuous communication and feedback is essential, especially during the early phases of the project (Macke et al., 1996). This is an assurance that the proper adoption of PSP is fully assimilated by students, and this will later provide positive and desirable output for measuring PSP effectiveness. Consensus exists on the previous assumption that individual discipline is the key factor for the effectiveness of PSP implementation; it is up to the instructor to not only provide a disciplined approach to programming but also to ensure that the students follow that discipline (Hou & Tomayko, 1998). Finally, the most common approach to measurement verification in PSP research is the manual inspection of the data by the instructor (Johnson & Disney, 1999), and this been claimed to act as a predetermined assurance for the production of quality software and tasks by the students. However, sometimes instructors also find it hard to keep track of student progress due to a lack of measurable assessment data across courses to track the effectiveness of the process in helping to improve student software quality (Suri & Sebern, 2004). This lack hinders the adoption process, and sometimes instructors must cover a large number of students, giving feedback for each assignment submitted and evaluating their projects; together, these may be too cumbersome for instructors. A more structured syllabus and simplified material help instructors to cope and give feedback on student assessments.

Onerous Manual Data Collection and Automated Tool Support

From lessons learned in the academic setting, we found that some universities perform manual data collection when implementing the PSP. It is agreed that manual data recording is one of the barriers to the adoption of the PSP in engineers, but for students there is no point of reference, as the results show that neither the use of manual recording nor the use of automated tool support result in desirable PSP adoption. As an example, the University of Montana, Drexel University, Oulu University, the Curtin University of Technology, Feng Chia University and the University of Queensland all reported a positive outcome for PSP implementation, even though all the universities used manual data recording, consisting of spreadsheets and the standard PSP form. This differs from Auburn University and Purdue University, where students tended to provide faulty data logging, consistent with a previous report (Lisack, 2000). However, with the use of automated support, the same negative result resurfaces, as in Umea University, where they decided that PSP implementation was not advisable even though the data was recorded via automated tool support. Middle East University, and another experiment conducted with volunteer graduate students (Prechelt & Unger,

2001), also concluded the same negative result as Umea University. Conversely, the University of Utah did not encounter the same result, as the PSP implementation was well adopted by the students. These diverse results make it difficult to conclude what the best data-collection option is with respect to facilitating PSP adoption for students; hence, while it is undeniable that automated tool support is a helping hand and can assist students in recording data, considering the defects, schedule management, measuring and size estimation, observing quality and also managing time (regardless all of interruptions), this support is not an assurance of better PSP adoption. Rather, individual effort and discipline are the main factors for the PSP to be fully adopted by students. Humphrey (Watts S. Humphrey, 1996) stated that he introduces PSP concepts one by one (in the PSP seven process levels) to help engineers learn a disciplined personal method. Moreover, automated tool supports can sometimes provide incorrect calculations, for example, at the Middle East University, where students found that errors were made by a locally developed tool, and this is crucial, as not only humans may make errors in defect recording; tools can also result in error, which can sometimes have a huge impact on software development.

Pair Programming Approach

Among the universities selected to measure PSP effectiveness, the University of Utah apply pair programming in putting the PSP into practice. Pair programming involves two programmers collaborating on design, coding and testing (Lui & Chan, 2006). Based on the results, they found that PSP implementation at the University of Utah was well received, and it seemed those involved in pair programming outperformed students working individually. Pairs produced higher quality code in essentially the same amount of time as did individuals (Williams, 2001). Fundamentally, future research should be performed with this approach, as only one university showed its efficiency. It is true that the PSP involves tasks to be done individually, but some universities have made few changes to the PSP to formulate the CSP (Collaborative Software Process) and so leverage the power of two programmers working together (Williams, 2001). As the PSP was initially implemented in courses and taught at university, it is important that several precautionary steps be included to ensure PSP effectiveness is perceived by the students. Pair programming may be good; however, further research is needed to determine the possibilities of its application. It was shown elsewhere that pair programming effectively helps developers solve unfamiliar programming problems (Lui & Chan, 2006). Hence, if the PSP might be unfamiliar to freshman, for example, pair programming is an option that may yield a better chance for PSP adoption, and it was well received by freshmen in implementing the PSP, not only in their present tasks but also in the near future. Regardless, as noted, future research is crucially important to measure it effectiveness further.

Barriers to PSP Adoption

Engineers are likely to be unwilling to adopt any new method in software development. As mentioned earlier in this chapter, engineers may be *doubting Thomases*, sceptical about changes to their work habits. When it is encouraged by management, they may be willing to make a few minor changes; however, engineers generally hold fairly closely to what has worked for them in the past. Engineers and also organisations may not recognise or believe that it is possible to develop low-defect, high-integrity and cost-effective software (Chapman, 2006). This matter has been elucidated as a barrier to the adoption of the PSP, as each engineer may have the mindset that a method acknowledged as successful should come with supporting evidence on its implementation within a recognised company. Engineers want to see either that the PSP is able to impact their organisation

before adopting the PSP method in their project. Additionally, engineers also want to see that the PSP is able to estimate their project completeness and also enables them to accomplish their tasks at a level equivalent to or better than their previous work. These limitations are indicators of whether or not to apply the use of the PSP. Moreover, this limitation becomes a dilemma for engineers when implementing the PSP method in their project. Finally, introduction of the PSP may consume too much time for training. A lengthy training time of 150 to 200 hours (Morisio, 2000) is also a barrier for developers to accommodate the PSP. Furthermore, recording various size and defect data can be onerous, leading to poor adoption and data quality (Sison, Diaz, Lam, Navarro, & Navarro, 2005). Additionally, (Johnson et al., 2003) also remarked on the same issues, and further implies that the PSP tools can be a barrier as well, given a low level of adoption of a toolkit that provides a great deal automated support. Even though the barrier can be overcome, another barrier may resurface, as in the example of context switching.

The implementation of the PSP requires a great deal of data collection, which consists of several log forms and scripts to be filled in by developers to accumulate data for future use. Each data set identifies defects from the development process rather than defects being identified during the testing phase. This overhead issue becomes a burden to engineers, as it consumes much of their time and increases their workload. (Johnson et al., 2003) and also (Johnson & Disney, 1998) realised that not only could the collection of forms be a problem but so also could the accuracy of data that was altered by students, for example, data for the defect recording log, where students also incorrectly identified defect types. (Sillitti, Janes, Succi, & Vernazza, 2003) also stated that manually collected data is often affected by errors, making it unusable. Thus, it is vital for developers to ensure that all data collection is accurate, as the data will become historical data that will be used to the same extent to predict later projects developed by their company. This is in accord with (Khajenoori & Hirmanpour, 1995), who stated that the collection and analysis of accurate data demonstrates the effectiveness of a new method or tool. This was verified by (Shin, Choi, & Baik, 2007), who affirmed that difficulties by the developer in collecting reliable data later lead to incorrect analysis results. Engineers must have reliable data for analysis, as his date may determine parameters not only for the ongoing project but also future projects. As affirmed by (Hassan, Nasir, & Fauzi, 2009), it is important to preserve accurate evaluations of productivity across diverse software development projects, as they are used as historical data later. This idea was also supported by (Sison et al., 2005), who concluded that the main hindrance to PSP adoption was the inconvenience of recording of the large quantity of size, effort and defect data. This data collection became a burden if it was recorded using paper-based tools. This is true not only for the industrial sectors; (Sison et al., 2005) added that students complained about the recording difficulty involving the use of paper-based script logs. To address this issue, a number of approaches have been introduced to overcome this barrier, such as the use of software tools to replace traditional data collection paperwork, although similar to the barrier mentioned earlier, the introduction of automation tools can also lead to context switching.

Currently, there are tools that enable software engineers to collect the necessary data to perform PSP quality assessment. However, recent research has shown that software engineers are not using these tools, and the main reason they cite for not using PSP tools is that the data collection process is too cumbersome (Watts S. Humphrey, 2000a). The use of such tools can immediately became a helping hand to engineers in some ways for gathering data when implementing the PSP process, but some tools were not fully automated and required the insertion of some data manually. Additionally, manual data recoding required the developer to context switch among applications

to insert data. Nevertheless, not every engineer is capable of handling multitasking jobs requiring them to switch between work and also enter data into tools, as this requires most of their time. Engineers also need time to learn about the usefulness of the provided tool(s), and they sometimes become unaware of the amount of time spent on tools compared with the time spent on developing the projects. (Johnson et al., 2003) indicated that context switching is still too intrusive for many users who desire long periods of uninterrupted focus for efficient and effective development work. Time consumption and the estimated time for project completion may increase or differ from expectations because engineers have to switch contexts between applications as data is required to be inserted. This effect was also noted by (Börstler et al., 2002), implying that tools should be convenient to use and not distracting from the work itself. Moreover, any automated tool selected must provide ease of use for the engineer rather than implementing a crucial framework with higher complexity that may cause engineers to spend more time on tools than their projects. Although numerous automated PSP tools can overcome the problems of high overhead, context switching and manual data recording, software engineers still face difficulties in visualising their performance to monitor and perform high-quality work in a given time (Hassan et al., 2009). This implies that automated tools may not ultimately provide support for engineers dealing with PSP adoption. Many tools have evolved, and many implemented tools have led to other barriers. Typically, context switching becomes a major hindrance with all tools. However, there are many currently available tools that can be used to overcome the mentioned barriers to PSP adoption, and the feedback collected is definitely positive, although some flaws have also been detected.

Other than the barriers mentioned above, further barriers may also be encountered to the implementation of the PSP. One of the challenges faced by the PSP is the ability to scale to large-scale development. From the beginning of PSP development, the PSP was introduced to solve the issues inherent in implementing the CMM framework for small organisations or small software teams. Thus, the PSP is not appropriate for implementation in large-scale development unless several changes are made to the framework or the PSP is integrated within another framework. This is supported by (Carrington et al., 2001), who stated that a limitation of the PSP is the focus on personal development, so the issue of scaling up to industrial practice requires extrapolation. Furthermore, the PSP requires a long period of time to gather reliable historical data to enable good predictions in future projects with respect to time, effort, size and defects. Thus, as the learning process may take time, it is not yet fully efficient, as the technology may change over the course of time. The lack of long-term commitment by management to support PSP efforts (Khajenoori & Hirmanpour, 1995) has been reported as another factor forming a barrier to PSP adoption. Management support also contributes to and becomes a mirror for determining the effectiveness of PSP adoption within an organisation. Hence, it is necessary to overcome these barriers, as they can become a major drawback in implementing the PSP into a project. As engineers may tend to see the evidence of the successful implementation of the PSP in projects that incorporated it, it is crucial to find relevant solutions to surmount these barriers and enhance the PSP method with essential automation tools or an outstanding integrated framework of the PSP with any other suitable framework.

Data Measurement

In the PSP, there are several basic measurements that must be noted by engineers in estimating the data to assure the accuracy of their estimations and so obtain reliable data for the project in development. (Saint-Amand & Hodgins, 2007) agreed, also clarifying that the measurements collected are used to improve the quality of the products being developed. Hence, data measurement is an important factor when implementing the PSP, as it is the key factor in determining PSP effectiveness. The basic measurements for the PSP are the time spent in each phase of development, the number of defects detected and removed during each phase, and the size of the resulting product (Johnson & Disney, 1999).

1.   Time

Time performing tasks is measured in minutes and tracked while the engineer is doing the work, because time recorded later is more likely to be logged incorrectly. Components in time measurement included start date, start time, end date, end time, interrupt time, off-task time, and delta time. The time is planned in phases or the actual time spent in each particular phase of the process. Interrupt time is not included in the time measurement for a task or process phase, because time interruption is defined as anything that takes one away from the task at hand, including answering phone calls and other office activities (Akinwale, Dascalu, & Karam, 2006). If there is an interruption during the work, that time is subtracted from the time measurement. Off-task time is the time spent doing things other than planned project tasks such as time spent in management and administrative meetings, attending training classes, reading email, or any of the other essential activities required of a team member. Off-task time for a given task or while perform work is calculated by subtracting the total delta time from the total elapsed time spent on a task. Delta time is the actual time that it took to complete a task or process phase and is calculated as end time minus start time (minus any interrupt time). It is important to determine delta time to perform a linear regression for size estimation (Johnson & Disney, 1999). Time data can be measured accurately when it is collected using an automated tool; however, the tool should be able to record start and stop times and dates, calculate the elapsed time, and subtract interrupt time from the elapsed time to calculate the delta time. Each entry for time data should also include the names of the process phase involved, the product and element being worked on, the project task being performed, and the person who is doing the work.

2. Size

A size measure is a measurement of the amount of work produced by an engineer. Size measures are selected such that they are suitable to and compatible with the work product, for example, using pages (instead of words or letters) as a measure for text pages or taking programming tasks and language into account for software component. Size data should be collected in real time because data collected after the fact are more likely to be inaccurate. Additionally, size determination is important and facilitates better planning and is useful in tracking development effort as well as in assessing program quality. Size measures apply not only to the final deliverable product, but also to its component parts and temporary versions of the product. Size data are most accurate when collected using an automated tool that records both the planned and actual sizes of the various product parts or components, using size accounting measure categories such as base, added, modified, deleted, and reused. The tool must calculate the totals for each category of size data or otherwise ensure self-consistency in the data being collected. To date, many tools have been developed for collecting size data to assist engineers with their work when implementing the PSP in their working environment.

3. Quality

To measure the quality of a product when implementing the PSP, engineers can determine it based on defects found while performing their tasks. It is also true that engineers cannot assure the release of a defect-free product is accepted by the user; as mentioned by (Schulmeyer, 2008), that the mere absence of defects is no guarantee of user satisfaction, but it is necessary to ensure that the product quality is achieved before releasing the product for public use. A defect is identified as something that is wrong in a program (or in a related artefact, such as the design for a program). In the PSP, defects can be found within the code construction, designs and specifications, requirements, etc., and should be recorded when they are identified. Currently, the efficiency of defect recording is facilitated by the existence of tools developed by engineers to assist them in this task. The following data should be collected for every defect detected: defect identifier number, date when the defect was discovered, phase when the defect was created, phase when the defect was removed, defect type, time to find and fix the defect, and a brief description of the defect. Defects normally reoccur, as when fixing one defect, a new defect may unconsciously be created. The time required to fix each defect includes the total time needed to find and fix the problem and also that to validate the correction. Fix time is recorded separately for each defect. As Humphrey noted (Watts S. Humphrey, 2005), poor quality performance damages a software development organisation's cost and schedule performance and produces troublesome products. Hence, quality is the most crucial measure in verifying the effectiveness of a PSP implementation.

4. Schedule

The schedule provides guidance to the engineer with respect to measures and plans when the project should be completed and in tracking progress against the plan. Schedules that more closely track plans have been shown to yield higher program quality (Bullers, 2004). Like other measurements, schedule data are also most accurate when collected using an automated tool that records planned task names and descriptions, phases in which the work is to be done, product/ element involved, applicable committed dates for completing tasks, and the dates on which tasks were completed. Schedule data should be collected in real time, particularly information on task completion dates, as this is the most important means of obtaining earned value credit that allows individuals to track their progress on work completed vs. the planned schedule.

Tools Supporting the PSP

In the PSP, the most commonly encountered issue is the adoption barrier among students or engineers, as mentioned earlier. However, these issues can be overcome with the help of tools developed as solutions for issues including context switching and overhead. Moreover, the existence of these tools can improve the software development process for engineers or students and significantly help them to collect reliable data that can be used later. Some of the tools and their features are described in detail below.

1.　Jasmine

(Shin et al., 2007) developed Jasmine as a tool to help overcome implementation barriers to the PSP such as context switching and overhead; Jasmine consists mainly of sensor-based automated tools, in which the sensors are attached to development-related tools (e.g., Eclipse, Microsoft Office and JBuilder). One of the subsystems in Jasmine is called PPMT (Personal Process Management Tool), which produces a report summary and generates analytic outcomes of project development. The analysis results are viewed as trend charts (trends of data vs. time) and earned value charts, which display planned value, earned value and predicted earned value vs. time. Any failed unit tests, bugs, and compiled errors are automatically collected as defects. All defects are finalised in a defect log, allowing for modifications and insertions when necessary.

Automated time logging is done by the developer, consisting of a set of consecutive time data stored as items in a time log. Additionally, the PPMT subsystem automatically records software size, as determined by the number of LOC, which is measured by line counting tools. Reliable data is automatically collected and analysed, avoiding any faulty recording and data accuracy problems. Jasmine is also a user-friendly tool, as it utilises a graphical user interface (GUI).

2.　PSPA

To address the issues of manual data recording, (Sison et al., 2005) introduced PSPA, which provides features allowing for automated data recording and other feasibility features. The PSPA environment involves open-source IDE, which has plug-ins that perform automatic LOC counting, defect recording, defect classification and defect ranking. An example of an IDE plug-ins is Eclipse, which also used in Jasmine. PSPA produces automated PSP reports and graphs and summarises project development at the end of software development. These documents include productivity per task reports, yield per task reports, defect density per task reports, size estimates versus actual size reports, time estimate versus actual time reports, team productivity reports and also allow the user to view a member's history, showing productivity and output quality for developed software. Moreover, PSPA also allows for automated defect recording (compiled), automated classification of discovered defects, and automated generation of a team's library of defects, in ranked order (as determined by the number of time each defect was encountered within a team). This tool also performs automated time recording, in which the developer can click on a task name to start or stop each timer. If the developer forgets to start/stop the timer, PSPA prompts the developer with a message as a reminder. Additionally, the developer is also able to edit the automated time recorded if they encounter any interruptions while working on the project. Details of any interruption encountered are embedded in the finalised reports. Defects encountered can be shared with other team members, who can consolidate their schedules, and any list of defects (encountered individually) can be uploaded into the library for the developer's team. This is similar to knowledge sharing, as it helps other developers within a team to avoid causing the same error in coding. PSPA also performs automated LOC counting, facilitating the estimation of project size and the time to project completion. The LOC counter excludes any blanks lines and comment lines in a program. Additionally, developers are able to create private tasks, as PSPA can distinguish among individual users. The details of a private task of a particular developer cannot be viewed by the project manager or other developers; however, the project progress status is viewable by all. Basically, all data is automatically collected with PSPA, even though some may appear to be manually recorded for some users. PSPA can be a good guidance tool, as it simplifies the data recording process associated with project development. The interface uses a GUI and pop-up windows. Furthermore, each individual's schedules and defects are accumulated into their team's schedules and defects.

3.   Hackystat

Hackystat was developed by (Johnson et al., 2003) as a solution to the drawbacks of first- and second-generation tools because most of these tools suffer from complexity and overhead issues. Hackystat has client-side sensors attached to the development tools, including sensors for Emacs and JBuilder IDE, the Ant builder system, and the JUnit testing tool. Hackystat generates summaries and graphs in finalised reports. It also automates defect data collection, recording every defect and compilation of defects, the time spent in removing each defect, defects created as a result of defects encountered, phase defects created and phase defects removed. In logging time, Hackystat defines

unique projects for every development activity and determines which phase is to be assigned. Development entries for individuals are recorded each time, and the developer able to switch between different tasks or projects automatically. Even idle time is recorded; any phone call or colleagues' appearance (interruptions) may generate additional recording activity. Hackystat provides a detailed log of a developer's activities. It is accessible by managers, and developers can control the accessibility of data by creating a password, which is maintained on a public Hackystat server (thus keeping data "off-site") and run locally on a Hackystat server. Hackystat implements Chidamber-Kemerer object-oriented metrics, a no-comment source LOC counter (Java). LOC are measured automatically, as Hackystat has a sensor-based attachment to tools that automatically capture LOC measures in the project under development. When the server sets up an account during registration, an email is sent to the developer consisting of an account password (randomly generated 12 character keys). This prevents others from accessing metric data (secured accessibility) and avoids others uploading unnecessary data into the developer's personal account. The tool automates data collection and analysis, eliminating any barriers to PSP implementation. Activity data is collected periodically, for example, as a current file modification in 30 second intervals. Hackystat uses a GUI as the main interface and also embeds other features not intend to act as user interfaces with the system, such as Daily Diary, which is used to visualise and explain the Hackystat representation of a developer's behaviour.

4.   PSP Studio (http://www-cs.etsu.edu/psp)

PSP Studio is an example of a PSP tool that is so far only compatible with the Microsoft Windows 95 operating system or Microsoft Windows NT Workstation 4.0. Reporting in PSP Studio involves the use of Project Plan Summary (PPS), providing a graphical analysis of time, defects and effort. In defect logging, each defect found during development is manually entered in a defect recording log, in which defect records can be added or edited. The number of defects found can be determined automatically, and the developer is able to choose from a drop-down menu the type of defect, defect created, etc., facilitating selections made by the developer. Descriptions of each defect should be entered in detail for future reference. Time logging is done automatically by starting a timer in the Time Recording Log. The developer must initially select "Start Time Log" in a pop-up menu, and PSP Studio begins recording the time performing tasks. Any interruptions encountered can be entered (developer must first pause the timer), and delta time is automatically calculated. In counting LOC with PSP Studio, for level PSP0.1 and higher level, the developer must enter the total LOC manually. Moreover, data is collected either manually or automatically. For example, time is recorded automatically but not defects and size, as each of these must be recorded manually by the developer. Provide simple and easy to learn interface even though quite basic and not interactive. However, PSP Studio also has pop-up windows prompting any necessary details required from the user. PSP Studio also supports all seven process levels of the PSP, and each of level is implemented well for proper adoption. Finally, PSP Studio provides a printing function; hence, the developer can print any necessary details of the developed projects for discussion purposes (for example).

5. Process Dashboard (http://processdash. sourceforge.net)

The Process Dashboard is a powerful and flexible tool for software process automation, released under the terms of the GNU General Public License. By automating and simplifying metrics collection and analysis, the Process Dashboard makes it easier to use high-maturity processes such as the Personal Software Process(SM). Process Dashboard is compatible with any platform, i.e., Windows, UNIX, Linux or Macintosh, and is a user-friendly tool, as it supports many platforms for execution. Report generation is in PPS, along with Graph Estimation and a summary of defects. Process Dashboard performs manual defect logging; however, in contrast with defects, time is logged automatically by Process Dashboard. This tool performs automatic LOC counting, but it is done offline, and utilises both manual and automatic data recording. The interface uses a GUI as to assist the developer.

6. DuoTracker

DuoTracker is implemented as non-stand-alone application using an integrated tool suit (IDE) for its development. This tool was developed by (Akinwale et al., 2006) and consists of several other tools that are useful in developing software products. DuoTracker also implements a Defect Classification Scheme (DCS) and follows IEEE Standard 1044-1993 to integrate a PSP defect tracking tool into an organisation-wide defect tracking application. This tool has a defect viewer that accumulates and displays project ID, defect record number, persons to whom defects are assigned, defect submitter and the status of reported defects. DuoTracker performs automated defect logging; hence, the developer can estimate fix and actual fix times for defects and automate time logging for defects submitted by the developer. This tool also provides user privacy, as all data collected have restricted viewing, and in performing any update of recorded PSP data, only people who have been assigned are able to perform this task. In data collection, this tool only enables the collection of defect data; the collected data is automatically collected and defect descriptions are entered into a defect description field based on IEEE Standards. The interface uses a GUI and a dialog box and also records defects occurring outside the PSP compiling phase; DuoTracker is able to compare the quality of projects developed by individuals and projects developed by organisations.

7.   PSP.NET

PSP.NET, compatible with the Windows and UNIX platforms, was created by (Nasir & Yusof, 2005) as a base for the tools to be executed. PSP.NET can generate a test report template for reviewing the components from the PSP1 level to the higher levels and a graphical report, which is a new component embedded in the PSP.NET module. Defect recording is performed manually, as developer must insert defects encountered in the Defect Recording Log, consisting of defect type, description of the defect and any proposed solutions (inject defect). PSP.NET automates time logging; the developer is not required to fill in time log entry fields, as this is automatically captured. However, the developer should be concerned about any time logged and should have the power to override or correct any of the automatically collected data. Defect sharing revolves among developers, as defects found can be shared in one extensive public library instead of a private library for personal use only. PSP.NET performs automate LOC counting including tracking added and deleted lines and any line of code changed involving multiversion programs. PSP. NET provides secure accessibility and authentication mechanisms, as each developer is assigned a unique user name associated with password. Support consists of a manual and automatic data recording. The interface uses a GUI and pop-up windows and also provides printing functions, so the developer is able to print forms related to development such as PSP forms, checklists, and project plan summaries.

8.   The LEAP Toolkit

The LEAP Toolkit is compatible with any platform and is executed in Windows NT, the system most recognised and widely used at the time it was developed. In its summary report, this tool developed by (Moore, 2000), uses He'e, a project summary tool. With He'e, a developer is able to summarise and review the project being developed, comparing their estimated values for collected data with the actual data. The LEAP Toolkit manually records defects, and most developers (or students implementing the LEAP toolkit in their PSP assessment) declare that the defect data they recorded were valuable for measuring project quality. All time logging and data collection are manually recorded, but some students have found that this tool eases the burden of data collection during development. The LEAP toolkit has a Dialog Box, in which students insert all necessary measures for defects, time and size of the projects

9.   PROM

This tool, created by (Sillitti et al., 2003), operates by using plug-ins embedded in IDE consisting of Microsoft Visual Studio 6, .NET, Eclipse, Emacs and NetBeans and also plug-ins for Microsoft Office and Together Central (for example Rational Rose and JBuilder). The tool generates a finalised report consisting of a System Status Report and an HTML Report. PROM performs automated time logging and data acquisition and analysis; collecting codes involves counting the total LOC and also process measures (e.g., editing of time logging, number and type of changes in class and files). PROM also provides user privacy features, as project managers are unable to access an individual developer's data, and only a summary of the status of developer's project is viewable by the project manager. In collecting data PROM performs auto tracking for projects done by developers and the project manager. The interface for the PROM Database is based on SOAP Services. However, this interface completely hides the DBMS and any low-level data model. Moreover, the accessibility of data is totally determined and controlled by the developer.

10. PSP-EVA

PSP-EVA is a tool developed by (Hassan et al., 2009) for connecting to web application platforms such as PHP and Ajax. In PSP-EVA, the reporting is viewed as a graphical analysis report that provides ease of tracking developers' performance and facilitates comparisons among developers' efforts. This tool automates defect logging, a significant functions to ease the burden of the developer in recording defects. PSP-EVA also automates time logging; when the developer wishes to start tracking time, the LOG Time Interface appears and the developer can start/stop the log timer by clicking on a button embedded within the interface. LOC counting is done automatically, as it has sensor-based LOC tracking. PSP-EVA provides user privacy, as each user has a unique user identity, with some data manually collected from the login page and some automated data recording (for example time and defects). This tool also has an interface agent that allows the whole process to be viewed by the developer, and PSP-EVA automates data storing for historical analysis and future reference

The existence of these tools has contributed a great deal to overcoming adoption barriers to the PSP. Certainly, there are more tools that have been developed or are in progress (Table 2). The tools mentioned above are only a sample of the tools used by students and engineers to collect PSP data. Each tool has its own unique and significant features that differentiate it from the others. The most important factor, regardless of whether the tools are manual, semi automated or fully automated, is whether they help engineers and students to analyse the PSP data they have collected.

FUTURE RESEARCH

In summary, PSP is a blessing in disguise. The benefit gained may not be recognised at first, but after the collected data is analysed and useable for future work, engineers and students appreciate the method. However, the implementation has so far only focused on academic settings, and it is hopeful that in the future the focus can be diversified to industrial settings as well. Throughout industrial settings, the implementation may vary with regard to the software project and efforts by engineers in undertaking their projects. Additionally, in academic settings, the coverage level in university courses should be standardised, and it is believed the target audience should be freshmen, as an earlier stage of exposure may positively influence students in implementing the PSP method later in their future work. This is also because freshmen attitudes are more easily impacted (Runeson, 2003). PSP implementation for sophomores, juniors, seniors and graduate students can have either negative or positive results. Some authors suggested that implementation at upper levels may be more reliable, because the students are more mature. From the analysis of target audiences, educational level was not a key factor in determining the successful adoption of the PSP; however, students did not fully understand the PSP and implement the PSP in their projects, as it was part of the course structure. For these students, the PSP constitutes an excessive workload, and some students logged unreliable data (Karagoz and Yildiz, 2004). Most universities developed their own tools with their own preferences, and some tended to use the PSP form appended in Humphrey's book (manual data recording). Similar to the coverage level, both of these criteria should be standardised to yield satisfactory results in PSP implementation. Hence, a standardised course structure and course environment (Prechelt & Unger, 2001), appropriate tools, and adequate lectures on PSP should be considered to ensure a well-implemented PSP. Moreover, instructors should also provide timely feedback to students on data that have been collected and submitted because it may improve the accuracy of the data.

Table 2. Specifications of different types of PSP tools

Tools	Environment	Reporting	Defect Logging	Time Logging	Defect Sharing	LOC Counter	User Privacy	Data Collection	Interface	Other Features
Jasmine	Eclipse, Ms Office, JBuilder	Test report Summary	Auto (sensors attached to JUnit and Bugzilla)	Auto	No	Auto (sensor-based)	No	Auto		
PSPA	open source IDE	PPS, graph (estimation defects), defect classification and ranking	Auto	Auto	Yes (Auto)	Auto	Yes (Login and Privacy Tasks)	Auto	GUI and Popup Window	Consolidation of individual schedules / defects into team schedules/ defects
Hackystat	Eclipse, Visual-Studio, Jbuilder, IntelliJ Idea	Summaries and Graph	Auto	Auto	No	Auto (sensor-based)	Yes	Metric data / Upload other data	GUI	Data collected by separate software tools
PSP Studio	Windows only (Win32 platform)	Graphical analysis report	Manual	Manual	No	No (Input from user)	No	Manual and Auto	Simple and Easy to learn	Support PSP0-PSP3, provides print functions
Process Dash-board	Windows, UNIX, Linux, Macintosh etc	PPS, Graph Estimation and Defects	Manual	Auto	No	Auto (but offline)	No	Manual and Auto	GUI	
DuoTracker	Integrated tool suite - IDE	DuoTracker Defect Viewer -displays (i)project ID (ii)defect record number (iii) persons defect assigned (iv)submitter of defect (v)status of reported defect	Auto	No	No	No	Yes	Auto	GUI, dialog box	records defects occur outside PSP compile phase, able to compare quality of work (individual and organisation)
PSP.NET	Windows and UNIX Platform	Test Report Template, Graphical Report		Auto	Yes	Auto	Yes	Manual and Auto	GUI and Popup Window	printing facility

continued on following page

Table 2. Continued

Tools	Environment	Reporting	Defect Logging	Time Logging	Defect Sharing	LOC Counter	User Privacy	Data Collection	Interface	Other Features
Leap Toolkit	Window NT and newer version of Windows		Manual						Dialog box where as students record effort, size and defect	
PROM	plug-ins into IDE(Microsoft Visual Studio 6, .NET, Eclipse, Emacs and NetBeans, Microsoft Office, Rational Rose, Jbuilder)	System Status Report and HTML Report	Not mentioned	Auto	Not mentioned	Auto	Yes	Auto	SOAP Services	Accessibility of data is determined and controlled totally by the developer
PSP-EVA	PHP and Ajax	Graphical analysis report	Auto	Auto	Not mentioned	Auto	Yes	Manual	has interface agent	

Furthermore, it will ensure that data collected later will be improved and reliable for future reference.

CONCLUSION

PSP implementation was undertaken in various settings to help engineers and students understand its benefits. Earlier in this chapter, a bit of history on the PSP and the processes involved in PSP was provided to enable a clear view of process flow in the PSP. The PROBE Method and the seven process levels in the PSP were also elaborated to ensure that students understood the PSP before implementing it in their projects. Humphrey intended at first to find a method that brings benefits to small software development projects and simultaneously wanted to ensure that the method can be easily implemented with both students and engineers. He successfully developed the PSP, but does that mean that it is well implemented with students and engineers? The literature reviewed shows that there have been mixed results on the outcome of PSP implementation with students at higher institutions; however, the outcome depends on a number of contributing factors. Several criteria were considered, such as the setting of the course environment, the coverage level for the course and the tools involved in measurements for determining the lesson learned afterwards. Finally, we discussed data measurement in the PSP and the adoption barriers that hinder PSP implementation for both students and engineers. Several solutions were proposed, and automated tools are one of the options recommended. Several tools were examined to highlight their features and understand how they can work to overcome the barriers.

REFERENCES

Abrahamsson, P., & Kautz, K. (2002). The personal software process: Experiences from Denmark. *Euromicro'02: 28th Euromicro Conference*, (pp. 367-374). doi: 10.1109/EURMIC.2002.1046223

Abrahamsson, P., & Kautz, K. (2006). Personal software process: Classroom experiences from Finland. *ECSQ 2002: Proceedings of the 7th International Conference on Software Quality*, (pp. 175-185). doi: 10.1007/3-540-47984-8_21

Akinwale, O., Dascalu, S., & Karam, M. (2006). DuoTracker: Tool support for software defect data collection and analysis. *ICSEA'06: Proceedings of the International Conference on Software Engineering Advances*, (p. 22). doi: http://doi.ieeecomputersociety.org/10.1109/ICSEA.2006.34

Börstler, J., Carrington, D., Hislop, G. W., Lisack, S., Olson, K., & Williams, L. (2002). Teaching the PSP: Challenges and lessons learned. *IEEE Software, 19*(5), 42-48. doi: http://doi.ieeecomputersociety.org/10.1109/MS.2002.1032853

Bullers, W. I. (2004). Personal software process in the database course. *ACE '04: Proceedings of the Sixth Conference on Australasian Computing Education, 30*, (pp. 25-31). Retrieved from http://portal.acm.org/citation.cfm?id=979968.979972

Carrington, D., McEniery, B., & Johnston, D. (2001). *PSPSM in the large class. CSEET '01: Proceedings of the 14th Conference on Software Engineering Education and Training*, (pp. 81-88). doi: http://dx.doi.org/10.1109/CSEE.2001.913824

Chapman, R. (2006). Correctness by construction: A manifesto for high integrity software. *SCS '05: Proceedings of the 10th Australian Workshop on Safety Critical Systems and Software, 55*, (pp. 43-44). Retrieved from http://portal.acm.org/citation.cfm?id=1151816.1151820

Hassan, H., Nasir, M. H. N. M., & Fauzi, S. S. M. (2009). Incorporating software agents in automated personal software process (PSP) tools. *ISCIT'09: Proceedings of the 9th International Conference on Communications and Information Technologies*. doi: http://dx.doi.org/10.1109/ISCIT.2009.5340991

Hayes, W., & Over, J. W. (1997). *The personal software process^sm (PSP^SM): An empirical study of the impact of PSP on individual engineers (No. CMU/SEI-97-TR-001ESC-TR-97-00)*. PA: Software Engineering Institute Carnegie Mellon University Pittsburgh.

Hou, L., & Tomayko, J. (1998). Applying the personal software process in CS1: An experiment. *SIGCSE Bulletin, 30*(1), 322–325. .doi:10.1145/274790.274322

Humphrey, W. S. (1994). The personal process in software engineering. *Third International Conference on the Software Process*, (pp. 67-77). Retrieved from ftp://ftp.cnam.fr/pub4/PAL/sei/documents/articles/ps/psp.swe.ps.Z

Humphrey, W. S. (1996). Using a defined and measured personal software process. *IEEE Softw., 13*(3), 77-88. doi: http://doi.ieeecomputersociety.org/10.1109/52.493023

Humphrey, W. S. (2000a). Guest editor's introduction: The personal software process-Status and trends. *IEEE Softw., 17*(6), 71-75. doi: http://doi.ieeecomputersociety.org/10.1109/MS.2000.895171

Humphrey, W. S. (2000b). *The personal software process ^SM (PSP^SM) (No. CMU/SEI-2000-TR-022ESC-TR-2000-022)*. PA: Software Engineering Institute Carnegie Mellon University Pittsburgh.

Humphrey, W. S. (2005). Acquiring quality software. *The Journal of Defense Software Engineering, 18*(12), 19–23. Retrieved from http://www.crosstalkonline.org/storage/issue-archives/2005/200512/200512-Humphrey.pdf.

Johnson, P. M., & Disney, A. M. (1998). The personal software process: A cautionary case study. *IEEE Softw., 15*(6), 85-88. doi: http://dx.doi.org/10.1109/52.730851

Johnson, P. M., & Disney, A. M. (1999). A critical analysis of PSP data quality: Results from a case study. *Empirical Software Engineering, 4*(4), 317–349. doi:10.1023/A:1009801218527

Johnson, P. M., Kou, H., Agustin, J., Chan, C., Moore, C., Miglani, J., et al. (2003). Beyond the personal software process: Metrics collection and analysis for the differently disciplined. *ICSE '03: Proceedings of the 25th International Conference on Software Engineering.* doi: http://dx.doi.org/10.1109/ICSE.2003.1201249

Karagöz, N. A., & Grubu, A. Y. B. (2004). *Experiences from teaching PSP,* (pp. 58-63). Retrieved from http://trese.cs.utwente.nl/workshops/improq2004/Papers/workshopReport-Improq-2004.pdf

Khajenoori, S., & Hirmanpour, I. (1995). Personal software process: An experiential report. *Software Engineering Education, 895,* 131–145. doi:10.1007/3-540-58951-1_100

Konsky, B. R. v., Ivins, J., & Robey, M. (2005). Using PSP to evaluate student effort in achieving learning outcomes in a software engineering assignment. *ACE '05: Proceedings of the 7th Australasian Conference on Computing Education,* (p. 42). Retrieved from http://portal.acm.org/citation.cfm?id=1082424.1082449

Lisack, S. K. (2000). The personal software process in the classroom: Student reactions (an experience report). *CSEET: Proceedings of the 13th Conference on Software Engineering Education & Training.* doi: http://dx.doi.org/10.1109/CSEE.2000.827035

Lui, K. M., & Chan, K. C. C. (2006). Pair programming productivity: Novice-novice vs. expert-expert. *Int. J. Hum.-Comput. Stud., 64*(9), 915-925. doi: http://dx.doi.org/10.1016/j.ijhcs.2006.04.010

Macke, S., Khajenoori, S., New, J., Hirmanpour, I., Coxon, J., Ceberio, A., et al. (1996). An industry/academic partnership that worked: An in progress report. CSEE: *Proceedings of the 9th Conference on Software Engineering Education.* doi: http://doi.ieeecomputersociety.org/10.1109/CSEE.1996.491375

Maletic, J. I., Marcus, A., & Howald, A. (2001). Incorporating PSP into a traditional software engineering course: An experience report. *CSEET: Proceedings of the 14th Conference on Software Engineering Education and Training.* doi: http://doi.ieeecomputersociety.org/10.1109/CSEE.2001.913825

Moore, C. A. (2000). Lessons learned from teaching reflective software engineering using the Leap Toolkit. *ICSE 2000: Proceedings of the 22nd International Conference on Software Engineering.* doi: http://dx.doi.org/10.1109/ICSE.2000.870464

Morisio, M. (2000). Applying the PSP in industry. *IEEE Softw., 17*(6), 90-95. doi: http://dx.doi.org/10.1109/52.895174

Nasir, M. H. N. M., & Yusof, A. M. (2005). Automating a modified personal software process. *Malaysian Journal of Computer Science, 18*(2), 11–27. Retrieved from http://ejum.fsktm.um.edu.my/ArticleInformation.aspx?ArticleID=337.

Prechelt, L., & Unger, B. (2001). An experiment measuring the effects of personal software process (PSP) training. *IEEE Trans. Softw. Eng., 27*(5), 465-472. doi: http://dx.doi.org/10.1109/32.922716

Runeson, P. (2001). Experiences from teaching PSP for freshmen. *Paper CSEET '01: Proceedings of the 14th Conference on Software Engineering Education and Training.* Retrieved from http://portal.acm.org/citation.cfm?id=794193.794906

Runeson, P. (2003). Using students as experimental subjects - An analysis of graduate and freshmen PSP student data. *Proc. Empirical Assessment in Software Eng.* Retrieved from http://citeseerx.ist.psu.edu/viewdoc/download?doi=10.1.1.99.6046&rep=rep1&type=pdf

Saint-Amand, D. C. H., & Hodgins, B. (2007). *Results of the software process improvement efforts of the early adopters in NAVAIR 4.0.* Naval Air Warfare Center Weapons Div., China Lake, CA. Retrieved from http://oai.dtic.mil/oai/oai?verb=getRecord&metadataPrefix=html&identifier=ADA482027

Schulmeyer, G. G. (2008). *Handbook of software quality assurance* (4th ed.). Artech House Publishers.

Shen, W.-H., Hsueh, N.-L., & Chu, P.-H. (2006). *An experience report of applying the personal software process methodology.* International Conference on Software Engineering Research and Practice, (pp. 184-190). Retrieved from http://iec.cugb.edu.cn/WorldComp2006/SER4081.pdf

Shin, H., Choi, H.-J., & Baik, J. (2007). Jasmine: A PSP supporting tool. *ICSP'07: Proceedings of the 2007 International Conference on Software Process.* Retrieved from http://portal.acm.org/citation.cfm?id=1763239.1763248

Sillitti, A., Janes, A., Succi, G., & Vernazza, T. (2003). Collecting, integrating and analyzing software metrics and personal software process data. *EUROMICRO '03: Proceedings of the 29th Conference on EUROMICRO,* (p. 336). doi: http://doi.ieeecomputersociety.org/10.1109/EURMIC.2003.1231611

Sison, R., Diaz, D., Lam, E., Navarro, D., & Navarro, J. (2005). Personal software process (PSP) assistant. *APSEC '05: Proceedings of the 12th Asia-Pacific Software Engineering Conference,* (pp. 687-696). doi: http://dx.doi.org/10.1109/APSEC.2005.87

Suri, D., & Sebern, M. J. (2004). Incorporating software process in an undergraduate software engineering curriculum: Challenges and rewards. *CSEET'04: Proceedings of the 17th Conference on Software Engineering Education and Training.* doi: http://doi.ieeecomputersociety.org/10.1109/CSEE.2004.1276505

Umphress, D. A., & Hamilton, J. A. (2002). Software process as a foundation for teaching, learning, and accrediting. *CSEET'02: Proceedings of the 15th Conference on Software Engineering Education and Training.* doi: http://doi.ieeecomputersociety.org/10.1109/CSEE.2002.995208

Williams, L. (2001). Integrating pair programming into a software development process. *CSEET '01: Proceedings of the 14th Conference on Software Engineering Education and Training.* Retrieved from http://portal.acm.org/citation.cfm?id=794193.794899

Xiaohong, Y., Percy, V., Huiming, Y., & Yaohang, L. (2008). A personal software process tool for Eclipse environment. Retrieved from http://abner.ncat.edu/yaohang/publications/eclipsepsp2.pdf

Zhong, X., Madhavji, N. H., & Emam, K. E. (2000). Critical factors affecting personal software processes. *IEEE Softw., 17*(6), 76-83. doi: http://dx.doi.org/10.1109/52.895172

Chapter 8
Managing Software Projects with Team Software Process (TSP)

Salmiza Saul Hamid
Two Sigma Technologies, Malaysia & University of Malaya, Malaysia

Mohd Hairul Nizam Md Nasir
University of Malaya, Malaysia

Shamsul Sahibuddin
Universiti Teknologi Malaysia, Malaysia

Mustaffa Kamal Mohd Nor
University of Malaya, Malaysia

ABSTRACT

Despite the widespread use of sound project management practices and process improvement models over the last several years, the failure of software projects remains a challenge to organisations. As part of the attempt to address software industry challenges, several models, frameworks, and methods have been developed that are intended to improve software processes to produce quality software on time, under budget, and in accordance with previously stipulated functionalities. One of the most widely practised methods is the Team Software Process (TSP). The TSP was designed to provide an operational framework for establishing an effective team environment and guiding engineering teams in their work. This chapter provides an overview of the TSP and its associated structures and processes. It also highlights how the TSP operational framework can assist project manager and software development team to deliver successful projects by controlling and minimizing the most common software failure factors. Comparative analysis between the TSP and conventional project management has also been presented. Additionally, the results of TSP implementation in industrial settings are highlighted with particular reference to scheduling, quality, and productivity. The last section indicates additional advantages of TSP and comments on the future of TSP in the global software development project.

DOI: 10.4018/978-1-61350-141-2.ch008

INTRODUCTION

In this day and age, many government organizations and information technology based companies develop and maintain software to support their daily operations. The software turns out to be their business product as well. The need for complex software products to support businesses operations are a very important issue nowadays. As projected by Boehm (2006), between now and 2025, the sustainability of the organizations and their products, systems and services are much depending heavily on software and this ever-increasing demands will cause major differences in the processes currently used to define, design, develop, deploy, and evolve a diverse variety of software-intensive systems. The statistics on software projects are discouraging, as there is high percentage of projects that fail, thereby not conforming to the requirements and causing deviations in time and cost. These result in poor quality products that lead to customer dissatisfaction.

In striving to address the software industries challenges, several frameworks and methods have been developed covering all aspects of improving project management practices and software processes purposely to produce quality software on time, under budget and within pre-agreed functionalities. One of the most widely practiced methods is Team Software Process (TSP), which has been implemented in wide range of organizations worldwide and gained positive results (Davis & Mullaney, 2003).

This chapter provides an overview of the TSP and its associated structures and processes. It also highlights how the TSP operational framework can assist project manager and software development team to deliver successful projects by controlling and minimizing the most common software failure factors. Comparative analysis between the TSP and conventional project management is also been presented. Additionally, the results of TSP implementation in industrial settings are highlighted with particular reference to scheduling, quality, and productivity. The last section indicates additional advantages of TSP and comments on the future of TSP in the global software development project.

BACKGROUND

Software Crisis

The term "software engineering" was coined at the first NATO Software Engineering Conference in Germany in 1968 (Naur & Randell, 1969) amid widespread consensus that there were problems with software development and maintenance. These problems were later discussed by Brooks (1975, 1987, 1995), and the term "software crisis" emerged to describe the software industry's inability to provide customers with high-quality products within schedule and under budget. Brooks concluded that there is no silver bullet to overcome this problem. Hardware costs were dropping, while software costs were rising rapidly. Major computer system projects were sometimes years late, and the resulting software was unreliable, hard to maintain and performed poorly.

Since the 1980s, in the medical field, for example, computers have been designed to help people, and most of the time, they do. However, in the case of Therac-25, computer errors could be fatal. Between 1985 and 1987, two people died and four others were seriously injured after they received massive radiation beamed via Therac-25 radiation therapy machines. Investigations revealed that defective software was among the various factors leading to this accident (Leveson & Turner, 1993). Another example is the delay of over 16 months in the opening of Denver International Airport, in addition to construction costs of over 100 million dollars in excess of the budget (Swartz, 1996). Indeed, *"one main reason for the delay and overrun was the presence of major bugs in the baggage handling control software"* (Glass, 1998). The explosion of the European

Table 1. Standish software project performance findings, 1994–2008

Benchmark/Year	1994	1996	1998	2000	2004	2006	2008
Succeeded (%)	16	27	26	28	29	35	32
Challenged (%)	53	33	46	49	53	46	44
Failed (%)	31	40	28	23	18	19	24

Space Agency rocket Ariane 5 40 seconds after lift-off in June 1996 is another example of an accident caused by software defects. The rocket and the four scientific satellites on board, which cost about 2.5 billion dollars, were completely destroyed. In-depth investigation uncovered that *"specification and design errors in the software, and poor analysis and testing of the failed subsystems, were to blame"* (Ariane 501 Inquiry Board, 1996).

Even today, this situation has not changed much. Software development projects are known for being completed far over budget and behind schedule (Gray & Larson, 2008). In the United States (US), a survey conducted by the Standish Group (1995) in 1994; the results included data from several thousand information technology (IT) projects and revealed a software project success rate of only 16%. Meanwhile, 31% of projects failed, whereas the remaining 53% had cost overruns, time overruns and impaired functionalities. Of these, the average cost overrun was 189%, and the average time overrun was 222%. A more recent report by the Standish Group (2009) showed a slight improvement in 2008; however, the figure remained troublesome, with a success rate of less than 40%. Table 1 tracks the progress of Standish software project performance findings for more than a decade from 1994 to 2008. These figures were published by a number of different authors in various journals and white papers (Standish Group, 1995, 1999, 2001, 2010; Othman, Zain, & Hamdan, 2010; Hass, 2007; Eveleens & Verhoef, 2010; Humphrey, 2005; Hartmann, 2006). It is important to note, however, that some researchers have argued and expressed concerns regarding the

reliability of the figures (Jorgensen & Molokken, 2006); some felt that the figures do not reflect reality (Glass, 2005, 2006), and some questioned their validity (Eveleens & Verhoef, 2010).

Another study conducted in the United Kingdom (UK) by Oxford University in collaboration with Computer Weekly in 2003 reported that only 16% of the 421 IT projects examined were finished on time within the estimated budget and with the agreed functionalities (Sauer & Cuthbertson, 2003). Moreover, only 55% of projects were completed on time, and 41% were completed within the agreed budget (Sauer & Cuthbertson, 2003). Similarly, another UK survey published by the British Computer Society (BCS) (Taylor, 2000) reported that only three out of the more than 500 development projects assessed met the survey's criteria for success. Although the success rate of software projects is improving each year, the general trend still suggests that software projects are hard to manage.

The processes for large-scale software development can themselves be quite large and complex, which may involve many software engineers, programmers and designers. As a result, they are often hard to define, difficult to understand, and even harder to establish. This is why software process improvement (SPI) models were developed. The use of SPI is based on the premise that mature and capable processes generate quality software products. Over decades, several models for improving the quality of software through management of the software process have become significant in the software industry. The importance of the software process concept is indicated by the widespread popularity of software process and software process improvement approaches in software development organisations around the world. Towards this end, in the last few years various efforts, initiatives, models, methodologies and standards have been developed, such as ISO/IEC 15504 (SPICE), Capability Maturity Model (CMM), Capability Maturity Model Integration(CMMI), International Standards Organization (ISO) 9000, Team Software Process (TSP), Personal Software Process (PSP) and there are quite exhaustive lists of models available. In this chapter we limit our topic for discussion to the TSP since it has been implemented in a wide range of organisations worldwide and have afforded positive results as well as are actively supported by the SEI. Several published studies have reported that TSP teams are delivering essentially defect-free software on schedule while improving productivity. To highlight a few recent results, Davis and Barbara (2009) reported that the TSP team at Adobe produced 5 million lines of code that was 20 times better than the industry average, as measured in terms of system test and test density. Wilson (2010) reported that a software trouble report at the final product evaluation test found no problems after the United States Naval Air Systems Command (NAVAIR) system engineering team adopted TSP. Another study reported by Battle (2009) found that the system test-delivered defects averaged 0.9 per kilo lines of code, and customer-delivered defects averaged less than 0.5 per kilo lines of code after the United States Naval Oceanographic Office (NAVO) adopted TSP.

An Overview of the TSP

Software engineering is progressively becoming a collaborative activity as it relies on the knowledge, expertise and experience of an ample and frequently dissimilar group of individuals. Although individuals can develop some software products, it is no longer practical for one person to do most software development jobs because the scale and the complexity of the systems have increased and

the demand for short time-to-deliver is high. System development is a team activity, and the quality of the software products are largely determined by the effectiveness of the team coordination. Yet, to be effective, teams must work in a trusting and supportive environment (Shellenbarger, 2000).

The Team Software Process (TSP) was developed in 1996 by Watts Humphrey, the founder of the Software Process Program (Humphrey, 1999) at the Software Engineering Institute (SEI) at Carnegie Mellon University, United States. TSP began as an attempt to make the Personal Software Process (PSP) a consistent practice for software engineers. The first version of TSPs, TSP0, was created in 1996. It was simple, was tested using two teams and ultimately helped engineers to do the work associated with their discipline. TSP0 included additional guidance necessary to teams regarding its processes. This initial trial indicated the importance of wider management support to TSP implementation. The enhanced version of TSP0, TSP0.1, provided extra information on process improvements and was tried using a larger number of teams. Within 3 years after TSP0.1 was released, another nine versions of TSP were gradually developed, beginning with TSP0.2 between the end of 1996 and early 1997. In these versions, the TSP process was slowly reduced and became significantly shorter than in TSP0.1. In 1999, the SEI introduced TSP as one of its products. TSP, which is a collection of PSP components taken from individual software developers' work processes and supplemented with selected engineering functions, was an excellent software process standard for use at the team level. The Capability Maturity Model (CMM), which was developed earlier at the SEI, indicates organizational best practices for software development and can be efficiently adopted using TSP. CMM and a later version known as the Capability Maturity Model Integration (CMMI) program are a worldwide recognized framework that provides organizations with the ability to reach high software development standards. Because TSP was originally based on the CMM model, which includes personal and team practices associated with the key CMM process areas (McHale & Wall, 2005), they complement each other in terms of design (Humphrey, 1998). While the CMM/CMMI is a descriptive model that highlights in detail the criteria for five levels of software process maturity, TSP is a prescriptive software process that drives the implementation of key CMM/CMMI practices.

The TSP is a prescriptive process for implementing projects consisting of a set of process scripts, forms, standards, procedures, methods and tools for project teams to produce high-quality software products on schedule and within pre-agreed budget constraints (Humphrey, 2000b, 2002a, 2006). It provides clear and concise guidance on software development processes, with emphasis on mutual support and leadership among software project team members. The purpose is to build effective teamwork through collaborative and disciplined work within productive team working environments, where everyone knows exactly what they are supposed to do and where roles and responsibilities are clearly defined. The outcome is a well-defined and well-planned work process. The operational processes in TSP are presented in the form of scripts, supplemented with specific forms to guide the team members throughout the project implementation.

TSP can be adopted by teams of 2 to 150 members (Humphrey, 2000a). However, it is especially advisable to split teams of more than 15 to 20 members into smaller sub-teams for better management and team coherence (Humphrey, 2006). The nature of the work will determine the level of interaction among the team members. To cater to different team structures and their work, there are three variations on TSP: Multi-team TSP (*TSPm*), Functional TSP (*TSPf*), and TSP+. TSPm is a TSP process meant for teams using different processes, teams whose members are in different locations or teams under separate management (Humphrey, 2006). Basically, it extends TSP to large project teams and geographically distributed project teams by treating the project team as a team of sub-teams and adding another layer to the core TSP process to coordinate the sub-team activities. TSPm provides mechanisms that can be used to coordinate collaboration, communication and management among unit teams. Meanwhile, functional TSP (TSPf) is for teams in which each member usually works independently. It modifies the basic TSP process for use by functional organisations that do not have a project structure. It is typically used when there is no project organisation present, usually for on-going activities such as maintenance of multiple products and product support. Maintenance project teams are a good example of where TSPf could be adopted, as each member normally handles separate features of a product enhancement that require them to work on their own. TSP+ on the other hand, extends core TSP and TSPm by including additional process scripts designed to improve compliance of TSP with the CMMI process improvement model. It was published as part of the 2010 TSP release, presumably to increase the appeal of TSP to organizations with a CMMI initiative. TSPm, TSPf and TSP+ are not in the public domain. They are proprietary to the SEI and provided under license to SEI partners only.

Structures and Processes

Team Software Process (TSP) provides clear and concise guidance for software development processes and emphasizes mutual support and leadership among software project team members. Its purpose is to build an effective team through collaborative and disciplined work within a productive environment in which everyone knows their roles and responsibilities. The outcome is well-defined and well-planning work processes. The operational processes included in TSP are presented in the form of scripts, together with specific forms that will guide the team members through the project.

TSP builds on the Personal Software Process (PSP); individual members must be familiar with PSP skills and knowledge before becoming part of a TSP team. PSP training helps individual software engineers to assume a structured and discipline approach in writing software and particularly in planning, tracking, measuring and manage the quality of their own work. It is vitally important for each team member to know and understand the principles underlying the TSP process to build a cohesive TSP team (Humphrey, 2000c). Humphrey (2000a) states the three conditions for effective team formation. First, the team members must truly understand what they are supposed to do, setting common goals and defining their roles. Secondly, all members must agree on how to execute those goals, determining process tasks and a detailed project plan that are common to the team. Last but not least, the team must believe that the plan is achievable; everyone must contribute to the production of the plan. Figure 1 presents these criteria for effective TSP team-building:

TSP teamwork, on the other hand, involves daily engineering practices related to project development that require mutual cooperation and precise supervision. For example, status tracking and reporting are provided by the team at regular intervals to maintain effective teamwork and are an important factor in project control. TSP team-building activities take place during the TSP launch preprocess, whereas the TSP teamwork processes continue for the entire project duration. Both components shape the overall principles of TSP team-building (Humphrey, 2000a).

TSP Team Launch and Process Flow

As illustrated in Figure 2, each TSP project begins with a team launch. TSP team launch is a four-day planning process led by a trained launch coach, and TSP launch scripts are used to drive the launch activities. The launch consists of nine development team meetings, with management and/or marketing/customer representatives at the first and ninth meeting. During the launch, the team members work together to develop strategies, processes and detailed plans for their project. The overall project plan will be presented for management approval during a management review meeting before the team proceeds with the project development process. The plan is updated and refined at periodic launch sessions known as '*re-launches*'

Figure 1. Principal components of TSP process (Schwalb, 2004)

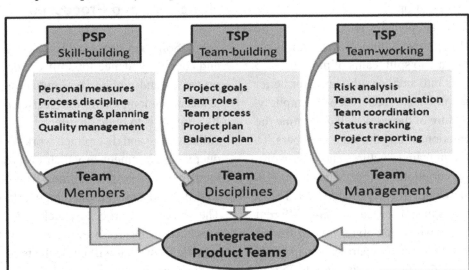

Figure 2. TSP launch process (Humphrey, 2000a)

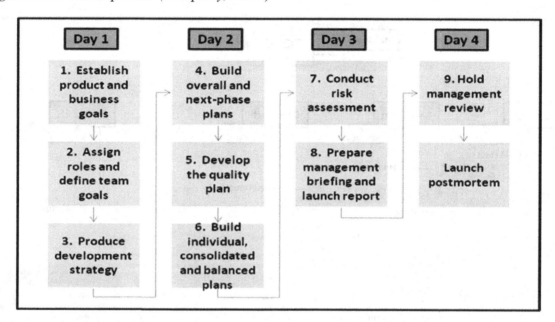

that take place every three to four months so that the plans remain accurate. The breakdown of tasks created during the initial launch is highly detailed (TSP provided forms for tasks designation) and broken down further into still more detailed sets of tasks for the next launch plan (Webb, 2002). During every launch cycle, the plan for the next launch phase is established in advance. Once the current development cycle is almost complete, the plan for the next phase is revised and refined according to the results achieved during the phase that is at an end.

In this way, TSP involves multiple development cycles (phases). Each cycle of three to four months includes detailed planning during the TSP launch process, development steps such as strategy, planning, requirements, design, coding and testing as in the traditional software development life cycle (SDLC) and a postmortem. The postmortem, which is the last step in each TSP development cycle, is used to evaluate the effectiveness of the current work plan and identify areas to be improved through process improvement proposals (PIPs) as described in TSP postmortem scripts.

The first cycle release should be the most limited workable version of the product and will gradually be enhanced through the subsequent subset of product releases. TSP provides scripts for each development step, and most come with forms that contain guidelines for walking through work processes. The TSP development strategy as a whole is an iterative and evolving process that continues until the intended finished product is delivered. Figure 3 illustrates the TSP process flow:

At the first TSP launch meeting, the project development team will be briefed on project objectives and goals related to the particular product/system to be developed and with reference to management targets, business needs and project constraints. This meeting includes senior management and marketing/customer representatives together with the project developers and ensures that overall project information is communicated and properly received by the project team and that everyone understands the overall TSP launch process. The TSP launch coach will be present to supervise the meeting and guide the participants, ensuring an effective meeting outcome. Project team members will be able to ask

Figure 3. TSP process flow

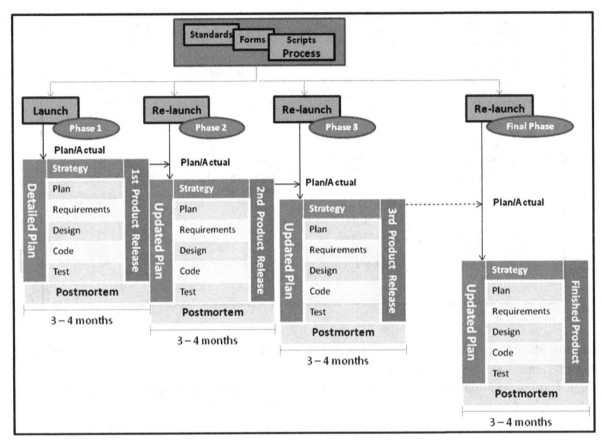

project-related question and will learn about both project constraints and areas of flexibility in terms of quality, schedule, budget and other considerations. The meeting materials are handed to the participants in advance so that they have time to study the necessary items and prepare thoroughly for the meeting.

In TSP, each team member is a manager, and everyone is assigned a specific managerial role based on his or her specific skills. The management positions include team leader, customer interface manager, design manager, implementation manager, test manager, planning manager, process manager, quality manager and support manager. Each role has its own set of goals and responsibilities. The team roles and goals are established in the second TSP launch meeting (Table 2). The team is intended to be self-directed, with its own

defined work processes in accordance with the software development project goal. A TSP team is comparable to a basketball team on which everyone's positions are dynamic, encompassing multiple specialties, and all members use their responsibilities to work toward a single objective (Humphrey, 2000a).

An overall project schedule in TSP is estimated using a top-down approach based on overall project size and average team productivity (Webb, 2000). Beginning in the third TSP launch meeting with the creation of the system's conceptual design, which indicates the general product structure, a list of manageable products to be developed is determined. A Work Breakdown Structure (WBS) is first produced by the team based on the conceptual design (Jain, 2009). The WBS is a list of product components grouped into

Table 2. TSP team launch (Webb & Humphrey, 1999; Humphrey, 2000a)

Launch Meeting 1 and 2	**Management** - Defines project goals. - Answers team questions. **Team** - Establishes team roles. - Defines team goals.
Launch Meeting 3	**Team** - Produces a conceptual system design and fix list (if needed). - Determines the development strategy and products to produce. - Defines the development process to be used. - Produces the process and support plans.
Launch Meeting 4 and 5	**Team** - Develops size estimates and overall plan. - Develops the quality plan.
Launch Meeting 6	**Team** - Allocates work to team members. - Creates overall and next-phase plans for each team member
Launch Meeting 7 and 8	**Team** - Identifies and evaluates project risks. - Defines risk assessment checkpoints and responsibilities. - Proposes ways to mitigate immediate high-impact risks. - Prepares management presentation (launch report).
Launch Meeting 9	**Team** - Presents project plan to management. - Defends plan to management. **Management** - Responds to the team's plan. - Resolves plan issues with the team.
Postmortem	- Walks through the weekly report preparation. - Gathers launch data and produces a launch report. - Enters this report in the project notebook. - Assesses the launch/phase process and prepares PIPs.

small groups of similar items. Once assembled, it provides a list of major products and indicates the order in which they should be built.

In TSP launch meeting 4, a project plan is developed in which the size of all of the parts of the final product is estimated based on the WBS. This information is usually estimated using lines of codes (LOC), and the existence of a sufficiently detailed conceptual design will simplify the estimation process. The tasks associated with the product components are listed before the estimations by the individual project team members. When a project is small, it is possible to include all team members in the process of estimating multiple tasks. However, on large software projects, it may be helpful to divide the team into several smaller teams that work on different set of WBS tasks and assign a moderator to each sub-team. It is necessary that those responsible for particular tasks work on estimating them. Thus, the estimation teams should be grouped based on individuals experience, exposure, ability and skills.

Once the estimation groups are formed, individual group members create their initial size estimations (based on historical productivity data if available). These figures will be iteratively refined and finalized once a consensus is reached with the moderator's guidance. Individual member estimations will be collected and compiled by the planning manager and reviewed by the team leader for the purpose of the final WBS list and estimation.

Based on the above information, the team computes the total hours necessary for their project given the resources available. The overall project schedule, however, will be influenced by actual productivity, including member availability during working hours. The team and individual task plans, which are generated assuming a 40-hour week, are supposed to exclude non-engineering activities such as email, training and holidays. Work productivity differs based on technology, complexity and domain. For instance, the time that it takes to write 10 lines of assembly language to develop a real-time mission-critical program for a military system is not equivalent to the time it takes to write 10 lines of C++ code to develop a windows-based application system. Work is done in assembly language due to the limited power availability when a small amount of RAM is available. The development environment is primitive, and there are extensive testing requirements because a software failure after system deployment could result in a catastrophic loss. In Windows-based application development, all work is done in C++ with few tools and no real-time or memory constraints. Testing is adequate but is nothing like that which occurs in the military system because there is no significant risk of financial loss associated with software failure. It would be completely meaningless to compare the productivity of military systems and that of windows-based application systems. However, the productivity figures in each domain could be compared to determine if a trend existed over time. Of course, statistically, at least 10-20 data points are needed for a trend to emerge, whereas comparing two successive productivity measurements is most likely meaningless even within a given domain.

TSP processes are designed to prevent problems before they occur through defect measurement (Humphrey, 2000a). During the fifth launch meeting, the project team estimates the percentage of defects detected and resolved based on the estimated size of the overall software product using historical data or TSP quality planning guidelines (if no historical data are available). Based on this estimation, the project quality plan is then produced and adjusted in accordance with the team's quality goal as established during launch meeting 2. The generation of the quality control plan and the identification and prevention of quality control problems are the three activities that fall under the heading of TSP quality management (Humphrey, 2000a).

As previously mentioned, individual task planning takes into account the productivity of each group member and his or her availability in terms of task hours. ”*Task hours are hours spent working only on the tasks in the task list*” (Webb & Humphrey, 1999). Tasks are distributed among project team members during TSP launch meeting 6. Because TSP emphasizes balanced workloads for all team members, the overall team workload will be reviewed as often as necessary to ensure that everyone has the same workload. If the accumulated task hours for a member are greater than his or her available hours, the extra task will be allocated to other members of the same group. Nevertheless, it is important for everyone to be in agreement regarding the tasks hours and resources provided as well as the task distribution so that the target completion date will remain a realistic goal.

The final project plan is generated by consolidating all of the individual plans. The individual group members' task hours are accumulated to create the overall project schedule. Using the earned value (EV) method, in which a value is assigned to each of the tasks based on the total project hours estimated, individual members' and whole teams' work progress can be tracked. For example, 29 hours of work when there are 1000 task hours to be completed in total will have a value of 2.9. Task completion is tracked daily on the individual level, whereas each team's work outcomes are tracked on a weekly basis. Even when tasks are completed out of order, the planned value attached to each of them will remain the same, so it will remain possible to determine project status at any point in time to prepare for any scheduling issues.

In TSP, project risk is identified early in the project phase. Risk is the threat of a serious problem at some point in the project life cycle. During the risk analysis at launch meeting 7, everyone's views regarding the risks involved in the project are listed. Then, the risks are further evaluated and ranked based on their likelihood of occurrence and impact, and the members responsible for monitoring each risk are identified. Plans are also made for mitigating major risks. The three most common risks in any project are the failure to meet deadlines, requirements, and quality standards, and all of these issues can be addressed appropriately using the TSP approach (Webb, 2000).

Individual group members are required to record all of their work activities. This includes task implementation time, interruptions and problems identified, along task execution and work output volume (Jain, 2009). To accurately log the details of their activities, employees can use the TSP support tool or other tracking programs. The use of these programs can also simplify the data collection process and increase its speed. TSP teams track their progress with reference to the plan on a weekly basis; a meeting is conducted every week at which the team discusses its current progress using EV, provides information on individual work output, reviews the risks noted during the launch, addresses any issues encountered and plans for the execution of the next set of tasks.

The four fundamental measures used in TSP execution are time, size, defects and task completion date (Schwalb, 2004). All of these data are collected, recorded and referred to for the purpose of current and future project development and improvement. Whereas we have already thoroughly discussed the question of size, the focus will now be on the other three elements. Overall project duration is calculated by summing the data on the efforts of all software engineers working to complete the development process. Figures for total effort are acquired after the size of each project task has been determined. Then, the completion date for each task is obtained using the EV method to determine project milestones. Thus, team actual effort used to complete weekly tasks can be compared with the estimates made at the beginning of the project so that any necessary adjustments to the primary plan can be made as early as possible to avoid further lapses in effort and/or scheduling issues (if any). To measure defects, TSP uses a technique for quality inspection that can be employed during each software development phases and during software use. This technique is called the Percent Defect Free (PDF) system. The PDF measure and data at the module level can demonstrate defects remarkably well and encourage developers to work effectively to improve PDF (Humphrey, 2006). For example, if there are 100 modules in a software product and 38 modules have no defects, the PDF rate will be 38 percent. Similarly, to measure defect injection, the number of defects in each project phase (including the requirements stage, the high-level design and detailed design phases, the coding stage and so on) should be carefully estimated. As Humphrey (2006) suggests, one can "*compare the total defect numbers with the team's PSP data for total defects injected and compare the estimated defects injected by phase with the members' PSP data on defect distribution*". The same occurs during the defect removal estimation plan; the percentage of defects to be removed will be allocated in advance to each project phase using yield data (Humphrey, 2000a) and later compared with the actual defects removed during those phases. Developing a defect estimation plan early will give the developers the opportunity to budget the time needed to address these defects and make them familiar with those that they are likely to encounter during each project phase so that they can take early action to prevent them from becoming much more costly (as may be the case if they are found or removed later in the project).

Indeed, this is the major aspect of quality control planning; the model simulates what is expected to occur (Humphrey, 2006).

TSP emphasises early problem inspection and measurement during each software development phases. A process that can be measured can surely be improved. TSP team members are encouraged to list the details of any changes that they would like to see or any problem that they can address by improving their work. Such ideas are routinely conveyed during the postmortem phase. Process improvement proposals (PIPs) are the outcome of postmortem sessions conducted at the end of TSP launch meetings or TSP project cycles (for re-launches). Postmortem meetings act as a learning vehicle for teams, and the purpose of the launch postmortem is to improve both the effectiveness and the efficiency of the launch process (Humphrey, 2006). Thus, one factor that should be discussed in this context is how the team's existing work processes affected the results it achieved.

ADOPTING TSP TO MINIMIZE AND AVOID SOFTWARE PROJECT FAILURE

Software projects hardly ever fail for just one or two factors. In fact, most failures are due to several combinations of people, project, process, and technical factors. Of course each of the factors, interact with each others in complex ways that contribute to the likelihood of software project failure. Among the most common failure factors that were reported by several articles and surveys are:

1. Vague requirements and specifications
2. Unclear objectives and goals
3. Unrealistic schedules and budgets
4. Lack of support from top management
5. Lack of user and client involvement
6. Ineffective communication and feedback
7. Poor reporting of the project's status
8. Ineffective project monitoring and control
9. Unclear assignment of roles and responsibilities
10. Sloppy project management skills and methodologies

In this section, we would like to highlight how the TSP operational framework can assist project manager and software development team to deliver successful projects by controlling and minimizing the most common software failure factors as listed above.

Vague Requirements and Specifications

TSP includes a requirements process as part of a package of included process scripts that are meant to be used as a starting point for tailoring a project specific development process. The TSP addresses this factor via the requirements process script (Script REQ). The purpose of the script is to produce a complete, valid, and accurate system requirements specification (SRS) and hardware/software engineering requirement specification (ERS). The process steps in the REQ script include Market Requirements Study, Requirements Elicitation, Requirements Prototypes, System Requirements Specification, User Manual Draft, System Test Plan, SRS Inspection, Engineering Requirements Specification, ERS Inspection, ERS Baseline, and requirements process post-mortem. Besides, TSP establishes Customer Interface Manager as one of the standard roles to be assigned to the team member. One of the main roles of Customer Interface Manager is to establish team standards and procedures for documenting and reviewing the product requirement. This task includes (1) leading the team in development, review and verification of the product requirements; (2) ensuring all the product requirements assumptions are identified, documented, tracked and verified with the customer; and (3) ensuring that the customer agrees with the requirements.

Besides, during TSP launch Meeting 4, the first planning step leaded by Design Manager is to check and asses the completeness and correctness of the requirement documentation. If all these activities performed and managed successfully by Customer Interface Manager and Design Manager, it will lead to clearer product requirements and specification.

Unclear Objectives and Goals

In TSP, unclear objectives and goals can be resolved during the first TSP Launch meeting i.e. Establish Product and Business Goals. It provides guidance to senior management and marketing representatives for preparing goals and objectives for presentation and discussion with the team, including answering team members' questions about goals and objectives. During this meeting, the sales or marketing representative presents a product overview, its intended usage, its existing competition, intended customer or user for the product, timeline and critical sets of product functions to the entire team. Then, it will continue by the management presentation on the business needs and goals for the product inclusive high-level budget, specific expectation, constraints, available resources and success criteria. The entire team has a chance to solicit management to gain more clarification on the business needs and goals. Besides, clarification on goal priorities to be required is sought during this meeting. Goals are re-stated in quantitative form. As consequences, the entire team is made aware of the goals and constraints producing better alignment, a more realistic assessment of the feasibility of meeting the goals and constraints, a broader sense of ownership, and ultimately a better plan. This helps the team to get the scope correct and avoid underestimating or gold plating. The team checks plan and any future revision to the plan against the goals to ensure compliance and to eliminate unnecessary steps. Instead of presenting the project objectives and goals to solely the project manager,

TSP requires high involvement by all the entire team members so that the project objectives and goals are understood by all the team members. In meeting 2 of the launch process, the team further reviews management's goals and objectives and defines measurements for the goals. Then the team defines its own additional goals and objectives and defines measurements for those as well.

Unrealistic Schedules and Budgets

To produce a realistic schedule and budget is a fundamental tenet of the TSP. There are several practices in the TSP that lead to a realistic schedule and budget:

1. The project team members understand business and product goals
2. The people who do the work plan the work
3. A defined estimation method (PRoxy Based Estimation or PROBE) is used
4. Quality is planned and is non-negotiable
5. Work is load-balanced amongst all team members
6. Risks are identified, mitigated, and tracked via up-to-date progress reporting

A realistic schedule and budget is an outcome of the TSP Launch process. The TSP Launch is conducted as a series of nine meetings which take place over a 3-to5-day period at the start of a project. During a launch, the software development team first meets with business and product leaders to understand the business and product goals for the project, then systematically follows a defined planning process to plan their work, and then meets with business and product leaders to present their plan (or alternate plans). The launch process is defined in eleven process scripts, which includes the overall launch script, a script for each of the nine launch meetings, and a script for the launch post-mortem (Script LAU, Scripts LAU1-LAU9, and Script LAUPM). During the launch, the team follows a defined estimation process to produce project estimates, then considers a development strategy, then produces a quality plan to make sure that poor quality does not impact schedule, and then load balances the work amongst team members to make sure all team members contribute to meeting the schedule. If the team finds that project goals cannot be met within the schedule, feature, quality, and resource constraints provided by management, then the team comes up with alternate plans to present to management. Alternate plans may ask for a more realistic schedule, more resources, and/or reduction in project scope.

In TSP, the team produces schedule and budget estimates during TSP launch meeting 4–Building Overall Team Plan. During this meeting, the team estimates everything including size, effort, bugs and time. High-level schedule will be prepared by the team once the size has been determined and estimated. The entire team will work together to create overall estimate for full project and also detailed plan covering for next 3 months and decide on the resources utilization accordingly. Schedule and budget estimation is derived based on historical data from past similar project which will provides productivity rates for the team and for also each individual. In case of historical productivity data is absent, the team should consider using data from some other project or the team can utilize expert judgment. Once the productivity rate is determined, the team can estimate overall hours required, plus with available resources the team can project a high-level schedule for the project. The overall plan is analyzed and reviewed by all the team members and team ensures that the task, dates, timeline, size and effort estimates are realistic and all the necessary works has been included and calculated. This helps catch omissions and inconsistencies that could result in an unrealistic plan. This process results in fewer missed and redundant tasks that if the project manager and one or two senior engineers compile a list for the team.

By this time, the team has justified information about the project schedule and budget. The project

schedule completion and estimated budget will be compared against management or customer expectation to see whether there is high deviation or not. In case of high deviation, the team will talk to management or customer about the approximate project schedule completion and estimated budget as well as explore alternatives. Any negotiations to scope, budget, staffing, etc. are performed in public as part of the out brief meeting. Team and management commitments are documented in the minutes of the meeting. This is explicitly included to prevent the project manager from privately acquiescing to unrealistic goals or constraints under pressure from management or the client. Indirectly, TSP provides a mechanism for commitment discipline by all parties and makes it more likely that all team members really commit to the plan.

Besides, the TSP also explicitly includes estimating effect Cost of Quality (COQ) as part of estimating process and forecasting the effect of the product quality delivered by the development process on cost and schedule. COQ is the cost of all project activities associated with defect prevention, defection, and removal expressed as a percentage of overall project cost. It consists of three components:

1. Failure Cost of Quality (FCOQ), the of finding and fixing defects in test
2. Appraisal Cost of Quality (ACOQ), the cost of performing reviews and fixing defects found in review
3. Prevention Cost of Quality (PCOQ), the cost of defect prevention activities such as root cause analysis.

COQ = PCOQ + ACOQ + FCOQ. A decrease in COQ corresponds to an increase in productivity since less effort is expended in dealing with failures and proportionally more effort is spend producing product. COQ is independent of language, product domain, etc. So it is an ideal measure for benchmarking the effect of process changes.

Lack of Support from Top Management

The TSP introduction strategy includes training for all levels of management: from senior executives to middle management to team leader. The first level of support required from top management is to attend the one-day TSP Executive Strategy Seminar. Top management is trained in the concepts of the TSP, and agrees to sponsor TSP by providing resources to train all levels of management, as well as TSP team members. Management also provides TSP coaching services for TSP teams. Support goes much beyond training and sponsorship, to personal involvement. Top management has to agree to meet with the teams to provide business and product goals in launch meeting 1, to be present when teams present their plan to management during launch meeting 9, to be involved in status review meetings at the end of each development cycle, and to be involved in periodic status review meetings. TSP also requires the top management to proactively providing sufficient resources to support the project by providing training necessary and assign key individuals to the project. Thus, there is no issue about the lack of support from top management in the TSP.

Lack of User and Client Involvement

In the TSP, the product manager role (also known as the marketing manager) represents the user/client to the team. The product manager meets with the development team to present the product goals, including user needs, during launch meeting 1 (Script LAU1). The team then builds a plan to meet these goals. The Customer Interface Manager role (Specification Customer Interface Manager) on a team also focuses on the user/client. The Customer Interface Manager's goals are to understand the customer's wants and needs, and to lead the team in providing a product that delights the customer. He or she has to build a rapport with the customer,

understand the customer's needs and lead the team to deliver as per customer expectations.

Ineffective Communication and Feedback

The TSP employs several methods and levels to ensure effective communication and feedback. All communication is supported by heavy use of data. The TSP encourages the use of data to help make decisions and provide feedback. Watts Humphrey calls this one of four aspects of rational management. Communication amongst team members takes place during the launches, re-launches, cycle post-mortems, project post-mortems, and weekly status review meetings. Role managers communicate by presenting role status during the team weekly meetings. Communication amongst team members and team coach occurs on an as-needed basis, and during TSP Checkpoints. Communication with management happens during launches and re-launches, and via status reporting (Specification STATUS).

Poor Reporting of the Project's Status

In TSP, project's status is reported at least once a week in the weekly project status meetings coordinated by Planning Manager. The TSP employs several methods and levels for progress reporting. Schedule status is planned, tracked, and reported via a simplified Earned Value reporting system. Cost status is planned, tracked, and reported via effort hours. Product quality status is reported by tracking planned versus actual defect injection and removal rates, and other quality measures such as defect density. Process quality is reported via measures such as time-in-phase ratios and process quality index. Feature status is reported via feature completion status. Progress reporting turn out to be easier if the organization adopting PSP/TSP automated tool to automatically track and analyze the project progress. This project's status reports provides many details to the team for understanding the status of the project, and if needed, necessary actions need to be taken to bring the project back on track.

Ineffective Project Monitoring and Control

There is no issue about ineffective project monitoring and control because the roles and responsibilities of project management are distributed among the team member. The team leader, the team coach, and the eight role managers (Planning, Process, Quality, Support, Customer Interface, Design, Implementation, and Test) monitor and control all aspects of the project (schedule, quality, cost, scope, features, and processes). The monitoring and control activities turn out to be easier and manageable. Individual team members monitor and control their own work, treating individual plans as mini-projects. Data is used to plan and track all work at all levels: individual, team, and multi-team. Senior management monitors the project less frequently than the team: on a periodic basis at the end and start of each project cycle, and via a weekly, monthly, or quarterly status reports. If the project is not on track, corrective actions will be taken to bring it back on track.

Unclear Assignment of Roles and Responsibilities

During TSP launch meeting 2, the roles and responsibilities will be defined and agreed by team members and are allocated for tracking them among the team members. Besides routines engineering responsibilities, project management responsibilities can be divided among the team members. Defined roles ensure that all team members can concentrate on specific aspects of the project e.g. quality, design, planning and etc. TSP establish nine standard roles i.e. team leader, customer interface manager, planning manager, quality manager, process manager, design man-

ager, implementation manager, test manager and support manager. All the roles and responsibilities are documented and communicated with the team. The team is built as a self-directed team as they come out with their own defined work processes in accordance to the established team goals. It takes particular care to distribute the roles and responsibilities across the entire team to avoid bottlenecks and promote career development. There are no issues about clarity who is doing what and conflicts due to overlapping responsibilities.

Sloppy Project Management Skills and Methodologies

TSP projects are self-directed. Based on management's business and product goals, teams plan and track their own work. The Team Leader role in the TSP corresponds to the project manager role on a traditional project. Prior to leading a TSP team, the team leader attends a mandatory three-day class called *Leading Development Teams*. This training teaches team leaders how to lead teams using the TSP. Additionally, team members help with different management aspects via the eight defined team roles on a TSP team: Customer Interface Manager, Design Manager, Implementation Manager, Test Manager, Support Manager, Process Manager, Planning Manager, and Quality Manager. Each role manager is responsible for all activities the team performs related to that role. All team members attend TSP training prior to participating on TSP teams. Developers complete a minimum of 5-days of training, titled *Personal Software Process (PSP) for Engineers*. Non-developers attend the 2-day *TSP Team Member Training*. All of this training addresses fundamental project management skills.

For additional reading, Nasir and Sahibbuddin (2011) conducted a Delphi study to determine the degree to which the Team Software Process (TSP) can address the identified critical success factors for software projects.

COMPARATIVE ANALYSIS OF CONVENTIONAL PROJECT MANAGEMENT VERSUS TSP

For the sake of providing a comparison, we assume a 10 person team that includes a full time project manager, a lead designer, and a lead tester that implements a software development project for approximately 1 year. For simplicity, we also assume that there are no subcontracts. All organisations are different, and there is much variation in the role of project manager from organisation to organisation. In this analysis, our choice of a "conventional" approach is based on assuming a dedicated project manager primarily responsible for planning, tracking, status reporting, and management. For easier visualisation, we provide a comparison according two perspectives, namely, planning and managing, as shown in Tables 3 and 4, respectively. The benefits of the TSP approach are also highlighted in these tables.

Table 3. Conventional project management versus TSP: A comparison from a planning perspective

Conventional Project Management	TSP Approach	Benefits of the TSP Approach
Project goals and constraints are provided to the project manager by the sponsoring management.	Project goals and constraints are discussed with the entire team, revised, and agreed upon during a project launch briefing.	1. The entire team is aware of goals and constraints, thereby producing better alignment, a more realistic assessment of the feasibility of meeting the goals and constraints, a broader sense of ownership, and ultimately a better plan. 2. Goals are re-stated in quantitative form. The team checks the plan; any future changes to the plan are checked against the stated goals to ensure compliance and eliminate unnecessary steps. 3. Team goals are included along with management goals, thus providing a mechanism for personal growth and career development.
The project manager produces a plan based on inputs from the lead designer and lead tester.	The entire team produces a plan facilitated by the project launch workshop that takes about four days. Each team member identifies a task list and generates estimates for items on that list. The team as a whole combines the individual task lists into a balanced plan. The team as a whole produces a list of prioritised risks using impact analysis.	1. Bottom-up task identification is coupled with a team review, which tends to result in fewer missed tasks. 2. Bottom-up risk identification also tends to result in fewer missed risks. 3. Bottom-up estimating tends to be more accurate due to use of individual-level historical data. 4. The use of a facilitator prevents one or two senior engineers from dominating the planning activities and biasing the estimates. 5. The resulting tends to have much greater detail and is usually produced faster. 6. Additional detail improves the plan's credibility with senior management. 7. The team usually has much more of a sense of ownership with respect to the plan.
The project manager assigns tasks to team members based on inputs from the lead designer and lead tester. Often, team members are assigned new tasks in an ad hoc way whenever a current task is completed.	Team members produce their own task lists and adjust the list as a team, negotiating tasks based on skills and availability.	1. A higher sense of plan ownership results from launch participation. 2. Each team member leaves the launch with a detailed list of tasks for the next three months. 3. Each team member has reviewed every other team member's task list. 4. Intimate knowledge of assumptions and dependencies across the entire team makes oversights and missed dependencies much less likely.
A copy of the approved plan is provided to team members.	The team produces the plan.	1. The team is intimately familiar with all plan details and is in a much better position to successfully execute it. 2. There is no need to spend additional effort to communicate the plan to team members.

continued on following page

Table 3. continued

Conventional Project Management	TSP Approach	Benefits of the TSP Approach
The project manager provides the plan to the lead designer and lead tester for review and then to sponsoring management for approval. Often, negotiations regarding the scope, budget, and delivery date are privately held between the project manager and the sponsoring management.	The entire team produces and reviews the plan together, identifies any proposed exceptions to management goals and constraints, and participates in the out brief to sponsoring management. Any negotiations regarding scope, budget, staffing and so on are held in public as part of the out brief meeting. The team and management commitments are documented in the minutes of the meeting.	1. This provides a mechanism to prevent organisations from adopting unrealistically optimistic plans. 2. This prevents the project manager from privately acquiescing to unrealistic goals or constraints under pressure from management. 3. This provides a mechanism for disciplined commitment by all parties. 4. This makes it more likely that all team members really commit to the plan.
The task granularity is typically on the order of one month.	The team produces a top-level plan covering the entire project with typical task durations of about one month. The team produces a detailed plan covering the next three months, with an average of two task completions per person per week. A new detailed plan is produced when the current one becomes obsolete or requires major changes.	1. The high level of task granularity makes it very easy to spot trends in Earned Value (EV) typically much sooner than with a lower-level granularity plan. Because adverse trends become apparent much sooner, there is more time to take corrective actions, thus producing a higher overall probability of meeting the project goals and constraints.
The plan typically assumes that planning, status tracking, status reporting, and team management are responsibilities of the project manager.	Management responsibilities are distributed across the entire team, and the project manager primarily serves as the team coach.	1. This prevents bottlenecks. 2. This provides backup. 3. Team members are able to perform planning, track their own personal status, and generate overall team status information. 4. This keeps the project manager available for coaching. 5. This facilitates career development.

We can observe that the strength of the TSP model lies in the characteristics of a self-directed team in which all team members have a high sense of project ownership, specifically regarding the project plan and processes. They are committed to meeting the stipulated goals, have the skills to develop a plan (much like a project manager) and have the discipline to follow the plan and the motivation to do superior work. The TSP model uses a distributed management model, whereby some of the responsibilities of a traditional project manager are distributed across the project team. The assignment of team roles and responsibilities is discussed in section 5, meeting 2, of (Humphrey, 2000), entitled "Roles and Responsibilities". The project manager is assigned the role of team leader. However, the roles of the customer interface manager, design manager, implementation manager, test manager, planning manager, process manager, quality manager, and support manager are explicitly assigned to other individuals to avoid creating a bottleneck, as often results from asking the project manager to undertake too many roles and responsibilities. The roles of planning manager, process manager, quality manager, customer interface manager, and

Table 4. Conventional project management versus TSP: A comparison from a managing perspective

Conventional Project Management	TSP Approach	Benefits of the TSP Approach
The project manager checks the status of individual team members once per week, which is rolled up into team level status. Earned value status is updated at most once a week, though often less frequently.	Each team member tracks effort expended on each task with an automated time-tracking tool. Individual EV status as well as team EV status is available in real-time from this tool. The team member that has been assigned a planning role presents team-level data during weekly status meetings and generates status reports. At the weekly status meetings, each team member his/her present personal EV status, and the planning lead presents the overall team EV status.	1. Tracking data are always available in real time. 2. The emphasis shifts from collecting tracking data to making decisions and then taking corrective action based on tracking data. 3. The presentation of individual-level EV data makes clarifies whether there are bottlenecks or adverse trends, thus allowing problems to be addressed early. 4. The presentation of individual-level EV data fosters a sense of ownership and accountability to other team members.
The project manager manages the risk list and updates risks before status meetings with senior management and/or before major milestone reviews.	The tasks of tracking specific risks are assigned to individual team members based on roles and responsibilities. New risks are identified by team members using a bottom-up approach at the weekly status meetings.	1. Risk status tends to be more current. 2. New risks tend to be identified and assigned more quickly. 3. Overall risk management works better.
The project manager performs status tracking and risk tracking, generates status reports, and coaches the team during his/her remaining time.	The management responsibilities are divided among the team members, freeing the manager for coaching and decision-making functions.	1. The manager has much more time to make decisions and address problems. 2. The project team typically performs better with high-quality coaching.

support manager are all part of the project management function, at least to some degree, in the conventional project management.

The fact that roles are distributed does not necessarily increase their scope beyond what is included in the conventional project management project management function, but in practise, distributed project management functions are more likely to be performed on time and in greater depth because they are not assigned to a single person. Distributed roles also provide a mechanism for developing new skills and team camaraderie, which is yet another responsibility under the project management function in the conventional project management. By using the TSP model to integrate team members into the project management function, individual practises and team performance can be defined, managed and measured, and accurate information on the project's progress and status can be made easily accessible to the management team.

TSP IMPLEMENTATION BENEFITS

TSP is designed for use on teamwork software projects in both industrial and academic environments. With equivalent notions and methods, TSPi is a smaller-scale version of TSP intended for graduate or undergraduate students, particularly those majoring in software engineering. By making use of the wide range of software project management and planning expertise in the industry (Humphrey, 2000b), TSPi may greatly help students in both their educational and future professional endeavours.

The study in this chapter, however, will focus only on TSP implementation outcomes in the industry. Our central discussion will consider the use of TSP to address four issues in software development: schedule, quality, cost and productivity.

TSP Implementation Outcome in the Industry

We surveyed 10 articles that highlight the experience of adopting TSP as analysed by practitioners and management teams. We limit our studied materials to 4 sources: namely, Crosstalk (The Journal of Defense Software Engineering), the SEI (Software Engineering Institute) Repository and Technical Report and TSP Symposium. These 4 sources are well known and presented a wide variety of cases in which TSP has been implemented; indeed, they include information on TSP use in different projects categories at 10 organizations between 2001 and 2009. These studies highlight cases of new software development and enhancement and maintenance projects while also providing information on company management. Thus, they highlight a range of instances of TSP implementation whose outcomes are almost identical (Table 5).

These studies indicate substantial improvements, particularly in terms of schedule performance, and/or development cost as well as software quality. For instance, Ciurczak (2001) reports 37 percent reduction in overall development time, and the U.S. Naval Air Systems Command/NAVAIR (Hefley, Schwalb & Pracchia, 2002), Microsoft (Grojean, 2005) and the Mexican company (Nichols & Salazar, 2009) are reported to have achieved higher-quality product delivery during a system test, with defect rates of 2.1 percent, 1.36 percent and 1.7 percent per thousand lines of code (KLOC). These outstanding results can be traced to the strengths of the TSP framework as tabulated in Table 5.

Within 5 years after TSP is introduced, average schedule delay of only 6 percent schedule delay is reported in a study of 20 TSP projects in 13 organizations (Davis & Mullaney, 2003). This percentage is obviously a great sign for the software industry given that a great number of organizations continue to operate behind schedule in their software development projects. For example, the Standish Group Report reported an average figure of 222% time overruns in software projects across various major industries in 1994 (Standish Group, 1995), followed by 63% in 2000 (Standish Group, 2001), 72% in 2006 and 79% in 2008 (Standish Group, 2009).

Using TSP, project developers can present and manage their planned project delivery timeline confidently after a rigorous estimation process that emphasizes each team's collective productivity. One program manager in the Department of Defense (DoD) who had been working on a large and complex military systems project had given his approval for a project delivery plan that included a first minimum-function software release after 13 months followed by two subsequent releases within another six months (as opposed to eight month as dictated by an earlier schedule earlier presented by the project developers) (Nichols, Carleton & Humphrey, 2009). Although he was disappointed with the dates, he has admitted that this was the best program plan he has ever seen and that a solid date was essential to the DoD commitment to the project.

Table 6 summarizes the timelines for the projects using TSP in the 10 cases examined. These projects finished either ahead of schedule, on time or slightly behind schedule.

Seven of the studied organisations explicitly mentioned either that TSP helps them to create realistic plans and accurate estimations or that such plans and estimations are their goal when they use TSP (Ciurczak, 2001; de Oca & Serrano, 2002; Trechter & Hirmanpour, 2005; Grojean, 2005; George & Janiszewski, 2005; Nichols et al., 2009; Nichols & Salazar, 2009; Battle, 2009). It has been suggested that unrealistic scheduling either leads to software failure or puts project at

Table 5. Compilation of TSP implementation outcomes

Outcome	Organization
Clear project objectives Clear customer requirements	QuarkSoft Microsoft
Accurate project plan / Excellent estimation plan / Realistic plan	QuarkSoft EBS Dealing Resources Sandia National Laboratories Microsoft PS&J Software Six Sigma Department of Defense (DoD) Mexican's Outsourcing Organizations
Early detection of problems and effective solutions	EBS Dealing Resources NAVAIR AV-8B JSSA NAVAIR AV-8B MSC Sandia National Laboratories Mexican's Outsourcing Organizations
Reductions in defect concentration	EBS Dealing Resources NAVAIR AV-8B JSSA NAVAIR AV-8B MSC Mexican's Outsourcing Organizations Naval Oceanographic Office (NAVO)
Improved communication	QuarkSoft Department of Defense (DoD)
Worker attrition enhanced / Team synergy improved / Good team participation and collaboration	PS&J Software Six Sigma Department of Defense (DoD) Mexican's Outsourcing Organizations
Sense of ownership and commitment	Sandia National Laboratories Microsoft Department of Defense (DoD)
Precise project tracking / good project control	NAVAIR AV-8B JSSA Sandia National Laboratories Department of Defense (DoD) Mexican's Outsourcing Organizations Naval Oceanographic Office (NAVO)
Reductions in bureaucracy / political force	Microsoft Department of Defense (DoD)
Process improvements via PIP	NAVAIR AV-8B JSSA Department of Defense (DoD) Naval Oceanographic Office (NAVO)

risk (Boehm & Ross, 1989; CMMI Product Team, 2002; Humphrey & Thomas, 2010). To cope with unrealistic project schedules, software developers skip over or shorten various steps in their process and rapidly move on to the coding and testing phases. However, this method can result in either scheduling problems and/or the delivery of poor-quality software when software requirements and design are not properly addressed. A great deal of errors or defects can cause testing to take lon-

ger than planned. Furthermore, it might be necessary to revisit earlier project phases, which might then double the amount of time needed to complete the project. The DoD project team found that non-coding defects related to incorrect or misunderstood requirements create over four hours of extra work each on average, whereas coding takes an average of one hour (Nichols et al., 2009). System tests are indicated to be the most time-consuming activity and to require higher effort

Table 6. Summary outcomes of TSP implementation–Schedule

#	Organization	Outcomes
1	EBS Dealing Resources (Ciurczak, 2002)	Certification test time reduced by approximately 50%
2	EBS Dealing Resources (Ciurczak, 2002)	Reduction of 37.5% in duration of execution stage (overall)
3	NAVAIR AV-8B MSC (Rickets, 2005)	Maintenance project finished ahead of schedule
4	Sandia National Laboratories (Trechter & Hirmanpour, 2005)	An 8-week project was 51% completed in week 3 as opposed to 30% as planned
5	Microsoft (Grojean, 2005)	First TSP pilot: 96% schedule accuracy
6	Microsoft (Grojean, 2005)	Second TSP project: Product was delivered on schedule
7	Department of Defense (DoD) (Nichols et al., 2009)	Project completed 3% ahead of schedule
8	Mexican's Outsourcing Organizations (Nichols & Salazar, 2009)	Delivered products 2% later than scheduled on average
9	Naval Oceanographic Office (NAVO) (Battle, 2009)	25% of 16 projects released ahead of schedule
10	Naval Oceanographic Office (NAVO) (Battle, 2009)	25% of 16 projects released on schedule

than average. Due to this reason, this stage is known to be the main cause for schedule slips (McDonald, Musson & Smith, 2008).

EBS Company managed to reduce its overall product delivery time by 37.5 percent by decreasing the duration of the testing phase by 67 percent. The firm was able to fewer defects by conducting an extensive review during the earlier project phases (Ciurczak, 2002). The TSP review process enables problems to be identified long before the testing phases. TSP review activities begin during the TSP launch process and extend until postmortem for each product release. The TSP development life cycle, as shown in Table 7 (Rickets, 2005), includes design review and code review, and design review in particular is stated to be very beneficial in improving product quality together with design inspection because it allows design problems to be identified and addressed that are known to be very critical for software development. Even on its own, design review can be executed well if software developers use

the previously defined design review process to evaluate their designs (Humphrey, 2006).This process is incorporated even on the individual level with PSP-trained engineers through *self design review*. The software team leader of AV-8B JSSA commented that "*You have got to have good design to get good code. One advantage of doing design in TSP is the design review process. These reviews help you find and fix potentially costly defects much sooner*" (Hefley at al., 2002).

The complexity of software has increased; it can now contain a million lines of codes while simultaneously experiencing decreasing average market life expectancy. Thus, the concerns for software quality have also increased. According to the National Institute of Standards and Technology (RTI, 2002), the core factor that contributes to the quality issues in the software industry is how difficult it is to define and measure software quality. In TSP, software quality is measured in terms of defect processing/total rate. Prior research

Table 7. TSP development life cycle phases

HLD	High-Level Design
HLDINSP	High-Level Design Inspection
DLD	Detailed-Level Design
DLDR	Detailed-Level Design Review
DLDINSP	Detailed-Level Design Inspection
CODE	Code
CR	Code Review
CODEINSP	Code Inspection
COMPILE	Compile
UT	Unit Test
IT	Integration Test
ST	System Test

has continually indicated how defects have influenced project duration and complexity.

Table 8 summarizes the outcomes of TSP in terms of quality, which is mostly exhibited through defect density. Half of the companies completed their projects well ahead of schedule or experienced significant improvement in overall project schedule performance because they had fewer defects to address in the testing phase. Usually, 40 to 60 percent of typical project schedules are dedicated to testing activities (Humphrey, 2002b).

Humphrey and Thomas (2010) regard a quality product a, "*a product that provides the capabilities that are most important to its users*" and

Table 8. Summary of outcomes of TSP implementation–Quality

#	Organization	Outcomes
1	EBS Dealing Resources (Ciurczak, 2002)	Average defect fix time decreased by 25% per defect
2	EBS Dealing Resources (Ciurczak, 2002)	Test defects dropped by a factor of 2 and resulted in 50% improvement in system integration
3	EBS Dealing Resources (Ciurczak, 2002)	EBS quality at certification was 6 times better than industry average
4	NAVAIR AV-8B JSSA (Hefley et al., 2002)	2.1 defects/thousand lines of code at time of system integration test
5	NAVAIR AV-8B JSSA (Hefley et al., 2002)	Developed application is robust and enjoys 100% up time
6	NAVAIR AV-8B MSC (Rickets, 2005)	Reduced defects by 38%
7	NAVAIR AV-8B MSC (Rickets, 2005)	Maintenance team has almost reached its project quality goal of 10% maximum defects as indicated in its problem report (PR) at system test; the actual percentage was 13%
8	Microsoft (Grojean, 2005)	First TSP pilot: 1.36 defects/thousands lines of code (KLOC) in system test Second TSP project: System test revealed 0.71 defect density
9	Microsoft (Grojean, 2005)	Second TSP project: UAT/Beta Acceptance Test revealed 0.08 defect density
10	Microsoft (Grojean, 2005)	Second TSP project: Production revealed 0.15 defect density High product quality
11	Department of Defense (DoD) (Nichols et al., 2009)	10% of defects due to incorrect or misunderstood requirements and another 10% identified during testing Delivered a quality product
12	Mexican's Outsourcing Organizations (Nichols & Salazar, 2009)	Several projects had no defects based on system and/or acceptance test Delivered high-quality products
13	Naval Oceanographic Office (NAVO) (Battle, 2009)	0.9 defects/KLOC on average in system test
14	Naval Oceanographic Office (NAVO) (Battle, 2009)	0.5 defects/KLOC on average delivered by customer

point out the need to precisely define the important accomplishments to be reached. In TSP, a quality plan is prepared in accordance with the earlier defined project and team quality goals during the project team launch, and this plan is used throughout the software development phases/process.

Software products must not merely be delivered on time and on budget; they must also be reliable and include all of the functionalities required by users. Although it is essential to develop clear requirements in the first place to meet users' functional needs, software that runs without error is a must if the functions required are to be utilized (Humphrey & Thomas, 2010). Errors in design and coding that fail to be corrected will result in defects in the operational systems. Thus, instead of concentrating to another project or the next cycle of the product, engineers will have to spend their time addressing defects in the software that has just been released. As a result, software engineers will not be able to commit to their planned work or proceed with a new project. If these sorts of issues arise continuously, they will affect firm productivity in the long term. Product may be released much later than expected, and organizations that choose to add or change software personnel later on in the project to solve the problem tend to experience significant cost overruns. Thus, poor-quality software means investing more time and more money.

Organizations that use TSP have shown to work the other way around because they have decreased the number of defects in their software during the product testing phases. EBS has achieved a 50% improvement in system integration since their test defects decreased by a factor of 2, which in turn has shortened certification testing time and lowered costs. EBS software execution is composed of two main stages: (1) development activities which that design, coding, unit testing and system integration and (2) certification testing. Under the TSP system, overall product execution at EBS operates at a superior level; EBS is certified at a level 6 times

higher than industry average. After Microsoft's first TSP pilot project, the IT manager who proposed the use of TSP commented that TSP training was worthwhile when their engineers performed well during the project (Grojean, 2005). Having struggled with uncontrollable development projects involving ever-increasing testing loops with high defect counts, the team discovered a mere 5 defects during the system integration test (SIT) for this project and achieved similar results on a user acceptance test (UAT) and at the release to customer (RTC) date for 4255 lines of code. Software engineers working on the NAVAIR AV-8B JSSA project have also admitted that their use of TSP provides a strong emphasis on higher quality software by enabling them to consistently track the quality of the system product under development and record it to create points of comparison with earlier production processes (Hefley et al., 2002). The fruits of the project were reported to have 2.1 defects on average per thousand LOC based on the SIT (Software Integration Test) test, and the product was the first to achieve 100% up time. Another report on the NAVAIR project has to do with software maintenance by AV-8B MSC; TSP-enhanced practices applied to maintenance activity have managed to reduce software defects by 38% (Rickets, 2005). The team responsible for the project, which was inexperienced in the problem domain, has successfully completed its main task of remedial maintenance (i.e., it has fixed the software defects in question) by adjusting the TSP life cycle to processes that fit the team and the particular maintenance activity. The maintenance project goals were defined during TSP launch meeting 1, and the team established its quality goal as a problem report (PR) rate of no more than 10%; it then almost reached the specified goal by achieving a rate of 13%. A problem report is "*a document describing where changes were made and why*" (Rickets, 2005). Work quality in TSP starts with a defined objective and goals that drive the project team's quality plan and quality results that include the size of defects encountered in their tasks. A software product can be produced through continuous improvement and defect measurement activity as provided in TSP to make improvement activity possible. As Trechter and Hirmanpour (2005) highlight, "*TSP reports provide a rich set of quality data and an early warning system related to the quality being built*". Such information can be supported by findings from the DoD project, where an earned value (EV) report provided by the project teams every week enables senior management to identify the rationale behind milestones skipped, such as in cases where the teams' actual work has progressed ahead of planned work, with some quality steps recognized as omitted (Nichols et al., 2009).

Defects are not only the main cause of project delay but help to increase project cost when it is identified late in a project. Table 9 provides in indication of how the TSP approach helps some of the studied companies from the perspective of cost.

It has been commented that actual project cost and project cost estimation plans are not provided in the TSP framework (Trechter & Hirmanpour, 2005). Although TSP do not directly supply a method of managing a project budget, so that practitioners can present a plan that parallels that for overall project cost, many aspects of the TSP approach encourage wise spending during the software development process. For instance, *self design review*, as previously mentioned earlier, is a cost-effective method in which each software engineer identifies defects in his or her work and fixes them when it is relatively inexpensive to do so (Jain, 2009). Another report suggests that detailed TSP plans and effort tracking provide the early detection of wasted project costs when hired part-timers are performing poorly (Nichols et al., 2009). The design review process in TSP has also been revealed to enable expensive defects to be identified much earlier (Hefley et al., 2002). The same has been true of review for EBS, which has been indicated as the main source of cost reduction in the company's certification test phase (Ciurczak, 2001). Hence, the emphasis on early problem detection and handling has proven to have benefited the firm in terms of project cost.

In TSP, individual developers devote a certain amount of time per week solely to development tasks depending on their agreed upon *task time availability*. Based on actual time, which does not include time spent on non-engineering tasks in the software development, an accurate estimation plan can be produced. The purpose is to create a realistic project schedule. Thus, it is not suggested

Table 9. Summary of outcomes of TSP implementation–Cost

#	Organization	Outcomes
1	EBS Dealing Resources (Ciurczak, 2002)	Reduced cost in certification test phases by reducing defects through extensive use of review in product development phase
2	EBS Dealing Resources (Ciurczak, 2002)	Variable costs controlled and predictable (based on number of defects in the product being tested)
3	NAVAIR AV-8B JSSA (Hefley et al., 2002)	Costly defects identified much earlier through design review process
4	Sandia National Laboratories (Trechter & Hirmanpour, 2005)	The use of the company's financial system to help in providing the overall project status has not been burdensome
5	Department of Defense (DoD) (Nichols et al., 2009)	Early detection of waste in project costs (part-time staffing)
6	Mexican's Outsourcing Organizations (Nichols & Salazar, 2009)	Hidden cost of assign multiple projects per developer discovered through TSP bottom-up plan (part-time staffing)
7	Mexican's Outsourcing Organizations (Nichols & Salazar, 2009)	Delivered products within budget

that a developer be assigned to multiple projects when this will reduce both his or her available time for a project and his or her work productivity. Both of these factors are core elements that guide software teams in their project estimation plans. Furthermore, this practice may eventually affect an organization's overall, long-term project performance. Trechter and Hirmanpour (2005) indicate that when a developer has limited resources as a result of having been assigned to as many as four to five projects at one point of time, this creates inefficiency. In the first TSP project, a development team in Mexico encountered problems synchronizing the efforts of part-time workers during the launch, and the result was a plan whose timeline exceeded the management's desired schedule by six weeks and required additional human resources (Nichols & Salazar, 2009). The firm learned during the launch that handing over multiple projects to a developer at once will impose hidden costs and that the TSP bottom-up plan revealed this. A TSP bottom-up plan represents the sixth step in the TSP project launch, the one in which the development work of the various project team members to determine the final work completion date.

Table 10 highlights the results of practicing TSP in terms of productivity. Mali (1978) defines productivity as "*the measure of how well resources are brought together in organizations and utilized for accomplishing a set of result. Productivity is reaching the higher level of performance with the least expenditure of resources*". The results of TSP adoption are clear in the case of EBS, as the firm increased productivity by managing to reduce its product cycle time and simultaneously produce better quality products; these were the two goals at hand (Ciurczak, 2002). These improvements enabled EBS to develop more products that would definitely improve revenue generation due to the successful reduction o time to market. Similarly, Microsoft's Chief Information Officer (CIO) has expresses the same ideas with reference to the first TSP pilot project at Microsoft. Referring to the

large amount of the IT shop's budget dominated by activities such as support and bug fixes (which was indeed cited as being as high as 60 to 70 percent), he stresses that "*the potential for this to not only reduce our product cycles and increase our quality, but ultimately freeing up much of our sustainer activities enables us to invest more in builder activities that drive more value to the business*" (Grojean, 2005). In fact, a large amount of money is used every year to support and maintain software systems around the world. Rickets (2005) notes that H2.0 maintenance software on the NAVAIR AV-8B MSC project team enabled the re-evaluation of additional PRs to be resolved within the time remaining on their project, which was completed ahead of schedule. Because the number of software problems fixed increased by 76% through TSP practices, the H2.0 team managed to complete over 180 problem reports instead of an estimated 102 during a two-year period.

Additional Advantages of TSP

Better Coordination and Control

Significant emphasis has been placed on the need for coordination and control in software development. Nidumolu (1995) regards project coordination and control as the most influential components of software project performance. The contribution of these two considerations to effective project management has been broadly discussed. Zmud (1980) and Rook (1986) point out the importance of controlled structures during the early project implementation phases, indicating that they make project progress more visible. Meanwhile, Lederer and Prasad (1995) identify the lack of management attention to project control in comparing actual and estimated project performance as a cause of inaccurate estimates, a factor that contributes to overruns. Subsequently, Kirsch (1997) examines project control from several angles, including its role in coordinating project tasks, and suggests that they are necessary on

Table 10. Summary of outcomes of TSP implementation–Productivity

#	Organization	Outcomes
1	EBS Dealing Resources (Ciurczak, 2002)	Because cycle time for products' releases have decreased, more products can be developed and revenue generation has increased
2	QuarkSoft (de Oca & Serrano, 2002)	Critical problems are handled in a timely manner
3	NAVAIR AV-8B JSSA (Hefley et al., 2002)	PSP/TSP has accelerated SW-CMM level 2 assessment by more than 40%
4	NAVAIR AV-8B MSC (Rickets, 2005)	76% increase in problems fixed
5	NAVAIR AV-8B MSC (Rickets, 2005)	Managed to complete over 180 problem report instead of the estimated 102 over a two-year period
6	Sandia National Laboratories (Trechter & Hirmanpour, 2005)	Early problems detections led to minor corrections only
7	Microsoft (Grojean, 2005)	Project team achieved a score of 10/10 in customer relations
8	PS&J Software Six Sigma (George & Janiszewski, 2005)	Effort (time) reduced by factor of 2 with a total error of 23% rather than 41% (as in historical data)

every project. Na, Li, Simpson and Kim (2004), on the other hand, discuss risk coordination and control as factors in software project performance. Wiredu (2006) presents an analytical framework for coordinating Global Software Development (GSD) as a coordination process in distributed software project environments, whereas Philip, Schwabe and Ewusi-Mensah (2009) highlight coordination as a critical factor in offshore project failures. This long string of examples clearly signifies the crucial roles of coordination and control in ensuring software project success. We can also conclude that project coordination can be strongly associated with project control.

In TSP, coordination is not merely the responsibility of the project manager or team leader. The Naval Oceanographic Office (NAVO), in its process of enhancing organizational change using TSP, discovered that it was no longer the project manager's full-time responsibility to assess project status at the team level (Cagle, 2002). Instead, everyone would contribute to coordinating the work of the project, and efficient project coordination in this way could lead to effective project control and smoother work processes. The need

for coordination was recognized that at the level of individual software developers and at the group and management levels so that everyone working on a project became devoted to his or her own responsibilities. Within the TSP project environment, each team member would take control of his or her own work, revising and changing his or her individual plan as often as necessary (Davis & Mullaney, 2003), and periodical reports on the overall performance and progress of the team would be provided to the management. Necessary decisions could be made by the senior management working on the DoD project based on these project status reports when coordination problems or approval delays were identified. At the same time, certain steps in the process were sometimes excluded to speed up the process based on the EV reports (Nichols et al., 2009). The importance of reporting to better project control has been addressed by Rook (1986); management teams require adequate information to identify project status and determine what assistance they might need to provide. Rook stresses that *"the information on measured achievement must be presented effectively to management and the customer so that project progress can be approved at critical points and the correct decisions made*" (Rook, 1986). A lack of quality information creates uncertainty for decision-makers when they need to make vital decisions. Facilitating the flow of information flow in such contexts is understood as a means of coping with the uncertainty problem (Zmud, 1980). The issue of uncertainty has been highlighted from time to time when uncertainty has been widely associated with project control (Na et al., 2004; Keil & Robey, 2001; Gibbs, 1994; Zmud, 1980). Project reports have been identified as the main outcome of TSP use at Sandia National Laboratories, as the system has provided for precise project tracking and control (Trechter & Hirmanpour, 2005). The key seems to have been that the information in the report was derived from data and metrics gathered by the developers themselves; the information was reasonably objective and therefore provided a realistic vision of project status. All in all, the powerful role of TSP reporting systems seems clear; it helps management teams to make sound decisions and adjustments or to provide necessary assistance to their project teams. This is essential because all aspects of the software project must be carefully coordinated achieve better project control.

Flexibility

The rapid changes in the business practices governing software development require for a flexible model (Standish Group, 1995). Flexibility is also needed to accommodate the inevitable phenomenon of unpredictable user demand with regard to software development. The management team (MT) at QuarkSoft chose TSP and adjusted its regular management practices accordingly (de Oca & Serrano, 2002). Using TSP, the MT developed their own standards and ways of strengthening their reporting and data collection processes. There were quite a number of qualitative improvements made by the MT in terms of both team process

and company management through the use of TSP. This first example of the use of TSP in a domain other than software domain clearly displays how TSP practitioners can use TSP according to their needs. Furthermore, in such cases, TSP is being used not only to manage projects but also to organize a company.

TSP promotes *self-directed teams*. On self-directed teams, "*the members sense what is needed without being told, pitch in to help, and do whatever is needed to get the job done*" (Humphrey, 2006). Under the TSP approach, a team will be guided by a TSP coach, who will direct each team member as to how to conduct his or her own well defined processes and plan for his or her independent development work. The aim is to establish a team that is motivated and committed to its work and to the very concept of team membership. Defining the team's unique processes, producing unique plans for the team, and tracking and reporting on the team's independent work will build a sense of ownership and provide the team with flexibility. For instance, a clear understanding of the customer requirements during the launch process enable the project team to convince the customer on the anticipated schedule (i.e. potential anticipated delay might be included) (Grojean, 2005). Nevertheless, the committed participation of the management team, which should include support, guidance and observation, will guarantee sufficient project control. This kind of method encourages developers to feel that the firm views them as trustworthy and disciplined workers. TSP creates a flexible work environment and flexible implementation together with control. Nichols and Salazar (2009) note one lesson learned regarding the critical role of TSP coaches at the beginning of the TSP adoption process as follows: "*Provide pragmatic judgment about when to be flexible and when to hold the line on TSP principles. TSP should be followed to the letter only when it makes sense to do so. Recognizing when guidelines should be flexible or tailored requires experience*". Still, of two teams performing maintenance projects that have successfully adopted TSP according to their maintenance project requirements, one team included software engineers inexperienced not only with TSP but also with maintenance work (Rickets, 2005; George & Janiszewski, 2005). Both of these projects exhibited excellent results; each project team created a new estimation scheme for maintenance activity. Similarly, a software engineer at Microsoft who was part of the first TSP pilot project mentions that *"during the launch, we also modified some of the processes to fit our needs, and it was clear that TSP could be modified to suit a team's needs. We have made small changes to the process over time to make it more efficient for us, while at the same time ensuring quality"* (Grojean, 2005). The flexibility offered by TSP provides space for practitioners to make necessary changes or enhancements, and the PIP provides a mechanism through which to help them convey their ideas or opinions. This is particularly visible in some research: *"It is important to understand that the PSP and TSP frameworks are flexible and should be evolved based on the team and organization's needs. The primary vehicle for this evolution is the process improvement proposal – a fundamental element of the TSP"* (Hefley et al., 2002).

CONCLUSION AND FUTURE RESEARCH

The remarkable outcomes of TSP use in the cases reported on here did not manifest overnight. They have been achieved via a process requiring consistent discipline. As stated by Humphrey (2006), *"Discipline is what separates the experts from the amateurs in any field. Their willingness to rehearse, to practice, and to continually improve is what makes them experts and what makes superior work so natural that they can devote their energies to being creative."*

TSP promotes the application of disciplined engineering practices by software development teams under broad management support and involvement to ensure consistent employment of quality work efforts. Many organizations have significantly improved their software project schedules, decreased costs, and improved quality and productivity as presented here. A disciplined but flexible approach that allows for process adaptations in accordance with project goals and project teams makes TSP incredibly fitting for modern software development environments. Earlier and clearer definitions of project goals by management and the production of rigorous project plan by project teams (followed by continuous tracking to ensure project progress and the detection and elimination of product defects) all enable TSP users to keep their actions consistent with their project plans. Furthermore, there are management controls put in place to provide timely warnings. Management teams provided with a clearer picture of project milestone through TSP practices. In all of these ways, TSP promotes sound project development practices.

The complexity of software is undeniable and presents issues not only in terms of its construction on a technical level but also in terms of related managerial practices (Brooks, 1987). There is no silver bullet here. Instead, Brooks emphasizes the need to use good modern practices and to build new organizations like the Software Engineering Institute (SEI) to reach this objective. TSP, the product of SEI, has targeted how software engineers work rather than the intricacies of software itself. To do good work in software engineering requires discipline (Humphrey, 2009). It has been identified in recent decades that a disciplined, structured and systematic approach to project management is not only preferable but also essential (Rook, 1986).

Based on this study, it is evident that improvements in scheduling, quality, cost-effectiveness and productivity accrue when every team member is committed to one work culture. The key to a unified work culture is trust. Every team member should trust that his or her colleagues will do their utmost under the leadership of a promising software engineering strategy; such conviction helps to create a positive and energetic community. Such a positive atmosphere will also help to unify software development teams that are globally distributed. As stated by Wiredu (2006), the implications of distribution are critical to both developer actions and the coordination of those actions. Future research should consider how TSP promotes the concept of a unified work culture within the context of global software development (GSD), which is known to be very challenging because of factors such as the geographical distribution of project teams, socio-cultural differences, language barriers and technological considerations. TSP should be the best strategy for GSD because it primes the work culture to fulfil the three aforementioned most important elements of effective team-building: that everyone must truly understand what they are supposed to do based on universal project goals and a unifying objective, that everyone must agree on how to achieve those goals using a detailed project plan, and finally, that everyone must believe in the achievability of the goals and plan. In addition, the TSP approach seems to address a significant portion of the problems addressed in the GSD project environment:

- TSP emphasizes early problem management and handling, the need to do the right thing at the earliest possible moment. Because re-planning, redesign and rework take significant effort and are not easily executed in the GSD context given the geographical distribution of the team members (Sangwan, Mullick, Bass, Paulish & Kazmeier, 2006), a detailed and promising plan should be put in place from the very beginning through the TSP launch process.
- Because software development is a non-routine activity in which most software systems are one-of-a-kind projects (Kraut & Streeter, 1995), some system features

are frequently incomplete during the initial design phase This is especially common for large software development process that are extremely complex. A top-down development approach will be perfect in such scenarios; the system can be developed or enhanced gradually via small, incremental phases so that gaps in earlier versions can be filled in subsequent software product releases.

- TSP provides direction and guidelines for geographically dispersed teams and integrated development teams alike (Humphrey, 2006), which will be a huge help in the GSD project environment.
- To reduce ambiguity, maximize stability, facilitate coordination and balance flexibility and rigidity is critical in the GSD project environment (Sangwan et al., 2006) are all offered through the practice of TSP.

These are some basic considerations regarding the use of TSP within the GSD project framework. Although TSP has provided mechanisms for the coordination of teamwork in tandem with distributed software development, various model-driven frameworks can be integrated in implementing TSP in that context to encourage visibility and the comprehension of both project requirements and design in the face of linguistic and culture differences. The future aim would be to unite everyone working on global software development projects into one work culture regardless of their background under the project management specifications presented by TSP. *"In order to eliminate the threats of a distributed environment, a strategy that addresses diversity minimization shall be implemented. A set of practices that helps to establish a common work environment for every team involved in the project shall form a shared domain for successful collaboration"* (Smite & Borzovs, 2006).

REFERENCES

Ariane 501 Inquiry Board. (1996). *Ariane 5: Flight 501 failure*. Retrieved from http://www.di.unito.it/~damiani/ariane5rep.html

Battle, E. (2009, September). *Using TSP at the MSG Level* [PowerPoint slides]. Paper presented at the Fourth Annual TSP Symposium, New Orleans, Louisiana. Retrieved from http://www.sei.cmu.edu/tspsymposium/2009/2009/index.html

Boehm, B. W. (2006). Some future trends and implications for systems and software engineering processes. *Systems Engineering, 9*(1), 1–19. doi:10.1002/sys.20044

Boehm, B. W., & Ross, R. (1989). Theory-W software project management: Principles and examples. *IEEE Transactions on Software Engineering, 15*(7), 902–916. doi:10.1109/32.29489

Brooks, F. P. (1975). *The mythical man-month: Essays on software engineering*. Reading, MA: Addison-Wesley.

Brooks, F. P. (1987). No silver bullet: Essence and accidents of software engineering. *IEEE Computer, 20*(4), 10–19. doi:10.1109/MC.1987.1663532

Brooks, F. P. (1995). *The mythical man-month: Essays on software engineering* (Anniversary ed.). Reading, MA: Addison-Wesley.

Cagle, L. (2002). *Enhancing organization change using TSP*. Carnegie Mellon University, Software Engineering Information Repository (SEIR), Software Engineering Institute. Retrieved from https://seir.sei.cmu.edu/seir/

Ciurczak, J. (2001). *The quiet quality revolution at EBS Dealing Resources, Inc*. Carnegie Mellon University, Software Engineering Information Repository (SEIR), Software Engineering Institute. Retrieved from https://seir.sei.cmu.edu/seir/

Ciurczak, J. (2002). *Team software process (TSP) experiences in the foreign exchange market*. Carnegie Mellon University, Software Engineering Information Repository (SEIR), Software Engineering Institute. Retrieved from https://seir.sei.cmu.edu/seir/

CMMI Product Team. (2002). *Capability maturity model integration (CMMI) version 1.1*. Carnegie Mellon University, Software Engineering Institute. Retrieved from http://www.sei.cmu.edu/reports/02tr029.pdf

Davis, N., & Barbara, S. (2009). *Experiences using the team software process at Adobe Systems*. Paper presented at the Fourth Annual TSP Symposium, New Orleans, Louisiana. Retrieved from http://www.sei.cmu.edu/tspsymposium/2009/2009/index.html

Davis, N., & Mullaney, J. (2003). *The team software process (TSP) in practice: A summary of recent results*. Carnegie Mellon University, Software Engineering Institute. Retrieved from http://www.sei.cmu.edu/reports/03tr014.pdf

de Oca, C. M., & Serrano, M. A. (2002). Managing a company using TSP techniques. *Crosstalk. The Journal of Defense Software Engineering, 16*(9), 17–21.

Eveleens, J. L., & Verhoef, C. (2010). The rise and fall of the chaos report figures. *IEEE Software, 27*(1), 30–36. doi:10.1109/MS.2009.154

George, A., & Janiszewski, S. (2005). Applying functional TSP to a maintenance project. *Crosstalk. The Journal of Defense Software Engineering, 18*(9), 24–27.

Gibbs, W. (1994). Software's chronic crisis. *Scientific American, 271*(3), 86–95. doi:10.1038/scientificamerican0994-86

Glass, R. L. (1998). *Software runaways: Lessons learned from massive software project failures*. Prentice Hall.

Glass, R. L. (2005). IT failure rates--70% or 10–15%. *IEEE Software, 22*(3), 110–112. doi:10.1109/MS.2005.66

Glass, R. L. (2006). The Standish report: does it really describe a software crisis? *Communications of the ACM, 49*(8), 15–16. .doi:10.1145/1145287.1145301

Gray, C. F., & Larson, E. W. (2008). *Project management: The managerial process* (4th ed.). Burr Ridge, IL: Irwin/McGraw-Hill.

Grojean, C. A. (2005). Microsoft's IT organization uses PSP/TSP to achieve engineering excellence. *Crosstalk. The Journal of Defense Software Engineering, 18*(3), 8–12.

Hartmann, D. (2006). *Interview: Jim Johnson of the Standish.* Retrieved from www.infoq.com/articles/Interview-Johnson-Standish-CHAOS

Hass, K. B. (2007). The blending of traditional and agile project management. *PM World Today, 9*(5), 1–8.

Hefley, B., Schwalb, J., & Pracchia, L. (2002). AV-8B's experience using the TSP to accelerate SW-CMM adoption. *Crosstalk. The Journal of Defense Software Engineering, 16*(9), 5–8.

Hilburn, T. B., & Humphrey, W. S. (2002). Teaching teamwork. *IEEE Software, 19*(5), 72–77. doi:10.1109/MS.2002.1032857

Humphrey, W. S. (1998). Three dimensions of process improvement, part III: The team process. *Crosstalk. The Journal of Defense Software Engineering, 11*(4), 14–17.

Humphrey, W. S. (1999). *Pathways to process maturity: The personal software process and team software process.* Carnegie Mellon University, Software Engineering Institute. Retrieved from http://www.sei.cmu.edu/library/abstracts/news-at-sei/backgroundjun99.cfm

Humphrey, W. S. (2000a). *The team software process (TSP).* Carnegie Mellon University, Software Engineering Institute. Retrieved from http://www.sei.cmu.edu/reports/00tr023.pdf

Humphrey, W. S. (2000b). *Introduction to the team software process.* Reading, MA: Addison-Wesley.

Humphrey, W. S. (2000c). Building productive teams. *Crosstalk. The Journal of Defense Software Engineering, 13*(6), 4–6.

Humphrey, W. S. (2002a). *Relating the Team Software Process SM (TSP SM) to the Capability Maturity Model for the Software (SW-CMM).* Software Engineering Institute.

Humphrey, W. S. (2002b). *Winning with software: An executive strategy.* Boston, MA: Addison-Wesley.

Humphrey, W. S. (2005). Why big software project fail: The 12 key questions. *CrossTalk. The Journal of Defense Software Engineering, 18*(3), 25–29.

Humphrey, W. S. (2006). *TSP: Coaching development teams.* Reading, MA: Addison-Wesley.

Humphrey, W. S. (2009). *The Watts New? Collection: Columns by the SEI's Watts Humphrey.* Carnegie Mellon University, Software Engineering Institute. Retrieved from http://www.sei.cmu.edu/reports/09sr024.pdf

Humphrey, W. S., & Thomas, W. R. (2010). *Reflections on management: How to manage your software projects, your teams, your boss, and yourself.* Retrieved from http://www.ebooksx.com/

Jain, M. (2009). *Delivering successful projects with TSP and Six Sigma: A practical guide to implementing team software process.* Retrieved from http://www.ebooksx.com/

Jorgensen, M., & Molokken, K. (2006). How large are software cost overruns? A review of the 1994 chaos report. *Information and Software Technology, 48*(4), 297–301. doi:10.1016/j.infsof.2005.07.002

Kirsch, L. J. (1997). Portfolios of control modes and IS project management. *Information Systems Research, 8*(3), 215–239. doi:10.1287/isre.8.3.215

Kraut, R. E., & Streeter, L. A. (1995). Coordination in software development. *Communications of the ACM, 38*(3), 69–81. doi:10.1145/203330.203345

Lederer, A. L., & Prasad, J. (1995). Causes of inaccurate software development cost estimates. *Journal of Systems and Software, 31*(2), 125–134. doi:10.1016/0164-1212(94)00092-2

Leveson, N. G., & Turner, C. S. (1993). An investigation of the Therac-25 accidents. *IEEE Computer, 26*(7), 18–41. doi:10.1109/MC.1993.274940

Mali, P. (1978). *Improving total productivity: MBO strategies for business, government and not-for-profit organizations*. New York, NY: John Wiley and Sons.

McDonald, M., Musson, R., & Smith, R. (2008). *The practical guide to defect prevention*. Retrieved from http://www.ebook3000.com/The-Practical-Guide-to-Defect-Prevention_66621.html

McHale, J., & Wall, D. S. (2005). *Mapping TSP to CMMI*. Carnegie Mellon University, Software Engineering Institute. Retrieved from http://www.sei.cmu.edu/reports/04tr014.pdf

Na, K., Li, X., Simpson, J. T., & Kim, K. (2004). Uncertainty profile and software project performance: A cross-national comparison. *Journal of Systems and Software, 70*(1-2), 155–163. doi:10.1016/S0164-1212(03)00014-1

Nasir, M. H. N. M., & Sahibuddin, S. (2011). Addressing a critical success factor for software projects: A multi-round Delphi study of TSP. *International Journal of the Physical Sciences, 6*(5), 1213–1232.

Naur, P., & Randell, B. (Eds.). (1969). *Software engineering: Report on a conference sponsored by the NATO Science Committee*. Belgium: NATO Science Committee. Retrieved from http://homepages.cs.ncl.ac.uk/brian.randell/NATO/nato1968.PDF

Nichols, W. R., Carleton, A. D., Humphrey, W. S., & Over, J. W. (2009). A distributed multi-company software project. *Crosstalk. The Journal of Defense Software Engineering, 22*(4), 20–24.

Nichols, W. R., & Salazar, R. (2009). *Deploying TSP on a national scale: An experience report from pilot projects in Mexico*. Carnegie Mellon University, Software Engineering Institute. Retrieved from http://www.sei.cmu.edu/reports/09tr011.pdf

Nidumolu, S. (1995). The effect of coordination and uncertainty on software project performance: Residual performance risk as an intervening variable. *Information Systems Research, 6*(3), 191–219. doi:10.1287/isre.6.3.191

Othman, M., Zain, A. M., & Hamdan, A. R. (2010). Review on project management and issues surrounding dynamic development environment of ICT project: Formation of research area. *International Journal of Digital Content Technology and its Applications, 4*(1). doi:10.4156/jdcta.vol4.issue1.10

Philip, T., Schwabe, G., & Ewusi-Mensah, K. (2009). *Critical issues of offshore software development project failures*. Paper presented at the Thirtieth International Conference on Information Systems, Phoenix, Arizona.

Rickets, C. A. (2005). A TSP software maintenance life cycle. *Crosstalk. The Journal of Defense Software Engineering, 18*(3), 22–24.

Robey, D. (2001). Blowing the whistle on troubled software projects. *Communications of the ACM, 44*(4), 87–93. .doi:10.1145/367211.367274

Rook, P. (1986). Controlling software projects. *Software Engineering Journal, 1*(1), 7–16. doi:10.1049/sej.1986.0003

RTI. (2002). *The economic impacts of inadequate infrastructure for software testing*. Research Triangle Park, NC: Author.

Sangwan, R., Mullick, N., Bass, M., Paulish, D. J., & Kazmeier, J. (2006). Critical success factors for global software development. In *Global software development handbook* (pp. 9-20).

Sauer, C., & Cuthbertson, C. (2003, April 15). The state of IT project management in the UK 2002-2003. *Computer Weekly*.

Schwalb, J. (2004, July). *Overview of the team software process & personal software process.* Paper presented at the Eight Annual PSM Users' Group Conference, Keystone, Colorado. Retrieved from http://www.psmsc.com/UG2004/Presentations/SchwalbJeff_PSMTSPBrief.pdf

Shellenbarger, S. (2000). To win the loyalty of your employees, try a softer touch. *The Wall Street Journal, 26*(1).

Smite, D., & Borzovs, J. (2006). A framework for overcoming supplier related threats in global projects. In Richardson, I., Runeson, P., & Messnarz, R. (Eds.), *Software process improvement* (*Vol. 4257*, pp. 50–61). Berlin, Germany: Springer. doi:10.1007/11908562_6

Standish Group International. (1995). *Chaos*. Standish Group International.

Standish Group International. (1999). *Chaos: A recipe for success*. Standish Group International.

Standish Group International. (2001). *Extreme chaos*. Standish Group International.

Standish Group International. (2009). *Chaos summary 2009: 10 laws of CHAOS*. Standish Group International.

Standish Group International. (2010). *Chaos summary for 2010*. Standish Group International.

Swartz, A. J. (1996). Airport 95: Automated baggage system? *ACM SIGSOFT Software Engineering Notes, 21*(2), 79–83. .doi:10.1145/227531.227544

Taylor, A. (2000). IT projects: Sink or swim. *The Computer Bulletin, 42*(1), 24–26. .doi:10.1093/combul/42.1.24

Trechter, R., & Hirmanpour, I. (2005). Experiences with the TSP technology insertion. *Crosstalk. The Journal of Defense Software Engineering, 18*(3), 13–16.

Webb, D. (2000). Managing risk with TSP. *Crosstalk. The Journal of Defense Software Engineering, 13*(6), 7–10.

Webb, D. (2002). All the right behavior. *Crosstalk. The Journal of Defense Software Engineering, 16*(9), 12–16.

Webb, D., & Humphrey, W. S. (1999). Using the TSP on the TaskView Project. *Crosstalk. The Journal of Defense Software Engineering, 12*(2), 3–10.

Wilson, D. (2010). *New TSP paths: System engineering team uses TSP to manage software test product development*. Paper presented at the TSP Symposium, Pittsburgh, PA. Retrieved from http://www.sei.cmu.edu/tspsymposium/2010/proceedings.cfm

Wiredu, G. O. (2006). A framework for the analysis of coordination in global software development. *Proceedings of the 2006 International Workshop on Global Software Development for the Practitioner, Shanghai, China*, (pp. 38-44). doi:10.1145/1138506.1138516

Zmud, R. W. (1980). Management of large software development efforts. *Management Information Systems Quarterly, 4*(2), 45–55. doi:10.2307/249336

Chapter 9
Software Process Improvement for Small and Very Small Enterprises

Mohammad Zarour
King Abdulaziz City for Science and Technology, Saudi Arabia

Alain Abran
École de Technologie Supérieure, Canada

Jean-Marc Desharnais
Boğaziçi University, Turkey

ABSTRACT

Software organizations have been struggling for decades to improve the quality of their products by improving their software development processes. Designing an improvement program for a software development process is a demanding and complex task. This task consists of two main processes: the assessment process and the improvement process. A successful improvement process requires first a successful assessment; failing to assess the organization's software development process could create unsatisfactory results. Although very small enterprises (VSEs) have several interesting characteristics such as flexibility and ease of communications, initiating an assessment and improvement process based on well-known Software Process Improvement (SPI) models such as Capability Maturity Model Integration (CMMI) and ISO 15504 is more challenging in such VSEs. Accordingly, researchers and practitioners have designed a few assessment methods to meet the needs of VSEs organizations to initiate an SPI process. This chapter discusses the assessment and improvement process in VSEs; we first examine VSEs characteristics and problems. Next, we discuss the different assessment methods and standards designed to fit the needs of such organizations and how to compare them. Finally, we present future research work perceived in this context.

DOI: 10.4018/978-1-61350-141-2.ch009

INTRODUCTION

The software industry has become an important economic activity in industrialized countries. Investments in this industry are in billions of dollars. In parallel, the number of software organizations has increased, varying in size, types of products produced and development processes used.

One of the important players in the software industry and world economy is organization with few employees. The majority of positions in the IT sector in industrialized countries are provided by small and very small organizations. Until the end of 1990s, it is mostly large organizations that have shown interest in improving their software processes using well-known SPI models. Unfortunately, models such as CMMI, ISO 15504 and others have not been adopted by small and very small organizations since their level of detail and comprehensiveness is more suitable for large organizations than small and very small organizations. Applying these models in such organizations leads to a number of challenges within a set of constraints; small and very small organizations which are fighting to survive and provide their customers with a working version of their products, must address daily challenges. These challenges leave organizations with little flexibility with respect to long-term planning. Small and very small organizations must be highly agile and reactive, and they have little control over longer lead times. Therefore, any process assessment conducted by such organizations and any improvement process they implement must also be agile, quick and inexpensive. Other challenges and problems will be discussed later on in the issues, controversies, and problems section; open issues will be also discussed in Future research directions.

BACKGROUND

Designing an improvement program for a software development process is a demanding and complex task. This task consists of two main processes: the assessment process and the improvement process. A successful improvement process requires first a successful assessment which identifies the exact weaknesses in the organization's software development process; failing to assess the organization's software development process could create unsatisfactory results.

Software processes assessment (SPA) can be used either to determine the capability of another organization, for subcontracting purposes, or to determine and understand the status of the organization's current processes to initiate an improvement process. Currently, several methods are available to assess the maturity and capability of a software development process based on well-known software process assessment and improvement frameworks such as CMMI and ISO-15504. The success of these assessment methods and improvement frameworks is supported by post-development studies on the validity, reliability and effectiveness of these methods. Unfortunately, many researchers consider that such methods are too large to implement in small and very small organizations. As a result, some researchers have studied process assessment and improvement in small and very small organizations and proposed assessment methods suitable to such organizations' needs, usually called lightweight SPA methods such as MARES, TOPS and FAME. These methods and others will be discussed in the solutions and suggestions section

There is no standard definition for small organizations size. The size is something relative, i.e. an organization having 100 employees considers another organization having 1000 employee as very large, while the organization having 1000 employee considers the organization having 100 employees as a small one, and perhaps will consider the organizations having 10 employees as "micro-organizations." So when discussing SPI in small and very small organizations we have, firstly, to define "what small and very small" mean to us.

In the Software Engineering Process Group conference (SEPG'98) on the Capability Maturity Model (CMM) and small projects held in 1998, small was defined as: three to four months of effort, among five or less staff (Hadden, 1998). (Orci & Laryd, 2000) have developed a dynamic model of CMM to be applied in small organizations, in which they made different classification for organizations based on size, and introduced new terms such as: eXtra small and eXtra eXtra small, Table 1 summarizes their classification.

Orci and Laryd believe that special conditions apply to organizations with one or two employees since it is easy to communicate between them and each one knows what the other is doing at certain time. The employees adding to the count are assumed to be development staff, management or marketing and sales, excluding administrative services and human resources staff. They classify such organizations as eXtra eXtra Small organizations. The organizations with 3-15 employees are classified as eXtra Small while organizations from 16-50 are considered to be Small ones.

Laporte and April (2005) discussed very small enterprises VSE as "any IT services, organizations and projects with between 1 and 25 employees." This definition has been adopted by the emerging standard ISO 29110 (ISO/IEC, 2010). In our discussion of SPI we concentrate on organization size rather than project size since none of the assessment work done for small organizations is made at the project level; assessments are made at the organization level. Moreover, the word project is not well-defined in the industry; as Paulk

wrote (Paulk, 1998) it could be "an hour project with one employee" or as defined by the Project Management Institute (PMI) (ANSI/PMI, 2004) a 3 year project with 40 employees.

The European Commission (European Commission, 2005) defined the small organizations as organizations that employ fewer than 50 persons, and whose annual turnover and/or annual balance sheet total does not exceed 10 million Euro" and Micro - "which employ fewer than 10 persons and whose annual turnover does not exceed 2 million euro."

Small and very small organizations form the majority of IT sector worldwide. In Europe, for instance, 85% of the Information Technology (IT) sector's companies have 1 to 10 employees. In the context of indigenous Irish software firms: 1.9% (10 companies) out of a total of 630 employed more than 100 people whilst 61% of the total employed 10 or fewer, with the average size of indigenous Irish software firms being about 16 employees (Coleman & O'Connor, 2008). In Canada, the Montreal area was surveyed (Laporte et al., 2005), and it was found that 78% of software development enterprises have less than 25 employees and 50% have fewer than 10 employees. In Brazil, small IT companies (less than 50 employees) represent about 70% of the total number of companies (Anacleto, Wangenheim, Salviano, & Savi, 2004b). The term "very small entity" had been defined by the ISO/IEC JTC1/SC7 Working Group (WG) 24 and subsequently adopted for use in the emerging ISO/IEC 29110 standard (ISO/IEC, 2010), as being "an entity (enterprise, organization, department or project) having up to 25 people."

MAIN FOCUS OF THE CHAPTER

Issues, Controversies, Problems

Small and very small organizations are encountering a number of problems when trying to adopt

Table 1. Organization sizes based on (Orci & Laryd, 2000)

Variant of "Small"	Number of People
XXS (eXtra, eXtra small)	1-2
XS (eXtra small)	3-16
S (Small)	16-50

an SPI approach, especially those approaches designed for large organizations. The main characteristics of this type of organizations are as follows (Varkoi & Makinen, 2000):

1. Flexible and fast to adopt new cultures.
2. Highly concentrated to their main business i.e. they have only a few products.
3. Lean organizations (some even without any administrative staff).
4. Extensively customer-oriented.
5. Undertaking small projects (typically 6-18 person months).
6. Networked with other small companies.
7. Dependant on skilful individuals.
8. Overloaded with work but enthusiastic.
9. With limited resources for business development or process improvement.

The main problems facing small as well as very small organizations are presented in the following paragraphs.

Financial Problems

Usually small and very small organizations are fighting to survive: they strive to provide the client with a working version of the software but without adequate funding to pay enough attention to the software quality and documentation processes. Hence, small organizations tend to be less focused on the process through which the software is written. A key reason for this unplanned software development process is that small organizations do not have enough financial support to cover the high cost of adopting an SPI approach. Adopting such an SPI approach is usually a costly process that also requires time, raising another problem which is the cost of time, i.e. small organizations suffer from the lack of financial support which is a major factor in improving their processes. Kautz (1998) has found that the external financial support is one of four critical success factors for SPI in small organizations.

Undefined Organizational Structure and Responsibilities

As an organization becomes larger, the need for Software Quality Management (SQM) becomes vital. SQM requires the creation of specialized teams or groups with specific responsibilities for designing, coding and testing. By doing so, the organization improve its control over the software development process.

Usually, large organizations and large software development projects are more likely to utilize SQM; the reason might be that larger organizations have more resources and therefore better possibilities for engaging in SQM (Kautz & Ramzan, 2001). Although SQM is as vital for small organizations as it is for large organizations, there is no evidence that SQM is utilized in small organizations as regularly as in large organizations (Kautz & Ramzan, 2001). For instance, there are no specialized teams in small organizations where the organizational structure is undefined and wide responsibilities are assigned to persons involved in the software development life cycle, as mentioned in (Ward, Laitinen, & Fayad, 2000): "The organizational chart, if one even exists, is delineated in broad, intuitive strokes and is composed of roles and responsibilities defined more by this week's crisis than by any reified notion of corporate structure."

Organizational Success is Based on Individual Skills

The lack of success of small organizations is related to talented people not working to a standardized development process: this is of course very risky for the survival of the VSEs. Knauber, Muthig, Schmid, and Widen (2000) have discussed the importance of these talented people in small organizations: "We found that one major factor to consider is the influence of a few key individuals— perhaps the company founder or those who play key roles because of their very strong skills."

Ward et al. (2000) has also indicated this critical factor when he said: "Small companies live and die on the engineering talent they are able to hire."

Long Term Return on Investment (ROI)

Richardson (2002) has stated that small organizations cannot make large investments in SPI and long term ROI, and suggests that having a fast ROI is one of the requirements in any SPI method designed for small organizations.

As a summary, the existing lightweight assessment models show some differences and similarities regarding their achievements and processes. A comparison between most of the lightweight assessments in terms of their achievements and processes is available in (Pikkarainen, 2006). Consequently, the following points summarize the findings regarding software process assessment.

1. From the literature review: most of the publications that discuss problems facing the SMEs, and VSEs when conducting SPI initiatives, mention the same points in terms of special organization structure, shortage of resources, cost and long term ROI associated with SPI initiatives. The severity of these problems becomes apparent as the organization's size becomes smaller.
2. The work in the SPI and SPA field either:
   a. Discuss the SPI and SPA implemented by large organizations where the comprehensive, heavy-weight assessment methods and improvement approaches are used.
   b. Discuss the lightweight SPA methods and improvement approaches to fit the needs of small and very small organizations.
3. Consequently, when discussing the assessment methods, one can recognize two main streams in this research field:

   a. Comprehensive or heavyweight assessment methods used mainly by large organizations.
   b. Tailored or lightweight assessment methods used by "non large organizations" including small and very small organizations.
4. Researchers of lightweight SPA methods usually alternate between small and medium size organization (SME) and very small organizations (VSE) during their discussion of the same SPA method which means that they do not differentiate between the needs and requirements of assessments used by SME or VSE organizations. Thus, the classification of assessments as comprehensive heavyweight SPA methods and tailored lightweight SPA methods is dominant.
5. The current research trend in software process assessment in SME is to provide different SPA methods without paying attention to objectively evaluating the success of such methods or to what degree these methods fulfil the requirements of engineering design principles.

For small and very small organizations, pursuing a software process improvement initiative (SPI) and discovering that its objectives have not been achieved is a significant waste of their limited resources. Pursuing an SPI initiative and failing is not uncommon: failures occur in two-thirds of initiatives where a CMM-based SPI has been pursued (Curtis, 1994). Moreover, these comprehensive and rigorous assessments, provided by well-known SPI approaches, are considered by many small hence by very small software development firms to be too expensive (Cater-Steel, 2004). Researchers in the SPI field have mentioned that the comprehensive SPI models, used mainly by large organizations, are difficult for small and very small organizations to use. For example:

1. Laryd and Orci (2000) believe that there is a need for models for small organizations: "The existing models for software process improvement, e.g. CMM, are overkill for several reasons, and moreover difficult to understand and comprehend for the management of small organizations."

2. Johnson and Brodman (1997) state: "The CMM largely reflects the software practices of large businesses and large software organizations; moreover, many of its practices are inappropriate to small projects, which are prevalent not only in small businesses and small software organizations but also in large businesses."

3. Kelly and Culleton (1999) are of the opinion that "smaller organizations often operate under different constraints compared to large organizations."

4. Laporte and April (2005) note that "ISO international standards were not written for small projects, small development organizations, or companies with between 1 and 25 employees, and are consequently difficult to apply in such settings."

5. Villalón et al. (2002) state: "Current software process improvement methods, i.e. ISO 15504, CBA-IP, are difficult to apply to small and medium-sized enterprises (SMEs) due to the cost, e.g. financial, time and recourses associated with their application."

These comments suggest that the barriers to assessment and improvement initiatives are much more challenging for small and very small organizations than for larger ones. This seems to be related to the structural, organizational, and managerial nature of small and very small organizations. These differences have motivated researchers and practitioners to investigate and design new assessment methods to meet the needs of small and very small organizations. These new methods are usually tailored from, and

conform to, the comprehensive methods used by larger organizations.

The tailored assessment methods are usually known as lightweight assessment methods. As a result of having many assessment methods, a question is usually raised by the organizations determined to initiate an assessment process: which assessment method is the most relevant to their needs? This question raises the need to have a comparison approach that defines the necessary criteria to compare between the different assessment methods and help organizations taking the decision of which assessment method is a suitable one for them, as will be discussed in the following sections.

SOLUTIONS AND RECOMMENDATIONS

The Tailored Lightweight Assessment Methods Available in 2010

The well-known SPI frameworks, as well as their related assessment methods, have been seen by many researchers as being too complicated to implement and require too much effort and cost (CETIC, 2006; FUNDP-CETIC–Software Quality Lab, 2006; Habra, Renault, Alexandre, & Lopez, 2002; Mäkinen, Varkoi, & Lepasaar, 2000; McCaffery, Taylor, & Coleman, 2007; Pettersson, Ivarsson, Gorschek, & Ohman, 2008; Rout, Tuffley, Cahill, & Hodgen, 2000; Wangenheim, Anacleto, & Salviano, 2004; Wangenheim, Varkoi, & Salviano, 2006). As a result, many researchers have studied process assessment and improvement in SME and VSE organizations and proposed assessment methods suitable for such organization's needs; such assessment methods are commonly known as Lightweight assessment methods. Examples of such lightweight assessment methods include the following:

MARES- A Methodology for Software Process Assessment in Small Software Companies

A Methodology for Software Process Assessment in Small Software Companies–the MARES model, has been built by researchers from the UNIVALI University and CenPRA research center in Brazil. MARES was designed to support process improvement in the context of small software organizations; considering their specific characteristics and limitations, this MARES model is built in conformity to ISO 15504 (ISO/IEC, 2003-2006). MARES enhanced the process assessment model mainly by integrating a context-process model in order to support the selection of relevant processes and a process-risk model to support the identification of potential risks and improvement suggestions. The MARES assessment method is divided into five main parts:

1. **Planning:** In this phase, the assessment is organized and planned; at the end of this phase the resulted assessment plan is revised and documented.
2. **Contextualization:** In this phase, the organization is characterized in order to understand its goals, products and software process. Questionnaires and interviews are used as a means to collect data.
3. **Execution:** The selected processes are assessed in detail.
4. **Monitoring and control:** All activities during the assessment are monitored and controlled. Corrective actions are initiated if necessary, and the plan is updated accordingly.
5. **Post-mortem:** Once the assessment is finished, a brief post-mortem session is held by the assessors to discuss and evaluate the performance of the assessment.

FAME–Fraunhofer IESE Assessment Method

FAME (Beitz, Emam, & Jarvinen, 1999) is a stand-alone assessment method which is based on the ISO 15504 (ISO/IEC, 1998) assessment method. The use of the FAME method aims to the following benefits (Hamann, Beitz, Müller, & Solingen, 2001):

1. Allows for the performance of either a SPICE, currently known as ISO 15504 standard, or a BOOTSTRAP Assessment;
2. Focuses on relevant business processes to guide process improvement efforts;
3. Provides a cost-efficient and reliable method to show a better return on investment for the improvement program;
4. Provides a tailorable approach for performing assessments;
5. Provides an approach that allows an organization to compare its results with similar businesses based upon ISO 15504;
6. Provides a method that is applicable for small to large organizations.

FAME contains supplementary added value elements that have been developed through practical experiences from the worldwide ISO 15504 trials and from Fraunhofer IESE research results. These added value elements are the business focus, efficiency, reliability and benchmarking.

TOPS–Toward Organized Process in SMEs

TOPS is a rapid software process assessment method created by Florence University in Italy, to promote innovation in IT small and medium enterprises. The TOPS method tries to find equilibrium between accurate results and low costs; this method is based on a two part questionnaire (Cignoni, 1999):

1. The first part is made by phone and is organized into five sections that collect general data about the enterprise, define company characteristics and information regarding regional industry survey to evaluate the knowledge of European initiatives to support enterprises in their SPI experiments;

2. The second part is the basis for the assessment and is compiled during a meeting with the enterprise. This part is organized into three sections: collecting general data about the software development unit; assessing the organizational and technological characteristics of the software development unit; and the assessment of software processes with respect to three specific processes including requirement analysis, verification and tests, and joint review. These processes are based on the ISO 15504 (ISO/IEC, 1998).

This approach restricts its assessment to three processes for time constraints, to provide more time for discussion. This method also avoids "the risk of difficult topics, as for instance configuration management, that may need explanation diverting the focus of meeting" (Cignoni, 1999).

RAPID–Rapid Assessment for Process Improvement for Software Development

RAPID, developed by the Software Quality Institute at Griffith University (Queensland, Australia), defines an approach to assessment that delivers consistent evaluations of process capability based upon an intensive investigation of the operations of the organization. The approach is based upon the following principles (Rout et al., 2000):

1. The assessment is conducted within a one-day timeframe.
2. The assessment is based upon an assessment model of limited scope, with a standard set of eight processes.

3. The competence and experience of the assessors is seen as of primary importance. A team of two assessors with experience in performing full-bodied assessments based upon ISO 15504. (ISO/IEC, 1998) is used for a RAPID assessment.

4. Data collection is limited to the single technique of moderated discussions by performers of the processes, the management team and other members of the organization.

5. Generation of ratings of capability is performed by a process of consensus-gathering involving all of the participants in the discussion, rather than by the judgment of the assessors. Restricting the assessment to a single day rather than a more intense three to four day assessment enables small organizations to participate in a process capability assessment. Most organizations are willing to invest a day of their time and resources.

The RAPID method employs a defined assessment model of restricted scope based upon, and compatible with, the Process Reference Model of ISO 15504-2. The model includes eight processes, including:

1. Requirements Gathering.
2. Software Development.
3. Project Management.
4. Configuration Management.
5. Quality Assurance.
6. Problem Resolution.
7. Risk Management.
8. Process Establishment.

Micro-Evaluation Assessment

The Micro-Evaluation assessment method is based on the OWPL assessment model (CETIC, 2006). The OWPL model has been developed based on the ISO 15504 model. The OWPL approach for software process assessment and improvement is known as the OWPL gradual framework. This gradual framework involves a series of gradual assessments (Alexandre, Renault, & Habra, 2006): a micro-evaluation, an OWPL-evaluation and a SPICE or CMM assessment. The nested assessments can be used either separately or in successive stages in the SPI process.

Micro-evaluation assessment is the first step in the gradual framework and is a simplified model designed to reduce costs as much as possible and to give a first look at the assessed organization. The purpose of this model is:

1. To make the assessed SME organizations aware of weaknesses as well as potential expected improvements;
2. To determine the priorities of subsequent stages of evaluation and improvement procedures.

This method is based on an interview with a person having sufficient knowledge of organizational activities through a questionnaire. The questionnaire covers six key processes, called axes, selected as the most pertinent and most important to the target organization. These axes are (Habra et al., 2002):

1. Quality assurance.
2. Customer's management.
3. Subcontractor's management.
4. Project management.
5. Product management.
6. Training and human resources management.

Although the Micro-Evaluation framework was initially developed for evaluating IT organizations in the Wallonia area in Belgium, a few other similar regions with a lot of similarities to Wallonia area have applied this framework. For example, in the province of Quebec in 2004, a research project was initiated at ETS called Amélioration de la Performance des Petites Entreprises Québécoises – APPEQ. The aim of this project was to help SME improve their quality, productivity and performance.

Express Process Appraisal (EPA) Assessment Methods

The Express Process Appraisal - EPA method (McCaffery, McFall, & Wilkie, 2005; Wilkie, McCaffery, McFall, Lester, & Wilkinson, 2007) was developed by the Centre for Software Process Technologies in the UK to assess software processes within SME organizations that have little or no experience in software process improvement programs. This method is conformant with the ARC 1.1 requirements for a CMMI class-C method. The designers of this EPA method selected the six most appropriate process areas (to software companies within Northern Ireland) at CMMI maturity level 2 since the justification for starting a process improvement exercise with these process areas was already well established, being present at the first level in the model. The following process areas were selected: Requirements Management; Configuration Management; Project Planning; Project Monitoring and Control; Measurement and Analysis; Process and Product Quality Assurance.

Software Process Improvement Initiation Framework–SPINI

SPINI is an ISO 15504 TR SPICE compatible assessment method (Mäkinen et al., 2000; Varkoi & Makinen, 2000). This method has been developed as part of the SataSPIN project which started in August 1998, to establish a software process improvement network (SPIN) in the Satakunta region in Western Finland. The core of the project was to help small and medium sized enterprises SMEs in the software business to develop their operations using international software process models.

The SataSPIN project tailored the SPI initiation phases according to the needs of the participating organizations. The SPI initiation framework consists of three steps:

1. First, the organization needs to understand the possibilities of SPI in achieving its business goals.
2. Second, the software processes are assessed.
3. Third, the SPI activities need to be planned and supported.

The assessment process has several steps including: holding start-up session, reviewing work product, holding assessment session of two hours on average, reporting results and finally, holding feedback session.

A Modular Software Process Mini-Assessment Method

The modular Mini Assessment MMA method has been developed at Kodak to fulfill the need of the SPI community in the company to have a common assessment method that uses a standard set of tools and procedures. The objective was to construct a mini-assessment architecture that could be tailored to each project's improvement objectives, life-cycle status, team size and time constraints (Wiegers & Sturzenberger, 2000).

The method consists of 8 main steps: planning, opening meeting, CMM orientation, questionnaire administration, questionnaire response analysis, participant discussions, findings generation and findings presentation.

S³ᵐ Mini-Assessment Method-S³ᵐᴬˢˢᵉˢˢ

S³ᵐ mini-assessment method (April, Abran, & Dumke, 2004; Paquette, April, & Abran, 2006) has been developed to assess software maintenance processes based on S³ᵐ model (April & Abran, 2008; April, Hayes, Abran, & Dumke, 2005). S³ᵐᴬˢˢᵉˢˢ was developed to obtain a reliable maturity rating for maintenance processes without

investing too much effort. Additionally, individual assessment components can be selected to focus the investigation on specific concerns and to scope the assessment and rating effort to a level relevant to software maintenance organizations.

A new version of the S³ᵐᴬˢˢᵉˢˢ as a mini-assessment method has been recently developed based on the research work of (Vincent, 2008), and a new assessment tool for S³ᵐᴬˢˢᵉˢˢ has been developed in (Tomaso, 2008).

Compare Different Lightweight Assessment Methods

When an organization decides to initiate an assessment process (either on their own or by hiring an external assessor), they must first figure out which of a number of different SPI assessment frameworks is the most relevant to them.

The available SPI models are comprehensive and contain detailed descriptions, and so it is a challenge to compare them. Halverson (Halvorsen & Reidar, 2001) has observed that "many people who work in the SPI domain have chosen one SPI framework as their favorite. This choice is mostly subjective and seldom based on objective evidence of appropriateness. A reason for this is that SPI frameworks are difficult to compare due to their comprehensiveness." A consequence of this is that comparing SPA assessment methods, which have been built based on these SPI frameworks, is also a difficult process. A comparison could be carried out from different points of view:

- **The author's point of view:** The author of a new assessment method would like to compare his method with other methods to determine the differences and similarities, as well as the way in which his method is aligned with other methods.
- **The organization's point of view:** Organizations with little SPI knowledge planning to conduct a self-assessment pro-

cess to evaluate the capability levels of their processes need to compare the various SPA methods currently available and choose one of them.

Moreover, some organizations may already be involved in an SPI process, but wish to use another SPA method. In such cases, a comparison of the available methods would be useful. This section investigates previous work on comparing SPI models and assessment methods, and proposes a framework for comparing assessment methods dedicated to small and very small organizations. A number of comparisons of several well-known SPI models, such as CMMI, ISO 15504 and ISO 9000, have already been performed. For instance:

- Detailed comparison of the CMM, ISO 9000 and the Malcolm Baldrige National Quality Award (MBA) (Tingey, 1997);
- Textual comparison of SPICE and ISO 9000 to show their differences also provides a mapping of the two standards (El-Emam, Drouin, & Walcélio, 1998);
- Comparison of ISO 9000 and the CMM (Paulk, 1995);
- Comparison of several lightweight process assessment methods for small companies (Anacleto, Wangenheim, Salviano, & Savi, 2004a); and
- Comparison of his proposed assessment method dedicated to small organizations to other lightweight assessment methods (McCaffery et al., 2005).
- Zarour, Desharnais, and Abran (2007) have proposed a comparison method dedicated to small and very small organizations. Appendix-A summarizes the result of comparing several lightweight assessment methods as in (Zarour et al., 2007).

Develop Standards Targeting the Needs of Small Organizations

The Mexican Standard

This standard has been developed at the request of the Ministry of Economy by the School of Sciences at the Universidad Nacional Autónoma de México. The Mexican standard consists of two main parts:

1. **MoProSoft:** A processes model that establishes the process requirements. This model incorporates best practices for management and software engineering. The organizations apply the MoProSoft by tailoring it to fit their needs in order to increase their capability to provide services with international levels of competitiveness.

2. **EvalProSoft:** Provides guidelines for processes assessment. It considers the activities of preparation for the assessment, planning, execution, generation and delivery of results. Closing and notification of the assessment results. The purpose of EvalProSoft is to provide the applicant organization a profile of the capability level of the implemented process into the organization, as well as a maturity level of the process capability. In the following sub-sections we consider these parts in more detail.

MoProSoft

The process model MoProSoft consists of three process categories: top management, management and operation which describe the organization structure. The MoProSoft uses a process pattern which is a framework of elements used to document each process in detail. The process pattern consists of three main parts:

1. **General Process Definition:** Identifies process's name, category, purpose, gen-

eral activity description, goals, indicators, quantitative objectives, responsibility and authority, sub-processes, related processes, inputs, outputs, internal products and bibliographical references.

2. **Practices:** Identify the roles involved in the process and the training required, describe activities in detail, associating them to process goals, present a work flow diagram, describe verifications and validations required, list products that are incorporated into the knowledge base, identify the infrastructure resources necessary to support activities, establish process measurements, as well as training practices, management of exceptional situations and use of lessons learned.

3. **Tailoring Guides:** Suggest process modifications that shall not affect its goals.

EvalProSoft

EvalProSoft grants the following to the applicant organization:

1. **Processes Capability level Profile:** A set of capability levels achieved by the processes into the evaluation scope; capability level is a 6 level ordinal scale (0-5).

2. **Maturity Level of processes capabilities:** Once all the processes in the process model are included in the evaluation scope, the organization is assigned a maturity level which is the maximum capability level achieved by all the processes evaluated.

The EvalProSoft can be used for one of the following purposes:

1. **Assessment to determine the process capabilities and the organizational maturity.** This is, when an organization asks a Certification Body for an assessment execution in order to obtain a capability level profile of the implemented processes and a maturity level of processes capabilities.

2. **Provider capabilities assessment.** The customer asks a certification body to assess the software development and maintenance provider. The customer chooses the processes to be assessed depending on the service to be contracted.

3. **Process capabilities self-assessment.** This is, when an organization performs an assessment by internal or external personnel. These personnel do not need to be a certified assessor.

ISO Standardization Work for VSEs

In 2005, ISO started a Working Group named WG24 to develop a set of standards and technical reports suitable to VSEs audience. WG24 has used the concept of ISO profiles (ISP – International Standardized Profile) in order to develop the new standard for VSEs entitled ISO 29110. As stated in (Laporte, Alexandre, & Renault, 2008) and from a practical point of view, a Profile is a kind of matrix that identifies precisely all elements that are taken from existing standards from those that are not. The overall approach followed by WG24 to develop this new standard for VSE consists of three steps:

- Select ISO/IEC 12207 process (ISO/IEC, 2008) subset applicable to VSEs of less than 10 employees
- Tailor the subset to fit VSE needs
- Develop guidelines

In order to develop the VSE profiles, WG24 analyzed international reference standards and models that could help subset ISO/IEC 12207 for low maturity VSEs. This include studying standards or models that could be tailored to fit the needs of VSEs e.g. MoProSoft which is a Mexican standard developed to assist Mexican small and medium enterprises (SMEs) has been selected in order to achieve this objective (Mexican Standard, 2005). Since the Mexican standard is not mainly dedicated to VSE, WG24 decided to tailor MoProSoft in order to address key characteristics of low maturity VSEs. The ISO 29110 series has five main documents defined as follows, (Laporte et al., 2008):

1. **Overview:** The first document, technical report (TR) TR 29110-1, introduces the major concepts required to understand and use the suite of documents. It introduces the business aspects, characteristics and requirements of VSEs, and clarifies the rationale for VSE-specific profiles, documents, standards and guides. It also introduces basic process, lifecycle and standardization concepts.

2. **Framework and Taxonomy:** The Framework and Taxonomy document (ISP29110-2) establishes the logic behind the definition and application of profiles. It specifies the elements common to all profiles (structure, conformance, assessment) and introduces the taxonomy of 29110 profiles.

3. **Assessment Guide:** This guide, TR 29110-3, describes the process to follow to perform an assessment to determine the process capabilities and the organizational process maturity. This is when an organization wants an assessment execution in order to obtain a process capability profile of the implemented processes and an organizational process maturity level. It is also applicable to the situation where a customer asks for a third-party assessment execution in order to obtain a capability level profile of the implemented process by the software development and maintenance provider. It is also suitable for self-assessment. The Assessment Guide is applicable to all profiles.

4. **Profile Specifications:** There is a profile specification document for each profile. Its purpose is to provide the definitive composition of a profile, provide normative links to the normative subset of standards (e.g. ISO/IEC 12207) used in profile, and provide informative links (references) to "input" documents (e.g. 90003, SWEBOK, PMI).

5. **Management and Engineering Guides:** The management and engineering guides provide guidance on its implementation and use or a profile. It is targeted at VSE (management and technical staff), VSE-related organizations (technology transfer centers, government industry ministries, national standards, consortiums and associations, academic use for training, authors of derived products (software, courseware, and acquirer and suppliers). There is one management and engineering guide document for each profile, identified as 29110-5.x, where x is the number assigned to the profile. This number matches the number assigned to the profile specification.

FUTURE RESEARCH DIRECTIONS

In the past few years, researchers have attempted to introduce software process assessment and improvement in small and very small organizations by proposing several assessment methods to initiate the improvement process. The current research focuses in proposing convenient and easy to use assessment methods without paying attention to some important issues which need farther research. These issues include:

1. The first issue is related to the efficiency and effectiveness of the current assessment and improvement approaches. Much of the research into this issue has been performed by consultants involved in their promotion (Card, 2004). To provide industry with objective and rigorous studies related to this issue, academic researchers should conduct more research into the efficiency and effectiveness of assessment and improvement approaches.

2. The second issue is related to repeatability and reproducibility of software process assessments. When conducting the same assessment with different groups, would the results be the same? Similarly, if an assessment with one group is conducted at different intervals, would the results be the same? What is the variation between the different assessment results and what is the acceptable range of such variations? These and other related questions should be addressed thoroughly.

3. The third issue is related to the validity of a software process. Viewing software development as a process has helped in identifying the different dimensions of software development and the problems that need to be addressed in order to establish effective practices (Fuggetta, 2000). Accordingly, several research initiatives have investigated different areas related to the software model, including software process modeling and support, process improvement and related measures and empirical studies. Unfortunately, and as a result of the complex nature of the software process, the literature on software process related areas has not yet provided a full understanding of the nature of the software process. Such an understanding is vital before pursuing further research to evaluate the software process. The need for such understanding has been highlighted by (Gray & Smith, 1998): "Full understanding of the nature of the software process should be in place before and to underpin the design of process evaluation schemes. It is the case that process assessment methods are here before the required understanding." Despite the amount of results produced so far in increasing the quality and effectiveness of software development processes, software process research is undergoing a crisis that is visible through a number of symptoms (Fuggetta, 2000):

a. Most technologies developed by the software process community have not been transferred into industrial use.

b. The number of papers on software process modeling and technology presented at conferences and published in journals is decreasing.

c. There is an increasing feeling that the community is unable to produce innovative and effective contributions: (Fuggetta, 2000) concluded that these crises in the software process emphasize the need to rethink the adopted approach in studying and supporting software processes.

d. The fourth issue is related to the data acquisition mechanisms used in software process assessment methods. SPA methods employ questionnaires to conduct the assessment. Unfortunately, questionnaires are problematic in the sense that questions can have semantics with different interpretations by different participants. One of the consequences of this problem is the impact on the repeatability of the assessment results as discussed in the second issue. Ambiguity and inconsistency in the interpretation of questions is currently the norm in practice augmenting the subjectivity on the part of auditors (Gray & Smith, 1998).

Consequently, these research issues for assessment and improvement in general are not only valid and raised for small and very small organizations, but also are still valid for SPI in large organizations.

CONCLUSION

Small and very small organizations play important role in the IT industry worldwide: such organizations employ the majority of employees in the IT sector. As software quality increasingly becomes a subject of concern, the software process assessment and improvement to produce such products become crucial.

Heavyweight assessment methods and well-known SPI models are difficult to implement in small and very small organizations. Consequently, researchers and practitioners have developed several assessment methods that fit the needs of such organizations to initiate their SPI programs. International standards organizations (e.g. ISO) has also give attention to develop standards to meet the needs of small organizations.

Several methods are also available to compare between the different assessment methods for small and very small organizations which would help organizations choose the method that is suitable to their needs. Although the research and development of standards is advancing in the domain of small and very small organizations, more research is still needed to provide answers to the research issues which are still open.

REFERENCES

Alexandre, S., Renault, A., & Habra, N. (2006). OWPL: A gradual approach for software process improvement in SMEs. In *32nd EUROMICRO Conference on Software Engineering and Advanced Applications (EUROMICRO-SEAA'06)*, (pp. 328-335).

Anacleto, A., Wangenheim, C. G., Salviano, C. F., & Savi, R. (2004a). *A method for process assessment in small software companies.* Paper presented at the 4th International SPICE Conference on Process Assessment and Improvement, Portugal.

Anacleto, A., Wangenheim, C. G., Salviano, C. F., & Savi, R. (2004b). *Experiences gained from applying ISO/IEC 15504 to small software companies in Brazil.* Paper presented at the 4th International SPICE Conference on Process Assessment and Improvement, Lisbon, Portugal.

ANSI/PMI. (2004). *A guide to the project management body of knowledge (PMBOK guide)* (3rd ed.). Newtown Square, PA: Project Management Institute.

April, A., & Abran, A. (2008). *Software maintenance management: Evaluation and continuous improvement.* Hoboken, NJ: John Wiley & Sons, Inc.

April, A., Abran, A., & Dumke, R. (2004). *Assessment of software maintenance capability: A model and its architecture.* Paper presented at the IASTED Conference on Software Engineering, Innsbruck, Austria.

April, A., Hayes, J. H., Abran, A., & Dumke, R. (2005). Software maintenance maturity model (SMmm): The software maintenance process model. *Journal of Software Maintenance and Evolution: Research and Practice, 17*(3), 197–223. doi:10.1002/smr.311

Beitz, A., Emam, K. E., & Jarvinen, J. (1999). *A business focus to assessments.* Paper presented at the European Conference on Software Process Improvement.

Card, D. N. (2004). *Research directions in software process improvement.* Paper presented at the 28th Annual International Computer Software and Applications Conference (COMPSAC'04), Hong Kong.

Cater-Steel, A. P. (2004). *Low-rigour, rapid software process assessments for small software development firms.* Paper presented at the Australian Software Engineering Conference, ASWEC'04.

CETIC. (2006). *OWPL software process improvement for VSE, SME and low maturity enterprises Version 1.2.2.* Namur, Belgium: University of Namur, Software Quality Lab.

Cignoni, G. A. (1999). *Rapid software process assessment to promote innovation in SMEs.* Paper presented at the EUROMICRO'99, Milan, Italy.

Coleman, G., & O'Connor, R. (2008). Investigating software process in practice: A grounded theory perspective. *Journal of Systems and Software, 81*(5), 772–784. doi:10.1016/j.jss.2007.07.027

Curtis, W. (1994). *At the plenary session: Setting an agenda for measurement research and practice*. Paper presented at the 2nd International Symposium on Software Metrics: Bridging the Gap Between Research and Practice.

El-Emam, K., Drouin, J.-N., & Walcélio, M. (1998). *SPICE - The theory and practice of software process improvement and capability determination*. Los Alamitos, CA: Wiley-IEEE Computer Society Press.

European Commission. (2005). *The new SME definition*. Retrieved from http://ec.europa.eu/enterprise/policies/sme/facts-figures-analysis/sme-definition/index_en.htm

Fuggetta, A. (2000). *Software process: A roadmap*. Paper presented at the Conference on The Future of Software Engineering, Limerick, Ireland.

FUNDP-CETIC – Software Quality Lab. (2006). *OWPL software process improvement for VSE, SME and low maturity enterprises version 1.2.2*. University of Namur.

Gray, E. M., & Smith, W. L. (1998). On the limitations of the software process assessment and the recognition of a required re-orientation for global process improvement. *Software Quality Journal, 7*, 21–34. doi:10.1023/B:SQJO.0000042057.89615.60

Habra, N., Renault, A., Alexandre, S., & Lopez, M. (2002). *OWPL micro assessment*. Paper presented at the Software Quality Workshop, 24rd International Conference on Software Engineering ICSE, Orlando, Florida USA.

Hadden, R. (1998). How scalable are CMM key practices? *CROSSTALK: The Journal of Defense Software Engineering*, April, 18-23.

Halvorsen, C., & Reidar, C. (2001). *A taxonomy to compare SPI frameworks. Proceedings of the 8th European Workshop on Software Process Technology, Lecture Notes In Computer Science, vol. 2077,* Witten, Germany.

Hamann, D., Beitz, A., Müller, M., & Solingen, R. v. (Eds.). (2001). *International Workshop on Software Measurement*. Berlin, Germany: Springer-Verlag.

ISO/IEC. (1998). *ISO/IEC TR 15504, Information Technology - Software process assessment - Parts 1-9*.

ISO/IEC. (2004). *ISO/IEC 15504-1 Information Technology — Process assessment — Part 1: Concepts and vocabulary*.

ISO/IEC. (2008). *ISO/IEC 12207:2008, Information technology – Software life cycle processes*. International Organization for Standardization/International Electrotechnical Commission. Geneva, Switzerland: International Organization for Standardization (ISO).

ISO/IEC. (2010). *ISO/IEC DTR 29110-1: Software engineering - Lifecycle profiles for very small entities (VSE) -- Part 1: VSE profiles overview*. Geneva, Switzerland: International Organization for Standardization (ISO).

ISO/IEC. (2003-2006). *ISO/IEC 15504 Information Technology - Process assessment - Parts 1-5*.

Johnson, D. L., & Brodman, J. G. (1997, Winter 1997). Tailoring the CMM for small businesses, small organizations, and small projects. *Software Process Newsletter, 8*.

Kautz, K. (1998). Software process improvement in very small enterprises: Does it pay off? *Software Process Improvement and Practice, 4*(4), 209–226. doi:10.1002/(SICI)1099-1670(199812)4:4<209::AID-SPIP105>3.0.CO;2-8

Kautz, K., & Ramzan, F. (2001). *Software quality management and software process improvement in Denmark.* Paper presented at the 34th Hawaii International Conference on System Sciences, Maui, Hawaii, USA.

Kelly, D. P., & Culleton, B. (1999). Process improvement for small organization. *Computer, 32*(10), 41–47. doi:10.1109/2.796108

Knauber, P., Muthig, D., Schmid, K., & Widen, T. (2000). Applying product line concepts in small and medium-sized companies. *IEEE Software,* 88–95. doi:10.1109/52.877873

Laporte, C., Alexandre, S., & Renault, A. (2008). Developing international standards for very small enterprises. *IEEE Computer, 41*(3).

Laporte, C., & April, A. (2005, October 19-20, 2005). *Applying software engineering standards in small settings: Recent historical perspectives initial achievements.* Paper presented at the International Research Workshop for Process Improvement in Small Settings, Software Engineering Institute, Pittsburgh.

Laporte, C., Desharnais, J. M., Abouelfattah, M., Bamba, J. C., Renault, A., & Habra, N. (2005). *Initiating software process improvement in small enterprises: Experiments with micro-evaluation framework.* Paper presented at the SWDC-REK International Conference on Software Development, Rekjavick, Iceland.

Laryd, A., & Orci, T. (2000). *Dynamic CMM for small organizations.* Paper presented at the First Argentine Symposium on Software Engineering - ASSE 2000, Tandil, Argentina.

Mäkinen, T., Varkoi, T., & Lepasaar, M. (2000). *A detailed process assessment method for software SMEs.* Paper presented at the European Software Process Improvement SPI and Assessments (EuroSPI 2000).

McCaffery, F., McFall, D., & Wilkie, F. G. (2005). Improving the express process appraisal method. *PROFES, 2005,* 286–298.

McCaffery, F., Taylor, P., & Coleman, G. (2007). Adept: A unified assessment method for small software companies. *IEEE Software Special Issue of "SE Challenges in Small Software Organizations,* (pp. 24-31).

Mexican Standard. (2005). *NMX-059-NYCE-2005, Information Technology-Software-models of processes and assessment for software development and maintenance, part 01: Definition of concepts and products; Part 02: Process requirements (MoProSoft); Part 03: Guidelines for process implementation; Part 04: Guidelines for Process Assessment (EvalProSoft).* Mexico: Ministry of Economy.

Orci, T., & Laryd, A. (2000, Nov. 2000). *Dynamic CMM for small organisations - Implementation aspects.* Paper presented at the European Software Process Improvement Conference-EuroSPI 2000, Copenhagen, Denmark.

Paquette, D., April, A., & Abran, A. (2006). Assessment results using the software maintenance maturity model (S3M). *16th International Workshop on Software Measurement - (IWSM-Metrikom 2006),* (pp. 147-160).

Paulk, M. C. (1995). How ISO 9001 compares with the CMM. *IEEE Software, 12*(1), 74–82. doi:10.1109/52.363163

Paulk, M. C. (1998). *Using the software CMM in small organizations.* Paper presented at the Pacific Northwest Software Quality Conference and the Eighth International Conference on Software Quality.

Pettersson, F., Ivarsson, M., Gorschek, T., & Ohman, P. (2008). A practitioner's guide to light weight software process assessment and improvement planning. *Journal of Systems and Software, 81,* 972–995. doi:10.1016/j.jss.2007.08.032

Pikkarainen, M. (2006). *Agile assessment approach (based on the eight case experiences), Technical Report: D4.2_v1.0* (Technical Report): Technical Research Centre of Finland, VTT.

Richardson, I. (2002). SPI models: What characteristics are required for small software development companies? *Software Quality Journal, 10*, 101–114. doi:10.1023/A:1020519822806

Rout, T. P., Tuffley, A., Cahill, B., & Hodgen, B. (2000, June 10 - 11, 2000). *The rapid assessment of software process capability.* Paper presented at the First International SPICE Conference, Limerick, Ireland.

Tingey, M. O. (1997). *Comparing ISO 9000, Malcolm Baldrige, and the SEI CMM for software: A reference and selection guide.* Upper Saddle River, NJ: Prentice-Hall, Inc.

Tomaso, C. D. (2008). *Analyse de contexte et évolution d'un outil expérimental de support aux évaluations de la maturité des processus de la maintenance: S3mAssess. Unpublished Mémoire de maître.* Belgium: Facultés Universitaires Notre-Dame de la Paix Namur.

Varkoi, T., & Makinen, T. (2000). *Software process improvement initiation in small organisations.* Paper presented at the 3rd European Software Measurement Conference, FESMA-AEMES

Villalón, J. A., Cuevas, A. G., San Feliu, G. T., De Amescua, S. A., García, S. L., & Pérez, C. M. (2002). Experiences in the application of software process improvement in SMES. *Software Quality Journal, 10*(3), 261–273. doi:10.1023/A:1021638523413

Vincent, L. (2008). *Méthode d'évaluation des processus de la maintenance du logiciel. Unpublished Mémoire de maître.* Belgium: Facultés Universitaires Notre-Dame de la Paix Namur.

Wangenheim, C., Anacleto, A., & Salviano, C. F. (2004). *MARES - A methodology for software process assessment in small software companies. Technical Report: LQPS001_04E.* Brazil: LPQS - Universidade do Vale do Itajai.

Wangenheim, C., Varkoi, T., & Salviano, C. F. (2006). Standard based software process assessments in small companies. *Software Process Improvement and Practice, 11*(3), 329–335. doi:10.1002/spip.276

Ward, R. P., Laitinen, M., & Fayad, M. E. (2000). Thinking objectively - Management in the small. *Communications of the ACM, 43*, 113–116. doi:10.1145/353360.353377

Wiegers, K. E., & Sturzenberger, D. C. (2000). A modular software process mini-assessment method. *IEEE Software, 17*(1), 62–69. doi:10.1109/52.819970

Wilkie, F. G., McCaffery, F., McFall, D., Lester, N., & Wilkinson, E. (2007). A low-overhead method for software process appraisal. *Software Process Improvement and Practice, 12*(4), 339–349. doi:10.1002/spip.321

Zarour, M., Desharnais, J.-M., & Abran, A. (2007). *A framework to compare software process assessment methods dedicated to small and very small organizations.* Paper presented at the International Conference on Software Quality - ICSQ'07.

ADDITIONAL READING

Bae, D. H. (2007). *Panel: Software Process Improvement for Small Organizations.* Paper presented at the 31st Annual International Computer Software and Applications Conference (COMPSAC 2007).

Cater-Steel, A. (2002). *Process capability assessments in small development firms.* Paper presented at the IASTED 6th International Conference Software Engineering and Applications, Cambridge, MA, USA.

Cater-Steel, A., Toleman, M., & Rout, T. (2006). Process improvement for small firms: An evaluation of the RAPID assessment-based method. *Information and Software Technology, 48,* 323–334. doi:10.1016/j.infsof.2005.09.012

Cater-Steel, A. P. (2001). *Process Improvement in Four Small Software Companies.* Paper presented at the 13th Australian Software Engineering Conference (ASWEC'01).

Cater-Steel, A. P. (2004). *An Evaluation of Software Development Practice and Assessment-Based Process Improvement in Small Software Development Firms.* Grifth University, Queensland - Australia. Cepeda, S., Garcia, S., & Conway, J. *Using the CMMI in Small Organizations,* http://www.eng.uab.edu/ME/ETLab/HSC04/abstracts/HSC026.pdf.

Dangle, K. C., Larsen, P., Shaw, M., & Zelkowitz, M. V. (2005). Software process improvement in small organizations: a case study. *IEEE Software, 22*(6), 68–75. doi:10.1109/MS.2005.162

Demirors, E., Demirors, O., Dikenelli, O., & Keskin, B. (1998). Process Improvement towards ISO 9001 Certification in a Small Software Organization. *IEEE,* 435-438.

Desharnais, J. M., Laporte, C. Y., Stambollian, A., Zarour, M., Habra, N., & Renault, A. (2007, 12-16 February, 2007). *Initiating Software Process Improvement with a light model for Small Enterprise: Our Experience.* Paper presented at the 3rd International Workshop on Quality of Information and Communication Technologies, Havana - Cuba.

Desharnais, J. M., Zarour, M., & April, A. (2007, 12-16 February, 2007). *Very Small Enterprises (VSE) Quality Process Assessment.* Paper presented at the 3rd International Workshop on Quality of Information and Communication Technologies, Havana - Cuba.

Dybå, T. (2000). Improvisation in Small Software Organizations. *IEEE Software,* 82–87. doi:10.1109/52.877872

Dybå, T. (2003). *Factors of Software Process Improvement Success in Small and Large Organizations: An Empirical Study in the Scandinavian Context.* Paper presented at the 9th European software engineering conference held jointly with 11th ACM SIGSOFT international symposium on Foundations of software engineering, Helsinki, Finland.

Gong, B., He, X., & Liu, W. (2005). *A Process Improvement Framework and a Supporting Software Oriented to Chinese Small Organizations.* Paper presented at the International Software Process Workshop (ISPW 2005), Beijing, China.

Grünbacher, P. (1997). *A software assessment process for small software enterprises.* Paper presented at the 23rd EUROMICRO Conference '97.

Guerrero, F., & Eterovic, Y. (2004). Adopting the SW-CMM in a Small IT Organization. *IEEE Software, 21*(4), 29–35. doi:10.1109/MS.2004.3

Wangenheim, C., Weber, S., Hauckc, J., & Trentind, G. (2006). Experiences on establishing software processes in small companies. *Information and Software Technology, 48*(9), 890–900. doi:10.1016/j.infsof.2005.12.010

Wangenheim, C. G., Anacleto, A., & Salviano, C. F. (2006). Helping small companies assess software processes. *IEEE Software, 23*(1), 91–98. doi:10.1109/MS.2006.13

Wangenheim, C. G. v., Varkoi, T., & Salviano, C. F. (2005). *Performing ISO 15504 Conformant Software Process Assessment in Small Software Companies*. Paper presented at the EUROS-PI'2005, Hungary.

Zarour, M. (2009). *Methods to Evaluate Lightweight Software Process Assessment Methods Based On Evaluation Theory and Engineering Design Principles*. Montreal: Unpublished PhD, École de Technologie Supérieure, Université du Québec.

Zarour, M., Abran, A., & Desharnais, J. M. (2009). *Analysis of the Design of Software Process Assessment Methods from an Engineering design Perspective*. Paper presented at the Industrial Proceedings of the 16th EuroSPI2 Conference, Alcala de Henares, Spain, pp. 6.37 – 6.44.

Zarour, M., Abran, A., Desharnais, J. M., & Buglione, L. (2010). *Design and Implementation of Lightweight Software Process Assessment Methods: Survey of Best Practices*. Paper presented at the Proceedings of the 10th Software Process Improvement & Capability determination conference (SPICE 2010), Pisa (Italy).

KEY TERMS AND DEFINITIONS

These terms are based on the definitions in the ISO 15504 part 1 standard (ISO/IEC: 2004).

Assessment Sponsor: The individual or entity, internal or external to the organizational unit being assessed, who requires the assessment to be performed, and provides financial or other resources to carry it out.

Assessment Team: One or more individuals who jointly perform a process assessment.

Process: Set of interrelated or interacting activities which transforms inputs into outputs.

Process Assessment: A disciplined evaluation of an organizational unit's processes against a 'Process Assessment Model'.

Process Assessment Model: A model suitable for the purpose of assessing process capability, based on one or more Process Reference Models.

Process Capability Determination: A systematic assessment and analysis of selected processes within an organization against a target capability, carried out with the aim of identifying the strengths, weaknesses and risks associated with deploying the processes to meet a particular specified requirement.

Process Improvement: Actions taken to change an organization's processes so that they more effectively and/or efficiently meet the organization's business goals.

Process Improvement Programme: All the strategies, policies, goals, responsibilities and activities concerned with the achievement of specified improvement goals.

Process Improvement Project: Any subset of the process improvement programme that forms a coherent set of actions to achieve a specific improvement.

Process Improvement Sponsor: The individual or entity, internal or external to the organizational unit being assessed, who requires the process improvement to be performed, and provides financial or other resources to carry it out.

Process Reference Model: A model comprising definitions of processes in a life cycle described in terms of process purpose and outcomes, together with an architecture describing the relationships between the processes.

APPENDIX A

Note 1: the Not Available (NA) means that this piece of information was not available one conducting this comparison.

Note 2: SPM: Software Process Matrix is an assessment method which, unlike the other mentioned assessment methods, is based on Quality Function Deployment concepts QFD, rather than well-known models like the CMMI and ISO 15504

Table 2.

Criteria	MARES	TOPS	FAME	RAPID	SPM	EAP	Micro-Evaluation
Geographic origin/ Spread	Brazil	Italy	Germany	Australia	Ireland	Ireland	Belgium
Scientific origin	ISO 15504	ISO 15504	ISO 15504/ Bootstrap	ISO 15504	Quality Function Deployment	CMMI Compliant with the ARC 1.1	OWPL
Cost	Low	Low	NA	Low	Low	Low	Low
Development/ Stability	NA	NA	NA	Since 1999	Since 1999	Since 2003	Since 1998
Popularity	Regional	Regional	Regional	Regional	Regional	NA	Belgium/Quebec/France
Analysis techniques	Interview	Interview	Interview	Interview	Questionnaire	Interview	Short interview
Number of processes assessed	26	3	4	8	47 Process with 135 practices	6	6
Number of processes to be improved	2-3	3	4	8	Max. 10 practices	6	6
Assessed processes	Selected after identifying strengths and weakness based on SWOT analysis	ENG.2, ENG. 5, CUS. 4	ENG.2, ENG.3, ENG.4, ENG.5	CUS. 3, ENG.1, MAN.2, SUP.2, SUP.3, SUP.4, MAN.4, ORG2.1	Selected according to a prioritized list based on QFD calculations	1-Requirement Management 2-Configuration Management 3-Project Planning 4-Project Management 5-Project monitor & control 6-Process & Product QA	1. Quality Assurance 2. Customer Management 3. Supplier Management 4. Project Management 5. Product Management 6. Training and Human Resource Management
Tool support	NA	Paper forms	Data collection, analyses and rating tools	Paper forms	NA	Paper forms + data collection & analysis tools	Paper forms + Excel sheet
Assessment duration	1 day	Half a day	NA	1 day	NA	1 day	Half an hour
Public availability	Yes	Yes	No	No	NA	No	No

continued on following page

Table 2. continued

Guidance for process selection	Yes By using a contextualization phase	No	NA	No	NA	No	No
Support for identification of risk and improvement suggestions	Yes By using a risk management Phase	Partially supported	Partially supported	No	NA	Yes	Partially supported
Need for specific SE knowledge on the part of the company representative	No	Yes	Yes	Yes	NA	No	No

Chapter 10
Towards an Integrated Personal Software Process and Team Software Process Supporting Tool

Ho-Jin Choi
Korea Advanced Institute of Science and Technology, South Korea

Sang-Hun Lee
Korea Advanced Institute of Science and Technology, South Korea

Syed Ahsan Fahmi
Korea Advanced Institute of Science and Technology, South Korea

Ahmad Ibrahim
Korea Advanced Institute of Science and Technology, South Korea

Hyun-Il Shin
Korea Advanced Institute of Science and Technology, South Korea

Young-Kyu Park
Korea Advanced Institute of Science and Technology, South Korea

ABSTRACT

Personal Software Process (PSP) and Team Software Process (TSP) have been developed and used to help individual developers and teams make high-quality products through improving their personal and team software development processes. For the PSP and TSP practices, data collection and analysis of software metrics need to be done at fine-grained levels. These tasks are not trivial, requiring tool support. This chapter aims to discuss issues to building such a tool, and introduce our on-going endeavor towards an integrated PSP and TSP supporting tool. In particular, features of sensor-based automated data collection for PSP, utilization of Six Sigma techniques into PSP and TSP activities, and incorporation of electronic process guide will be paid attention.

DOI: 10.4018/978-1-61350-141-2.ch010

INTRODUCTION

Continuous process improvement has been regarded as a solid solution to make high-quality products at the personal and team levels as well as at the project and organization levels. The Personal Software Process (PSP) was developed to help individual developers make high-quality products through improving their personal software development processes. PSP provides a set of methods and practices to assist individual software developers to improve product and process quality such as defined and measurable process, size and effort estimation based on historical data, code and design review, precise designs, process quality measures, detailed plan, and earned value tracking. The Team Software Process (TSP) guides team members and managers in applying process principles to consistently produce high-quality products on planned schedule at the team level. In particular, the TSP, along with the PSP, supports process improvement in small organizations which have difficulty in applying the so-called "heavy" process as defined by the Capability Maturity Model Integration (CMMI) because of limited resources to adopt CMMI. Among these methods and practices, the measurement and analysis is a central and core practice in identifying process deficiencies and providing a focus on process improvements. Sets of historical project data are used to make a reliable estimate on effort and quality.

While the PSP was proved to be an effective way to improve the accuracy of effort estimation and to reduce defects (Abrahamsson & Kautz, 2002; Hayes & Over, 1997; Prechelt & Unger, 2001) the manual, paper-based data recording and process guide has been recognized as the major barriers in using the PSP process (Disney & Johnson, 1998; Johnson et al., 2003). Due to the high-overhead and context-switching problems of manual data recording, developers have difficulties in acquiring reliable data, which can lead to misguided analysis results. These problems can be overcome through an automated tool for col-

lecting the PSP data and analyzing the collected data. Since an automated tool cannot collect all necessary data, however, manual data recoding should still be supported as well because data errors can be decreased to a few items. To help developers collect more reliable and necessary data, it is therefore required to develop a tool that can support both automated and manual data collection activities. One of the research objectives in this chapter is to investigate ways to automate the data collection activities to support the PSP. To address the problems of context switching and recording overhead which exists in the manual, time-log recording technique as suggested by the original PSP, we have developed a PSP supporting tool, called *Jasmine*, which uses various software sensors built in the integrated development environment (IDE) to collect data semi-automatically. Then, we have further investigated a way to utilize speech sensor and other information to collect and reason about activity times, which is a crucial step to PSP time recording.

Another aim of our research is to take this PSP supporting tool and add features to support various activities to support the TSP, leading to an integrated PSP and TSP supporting tool. For this purpose, we have surveyed existing TSP supporting tools and compared their pros and cons. The results of the survey are presented in this chapter. Although our endeavor to build such an integrated PSP/TSP tool is still an on-going business, we have made a few achievements thus far. First, we have developed a framework to utilize Six Sigma techniques in the PSP and TSP practices to support process improvement activities at the individual and team levels. Six Sigma techniques in general provide statistical analysis and decision-making supports that can be employed for data analysis, continuous improvement, and process control. On the other hand, only a few analysis techniques have been suggested for the PSP and TSP practices. Deploying Six Sigma techniques within a PSP/TSP supporting tool, therefore, can become beneficial for quantitative analysis to identify high leverage activities, evaluate the effectiveness of process changes, quantify cost and benefits, and control process performance. Second, we have introduced the notion of electronic process guide (EPG) into the design of our PSP/TSP supporting tool to help developers follow the PSP and TSP practices. The original PSP and TSP define a set of processes and provide materials such as scripts, templates, and checklists in a paper-based form which has problems in the usability and maintenance. To allow easy navigation of the PSP process information and to enable storing additional information, we have developed an EPG that enhances the contents and usability of the paper-based process guide.

BACKGROUND

The PSP was developed to help developers make high-quality products through improving their personal software development processes. With consistent measurement and analysis activities that the PSP suggests, developers can identify process deficiencies and make a reliable estimate on effort and quality. Nevertheless, we have observed that many developers have difficulties in obtaining correct data which are crucial to various analyses of the PSP practice, mainly because of the overhead of context-switching in manual data recording. That is, one has to stop working in his/her own activity in order to look at the watch and record into the PSP template sheet the exact times of the beginning and the ending points of each activity (e.g., design, code, test, debug, etc.) and any interrupt (e.g., answering phone calls, checking emails, etc.). Or one sometimes forgets to check times at the right points but record "guessed" time durations of activities based on recalling his/her memory.

Some researchers have already shared our experience and developed tools such as Hackystat (Johnson et al., 2003) and PROM (Sillitti, Janes, Succi, & Vernazza, 2003) to help the developers

with the overhead of context-switching in manual data collection. These tools collect automatically some PSP data and provide various analyses on the data. Using these tools developers do not require additional effort in data collection, apart from installation and configuration of the sensors used. Sensors, attached to software development tools such as Eclipse, Microsoft Office, and JBuilder, are central to the automated data collection. A sensor collects unobtrusively low-level data (e.g., information on files that developers are editing, results of unit test executions) by monitoring application-generated events of a development tool. Then, it sends the low-level data to a server where the data are stored and analyzed.

Although Hackystat and PROM collect data automatically, all data necessary for the PSP analysis cannot be collected automatically. For example, the time data collected automatically from these tools are mostly associated with modification activities of software artifacts such as source files and design documents. That is, times spent on implementation or design activities are the ones to be collected automatically, but times spent on such offline activities as meetings, design reviews cannot be collected. There is no way to collect defects automatically in design, design review, or code review phases where developers manually find defects. Moreover, it is sometimes difficult to identify which phase of software development the collected time data belong to. Data on defects are usually collected by sensors attached to unit testing tools such as JUnit or bug reporting tools such as Bugzilla. However, the defect data collected as such do not include information on the times spent on finding and fixing the defects, the phases when they were injected, and their defect types. In this chapter we will introduce a PSP supporting tool called *Jasmine* which uses various software sensors in the development tools and utilize a speech sensor to collect and reason about activity times to be used for the PSP.

With the aim of having an integrated PSP and TSP supporting tool, we have surveyed existing

TSP supporting tools. In the software engineering community, tool support has been an issue for practicing the TSP. According to (Rombach, Munch, Ocampo, Humphrey, & Burton, 2008), an ideal TSP tool should facilitate data collection, data validation, communication and discussion among team partners, access to process material (e.g., forms, templates, scripts, tools), visualization of performance indicators (for the group and the individual), visualization of previous experiences (e.g., previous interviews with students in video format), defect management, and configuration management. Described below are the TSP supporting tools that we have surveyed.

- **Team Dashboard** (Software Process Dashboard, 2009): An open source tool available in the web. It provides functionalities such as data rollup/analysis, hierarchical planning, simultaneous top-down and bottom-up planning, real-time multi-project coordination, dependency tracking, customizable forms and reports, custom process workflows. Using this tool requires knowledge in PSP and TSP.
- **tVista** (tVista, 2009): An open source web application for undergraduate and graduate level students. It provides TSP data collection forms such as Inspection Report, Issue Tracking Log, Defect Recording Log, and TSP summary reports such as Defects Injected Summary, Plan Summary, Quality Plan. tVista is still in alpha stages with its framework established and two modules defined (Defect Tracking and Time Tracking).
- **Point** (Point, 2004): A tool developed by students to facilitate multiple teams using and managing data. It provides features like central management for multi projects, management for finished team and personal data, and real time consolidated data.
- **TSPi Workbook** (TSPi, 2010): An excel file which covers all the forms provided

by SEI. This tool is comparatively easy to use for those having extensive knowledge about TSP.

When adopting the PSP and TSP practices within an organization for process improvement, basically two approaches can be taken. One is top-down approach, where the effort is made to improve software process from organizational level to individual level. The other is bottom-up approach, where the effort is made from individual level to organization level. In the bottom-up approach, Six Sigma techniques can support software process improvement activities in the personal and team levels, then a software company can make use of these data to achieve process improvement at organizational level. Despite the fact that PSP provides data that can be analyzed by Six Sigma techniques, few cases exist for software companies actually to apply Six Sigma to help improve software process at an individual level by providing in-process feedback. In this chapter, we provide some guidance about which Six Sigma techniques can be used in the PSP and TSP processes.

Six Sigma is a quality improvement approach to enhancing organization's performance using statistical analytic techniques. Six Sigma aims to eliminate variability and defects which interfere with customer satisfaction and cost reduction. Six Sigma has been embodied in the management strategy for quality improvement to quantitatively evaluate organization's processes and to reduce process variability.

As part of our aim to develop an integrated PSP and TSP supporting tool, we have considered the option to implement an EPG to facilitate easy usage of the tool. A process guide is a reference document to help process participants understand and execute a given process, providing guidance of the process and other useful information (Kellner, Becker-Kornstaedt, Riddle, Tomal, & Verlage, 1998). Basic information of process guides are details regarding activities, artifacts, roles, and

Table 1. Comparison of TSP supporting tools

Tools → Criteria↓	Team Dashboard	Point	TSPi Workbook	tVista
Data Collection	Partially Automatic	Manual	Manual	Automatic
Data Validation	No	No	No	Info. not available
Statistical Analysis Tool	Some	No	No	
Communication/ Discussion among Team Members	No			
Access to Potential Materials (forms, template)	No	Partially	Partially	Yes
Visualization of Performance Indicators	Numeric mainly with some Graphs & Charts	Numeric only	Numeric only	Info. not available
Experience Repository	Database backup only	No	No	No
Defect Management	Yes	Yes	Yes	Yes
Configuration Management	Yes	Yes	No	Yes
Process guide/ User Manual	User manual Provided	No	1 page manual provided	Info. not available
User Friendliness	Minimal	Nominal	Nominal	Info. not available
Follow SEI provided forms and templates	Partially	Fully	Fully	Info. not available

relationships between them. Process guides are necessary for software process improvements where process knowledge transfer is crucial. Process guides traditionally were offered in a paper form, but it is said that they are not useful in their contents and layouts (Kellner et al., 1998). It is hard to navigate and search easily process information and to put related information together (e.g., an activity and its input and output artifacts) in paper-based process guides, because its layout is linear and static. Also, it is difficult to modify existing information or add new process information because it requires publishing a new edition of its process handbook. These problems of paper-based process guides can be mitigated by an EPG which provides a process guide using the web technology (Kellner et al., 1998; Scott, Carvalho, Jeffery, D'Ambra, & Becker-Kornstaedt, 2002). However, simply providing a process guide in forms such as PDF, Microsoft Word, or other electronic formats or converting the contents of a process guide into HTML is not treated as an

EPG. Basic requirements which an EPG should meet are as follows (Kellner et al., 1998).

- It should provide all information contained in a good paper process guide.
- It should provide hyperlinks, a graphical overview, and hierarchical activity decompositions for flexible navigation and easy access. Also, related information such as an activity and its associated artifacts should be linked together using hyperlinks.
- Each web page should contain so small manageable unit that process participants can easily understand and digest.
- All web pages should have the same basic structure in order to facilitate the usage.

PSP Supporting Tool

In this section, we present *Jasmine*–a PSP supporting tool that we have developed. Aiming at supporting personal process and quality management,

Jasmine provides capabilities to collect reliable data automatically and analyze the collected data. It also provides an EPG for the PSP guide for easy access, modification and addition of information.

Sensor-Based Automated Data Collection

Jasmine consists of two sub-systems, PPMT (Personal Process Management Tool) and PSPG/ER (PSP Guide/Experience Repository) as shown in Figure 1. PPMT supports project planning, earned value tracking, and quality management by facilitating data collection and analyses. It automates large parts of data collection to reduce the high overhead and context switching. It also provides various data analyses in forms of charts, graphs, or tables. In PSPG/ER, the EPG provides the PSP process guide in the web and the ER is used to store and share development experience which can be linked to the EPG contents.

PPMT is designed using a client-server architecture, where the client consists of sensors developed for automated data collection. The server provides all functionalities except automated data collection. It was implemented as a web application which interacts with users through

a web browser. The main components of PPMT are described as follows.

- **Sensor:** It is attached to a development-related application. It collects automatically data by monitoring the application and then sends the data to the PPMT Client.

- **PPMT Client:** The main functionality of the PPMT Client is to receive sensor data from the sensors and to send them to the PPMT Server. It plays a temporary storage for collected sensor data when it is not connected to the server, and sends them to the server when the connection to the server is re-established. If necessary, it can preprocess sensor data before sending them to the PPMT Server.

- **PPMT Server:** It provides most of functionalities for PPMT: manual data recording, data storage, data analyses, earned value calculation, and users/projects administration. The implementation is based on Java technologies (such as Java Servlet, JSP, Java Beans, and JDBC), and on Apache Tomcat to execute Java Servlets and JSP.

Figure 1. The architecture of Jasmine–the PSP supporting tool

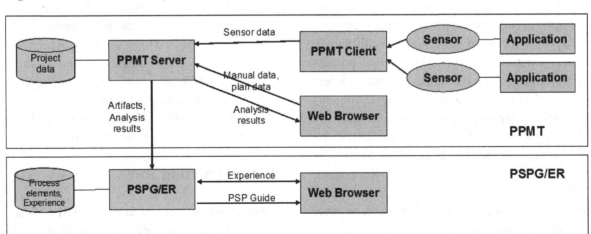

- **Database:** It stores the collected PSP data from sensors and manual recording such as time and defect logs, task and schedule plan data, and information on users/ projects. MySQL is used for the database implementation.

XML is used to send and receive sensor data among sensors, the PPMT Client, and the server. Its language-independent characteristic simplifies sensor data transmission because sensors are implemented using various programming languages.

To facilitate recording time, defects, and software size, PPMT provides a sensor-based automated data collection mechanism as in Hackystat and PROM. Time and defect data collected are recorded in the time and defect log respectively, which allows modification and insertion of the data when necessary. By monitoring software artifacts or tools, times spent on design, coding, review, and testing can be collected automatically. The current version of the Jasmine collects times spent on source code modification by monitoring continuously source files' size; manual testing of windows applications and web applications by monitoring mouse or key events occurred in the target application. An Eclipse sensor tracks Java source code modification and manual testing of a windows application executed in Eclipse. Testing web applications using Internet Explorer (IE) is tracked by an IE sensor. A set of consecutive time

data is stored as an item in the time log. Failed unit tests, bugs, compile errors and so on can be automatically collected as defects. Jasmine collects automatically failed unit tests, compile errors, and run-time errors, each of which is stored as a defect in the defect log. The Eclipse sensor collects the results of unit tests executed by JUnit, Java compile errors, and Java exceptions. As described in Table 2, information on removal phase, description, defect type, and found date are automatically recorded. Software size can be automatically collected as lines of code (LOC) measured by a line counting tool. The current implementation collects LOC measured by LOCC.

Support for Planning and Earned Value Tracking

Developers should make a detailed plan in the planning phase and track the progress with the earned value. In order to assist the project planning and tracking, PPMT provides forms to prepare the standard task and schedule planning templates, and automatically calculates the earned value of all planned tasks using planned data that a developer enters and actual data calculated from the recorded time log.

Data Analyses and Report Generation

PPMT provides various analyses over the collected data in forms of charts or tables. It reports

Table 2. Defect information of failed unit tests, compile errors, and runtime errors

	Failed unit tests	**Compile errors**	**Runtime errors**
Remove phase	"Test"	"Compile"	"Test"
Description	The stack trace of the exception	The description of the syntax error	The stack track of the exception
Defect type	The exception type	"Syntax"	The exception type
Found date	(automatic)	(automatic)	(automatic)
Inject phase	(manual)	(manual)	(manual)
Fix time	(manual)	(manual)	(manual)

a summary of analyses results. Available analyses include trend charts which show the trend of data over time and an earned value chart which displays the planed value, the earned value, and the predicted earned value over time. It also provides Pareto charts for defect analysis and quality measures such as process yield, A/FR (Appraisal to Failure Ratio), and phase ratio. Also, it can generate a weekly report which summarizes project data during a given week and a project report which summarizes project data during the whole period.

Comparative Analysis of Related Tools

Several PSP support tools have been developed such as Process Dashboard (Software Process Dashboard, 2009), Hackystat (Johnson et al., 2003), and PSPA (Sison, Diaz, Lam, Navarro, & Navarro, 2005) to help automatic data collection and analyses. Among those tools, Hackystat provides the most similar functionalities to Jasmine in that both tools provide sensor-based automated data collection. The primary difference between Jasmine and Hackystat lies in the goal that each aims for. Hackystat is a tool for data collection and analyses rather than a PSP supporting tool since it focuses on only automated data collection and analyses. Therefore, Hackystat does not support the other PSP activities such as planning, plan tracking, and estimation. It also provides the limited data analysis capabilities. This insufficiency of Hackystat is caused by not supporting manual data recording and not collecting automatically all necessary information of the PSP data. On the other hand, Jasmine aims for supporting the whole PSP activities. In Jasmine, the automatically collected time and defect data are recorded in the time and defect log respectively in order to allow developers to modify the data or insert necessary information to the data, which enables more various data analyses compared to Hackystat. Also, it provides an EPG for the PSP guide incorporating with an ER. While Jasmine does not support as many development tools as Hackystat does, it col-

lects automatically time spent on manual testing, compile and runtime errors which Hackystat does not collect. Jasmine would be easily extended to support various tools by reusing the Hackystat sensors, since Hackystat has been developed as an open source.

Activity Time Collection and Analysis Using Speech Sensor

An important aspect of the PSP practice is to keep track of the times spent on software development activities (known as PSP time recording log). A software developer can use this information to improve his performance in several ways. One can calculate the time difference between the actual times spent versus the planned times spent while doing some activity. One can also check if he/she is spending more time on certain activities than others. The times recorded can also be used to detect the interruption problem (Disney & Johnson, 1998). Despite these advantages of recording the time log, recording the time log itself is a major hurdle for the software developer. In order to keep the recorded times as accurate as possible, the PSP practice asks the developer to record the times right at the starting and the stopping points of any activity. Even if the user forgets to record the activity, the PSP practice suggests making the best guess about the activity start and ending times and recording that information. The difficulty in data recording is found to be main reason behind adaptation of PSP (Sison et al., 2005). The problem of recording the activity times exactly at the start or at the end is an overhead for the user. The user has to constantly keep in mind what activities he is doing and for each activity did he recorded the current activity start time, or previous activity end time. This practice of formally recording the activity at the start and at the end can interrupts the user thought process. Researchers have classified this problem as context switching and recording overhead problem (Johnson et al., 2003; Sison et al., 2005). To solve this problem, researchers have

Table 3. An example of user defined activities

Name	Description
Analysis	Working on requirement analysis
Architecture	Designing a Software architecture
Coding	Writing a source code
Debugging	Debugging a software
Design	Designing a Software
Documentation	Writing a documentation for the project
Lunch	Going on lunch
Presentation	Giving a project presentation
Report	Writing a project report
……	……

proposed sensor based automated time data collection techniques. Although sensors provide useful information about user activities but they cannot record the times for some activities which cannot be captured automatically. If the user is doing the activity "meeting" and not using any computer applications, for example, then that activity will not be automatically recorded. Moreover, information captured from the sensors cannot exactly tell what the user was actually doing at that time. For example, data from Microsoft Word can only tell that the user used this application from 9:00 to 10:00 AM, but they cannot tell whether the user was doing "documentation", "assignment", or "design" using the word processor.

We have investigated ways to deal with this problem, including a method of using speech sensor to record the user activity times. Assuming to have a mobile speech recognition device (e.g., a smart phone), our approach directs the user to speak the name of the activity (i.e., the registered "keyword" of the activity; see Table 3 for example) from time to time while he/she is performing that activity. Then, the speech recognizer will record the times for each activity. We envisage an intelligent temporal reasoning system so that the user does not need to tell the system the activity times punctually at the starting or ending moment of an activity, but spell the name of the activity at least

once during the activity. (Of course, the more times the user spells the name, the more accurately the system can infer the exact time during which the activity is performed.) We believe that this approach will give flexibility to software developers in that one needs not stop the current work and record the PSP time log. Instead, one just needs to spell the activity name to the speech sensor while continuing to work, thus reducing the overhead of context switching.

Since our goal is to free the software developers from the burden of keeping the time log punctually, we have assumed that the developer spells the activity name occasionally and irregularly any time during the activity. As a result, the time log recorded by the speech sensor lacks the exact record of the starting and ending points of the activities as illustrated by Table 4. For example, the log only shows that the "Design" activity was recorded three times but it does not tell exactly at which time the activity started or ended. Based on the partially "time-stamped" activities as recorded by the speech sensor, therefore, the system has to infer the actual durations of the activities recorded.

To facilitate the activity duration estimation, we consider some additional sources of information which are easily obtainable. Broadly, there are two kinds of additional information sources: those sources obtainable from sensors (other than speech sensors) and those sources obtainable from database (e.g., organizational and/or personal schedules). Sensors such as IDE sensors, OS sensors, etc. contain temporal information, so do the databases such as meeting schedule, project schedule, etc. The OS sensor records the current application a user is running. It records the title of currently active application on some delay basis (1 sec, 2 sec, etc.) and if there is no user activity for a certain period, say 5 min., it will stop recording. The schedule information provided by the database is assumed to contain definite start and end times of an activity. For the implementation of the speech sensor (Ibrahim &

Table 4. An example of time log recorded by speech sensor

UserID	ProjectID	Activity	TimeInstance	Date
Alice	Speech	Report	10:10:32	12/9/2008
Alice	Speech	Report	10:40:24	12/9/2008
Alice	Speech	Design	10:42:55	12/9/2008
Alice	Speech	Design	10:52:33	12/9/2008
Alice	Speech	Design	11:04:51	12/9/2008
Alice	Speech	Presentation	11:14:21	12/9/2008
Alice	Speech	Presentation	11:38:57	12/9/2008
Alice	Speech	Presentation	11:50:05	12/9/2008

Choi, 2009), we have used the third party library (i.e., Microsoft speech recognition API (Microsoft, 2008)). For the simplicity of experimentation, we assume that the speech sensor is noise free and will continuously run in the background such that it can record the user activity any time and provide more coverage than any other sensor since it can be implemented in a mobile phone environment.

PSP/TSP Supporting Tool

In this section we present a framework to guide how to use Six Sigma techniques can be used in the PSP and TSP practices. Then, we present the EPG functionalities of Jasmine that enhance the contents and usability of the paper-based process guide.

Using Six Sigma Techniques in PSP/TSP Supporting Tool

Six Sigma techniques are generally regarded as a useful means for process improvement, but there lacks a framework to guide where and how to use Six Sigma techniques for the PSP and/or TSP. In the Six Sigma community, no standard Six Sigma toolsets are defined but toolsets vary by approach, by company, and by organization. Some Six Sigma techniques such as Pareto analysis, scatter plot, and control chart are proven to be useful for software development. On the other hand, techniques such as DOE, MSE, and lean manufacturing have less applicability to software development. For selecting Six Sigma techniques suitable for PSP/TSP, we have considered various elements in the PSP and TSP process such as measures and estimation models. Then, Six Sigma techniques providing functionalities for analyzing these elements are included in our list. For example, defects data collected throughout the PSP/TSP process need to be prioritized to find most frequent defects, which will then be used to devise defect prevention strategies. In this case, Pareto analysis shall give the functionality for prioritizing defects types. Table 5 summarizes thirteen Six Sigma techniques we have selected for use in the PSP/TSP processes. In the table, the first column lists up the PSP/TSP elements necessary for effective and continuous process improvement, the second column how they should be analyzed, and the third column Six Sigma techniques providing corresponding functionalities.

It should be noted that some of the Six Sigma techniques are team-based, thus not applicable to PSP. They are affinity diagram, SQFD, Kano analysis and SWFMEA. As a result, Six Sigma techniques useful for PSP remain to include Pareto analysis, cause and effect diagram, control charts, ANOVA, two-sample t-test, scatter plots, correlation analysis, and regression analysis. On the other hand, all of the selected Six Sigma techniques are applicable to TSP.

Table 5. PSP/TSP elements and corresponding Six Sigma techniques

PSP/TSP Elements		Functions	Corresponding Six Sigma Tools
PSP/TSP measures	Defect measure	Prioritization of defects types to find most frequent defects	Pareto analysis
		Cause identification of defects	Cause and effect diagram
		Assessment of process stability	Control charts
	Other measures	Analysis of a relationship between measures	Scatter plots, correlation analysis, regression analysis
PROBE		Determination of goodness of "fit" of PROBE	ANOVA
Process		Documentation of process flow to make complex process easier to understand	Process mapping
customer needs		Requirements elicitation, prioritization, and analysis	Kano analysis, SQFD, affinity diagram
Estimation data		Determination of estimation accuracy	Two-sample t-test
Project risks		Risk assessment	SWFMEA

Figure 2. Association of Six Sigma techniques to PSP activities

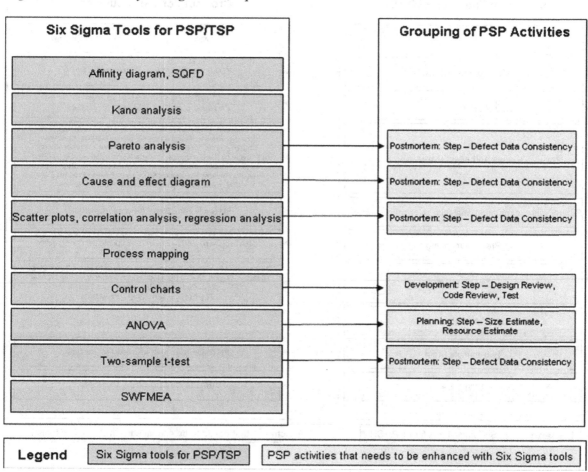

215

Based on this understanding, we have associated PSP and TSP activities with relevant Six Sigma techniques by grouping together those PSP/TSP activities which provide input data to the same Six Sigma technique. Figure 2 shows the result of grouping and association for the case of PSP, where the selected Six Sigma techniques are listed in the left and the associated PSP activities in the right. As shown in the figure, the Postmortem phase activities of PSP will get most benefits from various analysis techniques of Six Sigma, whereas process mapping technique of Six Sigma will not get applicability because PSP has no complex process to be documented visually by process mapping.

We have also performed similar analysis for TSP activities, and obtained the result shown as Figure 3, where the Six Sigma techniques are listed in the left and the associated TSP activities in the right. TSP is composed of many phases: Team Launch, Development Strategy, Development Plan, Requirements Development, Design, Implementation, Integration and System Test, and Postmortem. Each phase has 2 scripts, one for cycle 1 and one for cycle n. It should be noted that activities in cycle n are different from those in cycle 1; therefore, difference between two scripts should be taken into account when grouping TSP activities. As for TSP, all phases need to be enhanced by Six Sigma techniques. The Post-

Figure 3. Association of Six Sigma techniques to TSP activities

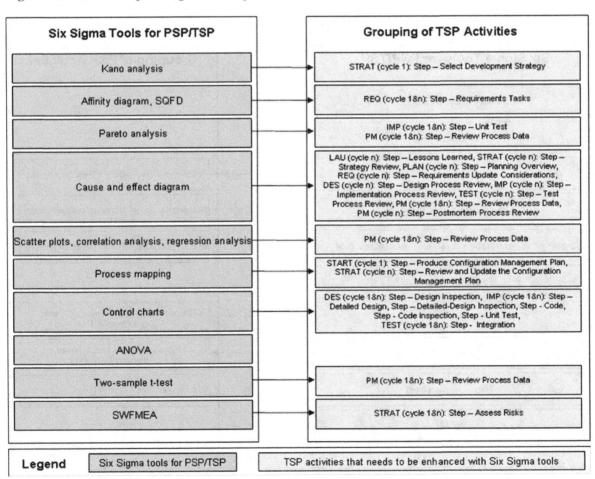

mortem phase activities will get most benefits, whereas ANOVA has less applicability since the use of linear regression is not part of TSP.

EPG Implementation for PSP/TSP Supporting Tool

As mentioned earlier, the problems of paper-based process guides can be mitigated by providing within the tool an electronic process guide, or EPG. However, simply providing a process guide in forms of PDF, HTML, or other electronic formats is not treated as an EPG. In addition to the basic requirements discussed earlier, an EPG should also contain process information such as examples of a document, personal annotation, or discussion, which leads to more general knowledge and experience management. As a result it is recommended to integrate an EPG with an experience repository (ER) (Kurniawati & Jeffery, 2004; Schneider & von Hunnius, 2003; Scott, Carvalho, & Jeffery, 2002). An ER is a system used to collect, structure, and reuse key management and development experience, and to make it quickly and easily accessible to users (Schneider & von Hunnius, 2003). An ER plays a crucial role in knowledge and experience management where past knowledge and experience is seen as resources to solve today's problems. Some works have been done to integrate an EPG with an ER. In (Kurniawati & Jeffery, 2004; Scott, Carvalho, & Jeffery, 2002), a successful implementation of coupling an EPG with an ER in a small organization is presented. In the combined tool, an experience entity is attached to its related process element for easy access to a large number of collected experience data. The idea to structure experience data to related process elements is also supported by (Schneider & von Hunnius, 2003), which proposes that a good experience repository should be organized to its related process.

In the case of our implementation, Jasmine has the PSPG/ER sub-system for this purpose (as shown in Figure 1). The main elements provided by PSPG are the PSP activities (e.g., planning, design, and design review), artifacts (e.g., task and schedule plan, project plan summary), and the PSP processes (e.g., PSP0, PSP0.1). The PSPG/ER homepage provides a single point access to the PSP processes. A number of activity and artifact pages provide the guides of the PSP activities and artifacts, respectively. Each activity page consists of a diagrammatic process flow and a description section (see Figure 4). The diagrammatic process flow shows a flow of activities highlighting the selected activity and supports fast navigation to other activities. The description section contains the description of the selected activity, links to its related artifact pages, and links to experience data associated to it. Each artifact page consists of a list of artifacts and a description section (see Figure 5). The list frame contains a list of all the artifacts which must be produced in the selected PSP process. The description section includes the description of the selected artifact, its templates, and links to experience data related to it.

The ER enables developers to collect development experiences gained from previous projects by following the PSP process and to share them among team members. To provide easy access to a number of collected experiences, they are structured according to relevant process elements. That is, developers should insert an experience data to its related activity or artifact page. For example, a document example should be linked to its related artifact page. Experience data are categorized into examples, generic experiences, and discussions: examples of an artifact are stored in the forms of files such as PDF, Microsoft Word, or other file formats, or HTML pages which are generated in PPMT; generic experiences can include any helpful information such as lessons learned, code fragments, and links to useful web pages; discussions allow developers to discuss process elements with other developers.

Figure 4. An example of an activity page

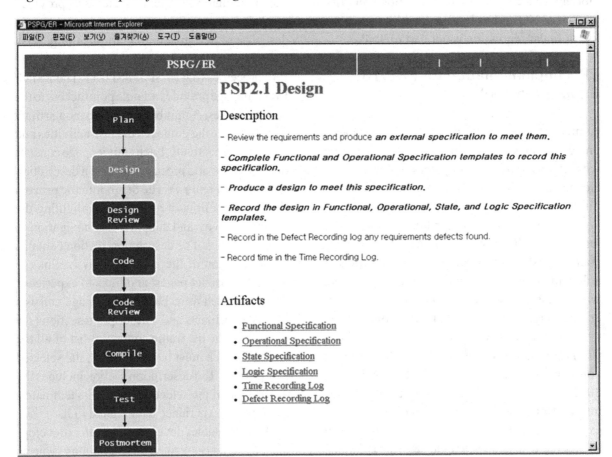

One of main features in PSPG/ER is to store examples of artifacts such as time logs, defect logs, and task/schedule plan. Examples can be stored in a HTML format which is produced in PPMT. Developers can store their artifacts such as time/ defect logs and task/schedule plan in an example category of a relevant artifact and their analyses results such as charts, tables, and reports in any experience category. This feature would make it easy to store development experience. Another way of interaction is to provide links to relevant pages. For example, the time log artifact page has a link to the time recording form of PPMT, and in reverse the form contains a link to the artifact page of PSPG/ER. This feature would allow developers to access easily relevant process information.

FUTURE RESEARCH DIRECTIONS

The PSP and TSP supporting tool we have built is yet to be further developed into a fully integrated system. Thus far, the major features discussed in this chapter have been developed rather separately without having an overall design of the entire system. That is, the Jasmine tool was developed first with emphasis on automated data collection using IDE sensors, from which we learnt the need for a mechanism to collect times for off-line activities, leading into the research of using speech sensors. Although substantial data can now be collected automatically using both IDE and speech sensors, we have not yet fully automate the time log recording required by PSP. The speech sensor-based time collection method has relieved the burden

Figure 5. An example of an artifact page

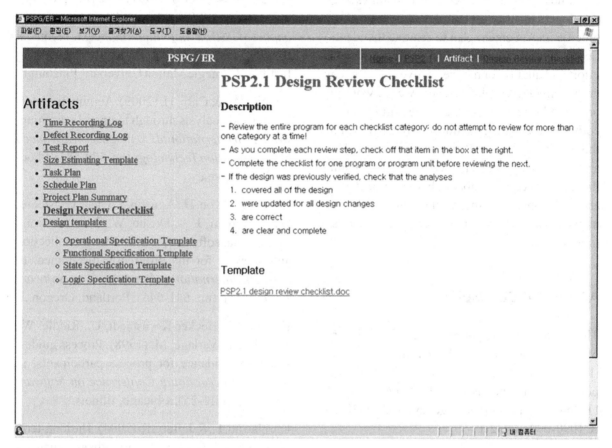

of context switching partially, because the user still has to "speak within the activity duration" to provide enough information to the temporal reasoning system. Alternative solutions to this problem need to be investigated further.

Another area of future research would be the issue of integrating the PSP/TSP tool into a process-centered software engineering environment (PSEE), namely a software development environment in which the processes used to produce and maintain software products are explicitly modeled in the environment (Garg & Jazayeri, 1995). After all, the goals of PSP and TSP are to help developers and teams enable a significant increase in both software productivity and quality, and these goals can only be achieved by cooperating with other teams and project managers, and process groups

in the organization. Thus, the usage of the PSP/TSP tool should be defined as part of PSEE.

CONCLUSION

This chapter has described our experience on developing a PSP and TSP supporting tool, and discussed major issues and the rationales behind our design. Especially, we have focused on the issues of sensor-based data collection, Six Sigma techniques for PSP and TSP activities, and incorporation of electronic process. Although not discussed in detail, Jasmine not only automates large parts of data collection to mitigate the problems of manual data recording, but also supports planning and plan tracking. It also provides various kinds of data analyses. These features help developers identify process deficiencies, make a process improvement plan to remove the identified deficiencies, and make a reliable estimate on effort and quality for more effective and efficient process management. Currently, we are working on extending the electronic process guide to incorporate the Six Sigma framework discussed in this chapter into the TSP supporting functionality, and providing more examples on TSP usage into the experience repository. This integrated PSP and TSP supporting tool would help developers understand the software development process more effectively.

ACKNOWLEDGMENT

This research was supported by the MKE (Ministry of Knowledge Economy), Korea, under the ITRC (Information Technology Research Center) support program supervised by the NIPA (National IT Industry Promotion Agency) (NIPA-2009-(C1090-0902-0032)).

REFERENCES

Abrahamsson, P., & Kautz, K. (2002). Personal software process: Classroom experiences from Finland. In *Quality Connection - 7th European Conference on Software Quality, Lecture Notes in Computer Science, vol. 2349* (pp. 175-185). Helsinki, Finland.

Disney, A. M., & Johnson, P. M. (1998). Investigating data quality problems in the PSP. *Software Engineering Notes, 23*(6), 143–152. doi:10.1145/291252.288292

Garg, P. K., & Jazayeri, M. (Eds.). (1995). *Process-centered software engineering environments*. Los Alamitos, CA: IEEE Computer Society Press.

Hayes, W., & Over, J. (1997). *The personal software process (PSP): An empirical study of the impact of PSP on individual engineers*. Technical Report SEI-97-TR-001, Software Engineering Institute, Carnegie Mellon University, Pittsburgh.

Ibrahim, A., & Choi, H. (2009). Activity time collection and analysis through temporal reasoning. In *the 11th International Conference on Advanced Communication Technology* (pp. 579-584). Phoenix Park, Korea.

Johnson, P., Kou, H., Agustin, J., Chan, C., Moore, C., & Miglani, J. ... Doane, W. (2003). Beyond the personal software process: Metrics collection and analysis for the differently disciplined. In *the 25th International Conference on Software Engineering* (pp. 641-646). Portland, Oregon.

Kellner, M., Becker-Kornstaedt, U., Riddle, W., Tomal, J., & Verlage, M. (1998). Process guides: Effective guidance for process participants. In *the Fifth International Conference on Software Process* (pp. 11-25). Chicago, Illinois.

Kurniawati, F., & Jeffery, R. (2004). The long-term effects of an EPG/ER in a small software organization. In *the 15th Australian Software Engineering Conference* (pp. 128-136). Melbourne, Australia.

Microsoft. (2008). *Developing speech applications*. Microsoft Speech Technologies. Retrieved June 2009, from http://www.microsoft.com/speech/

Point. (2004). *TSP tool development*. MSE Studio, Carnegie Mellon University. Retrieved June 2009, from http://dogbert.mse.cs.cmu.edu/mse2004korea/projects/point/index.html

Prechelt, L., & Unger, B. (2001). An experiment measuring the effects of personal software process (PSP) training. *IEEE Transactions on Software Engineering, 27*(5), 465–472. doi:10.1109/32.922716

Rombach, D., Munch, J., Ocampo, A., Humphrey, W., & Burton, D. (2008). Teaching disciplined software development. *Journal of Systems and Software*, *81*, 747–763. doi:10.1016/j.jss.2007.06.004

Schneider, K., & von Hunnius, J.-P. (2003). Effective experience repositories for software engineering. In *the 25th International Conference on Software Engineering* (pp. 534-539). Portland, Oregon.

Scott, L., Carvalho, L., & Jeffery, R. (2002). A process-centered experience repository for a small software organization. In *the Ninth Asia-Pacific Software Engineering Conference* (pp. 603-610). Gold Coast, Australia.

Scott, L., Carvalho, L., Jeffery, R., D'Ambra, J., & Becker-Kornstaedt, U. (2002). Understanding the use of an electronic process guide. *Information and Software Technology*, *44*(10), 601–616.

Sillitti, A., Janes, A., Succi, G., & Vernazza, T. (2003). Collecting, integrating and analyzing software metrics and personal software process data. In *the 29th EUROMICRO Conference* (pp. 336-342). Belek, Turkey.

Sison, R., Diaz, D., Lam, E., Navarro, D., & Navarro, J. (2005). Personal software process (PSP) assistant. In *the 12th Asia-Pacific Software Engineering Conference* (pp. 687-696). Taipei, Taiwan.

Software Process Dashboard. (2009). *The software process dashboard*. The Software Process Dashboard Initiative. Retrieved September 2009, from http://www.processdash.com/

TSPi. (2010). *Introductory team software process (TSPi)*. Software Engineering Information Repository, Software Engineering Institute, Carnegie Mellon University. Retrieved January 2010, from http://www.sei.cmu.edu/tsp/tools/tspi/

tVista. (2009). *Web application to support the team software process*. Open Source Software Engineering Tools. Retrieved September 2009, from http://tvista.tigris.org/

ADDITIONAL READING

Casallas, R., Osorio, L., & Lozano, A. (2005). The challenge of teaching a software engineering first course. In De Graaf, E., Saunders-Smits, G., & Nieweg, M. (Eds.), *Research and Practice of Active Learning in Engineering Education* (pp. 170–177). Amsterdam: Amsterdam University Press.

Ceberio-Verghese, A. C. (1996). *Personal Software Process: A User's Perspective*. Los Alamitos, CA: IEEE Computer Society Press.

Chrissis, M. B., Konrad, M., & Shrum, S. (2006). *CMMI(R): Guidelines for Process Integration and Product Improvement* (2nd ed.). Reading, MA: Addison-Wesley Publishers.

El Emam, K., Shostak, B., & Madhavji, N. H. (1996). *Implementing Concepts from the Personal Software Process in an Industrial Setting*. Los Alamitos, CA: IEEE Computer Society Press.

Humphrey, W. S. (1989). *Managing the Software Process*. Reading, MA: Addison-Wesley.

Humphrey, W. S. (1995). *A Discipline for Software Engineering: The Complete PSP Book*. Reading, MA: Addison-Wesley Publishers.

Humphrey, W. S. (1997). *Introduction to the Personal Software Process*. Reading, MA: Addison-Wesley Publishers.

Humphrey, W. S. (1997). *Managing Technical People: Innovation, Teamwork, and the Software Process*. Reading, MA: Addison-Wesley Publishers.

Humphrey, W. S. (2000). *Introduction to the Team Software Process*. Reading, MA: Addison-Wesley Publishers.

Humphrey, W. S. (2002). *Winning with Software: An Executive Strategy*. Boston, MA: Addison-Wesley Publishers.

Humphrey, W. S. (2005). *PSP: A Self-Improvement Process for Software Engineers*. Boston, MA: Addison-Wesley Publishers.

Humphrey, W. S. (2005). *TSP: Leading a Development Team*. Reading, MA: Addison-Wesley Publishers.

Ibrahim, A., & Choi, H. (2008). An approach for PSP time log processing. In *the Third International Conference on Convergence Information Technology* (pp. 676-679). Busan, Korea.

Ibrahim, A., & Choi, H. (2008). A framework for analyzing activity time data. In *the Fourth IEEE International Symposium on Service-Oriented System Engineering* (pp. 14-18). Jhongli, Taiwan.

Janieszewski, S., & George, E. (2004). Integrating PSP, TSP and Six Sigma. *Software Quality Professional, 6*(4), 4–13.

Johnson, P., Kou, H., Agustin, J., Zhang, Q., Kagawa, A., & Yamashita, T. (2004). Practical automated process and product metric collection and analysis in a classroom setting: lessons learned from Hackystat-UH. In *ACM-IEEE International Symposium on Empirical Software Engineering* (pp. 136-144). Redondo Beach, CA.

Kemerer, C. F., & Paulk, M. C. (2009). The impact of design and code reviews on software quality: An empirical study based on PSP data. *IEEE Transactions on Software Engineering, 35*(4), 534–550. doi:10.1109/TSE.2009.27

Macke, S. (1996). An Industry/Academic Partnership that Worked: An. In *Progress Report*. Los Alamitos, CA: IEEE Computer Society Press. doi:10.1109/CSEE.1996.491375

Pande, P., & Holpp, L. (2002). *What Is Six Sigma?* New York, NY: McGraw-Hill.

Pyzdek, T. (2003). *The Six Sigma Handbook: The Complete Guide for Greenbelts, Blackbelts, and Managers at All Levels, Revised and Expanded Edition*. New York, NY: McGraw-Hill.

Rupa, M., & Jiju, A. (2005). Confluence of six sigma, simulation and software development. *Managerial Auditing Journal, 20*(7), 739–762. doi:10.1108/02686900510611267

Shin, H., Choi, H., & Baik, J. (2007). Jasmine: A PSP supporting tool. In *IEEE International Conference on Software Process, Springer LNCS 4470* (pp. 73-83). Minneapolis, USA.

Syu, I., Salimi, A., Towhidnejad, M., & Hilburn, T. (1997). *A Web-Based System for Automating a Disciplined Personal Software Process (PSP)*. Los Alamitos, CA: IEEE Computer Society Press.

Towhidnejad, M., & Salimi, A. (1996). *Incorporating a Disciplined Software Development Process into Introductory Computer Science Programming Courses: Initial Results*. New York, NY: IEEE.

Van Duine, D. S. (2006, September). *Experiences integrating PSP and TSP with Six Sigma*. Presented at the meeting of the TSP Symposium 2006, San Diego, CA.

KEY TERMS AND DEFINITIONS

Data Collection: A process of collecting data as part of a process improvement to obtain information for making decisions about important issues.

Personal Software Process (PSP): A structured software development process to help software engineers understand and improve their performance by using a disciplined and data-driven procedure. PSP was created by Watts Humphrey, and "Personal Software Process" and "PSP" are registered service marks of the Carnegie Mellon University.

Process Improvement: A series of actions taken by an organization, by a team, or by an individual, in order to identify, analyze and improve existing processes to meet new goals or objectives.

Sensor: A device to measure a physical quantity and convert it into a signal that can be read by an instrument.

Six Sigma: A management strategy developed by Motorola for improving the quality of process output by removing the causes of errors in a business process.

Software Process: A structure of tasks or activities that take place during the development of a software product.

Team Software Process (TSP): A defined operational process framework to help teams of software engineers organize and improve the levels of quality and productivity of software development project. TSP was created by Watts Humphrey, and "Team Software Process" and "TSP" are registered service marks of the Carnegie Mellon University.

Chapter 11
Benefits of CMM and CMMI–Based Software Process Improvement

Maged Abdullah
University of Malaya, Malaysia

Rodina Ahmad
University of Malaya, Malaysia

Lee Sai Peck
University of Malaya, Malaysia

Zarinah Mohd Kasirun
University of Malaya, Malaysia

Fahad Alshammari
University of Malaya, Malaysia

ABSTRACT

Software Process Improvement (SPI) has become the survival key of numerous software development organizations who want to deliver their products cheaper, faster, and better. A software process ultimately describes the way that organizations develop their software products and supporting services; meanwhile, SPI on the other hand, is the act of changing the software process and maintenance activities. This chapter purposefully describes the benefits of software process improvement. The Capability Maturity Model (CMM) and the Capability Maturity Model Integration (CMMI) are briefly surveyed and extensively discussed. Prior literature on the benefits and impacts of CMM and CMMI-based software process improvement is also highlighted.

DOI: 10.4018/978-1-61350-141-2.ch011

INTRODUCTION

A new set of ideas on how to enhance the productivity and quality in software development organizations has emerged over the last decade under the term of Software Process Improvement (SPI) (Aaen, Arent, Mathiassen, & Ngwenyama, 2001). SPI has become the survival key of numerous software development organizations who want to deliver their products cheaper, faster, and better. A software process ultimately describes the way that organizations develop their software products and supporting services. Processes define what kind of steps the software development organizations should undertake at each phase of production and provide assistance in making good effort and schedule estimates, measuring quality, and developing plans (Gerry & Rory, 2007). Rico (2004) defines the software process improvement as "an approach to designing and defining a new and improved software process to achieve basic business goals and objectives." SPI is simply the act of changing the software process and maintenance activities. The aims are normally to decrease costs, increase efficiency, and also to increase profitability. For instance, SPI could be employed to create a new and enhanced process for software development organizations.

There is a widespread belief that a good software product is a result of mature and repeatable software processes, which have led to more focus on SPI to assist software development organizations realize its potential benefits. Thus, the search for new methodologies, ideas and innovations to enhance software development continues to be an essential focus for both academic and industrial research. In order to improve software development practices, many attempts have concentrated on defining, measuring, and monitoring development activities in an effort to identify and verify improvement areas. These attempts have led to the emergence of the term Process Model. A Process Model is defined as "a structured collection of practices that describe the characteristics of

effective processes" (SEI, 2007). An organization can define a process improvement priorities and objectives and make its processes capable, stable, and mature by the help of a process model. Moreover, a process model provides a guideline for an organization to realize its current state; also to identify relevant improvement activities and to identify how to start these activities (SEI, 2007).

Effort spent in this area has resulted in several SPI models and standards such as Personal Software Process (PSP), Team Software Process (TSP) (Humphrey, 1995), ISO 9001 (Paulk, 1995), Six Sigma (Pyzdek, 2003) and the Carnegie Mellon Software Engineering Institute's Capability Maturity Model for Software (SW-CMM) (Paulk, Weber, Curtis, & Chrissis, 1995) and its most recent version, the Capability Maturity Model Integration (CMMI) (Chrissis, Konrad, & Shrum, 2007). The motivation for selecting CMM and CMMI as the base of this chapter is that they are influential, long-standing, and often-studied standard to SPI (Staples & Niazi, 2008). Moreover, CMMI-based SPI has led to quantifiable enhancement in how processes of software engineering are performed (Bollinger & McGowan, 2009). According to Jones and Soule (2002), among the software process improvement frameworks, CMMI became a standard model with high rate of acceptance.

This chapter is organized as follows; a brief introduction of software process improvement is introduced in Section 1. Section 2 describes the benefits of software process improvement. The Capability Maturity Model (CMM) and the Capability Maturity Model Integration (CMMI) are briefly surveyed in Section 3. Section 4 extensively discusses numerous prior literatures on the benefits and impacts of CMM and CMMI-based software process improvement. Section 5 gives a summary of this chapter. Finally, Section 6 presents our conclusions and recommendations.

BENEFITS OF SOFTWARE PROCESS IMPROVEMENT (SPI)

SPI is significant because it is the primary means by which a new and enhanced software development process is created. This is done in order to achieve important economic benefits at the least costs. Research shows that well designed software development process has a positive impact on the economic performance of software projects. Performance is usually measured in terms of productivity as well as the efficiency of the cost (Rico, 2004). On the other hand, poorly designed software development processes have negative consequences on the economic performance of software projects because poor software development process results in high operations cost, ineffective use of available resources, and lost opportunities in the market. According to Rico (2004), poorly designed processes result in a lack of quality and reliability, and poor customer satisfaction. That is why "Software Process improvement has emerged as an important paradigm for managing software development" (Ravichandran & Rai, 2003).

There are several benefits of that can be gained from the adoption of one or more SPI models or standards. As seen in Figure 1, Gibson, Gold-enson, and Kost, (2006) described the effect of process improvement. It is used in this chapter for CMM and CMMI-based software process improvement; anyhow, the same depiction can be applied anywhere else. The left box illustrates the cost of process improvement. Some of these might be some planned investments for process improvement; others might be expenses indirectly or directly related to process improvement. Process capability and organizational maturity are shown in the upper center box. Organizations enhance their processes in order to achieve other benefits, and they use process capability and organizational maturity to compare and evaluate their results. The box on the right hand side illustrates different categories of benefits that organizations most frequently struggle to attain as a result of their efforts in process improvement. Also a combination of the costs and benefits can be done to calculate Return on Investment (ROI) or some related measures, as shown in the bottom center box of the Figure 1.

As shown in Figure 1, potential benefits of process improvement may be achieved and classified in six categories; cost, schedule, productivity, quality, customer satisfaction, and the return on investment (ROI). According to (Gibson et al., 2006), enhancement in the above six categories

Figure 1. High-level model of CMMI impact (Gibson et al., 2006)

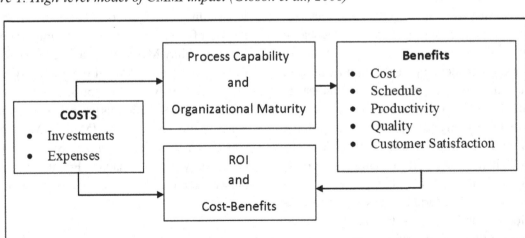

Table 1. Description of the six performance category

Category	Description
Cost	The cost category covers instances where organizations report changes in the cost of final or intermediate work products, changes in the cost of the processes employed to produce the products, and general savings attributed to model-based process improvement. It also includes increased predictability of costs incurred and other measures of variation.
Schedule	This category covers improvements in schedule predictability and reductions in the time required to do the work.
Productivity	This category includes various measures based on the amount of work accomplished in a given period of time.
Quality	Improvement in product quality is most frequently measured by reductions in numbers of defects.
Customer Satisfaction	This category generally includes changes based on customer surveys. Award fees also are sometimes used as surrogate measures.
Return on Investment	In addition to benefit-to-cost ratios, this category includes companion measures of net present value, internal rate of return, payback periods, and break even points.

can participate to further business goals, such as, reduced productivity time, lower cost for products, and higher quality.

Organizations typically seek to adopt some combination of the five basic categories of benefits which are shown in the box on the right hand side; any of the five benefits can be refined to include a variety of more particular measures. For example, an organization might be more concerned in decreasing the costs of its services and products while another organization might be interested in having more reliable predictable project costs, effort, or schedules. The above six categories of performance will be the primary focus of this chapter and it is described in Table 1.

OVERVIEW ON CMM AND CMMI

The Capability Maturity Model (CMM)

The Capability Maturity Model (CMM) focuses on the various processes involved in software development. It presents the key elements of an effective software process in describing an evolutionary improvement path for software organizations from ad hoc, immature processes to mature disciplined one (Paulk et al., 1995). It was created

and developed by attentive observations of best practices in both software and non software organizations. The framework is thus based on actual practices while reflecting the best of the state of the practice as well as the needs for individuals performing software process improvement and software process appraisal (Paulk et al., 1995).

The Software Engineering Institute (SEI), at Carnegie Mellon University has released the Software Capability Maturity Model (SW-CMM) in 1991 as a model for enhancing the organization's software processes capabilities, and it is widely used by software organizations. The Capability Maturity Model is a staged evolutionary model. It categorized software process maturity into five levels; Level 1 (Lowest) to Level 5 (Highest), and a set of 18 Key Process Areas (KPA). The organization must demonstrate a capability in a certain number of KPA's assigned to a specific Level in order to be rated at that level. At different maturity levels, key process areas can be used for assessing the capability of existing processes as well as for identifying the area that need to be strengthened so as to move the process to a higher level of maturity. The five maturity levels of CMM are Initial, Repeatable, Defined, Managed, and Optimized.

Since (SW-CMM) was released, it was applied to number of areas; therefore, several capability maturity models have been provided. These included people CMM (P-CMM) (Curtis, Hefley, & Miller, 1995), system engineering CMM (SE-CMM) (EPIC, 1995), the software acquisition CMM (SA-CMM) (Cooper & Fisher, 2002), and the integrated product development CMM (IPD-CMM) (SEI, 1996). As these different models were built by deferent organizations, there were an overlapping in the application's scopes in addition to the lack of consistency in the terminology, assessment approach, and architecture. These problems led to increase the time and cost to adopt multiple models. Therefore, the Software Engineering Institute, SEI, has released in 2000 the Capability Maturity Model Integration (CMMI) in order to integrate all existing capability maturity models. On August, 2000, (CMM) was replaced by a new process model, which is the Capability Maturity Model Integration (CMMI). The Capability Maturity Model Integration (CMMI) was created to reduce redundancy, to support product and process improvement, and to eliminate undesired inconsistency that experienced by organizations that are using multiple models. The CMMI join all relevant process models found in CMM into one product suite (SEI, 2007).

The Capability Maturity Model Integration (CMMI)

CMMI can be described as a group of optimum practices collected from the previous experiences with the preceding CMM, and other models and standards. CMMI defies how influential process must look like. It offers the practitioners with a suitable framework so that enhancement activities can be defined and organized. Moreover, CMMI enables the organization to deal with multi-disciplined activities and to easily combine process improvement aims with organizational business goals (SEI, 2007). The CMMI's product suite consists of process improvement models, training materials, and appraisal methods. Its models cover several disciplines, which are System Engineering (SE), Software Engineering (SW), Supplier Sourcing (SS), and Integrated Product and Process Development (IPPD) (Chrissis et al., 2007).

The Process Areas

The term Key Process Area (KPA) in CMM has been replaced with Process Area (PA) in CMMI model. PA is "a cluster of related practices in an area that, when implemented collectively, satisfies a set of goals considered important for making significant improvement in that area" (Chrissis et al., 2007). In CMMI there are 22 process areas, divided into four categories of process management, project management, Engineering and support.

Choosing a Representation

In CMMI, there are two CMMI models that can be selected for implementation by an organization, Staged and Continuous representation.

Staged Representation

The process areas in staged representation of CMMI are organized into five levels of maturity, which are: Initial (Maturity Level 1, ML1), Managed (Maturity Level 2, ML2), Defined Maturity Level 3, ML3), quantitatively managed (Maturity Level 4, ML4), and Optimizing (Maturity Level 5, ML5). According to Chrissis et al. (2007), the staged representation "prescribes the order for implementing each process area according to maturity levels, which define the improvement path for an organization from the initial level to the optimizing level."

Continuous Representation

The CMMI continuous representation provides the same process areas like the staged representation. However, no process area is allocated to a certain maturity level. The continuous representation grants software firms the flexibility to choose any process area they want to enhance and enable them to choose the order that meet their business objectives or reduces development risk. To measure the achievement of a certain process area for an organization, the continuous representation offers six capability levels, which are: Initial (Capability Level 0, CL 0), Performed (Capability Level 1, CL 1), Managed (Capability Level 2, CL 2), Defined (Capability Level 3, CL 3), Quantitatively managed (Capability Level 4, CL 4), and Optimizing (Capability Level 5, CL 5). The continuous representation offers organizations the flexibility to improve various processes at various rates. As an example, the organization may want to achieve CL 2 in a certain process area and CL 4 in another one.

The term "Maturity Level" is only belongs to staged representation and denotes to an organization's *overall* Process capability and organizational maturity, whereas the term "Capability Level" is only belongs to continuous representation and denotes to an organization's process improvement achievement for *each* process area (Kulpat & Johnson, 2008).

LITERATURE REVIEW ON THE BENEFITS OF CMM AND CMMI-BASED SPI

Much has been discussed on the benefits of increasing organizational process maturity levels as well as the impact and benefits of CMM and CMMI-based software process improvements as surveyed in the two subsequent sections.

Benefits of CMM-Based SPI

Numerous case studies in the SW-CMM have showed benefits from increasing organization's process maturity (Isacsson, Pedersen, & Bang, 2001; Keeni, 2000, Kuilboer & Ashrafi, 2000;

Pitterman, 2000; Russwurm & Meyer, 2000; Krasner, 1999; Yamamura, 1999; Diaz & Sligo, 1997; Velden, Vreke, Wal, & Symons, 1996; Deephouse, Mukhopadhyay, Goldenson, & Keller 1996; Haley, 1996; Wohlwend & Rosenbaum, 1994b). Also researchers showed that software organizations adopting the CMM-based SPI tend to have higher quality software, higher development productivity, accurate predictability, and a faster schedule (Humphrey, Snyder, & Willis, 1991; Lipke & Butler 1992; Dion, 1993). Based of an investigation of 31 historical projects, the benefits of the SW-CMM adoption were studied with two primary measures (cost and schedule) which were extracted from U.S. Air Force contracts (Flowe, Lawlis, & Thordahl, 1996). The results of that investigation revealed that projects with more capable and mature processes typically perform much better in term of both cost and schedule performance in compared to those with lower levels of process maturity. Herbsleb and Goldenson (1996) showed solid evidence, in a sample of 61 software organizations, that high CMM-based software process maturity is associated with high performance.

Another survey-based study of individuals from SW-CMM-assessed software organizations revealed that higher maturity organizations is associated with better performance, including the ability to meet budget and schedule, and increase staff productivity, product quality, and customer satisfaction (Goldenson & Herbsleb, 1995). According to Diaz and Sligo (1997), each CMM level enhances the quality of the product and generally reduces the development schedule. They reported that the process maturity level also has some effect on software development schedule by indicating how software process improvement helped Motorola. Based on some measurements, Motorola's software development schedule was around eight times faster at CMM level 5 than at CMM level 1. A study analyzing the development of 30 software products revealed that high software process maturity is positively associated with high software quality (Harter & Slaughter, 2003).

El Emam and Goldenson (2000), in an comprehensive review of studies and publications on the implementation of SPI methodologies, including CMM, reported qualitative performance improvements in terms of, higher quality, higher productivity, improved ability to meet development schedules, and higher customer satisfaction.

In his PhD dissertation, Clark (1997) has reported "the motivation behind the CMM is that a mature software development process will deliver the product on time, within budget, within requirements, and of high quality." He also used six mathematical models to determine the extent that CMM process maturity affects software development effort with the presence of some other factors. He conducted his work by the aid of 112 historical data which completed in 1990, and his results demonstrated that on level change in organizational process maturity results in a 15% to 20% increase in effort reduction. Based on this improvement, Clark proved that process maturity has a great effect on software development effort, and a measure of process maturity should be included in all software cost estimation models. He reported that the positive effects of process maturity are 1) a net saving in effort due to reduction in rework produced by implementing most CMM's key process areas (KPAs); 2) positional high saving in effort for some KPAs such as Peer Review process area. He also indicated that many KPAs are overlapped and should be considered in a certain implementation sequence to take the advantage of this overlap. Girish, James, and Klein (2007) conducted an empirical study to investigate the effects of the CMM on two critical factors in information systems (IS) implementation strategy, which are project performance and software quality. They claimed that CMM levels are associated with IS implementation strategies and higher CMM levels are relate to higher project performance and software quality. This would lead to noticeable

reduction in software development effort and schedule. Manish and Kaushal (2007) focused exclusively on CMM level 5 software projects from several organizations to investigate the effects of highly matured processes on development effort, quality, and schedule. Based on historical data projects from 37 CMM level 5 of four software development organizations and by using a linear regression model, they found that high process maturity levels reduce the impacts of factors that were believed to affects software development quality, effort, and schedule such as personnel capability, requirements volatility, and requirements specifications. They also claimed that the only factor found to be important in determining effort, schedule, and quality was the software size. On the average, their developed models estimated effort and schedule around 12% and defects to about 49% of the actuals, across organizations. In general, their results indicated that some of the biggest advantages from high levels of organizational process maturity come from the obvious reduction in variance of software development outcomes that were previously caused by some factors other than size of the software. In a 2004 article, Jiang, Klein, Hwang, Huang, and Hung examined the relationship between CMM-based SPI activities and project performance. From the responses of 154 software project developers, the results revealed that CMM-based SPI is positively associated with project performance.

In order to explore the impact of process maturity on software development effort, and based on CMM with the aid of 161-project sample, Clark (2000) isolated the effects on effort of process maturity versus effects of other factors, and found that an increasing of one organizational process maturity level can result in a reduction in software development effort by 4% to 11%. But this reduction seemed like a generalization across all five levels of CMM process maturity, i.e. the percentage of effort reduction is not the same among all levels. Despite several researches and case studies have shown many benefits of enhancing organizational process maturity by using different assessment approaches (Humphrey et al., 1991; Herbsleb, Carleton, Rozum, Siegel, & Zubrow, 1994; Wohlwend & Rosenbaum, 1994b; Butler, 1995; McGibbon, 1996), none of them attempts to isolate an individual factors that affect productivity like what Clark did when he separated the impacts of process maturity on development effort versus other factors. Nevertheless, they indicated that increasing organizational maturity levels will generally have some considerable effects. Donald, Krishnan, and Slaughter (2000) have conducted an empirical research to find out the relationship between quality of the products, organizational process maturity, development effort, and project schedule for a set of 30 software products in software development firms. Their findings indicated that process maturity has an effect in reducing software development schedule and effort. Diaz and King (2003) claimed that increase in CMM process maturity results in an improvement in for quality, phase containment, productivity and rework. Herbsleb, Zubrow, Goldenson, and Paulk (1997) showed that organizations with high maturity levels have "excellent" or "good'" ratings in a number of project performance dimensions such as the ability to stay within budgets, ability to meet schedules, etc. Recently, a review study of seventeen published articles, Galin and Avrahami (2006) explored CMM-based benefits such as defects, rework, schedule, productivity, error defection effectiveness, and return on investment (ROI), concluding that a good investment in CMM programs leads to enhanced software development and maintenance.

Benefits of CMMI-Based SPI

Despite numerous studies which have investigated the performance assessment results of CMM-based software process maturity and its impact on software development effort and schedule, there are still very limited works on the overall CMMI-based software process maturity (Huang,

Sheng, Ching, & Tsen, 2006). (SEI, 2007) reported several benefits of the CMMI-based process improvement, which include:

- Enhanced schedule and budget estimation.
- Enhanced cycle time.
- Increased productivity.
- Enhanced the product's quality.
- Increased the customer satisfaction.
- Enhanced employee morale.
- Increased return on investment.
- Decreased proposed cost of quality.

Case studies have also shown benefits from CMMI-base SPI (El Emam, 2007; Liu, 2007; Sapp, Stoddard, & Christian, 2007; Peter & Rohdi, 2007; Garmus & Iwanicki, 2007; McGibbon, Grader, & Vienneau, 2007; Gibson et al., 2006; Huang et al., 2006; and Goldenson & Gibson, 2003). Unlike previous studies in the literature that addressed the benefits of CMMI-based software process maturity and in terms of six performance dimensions of Customer, Finance, Quality, Process, Organization, and Employee, Huang et al. (2006) considered performance assessment for both tangible and intangible benefits of CMMI adoption. They presented the results of performance assessment of the CMMI-based Software process improvement based on an empirical study from 18 software firms in Taiwan, which have already obtained CMMI maturity level 2 and 3 certifications. They argued that their empirical study revealed that the CMMI-based software process improvement generally has a positive effect on the six performance dimensions in their investigated software firms but some assessment items do not revealed an important improvement.

Goldenson and Gibson (2003) reported some great and credible quantitative evidence that Capability Maturity Model Integration CMMI-based software process improvement can help an organization achieve higher quality products and better project performance with lower cost and decreased project schedule. The reported

Table 2. Summary benefits and impact from CMMI adoption–Cost

#	Results	Organization
1	33% decrease in the average cost to fix a defect	Boeing, Australia
2	20% reduction in unit software costs	Lockheed Martin M&DS
3	15% decrease in defect find and fix costs	Lockheed Martin M&DS
4	4.5% decline in overhead rate	Lockheed Martin M&DS
5	Improved and stabilized Cost Performance Index	Northrop Grumman IT1

results were drawn from a set of 12 cases from 11 independent firms. Most of the case studies mentioned in this report are provided by organizations that are adopting the CMMI Product Suite. Their results are categorized into four basic categories: cost, schedule, quality, and customer satisfaction. Only the cost and schedule categories are shown here since it is the most relevant to this research. Table 2 summarizes, according to Goldenson and Gibson's results (2003), the benefits and impact of CMMI-based software process improvements from the Cost perspective. The cost category "covers instances where organizations report reductions in the cost of final or intermediate work products, reductions in the cost of the processes employed to produce the products, and general savings attributed to model-based process improvement" (Goldenson & Gibson, 2003).

Table 3 summarizes the results of Goldenson and Gibson (2003) in terms of the benefits and impact of CMMI-based software process improvements from the Schedule perspective. The sched-

ule category "covers two aspects of schedule: improvements in schedule predictability and reductions in the time required to do the work" (Goldenson & Gibson, 2003).

Since the performance results provided by Goldenson and Gibson (2003) are limited, Gibson et al. (2006) continued the assessment performance of CMMI-based software process improvement and provide empirical tangible evidence about the performance results that can achieved as a outcome of CMMI-based process improvement. They reported "There now is ample evidence that process improvement using the CMMI Product Suite can result in marked improvements in schedule and cost performance, product quality, return on investment, and other measures of performance outcome." Results are drawn from a variety of small and huge organizations around the world. They reported that most of their results come from higher maturity organizations, but some notable enhancements also have been achieved by lower maturity organizations. In their

Table 3. Summary benefits and impact from CMMI adoption– Schedule

#	Results	Organization
1	Reduced by half the amount of time required to turn around releases	Boeing, Australia
2	60% reduction in work and fewer outstanding actions following pre-test and post-test audits	Boeing, Australia
3	Increased the percentage of milestones met from approximately 50% to approximately 95%	General Motors
4	Decreased the average number of days late from approximately 50 to fewer than 10	General Motors
5	Increased through-put resulting in more releases per year	JP Morgan Chase
6	30% increase in software productivity	Lockheed Martin M&DS
7	Improved and stabilized Schedule Performance Index	Northrop Grumman IT1

Table 4. CMMI performance results summary

Percentage Category	Median Improvement	Number of Data Points	Lowest Improvement	Highest Improvement
Cost	34%	29	3%	87%
Schedule	50%	22	2%	95%
Productivity	61%	20	11%	329%
Quality	48%	34	2%	132%
Customer Satisfaction	14%	7	-4%	55%
Return on Investment	4.0:1	22	1.7:1	27.7:1
Note: The performance results in this table express change over varying periods of time.				

results, the quantitative results obtained for all six performance categories discussed earlier which are Cost, Schedule, Productivity, Quality, Customer Satisfaction, and Return on Investment. The quantitative performance results of Gibson et al. (2006) are summarized in terms of percentage change in Table 4.

CHAPTER SUMMARY

Improving software development or software processes is a primary challenge for present community since the software has become the core and the crucial component of any modern service or product. Therefore, ensuring its quality is essential and should not be ignored. Consequently, SPI is one of the most important and critical efforts that any software development organization pursues.

The Software Engineering Institute (SEI), at Carnegie Mellon University, recommended a set of key software process improvement (SPI) areas. Later on, these new activities were composed into a framework called the Capability Maturity Model (CMM). Since the release of CMM, it has been received wide acceptance and interest in the software engineering community. It has also spread beyond its origins and has been used by thousands of major software development organizations all over the world (Fltzgerald & O'Kane, 1999). After the emergence of CMMI in 2000, it became

one of the widely adopted standards for SPI as many software organizations shifted to adopting it (Huang et al., 2006). CMMI has tremendously proven itself as an influential and successful SPI model, and "we can regard the currently matured CMMI as being a pragmatically proven model" (Bollinger & McGowan, 2009). Therefore, it is not surprising to see an increasing number of software development organizations worldwide adopt CMMI-based SPI. Some researchers argued that current SPI frameworks have not yet proven its effectiveness and successfulness. Conradi and Fuggetta (2002) assert that existing SPI initiatives (including CMM and CMMI) are incapable of handling the critical challenges of software organizations. Nevertheless, reviewing the literature on CMM and CMMI-based SPI do indicate its expected benefits. The literature has also has supported the basic hypothesis behind CMM and CMMI which is improving the maturity of the processes should result in better project performance and product quality.

In order to simplify the picture to the reader and to summarize the extensive literature reviewed in this chapter, Table 5 and 6 respectively classify the literature according to the six performance categories discussed in Gibson et al., (2006). In Table 5 and 6, the symbol "×" denotes a certain study has addressed the correspondent performance category. For example, as shown in Table 5, Wohlwend and Rosenbaum (1994a) addressed

Table 5. Summary of the literature on CMM-based SPI

Study	Performance categories					
	Cost	Schedule	Productivity	Quality	customer satisfaction	Return on Investment (ROI)
(Wohlwend & Rosenbaum, 1994a)	-	×	-	×	-	×
(Herbsleb et al., 1994)	×	×	×	×	-	-
(Goldenson & Herbsleb, 1995)	×	×	×	×	×	-
Haley, Ireland, Wojtaszek, Nash, & Dion, 1995)	×	-	×	×	-	×
(Flowe et al., 1996)	×	×	-	-	-	-
(Herbsleb & Goldenson, 1996)	×	×	×	×	×	-
(Lowe & Cox, 1996)	×	×	-	-	×	×
(Krishnan, 1996)	×	×	-	×	-	-
(Yamamura & Wigle, 1997a)	×	×	×	×	-	×
(Yamamura & Wigle, 1997b)	×	×	×	×	-	×
(Herbsleb et al., 1997)	-	×	×	×	-	-
(Vu, 1997)	×	×	×	×	-	×
(Diaz & Sligo, 1997)	-	×	-	×	-	×
(McGarry et al., 1999)	-	×	×	×	-	-
(Oldham, Putman, Peterson, Rudd, & Tjoland, 1999)	-	×	-	-	-	×
(Ferguson, Leman, Perini, Renner, & Sehagiri, 1999)	×	×	×	×	-	×
(Keeni, 2000)	×	×	-	-	-	-
(Clark, 1997; 2000)	×	-	×	-	-	-
(Donald et al., 2000)	×	×	×	×		-
(Curtis, 2000)	-	×	-	-	-	-
(El Emam & Goldenson, 2000)	-	×	×	×	×	-
(Pitterman, 2000)	-	×	-	×	-	×
(Blair, 2001)	×	×	×	-	-	×
(McGarry & Decker, 2002)	-	-	×	×	-	×
(Reo, 2002)	-	-	×	-	-	-
(Isaac, Rajendran, & Anantharaman, 2003)	-	-	-	×	-	×
(Diaz & King, 2003)	×	-	×	×	-	×
(Ashrafi, 2003)	-	-	-	×	-	-
(Harter & Slaughter, 2003)	-	-	-	×	-	-
(Girish et al., 2007)	-	-	-	×	-	-
(Manish & Kaushal, 2007)	×	×	-	×	-	-

the benefits of CMM-based SPI on three categories of performance, which are Schedule, Quality, and Return on Investment (ROI). While Goldenson and Gibson (2003) studied the impact of CMMI-based SPI on the whole six categories of performance, as shown in Table 6.

Table 6. Summary of literature on CMMI-based SPI

Study	Performance categories					
	Cost	Schedule	Productivity	Quality	customer satisfaction	Return on Investment (ROI)
(Goldenson & Gibson, 2003)	×	×	×	×	×	×
(Huang et al., 2006)	×	×	×	×	×	-
(Gibson et al., 2006)	×	×	×	×	×	×
(El Emam, 2007)	×	×	-	×	-	-
(Liu, 2007)	×	-	-	×	×	-
(Sapp et al., 2007)	×	×	-	×	-	-
(Peter & Rohde, 2007)	×	-	×	-	-	-
(Garmus & Iwanicki, 2007)	×	×	×	×	-	-
(McGibbon et al., 2007)	-	-	×	×	-	×

CONCLUSION AND RECOMMENDATIONS

At the end of this chapter, a number of observations can be concluded:

- Although numerous research and case studies have reported the performance assessment results and benefits of CMM-based SPI since its release in 1991 till recently, there are still very limited studies on the impacts and benefits of the CMMI-based SPI. Despite the release of CMMI in 2000, it seems that CMM still receiving much attention than CMMI.

- Most of the available studies and paper research which focus the effects and benefits of CMMI-based SPI are case studies which based on quantitative data. Qualitative studies on CMMI-based SPI are rare in the literature and should be further addressed in future research.

- Various researchers have investigated the effect of CMM and CMMI-based SPI on a variety of performance measures such as cost, schedule, and quality. To the best of our knowledge, no previous study has explicitly studied the impact of CMM or CMMI-based SPI on one of the aforementioned classes of performance, which is "Customer satisfaction."

- Prior literatures indicate great improvement in different performance categories when adopting CMM or CMMI-based SPI. It is not yet obvious the kind of correlation which exists between the six performance measures discussed in this chapter. This is a potential topic which deserves more attention in future investigations.

- Future work in the area of CMMI-Based process maturity requires collecting historical data for each of the 22 process areas used in CMMI in order to examine which process area or key practice has a greater impact on software development effort, productivity of the development team, and diseconomy of scale.

- The literature lack research on the CMMI-based SPI from continuous representation's point of view. All attention is being paid to CMMI staged representation.

- While available and limited case studies on CMMI-based SPI provide great and positive performance results, (Gibson et al., 2006) stated that these results "cannot necessarily be generalized elsewhere." Therefore, studies are needed to explore the reasons for varying success in varying environment.

From the literature reviewed in this chapter, much has been learned on the effect and benefits of CMM and CMMI-based software process improvement. Now, there is substantial evidence that software process improvement based on CMM and CMMI can result in a considerable improvements in cost, schedule, return on investment (ROI), product quality, and other performance measures.

REFERENCES

Aaen, I., Arent, J., Mathiassen, L., & Ngwenyama, O. (2001). A conceptual map of software process improvement. *Scandinavian Journal of Information Systems, 12*, 123–146.

Ashrafi, N. (2003). The impact of software process improvement on quality: In theory and practice. *Information & Management, 40*(7), 677–690. doi:10.1016/S0378-7206(02)00096-4

Blair, R. B. (2001, April). *Software process improvement: What is the cost? What is the return on investment?* Paper presented at the Pittsburgh PMI Chapter meeting.

Bollinger, T., & McGowan, C. (2009). A critical look at software capability evaluations. *IEEE Software, 17*(4), 89–96.

Butler, K. (1995). The economic benefits of software process improvement. *Crosstalk, The Journal of Defense Software Engineering*, 14-17.

Chrissis, M., Konrad, M., & Shrum, S. (2007). *CMMI: Guidelines for process integration and product improvement* (3rd ed.). Addison-Wesley.

Clark, B. (1997). *The effects of software process maturity on software development effort* (Doctoral dissertation, University of Southern California).

Clark, B. (2000). Quantifying the effects of process improvement on effort. *IEEE Software, 17*(6), 65–70. doi:10.1109/52.895170

Conradi, H., & Fuggetta, A. (2002). Improving software process improvement. *IEEE Software, 19*(4), 92–99. doi:10.1109/MS.2002.1020295

Cooper, J., & Fisher, M. (2002). *Software acquisition capability maturity model (SA-CMM)*. (Technical Report CMU/SEI-2002-TR-010). Carnegie Mellon University Software Engineering Institute.

Curtis, B. (2000). The cascading benefits of software process improvement. *Proceedings of the Second International Conference on Product Focused Software Process Improvement. Lecture Notes In Computer Science, vol. 1840, PROFES 2000*. Oulu, Finland: Springer-Verlag.

Curtis, B., Hefley, W. E., & Miller, S. (1995). *People capability maturity model*. (Technical Report CMU/SEI-95-MM-02). Carnegie Mellon University Software Engineering Institute.

Deephouse, C., Mukhopadhyay, T., Goldenson, D. R., & Keller, M. I. (1996). Software processes and project performance. *Journal of Management Information Systems, 12*(3), 187–205.

Diaz, M., & King, J. (2003). How CMM impacts quality, productivity, rework, and the bottom line. *Crosstalk. The Journal of Defense Software Engineering, 15*(3), 9–14.

Diaz, M., & Sligo, J. (1997). How software process improvement helped Motorola. *IEEE Software, 14*(5), 75–81. doi:10.1109/52.605934

Dion, R. (1993). Process improvement and the corporate balance sheet. *IEEE Software, 10*(4), 28–35. doi:10.1109/52.219618

Donald, H., Krishnan, M., & Slaughter, A. (2000). Effects of process maturity on quality, cycle time, and effort in software product development. *Management Science, 46*(4), 451–466. doi:10.1287/mnsc.46.4.451.12056

El Emam, K. (2007). TrialStat Corporation: On schedule with high quality and cost savings for the customer. *SoftwareTech, 10*(1), 24–29.

El Emam, K., & Goldenson, D. R. (2000). An empirical review of software process assessments. *Advances in Computers, 53*, 319–422. doi:10.1016/S0065-2458(00)80008-X

Enterprise Process Improvement Collaboration (EPIC). (1995). *Systems engineering capability maturity model,* version 1.1. *(*Technical Report CMU/SEI-95-MM-003). Carnegie Mellon University Software Engineering Institute.

Ferguson, P., Leman, G., Perini, P., Renner, S., & Sehagiri, G. (1999). *Software process improvement works! (*Technical Report CMU/SEI-99-TR-027). Carnegie Mellon University Software Engineering Institute.

Flowe, R., Lawlis, P., & Thordahl, J. (1996). A correlational study of the CMM and software development performance. *Crosstalk. The Journal of Defense Software Engineering, 8*(8), 21–25.

Fltzgerald, B., & O'Kane, T. (1999). A longitudinal study of software process improvement. *IEEE Software, 16*(3), 37–45. doi:10.1109/52.765785

Galin, D., & Avrahami, M. (2006). Are CMM program investments beneficial? Analyzing past studies. *Software IEEE, 23*(6), 81–87. doi:10.1109/MS.2006.149

Garmus, D., & Iwanicki, S. (2007). Improved performance should be expected from process improvement. *SoftwareTech, 10*(1), 14–17.

Gerry, C., & Rory, O. (2007). Using grounded theory to understand software process improvement: A study of Irish software product companies. *Information and Software Technology, 49*(6), 654–667. doi:10.1016/j.infsof.2007.02.011

Gibson, D., Goldenson, D., & Kost, K. (2006). *Performance results of CMMI-based process improvement. (*Technical Report CMU/SEI-2006-TR-004 ESC-TR-2006-004). Carnegie Mellon University Software Engineering Institute.

Girish, H., James, J., & Klein, G. (2007). Software quality and IS project performance improvements from software development process maturity and IS implementation strategies. *Journal of Systems and Software, 80*, 616–627. doi:10.1016/j.jss.2006.06.014

Goldenson, D., & Gibson, D. (2003). *Demonstrating the impact and benefits of CMMI: An update and preliminary results.* (Technical Report CMU/SEI-2003-SR-009). Carnegie Mellon University Software Engineering Institute.

Goldenson, D., & Herbsleb, J. (1995). *After the appraisal: A systematic survey of process improvement, its benefits, and factors that influence success.* (Technical Report CMU/SEI-95-TR-009). Carnegie Mellon University Software Engineering Institute.

Haley, T. (1996). Software process improvement at Raytheon. *IEEE Software, 13*(6), 33–41. doi:10.1109/52.542292

Haley, T., Ireland, B., Wojtaszek, E., Nash, D., & Dion, R. (1995). *Raytheon electronic systems experience in software process improvement. (Technical Report CMU/SEI 95-TR-17).* Carnegie Mellon University Software Engineering Institute.

Harter, D. E., & Slaughter, S. A. (2003). Quality improvement and infrastructure activity costs in software development: Longitudinal analysis. *Management Science, 49*, 784–800. doi:10.1287/mnsc.49.6.784.16023

Herbsleb, J., Carleton, A., Rozum, J., Siegel, J., & Zubrow, D. (1994). *Benefits of CMM-based software process improvement: Initial results.* (Technical Report CMU/SEI-94-TR-13). Carnegie Mellon University Software Engineering Institute.

Herbsleb, J., Zubrow, D., Goldenson, D., & Paulk, M. (1997). Software quality and the capability maturity model. *Communications of the ACM, 40*(6), 30–40. doi:10.1145/255656.255692

Herbsleb, J. D., & Goldenson, D. R. (1996). A systematic survey of CMM experience and results. In *Proceedings of the 18th International Conference on Software Engineering* (pp. 323–330). Washington, DC: IEEE Computer Society.

Huang, S., Sheng, T., Ching, C., & Tsen, Y. (2006). Assessing the adoption performance of CMMI-based software process improvement in 18 Taiwanese firms. *Journal of Software Engineering Studies, 1*(2), 96–104.

Humphrey, W. S. (1995). *A discipline for software engineering.* Addison-Wesley.

Humphrey, W. S., Snyder, T. R., & Willis, R. R. (1991). Software process improvement at Hughes Aircraft. *IEEE Software, 8*(4), 11–23. doi:10.1109/52.300031

Isaac, G., Rajendran, C., & Anantharaman, R. N. (2003). Do quality certifications improve software industry's operational performance?—Supplemental material. *Software Quality Professional, 6*(1).

Isacsson, P., Pedersen, G., & Bang, S. (2001). Accelerating CMM-based improvement programs: The accelerator model and method with experiences. *Software Process Improvement and Practice, 6*, 23–34. doi:10.1002/spip.133

Jiang, J., Klein, G., Hwang, G., Huang, J., & Hung, S. (2004). An exploration of the relationship between software development process maturity and project performance. *Information & Management, 41*, 279–288. doi:10.1016/S0378-7206(03)00052-1

Jones, L., & Soule, A. (2002). *Software process improvement and product line practice: CMMI and the framework for software product line practice.* (Technical Report CMU/SEI-2002-TN-012). Carnegie Mellon University Software Engineering Institute.

Keeni, G. (2000). The evolution of quality processes at Tata Consultancy Services. *IEEE Software, 17*(4), 79–88. doi:10.1109/52.854073

Krasner, H. (1999). The payoff for software process improvement: What it is and how to get it. In El Emam, K., & Madhavji, N. H. (Eds.), *Elements of software process assessment and improvement* (pp. 151–176). Los Alamitos, CA: IEEE Computer Society Press.

Krishnan, M. S. (1996). *Cost and quality considerations in software product management* (Doctoral dissertation, Graduate School of Industrial Administration, Carnegie Mellon University).

Kuilboer, J. P., & Ashrafi, N. (2000). Software process and product improvement: An empirical assessment. *Information and Software Technology, 42*, 27–34. doi:10.1016/S0950-5849(99)00054-3

Kulpat, M., & Johnson, K. (2008). *Interpreting the CMMI: A process improvement approach* (2nd ed.). Germany: Auerbach Publications.

Lipke, W. H., & Butler, K. L. (1992). Software process improvement: A success story. *Crosstalk. The Journal of Defense Software Engineering, 38*, 29–31.

Liu, A. Q. (2007). Motorola Software Group's China center: Value added by CMMI. *SoftwareTech, 10*(1), 18–23.

Lowe, D. E., & Cox, G.M. (1996). Implementing the capability maturity model for software development. *Hewlett- Packard Journal*, 1–11.

Manish, A., & Kaushal, C. (2007). Software effort, quality, and cycle time: A study of CMM level 5 projects. *IEEE Transactions on Software Engineering*, *33*(3), 145–156. doi:10.1109/TSE.2007.29

McGarry, F., & Decker, B. (2002). Attaining level 5 in CMM process maturity. *IEEE Software*, *19*(6), 87–96. doi:10.1109/MS.2002.1049397

McGarry, F., Pajerski, R., Page, G., Waligora, S., Basili, V., & Zelkowitz, M. (1999). *Software process improvement in the NASA Software Engineering Laboratory.* (Technical Report CMU/SEI-94-TR-22). Carnegie Mellon University Software Engineering Institute.

McGibbon, T. (1996). *A business case for software process improvement.* Utica, New York: Data and Analysis Center for Software, Kaman Sciences Corporation.

McGibbon, T., Grader, M., & Vienneau, R. (2007). The DACS ROI dashboard-Examining the results of CMMI® improvement. *SoftwareTech*, *10*(1), 30–35.

Oldham, G., Putman, B., Peterson, M., Rudd, B., & Tjoland, K. (1999). Benefits realized from climbing the CMM ladder. *Crosstalk. The Journal of Defense Software Engineering*, *12*(5), 7–10.

Paulk, M., Weber, C., Curtis, B., & Chrissis, M. (1995). *The capability maturity model: Guidelines for improving the software process.* Addison-Wesley.

Paulk, M. C. (1995). How ISO 9001 compares with the CMM. *IEEE Software*, *12*(1), 74–83. doi:10.1109/52.363163

Peter, J., & Rohde, L. (2007). Performance outcomes of CMMI®-based process improvements. *SoftwareTech*, *10*(1), 5–8.

Pitterman, B. (2000). Telcordia Technologies: The journey to high maturity. *IEEE Software*, *17*(4), 89–96. doi:10.1109/52.854074

Pyzdek, T. (2003). *The Six Sigma handbook: The complete guide for greenbelts, blackbelts, and managers at all levels.* McGraw-Hill.

Ravichandran, T., & Rai, A. (2003). Structural analysis of the impact of knowledge creation and knowledge embedding on software process capability. *IEEE Transactions on Engineering Management*, *50*(3), 270–284. doi:10.1109/TEM.2003.817278

Reo, D. (2002, April). *CMM for the right reasons.* Paper presented at the ASQF CMM Day, European Software Institute.

Rico, D. F. (2004). *ROI of software process improvement: Metrics for project managers and software engineers.* J. Ross Publishing.

Russwurm, W., & Meyer, L. (2000). Integrated evaluation procedure for software/hardware system development processes based on the software capability maturity model. *Software Process Improvement and Practice*, *5*, 231–242. doi:10.1002/1099-1670(200012)5:4<231::AID-SPIP128>3.0.CO;2-#

Sapp, M., Stoddard, R., & Christian, T. (2007). Cost, schedule and quality improvements at Warner Robins Air Logistics Center. *SoftwareTech*, *10*(1), 10–13.

Software Engineering Institute. (1996). *EPIC: An integrated product development capability maturity model,* version 0.9. Carnegie Mellon University, Software Engineering Institute. Retrieved from http://www.sei.cmu.edu

Software Engineering Institute. (2007). *Capability maturity model integration (CMMI.) version 1.2.* Carnegie Mellon University, Software Engineering Institute. Retrieved from http://www.sei.cmu.edu

Staples, M., & Niazi, M. (2008). Systematic review: Systematic review of organizational motivations for adopting CMM-based SPI. *Information and Software Technology, 50*(7-8), 605–620. doi:10.1016/j.infsof.2007.07.003

Velden, M., Vreke, J., Wal, B., & Symons, A. (1996). Experiences with the capability maturity model in a research environment. *Software Quality Journal, 5*, 87–95. doi:10.1007/BF00419772

Vu, J. D. (1997). *Software process improvement journey (from level 1 to level 5)*. Paper presented at the 2nd Annual European Software Engineering Process Group Conference.

Wohlwend, H., & Rosenbaum, S. (1994a). Software improvements in an international company. *Proceedings of the 15th International Conference on Software Engineering.*

Wohlwend, H., & Rosenbaum, S. (1994b). Schlumberger's software improvement program. *IEEE Transactions on Software Engineering, 20*(11), 833–839. doi:10.1109/32.368125

Yamamura, G. (1999). Process improvement satisfies employees. *IEEE Software, 16*(5), 83–85. doi:10.1109/52.795105

Yamamura, G., & Wigle, G. B. (1997a). SEI CMM level 5: For the right reasons. *Crosstalk. The Journal of Defense Software Engineering, 10*(8), 3–6.

Yamamura, G., & Wigle, G. B. (1997b). Practices of an SEI CMM level 5 SEPG. *Crosstalk. The Journal of Defense Software Engineering, 10*(11), 19–22.

Compilation of References

Aaen, I., Arent, J., Mathiassen, L., & Ngwenyama, O. (2001). A conceptual map of software process improvement. *Scandinavian Journal of Information Systems, 12*, 123–146.

ABNT. (1998). *Associação Brasileira de Normas Técnicas.* Retrieved March 24, 2006, from http://www.abnt.org.br

Abrahamsson, P. (2001). Commitment development in software process improvement: Critical misconceptions. *Paper presented at the 23rd International Conference on Software Engineering.* Los Alamitos, CA: IEEE Computer Society.

Abrahamsson, P., & Kautz, K. (2002). The personal software process: Experiences from Denmark. *Euromicro'02: 28th Euromicro Conference*, (pp. 367-374). doi: 10.1109/EURMIC.2002.1046223

Abrahamsson, P., & Kautz, K. (2006). Personal software process: Classroom experiences from Finland. *ECSQ 2002: Proceedings of the 7th International Conference on Software Quality*, (pp. 175-185). doi: 10.1007/3-540-47984-8_21

Abran, A., & Palza, E. (2003). *Design of a generic performance measurement repository in industry.* 13th International Workshop on Software Measurement, Montréal (Québec).

Abran, A., Bourque, P., Dupuis, R., Moore, J. W., Tripp, L. L., Abran, A., et al. (2004). *Guide to the software engineering body of knowledge - SWEBOK (2004 version ed.).* Piscataway, NJ: IEEE Press.

Ahern, D. M., Armstrong, J., Clouse, A., Ferguson, J. R., Hayes, W., & Nidiffer, K. E. (2005). *CMMI SCAMPI distilled: Appraisals for process improvement.* Addison-Wesley Professional.

Akinwale, O., Dascalu, S., & Karam, M. (2006). Duo-Tracker: Tool support for software defect data collection and analysis. *ICSEA'06: Proceedings of the International Conference on Software Engineering Advances,* (p. 22). doi: http://doi.ieeecomputersociety.org/10.1109/ICSEA.2006.34

Alexandre, S., Renault, A., & Habra, N. (2006). OWPL: A gradual approach for software process improvement in SMEs. In *32nd EUROMICRO Conference on Software Engineering and Advanced Applications (EUROMICRO-SEAA'06)*, (pp. 328-335).

Anacleto, A., Wangenheim, C. G., Salviano, C. F., & Savi, R. (2004a). *A method for process assessment in small software companies.* Paper presented at the 4th International SPICE Conference on Process Assessment and Improvement, Portugal.

Anacleto, A., Wangenheim, C. G., Salviano, C. F., & Savi, R. (2004b). *Experiences gained from applying ISO/IEC 15504 to small software companies in Brazil.* Paper presented at the 4th International SPICE Conference on Process Assessment and Improvement, Lisbon, Portugal.

Andrade, J. M., Albuquerque, A. B., Campos, F. B., & Rocha, A. R. C. (2004). *Conseqüências e características de um processo de desenvolvimento de software de qualidade e aspectos que o influenciam: Uma avaliação de especialistas.* Paper presented at the 3rd Brazilian Symposium on Software Quality, Brasilia, Brazil.

ANSI/PMI. (2004). *A guide to the project management body of knowledge (PMBOK guide)* (3rd ed.). Newtown Square, PA: Project Management Institute.

April, A.Laporte, Laporte, C.Y., Renault, A., Alexandre, S., Applying ISO/IEC Software Engineering Standards in Very Small Enterprises. In *Software Process Improvement for Small and Medium Enterprises: Techniques and Case Studies*. Hershey: Idea Group Inc.

April, A., & Abran, A. (2008). *Software maintenance management: Evaluation and continuous improvement*. Hoboken, NJ: John Wiley & Sons, Inc.

April, A., Hayes, J. H., Abran, A., & Dumke, R. (2005). Software maintenance maturity model (SMmm): The software maintenance process model. *Journal of Software Maintenance and Evolution: Research and Practice, 17*(3), 197–223. doi:10.1002/smr.311

April, A., Abran, A., & Dumke, R. (2004). *Assessment of software maintenance capability: A model and its architecture*. Paper presented at the IASTED Conference on Software Engineering, Innsbruck, Austria.

Ariane 501 Inquiry Board. (1996). *Ariane 5: Flight 501 failure*. Retrieved from http://www.di.unito.it/~damiani/ariane5rep.html

Ashrafi, N. (2003). The impact of software process improvement on quality: In theory and practice. *Information & Management, 40*(7), 677–690. doi:10.1016/S0378-7206(02)00096-4

Badariah, S., Sahibuddin, S., & Azim, A. A. A. (2009). Requirements engineering problems and practices in software companies: An industrial survey. In *Proceedings of International Conference on Advanced Software Engineering and Its Application, ASEA 2009 Held as Part of the Future Generation Information Technology, FGIT 2009* (pp. 70-77). Jeju Island, Korea.

Baddoo, N., & Hall, T. (2002). Motivators of software process improvement: An analysis of practitioner's views. *Journal of Systems and Software*, (62): 85–96. doi:10.1016/S0164-1212(01)00125-X

Baddoo, N., & Hall, T. (2003). De-motivators of software process improvement: An analysis of practitioner's views. *Journal of Systems and Software, 66*(1), 23–33.

Barbour, R., Benhoff, M., Gallagher, B., Eslinger, S., Bernard, T., Ming, L., et al. (2002). *Handbook CMU/SEI-2002-HB-002*.

Basili, V. R., McGarry, F. E., Pajerski, R., & Zelkowitz, M. V. (2002). *Lessons learned from 25 years of process improvement: The rise and fall the NASA Software Engineering Laboratory*. Paper presented at the Proceedings of the 24th International Conference on Software Engineering. Orlando, Florida: ACM.

Battle, E. (2009, September). *Using TSP at the MSG Level* [PowerPoint slides]. Paper presented at the Fourth Annual TSP Symposium, New Orleans, Louisiana. Retrieved from http://www.sei.cmu.edu/tspsymposium/2009/2009/index.html

Beecham, S., Hall, T., Britton, C., Cottee, M., & Rainer, A. (2005). Using an expert panel to validate a requirements process improvement model. *Journal of Systems and Software, 76*, 251–275. doi:10.1016/j.jss.2004.06.004

Beecham, S., Hall, T., & Rainer, A. (2003b). Software process improvement problems in twelve software companies: An empirical analysis. *Empirical Software Engineering, 8*(1), 7–42. doi:10.1023/A:1021764731148

Beecham, S., Hall, T., & Rainer, A. (2005). Defining a requirements process improvement model. *Software Quality Journal, 13*(3), 247–279. doi:10.1007/s11219-005-1752-9

Beecham, S., Hall, T., & Rainer, A. (2003a). *Defining a requirements process improvement model* (Technical Report No. 379). University of Hertfordshire, Hatfield.

Beitz, A., Emam, K. E., & Jarvinen, J. (1999). *A business focus to assessments*. Paper presented at the European Conference on Software Process Improvement.

Bertrand, C., & Fuhrman, C. P. (2008). *Towards defining software development processes in DO-178B with openup*. Paper presented at the Canadian Conference on Electrical and Computer Engineering (CCECE 2008).

Blair, R. B. (2001, April). *Software process improvement: What is the cost? What is the return on investment?* [PowerPoint slides]. Paper presented at the Pittsburgh PMI Chapter meeting.

Boehm, B. W. (2006). Some future trends and implications for systems and software engineering processes. *Systems Engineering, 9*(1), 1–19. .doi:10.1002/sys.20044

Boehm, B. W., & Ross, R. (1989). Theory-W software project management: Principles and examples. *IEEE Transactions on Software Engineering, 15*(7), 902–916. .doi:10.1109/32.29489

Bollinger, T., & McGowan, C. (2009). A critical look at software capability evaluations. *IEEE Software, 17*(4), 89–96.

Börstler, J., Carrington, D., Hislop, G. W., Lisack, S., Olson, K., & Williams, L. (2002). Teaching the PSP: Challenges and lessons learned. *IEEE Software, 19*(5), 42-48. doi: http://doi.ieeecomputersociety.org/10.1109/MS.2002.1032853

Brietzke, J., & Abraham. R. (2006). Resistance factors in software process improvement. *Clei Electronic Journal, 9*(1).

Brodman, J. G., & Johnson, D. L. (1994). What small businesses and small organizations say about the CMMI. In *Proceedings of 16th International Conference on Software Engineering* (pp. 331-340). IEEE Computer Society Press.

Brooks, F. P. (1975). *The mythical man-month: Essays on software engineering.* Reading, MA: Addison-Wesley.

Brooks, F. P. (1987). No silver bullet: Essence and accidents of software engineering. *IEEE Computer, 20*(4), 10–19. .doi:10.1109/MC.1987.1663532

Bullers, W. I. (2004). Personal software process in the database course. *ACE '04: Proceedings of the Sixth Conference on Australasian Computing Education, 30,* (pp. 25-31). Retrieved from http://portal.acm.org/citation.cfm?id=979968.979972

Butler, K. (1995). The economics benefits of software process improvement. *CrossTalk. The Journal of Defense Software Engineering, 8*(7).

Cagle, L. (2002). *Enhancing organization change using TSP.* Carnegie Mellon University, Software Engineering Information Repository (SEIR), Software Engineering Institute. Retrieved from https://seir.sei.cmu.edu/seir/

Card, D. N. (2004). *Research directions in software process improvement.* Paper presented at the 28th Annual International Computer Software and Applications Conference (COMPSAC'04), Hong Kong.

Carrington, D., McEniery, B., & Johnston, D. (2001). *PSPSM in the large class. CSEET '01: Proceedings of the 14th Conference on Software Engineering Education and Training,* (pp. 81-88). doi: http://dx.doi.org/10.1109/CSEE.2001.913824

Cater-Steel, A. P. (2004). *Low-rigour, rapid software process assessments for small software development firms.* Paper presented at the Australian Software Engineering Conference, ASWEC'04.

CETIC. (2006). *OWPL software process improvement for VSE, SME and low maturity enterprises Version 1.2.2.* Namur, Belgium: University of Namur, Software Quality Lab.

Chapman, R. (2006). Correctness by construction: A manifesto for high integrity software. *SCS '05: Proceedings of the 10th Australian Workshop on Safety Critical Systems and Software, 55,* (pp. 43-44). Retrieved from http://portal.acm.org/citation.cfm?id=1151816.1151820

Chrissis, M. B., Konrad, M., & Shrum, S. (2006). *CMMI guidelines for process integration and product improvement.* Addison Wesley.

Chrissis, M., Konrad, M., & Shrum, S. (2007). *CMMI: Guidelines for process integration and product improvement* (3rd ed.). Addison-Wesley.

Cignoni, G. A. (1999). *Rapid software process assessment to promote innovation in SMEs.* Paper presented at the EUROMICRO'99, Milan, Italy.

Ciurczak, J. (2001). *The quiet quality revolution at EBS Dealing Resources, Inc.* Carnegie Mellon University, Software Engineering Information Repository (SEIR), Software Engineering Institute. Retrieved from https://seir.sei.cmu.edu/seir/

Ciurczak, J. (2002). *Team software process (TSP) experiences in the foreign exchange market.* Carnegie Mellon University, Software Engineering Information Repository (SEIR), Software Engineering Institute. Retrieved from https://seir.sei.cmu.edu/seir/

Clark, B. (2000). Quantifying the effects of process improvement on effort. *IEEE Software, 17*(6), 65–70. doi:10.1109/52.895170

Clark, B. (1997). *The effects of software process maturity on software development effort* (Doctoral dissertation, University of Southern California).

Clements, P., & Northrop, L. (1999). *A framework for software product line practice*. Retrieved Dec 2009, from http://www.sei.cmu.edu/library/abstracts/news-at-sei/backgroundsep99pdf.cfm

CMMI Product Team. (2001). *Capability maturity model® integration (CMMI SM), version 1.1 (No. CMU/SEI-2002-TR-001)*. Pittsburgh, PA: Carnegie Mellon University.

CMMI Product Team. (2006). *CMMI® for development*, version 1.2. Carnegie Mellon University, Software Engineering Institute. Retrieved from http://www.sei.cmu.edu

CMMI Product Team. (2006). *Capability maturity model integration*. Retrieved March 24, 2006, from http://www.sei.cmu.edu/cmmi

CMMI Product Team. (2002). *Capability maturity model integration (CMMI) version 1.1*. Carnegie Mellon University, Software Engineering Institute. Retrieved from http://www.sei.cmu.edu/reports/02tr029.pdf

CMMI-Product-Team. (2001). *Appraisal requirements for CMMI, version 1.1*. Technical Report CMU/SEI-2001-TR-034, Carnegie Mellon University Software Engineering Institute.

Codd, E. F., Codd, S. B., & Salley, C. T. (1993). *Providing OLAP to user-analysts: An IT mandate*. Codd & Date, Inc.

Coleman, G., & O'Connor, R. (2008). Investigating software process in practice: A grounded theory perspective. *Journal of Systems and Software, 81*, 772–784. doi:10.1016/j.jss.2007.07.027

Conradi, R., & Fuggeta, A. (2002). Improving software process improvement. *IEEE Software, 19*(4), 92–99. doi:10.1109/MS.2002.1020295

Cooper, J., & Fisher, M. (2002). *Software acquisition capability maturity model (SA-CMM)*. (Technical Report CMU/SEI-2002-TR-010). Carnegie Mellon University Software Engineering Institute.

Curtis, B. (2000). The cascading benefits of software process improvement. *Proceedings of the Second International Conference on Product Focused Software Process Improvement. Lecture Notes In Computer Science, vol. 1840, PROFES 2000*. Oulu, Finland: Springer-Verlag.

Curtis, B., Hefley, W. E., & Miller, S. (1995). *People capability maturity model*. (Technical Report CMU/SEI-95-MM-02). Carnegie Mellon University Software Engineering Institute.

Curtis, W. (1994). *At the plenary session: Setting an agenda for measurement research and practice*. Paper presented at the 2nd International Symposium on Software Metrics: Bridging the Gap Between Research and Practice.

Daskalantonakis, M. K. (1994). Achieving higher SEI levels. *IEEE Software, 11*(4), 17–24. doi:10.1109/52.300079

Davis, N., & Barbara, S. (2009). *Experiences using the team software process at Adobe Systems* [PowerPoint slides]. Paper presented at the Fourth Annual TSP Symposium, New Orleans, Louisiana. Retrieved from http://www.sei.cmu.edu/tspsymposium/2009/2009/index.html

Davis, N., & Mullaney, J. (2003). *The team software process (TSP) in practice: A summary of recent results*. Carnegie Mellon University, Software Engineering Institute. Retrieved from http://www.sei.cmu.edu/reports/03tr014.pdf

de Oca, C. M., & Serrano, M. A. (2002). Managing a company using TSP techniques. *Crosstalk. The Journal of Defense Software Engineering, 16*(9), 17–21.

Deephouse, C., Mukhopadhyay, T., Goldenson, D. R., & Keller, M. I. (1996). Software processes and project performance. *Journal of Management Information Systems, 12*(3), 187–205.

Diaz, M., & King, J. (2003). How CMM impacts quality, productivity, rework, and the bottom line. *Crosstalk. The Journal of Defense Software Engineering, 15*(3), 9–14.

Diaz, M., & Sligo, J. (1997). How software process improvement helped Motorola. *IEEE Software, 14*(5), 75–81. doi:10.1109/52.605934

Dion, R. (1993). Process improvement and the corporate balance sheet. *IEEE Software, 10*(4), 28–35. doi:10.1109/52.219618

Disney, A. M., & Johnson, P. M. (1998). Investigating data quality problems in the PSP. *Software Engineering Notes, 23*(6), 143–152. doi:10.1145/291252.288292

Donald, H., Krishnan, M., & Slaughter, A. (2000). Effects of process maturity on quality, cycle time, and effort in software product development. *Management Science*, *46*(4), 451–466. doi:10.1287/mnsc.46.4.451.12056

Dorling, A. (1993). SPICE: Software process improvement and capability determination. *Software Quality Journal*, *2*(4), 209–224. doi:10.1007/BF00403764

Drouin, J. (1999). The SPICE project. In Emam, K. E., & Madhavji, N. H. (Eds.), *Elements of software process assessment and improvement* (pp. 45–56). California: IEEE Computer Society.

El Emam, K. (2007). TrialStat Corporation: On schedule with high quality and cost savings for the customer. *SoftwareTech*, *10*(1), 24–29.

El Emam, K., & Goldenson, D. R. (2000). An empirical review of software process assessments. *Advances in Computers*, *53*, 319–422. doi:10.1016/S0065-2458(00)80008-X

El-Emam, K., Drouin, J.-N., & Walcélio, M. (1998). *SPICE - The theory and practice of software process improvement and capability determination.* Los Alamitos, CA: Wiley-IEEE Computer Society Press.

El-Emam, K., Fusaro, P., & Smith, B. (1999). Success factors and barriers for software process improvement. In Messnarz, R., & Tully, C. (Eds.), *Better software practice for business benefit: Principles and experience* (pp. 355–371). Los Alamitos, CA: IEEE Computer Society.

Enterprise Process Improvement Collaboration (EPIC). (1995). *Systems engineering capability maturity model, version 1.1.* (Technical Report CMU/SEI-95-MM-003). Carnegie Mellon University Software Engineering Institute.

ESICENTER. (2003). *ESICenter UNISINOS*. Retrieved March 24, 2006, from http://www.esicenter.unisinos.br

European Commission. (2005). *The new SME definition.* Retrieved from http://ec.europa.eu/enterprise/policies/sme/facts-figures-analysis/sme-definition/index_en.htm

Eveleens, J. L., & Verhoef, C. (2010). The rise and fall of the chaos report figures. *IEEE Software*, *27*(1), 30–36. .doi:10.1109/MS.2009.154

Farias, L. D. L. (2002). *Planejamento de riscos em ambientes de desenvolvimento de software orientados à organização* (Unpublished master's dissertation). Instituto Alberto Luiz Coimbra de Pós-graduação e Pesquisa de Engenharia, Brazil.

Ferguson, P., Leman, G., Perini, P., Renner, S., & Sehagiri, G. (1999). *Software process improvement works!* (Technical Report CMU/SEI-99-TR-027). Carnegie Mellon University Software Engineering Institute.

Florence, A. (2001). Lessons learned in attempting to achieve software CMM Level 4. *CrossTalk, The Journal of Defense Software Engineering*, 29-30.

Flowe, R., Lawlis, P., & Thordahl, J. (1996). A correlational study of the CMM and software development performance. *Crosstalk. The Journal of Defense Software Engineering*, *8*(8), 21–25.

Fltzgerald, B., & O'Kane, T. (1999). A longitudinal study of software process improvement. *IEEE Software*, *16*(3), 37–45. doi:10.1109/52.765785

Forster, F. (2006). *Business process improvement patterns.* Doctoral dissertation, Queensland University of Technology & Technische Universitat, Munich.

Fuggetta, A. (2000). *Software process: A roadmap.* Paper presented at the Conference on The Future of Software Engineering, Limerick, Ireland.

Fuhrman, C., Djlive, F., & Palza, E. (2003). *Software verification and validation within the (rational) unified process.* Paper presented at the 28th Annual NASA Goddard Software Engineering Workshop (SEW 2003).

Fuhrman, C., Palza, E., & Do, K. L. (2004). *Optimizing the planning and executing of software independent verification and validation (IV&V) in mature organizations.* Paper presented at the 28th Annual International Computer Software and Applications Conference (COMPSAC 2004).

FUNDP-CETIC – Software Quality Lab. (2006). *OWPL software process improvement for VSE, SME and low maturity enterprises version 1.2.2.* University of Namur.

Galin, D., & Avrahami, M. (2006). Are CMM program investments beneficial? Analyzing past studies. *Software IEEE*, *23*(6), 81–87. doi:10.1109/MS.2006.149

Garg, P. K., & Jazayeri, M. (Eds.). (1995). *Process-centered software engineering environments*. Los Alamitos, CA: IEEE Computer Society Press.

Garmus, D., & Iwanicki, S. (2007). Improved performance should be expected from process improvement. *SoftwareTech, 10*(1), 14–17.

George, A., & Janiszewski, S. (2005). Applying functional TSP to a maintenance project. *Crosstalk. The Journal of Defense Software Engineering, 18*(9), 24–27.

Gerry, C., & Rory, O. (2007). Using grounded theory to understand software process improvement: A study of Irish software product companies. *Information and Software Technology, 49*(6), 654–667. doi:10.1016/j.infsof.2007.02.011

Gibbs, W. (1994). Software's chronic crisis. *Scientific American, 271*(3), 86–95. .doi:10.1038/scientificamerican0994-86

Gibson, D., Goldenson, D., & Kost, K. (2006). *Performance results of CMMI-based process improvement.* (Technical Report CMU/SEI-2006-TR-004 ESC-TR-2006-004). Carnegie Mellon University Software Engineering Institute.

Girish, H., James, J., & Klein, G. (2007). Software quality and IS project performance improvements from software development process maturity and IS implementation strategies. *Journal of Systems and Software, 80*, 616–627. doi:10.1016/j.jss.2006.06.014

Glass, R. L. (1998). *Software runaways: Lessons learned from massive software project failures*. Prentice Hall.

Glass, R. L. (2005). IT failure rates--70% or 10–15%. *IEEE Software, 22*(3), 110–112..doi:10.1109/MS.2005.66

Glass, R. L. (2006). The Standish report: does it really describe a software crisis? *Communications of the ACM, 49*(8), 15–16. .doi:10.1145/1145287.1145301

Goldenson, D. R., & Herbsleb, J. D. (1995). *After the appraisal: A systematic survey of process improvement, its benefits, and factors that influence success* (No. CMU/SEI-95-TR-009, Software Engineering Institute, USA): SEI.

Goldenson, D., & Gibson, D. (2003). *Demonstrating the impact and benefits of CMMI: An update and preliminary results.* (Technical Report CMU/SEI-2003-SR-009). Carnegie Mellon University Software Engineering Institute.

Gomes, A., & Pettersson, A. (2007). *Market-driven requirements engineering process model – MDREPM* (Master's thesis). Blekinge Institute of Technology, Sweden.

Gorschek, T., & Tejle, K. (2002). *A method for assessing requirements engineering process maturity in software projects* (Master's thesis). Blekinge Institute of Technology, Sweden.

Gray, C. F., & Larson, E. W. (2008). *Project management: The managerial process* (4th ed.). Burr Ridge, IL: Irwin/McGraw-Hill.

Gray, E. M., & Smith, W. L. (1998). On the limitations of the software process assessment and the recognition of a required re-orientation for global process improvement. *Software Quality Journal, 7*, 21–34. doi:10.1023/B:SQJO.0000042057.89615.60

Grojean, C. A. (2005). Microsoft's IT organization uses PSP/TSP to achieve engineering excellence. *Crosstalk. The Journal of Defense Software Engineering, 18*(3), 8–12.

Haase, V., Messnarz, R., Koch, G., Kugler, H., & Decrinis, P. (2002). Bootstrap: Fine-tuning process assessment. *Software, IEEE, 11*(4), 25–35. doi:10.1109/52.300080

Habra, N., Alexandre, S., Desharnais, J., Laporte, C. Y., & Renault, A. (2008). Initiating software process improvement in very small enterprises experience with a light assessment tool. *Information and Software Technology, 50*(7-8), 763–771. doi:10.1016/j.infsof.2007.08.004

Habra, N., Renault, A., Alexandre, S., & Lopez, M. (2002). *OWPL micro assessment.* Paper presented at the Software Quality Workshop, 24rd International Conference on Software Engineering ICSE, Orlando, Florida USA.

Hadden, R. (1998). How scalable are CMM key practices? *CROSSTALK: The Journal of Defense Software Engineering*, April, 18-23.

Haley, T. (1996). Software process improvement at Raytheon. *IEEE Software, 13*(6), 33–41. doi:10.1109/52.542292

Haley, T., Ireland, B., Wojtaszek, E., Nash, D., & Dion, R. (1995). *Raytheon electronic systems experience in software process improvement. (Technical Report CMU/SEI 95-TR-17)*. Carnegie Mellon University Software Engineering Institute.

Hall, T., Beecham, S., & Rainer, A. (2002). Requirements problems in twelve software companies: An empirical analysis. *IEEE Proceedings of Software*, *149*(5), 153–160. doi:10.1049/ip-sen:20020694

Halvorsen, C., & Reidar, C. (2001). *A taxonomy to compare SPI frameworks. Proceedings of the 8th European Workshop on Software Process Technology, Lecture Notes In Computer Science, vol. 2077,* Witten, Germany.

Hamann, D., Beitz, A., Müller, M., & Solingen, R. v. (Eds.). (2001). *International Workshop on Software Measurement.* Berlin, Germany: Springer-Verlag.

Hansen, B., Rose, J., & Tjørnehøj, G. (2004). Prescription, description, reflection: The shape of the software process improvement field. *International Journal of Information Management*, *24*(6), 457–472. doi:10.1016/j.ijinfomgt.2004.08.007

Harrison, W. (2000). *A universal metrics repository.* Paper presented at the 18th Annual Pacific Northwest Software Quality Conference, Portland, Oregon.

Harter, D. E., & Slaughter, S. A. (2003). Quality improvement and infrastructure activity costs in software development: Longitudinal analysis. *Management Science*, *49*, 784–800. doi:10.1287/mnsc.49.6.784.16023

Hartmann, D. (2006). *Interview: Jim Johnson of the Standish.* Retrieved from www.infoq.com/articles/Interview-Johnson-Standish-CHAOS

Hass, K. B. (2007). The blending of traditional and agile project management. *PM World Today*, *9*(5), 1–8.

Hassan, H., Nasir, M. H. N. M., & Fauzi, S. S. M. (2009). Incorporating software agents in automated personal software process (PSP) tools. *ISCIT'09: Proceedings of the 9th International Conference on Communications and Information Technologies.* doi: http://dx.doi.org/10.1109/ISCIT.2009.5340991

Hayes, W., & Over, J. W. (1997). *The personal software process^sm (PSP^SM): An empirical study of the impact of PSP on individual engineers (No. CMU/SEI-97-TR-001ESC-TR-97-00).* PA: Software Engineering Institute Carnegie Mellon University Pittsburgh.

Hayes, W., & Over, J. (1997). *The personal software process (PSP): An empirical study of the impact of PSP on individual engineers.* Technical Report SEI-97-TR-001, Software Engineering Institute, Carnegie Mellon University, Pittsburgh.

Hefley, B., Schwalb, J., & Pracchia, L. (2002). AV-8B's experience using the TSP to accelerate SW-CMM adoption. *Crosstalk. The Journal of Defense Software Engineering*, *16*(9), 5–8.

Herbsleb, J., Zubrow, D., Goldenson, D., & Paulk, M. (1997). Software quality and the capability maturity model. *Communications of the ACM*, *40*(6), 30–40. doi:10.1145/255656.255692

Herbsleb, J. D., & Goldenson, D. R. (1996). *A systematic survey of CMM experience and results.* Paper presented at the 18th International Conference on Software Engineering (ICSE-18), Berlin, Germany.

Herbsleb, J., Carleton, A., Rozum, J., Siegel, J., & Zubrow, D. (1994). *Benefits of CMM-based software process improvement: Initial results.* (Technical Report CMU/SEI-94-TR-13). Carnegie Mellon University Software Engineering Institute.

Hilburn, T. B., & Humphrey, W. S. (2002). Teaching teamwork. *IEEE Software*, *19*(5), 72–77. .doi:10.1109/MS.2002.1032857

Hou, L., & Tomayko, J. (1998). Applying the personal software process in CS1: An experiment. *SIGCSE Bulletin*, *30*(1), 322–325. .doi:10.1145/274790.274322

Huang, S., Sheng, T., Ching, C., & Tsen, Y. (2006). Assessing the adoption performance of CMMI-based software process improvement in 18 Taiwanese firms. *Journal of Software Engineering Studies*, *1*(2), 96–104.

Humphrey, W. (1989). *Managing the software process.* Addison-Wesley.

Humphrey, W. S. (2000b). *The personal software process ^SM (PSP^SM) (No. CMU/SEI-2000-TR-022ESC-TR-2000-022).* PA: Software Engineering Institute Carnegie Mellon University Pittsburgh.

Humphrey, W. S. (2005). Acquiring quality software. *The Journal of Defense Software Engineering*, *18*(12), 19–23. Retrieved from http://www.crosstalkonline.org/storage/issue-archives/2005/200512/200512-Humphrey.pdf.

Humphrey, W. S. (1998). Three dimensions of process improvement, part III: The team process. *Crosstalk. The Journal of Defense Software Engineering, 11*(4), 14–17.

Humphrey, W. S. (2000b). *Introduction to the team software process*. Reading, MA: Addison-Wesley.

Humphrey, W. S. (2000c). Building productive teams. *Crosstalk. The Journal of Defense Software Engineering, 13*(6), 4–6.

Humphrey, W. S. (2002a). *Relating the Team Software Process SM (TSP SM) to the Capability Maturity Model for the Software (SW-CMM)*. Software Engineering Institute.

Humphrey, W. S. (2002b). *Winning with software: An executive strategy*. Boston, MA: Addison-Wesley.

Humphrey, W. S. (2005). Why big software project fail: The 12 key questions. *CrossTalk. The Journal of Defense Software Engineering, 18*(3), 25–29.

Humphrey, W. S. (2006). *TSP: Coaching development teams*. Reading, MA: Addison-Wesley.

Humphrey, W. S. (1995). *A discipline for software engineering*. Addison-Wesley.

Humphrey, W. S., Snyder, T. R., & Willis, R. R. (1991). Software process improvement at Hughes Aircraft. *IEEE Software, 8*(4), 11–23. doi:10.1109/52.300031

Humphrey, W. S. (1994). The personal process in software engineering. *Third International Conference on the Software Process*, (pp. 67-77). Retrieved from ftp://ftp.cnam.fr/pub4/PAL/sei/documents/articles/ps/psp.swe.ps.Z

Humphrey, W. S. (1996). Using a defined and measured personal software process. *IEEE Softw., 13*(3), 77-88. doi: http://doi.ieeecomputersociety.org/10.1109/52.493023

Humphrey, W. S. (1999). *Pathways to process maturity: The personal software process and team software process*. Carnegie Mellon University, Software Engineering Institute. Retrieved from http://www.sei.cmu.edu/library/abstracts/news-at-sei/backgroundjun99.cfm

Humphrey, W. S. (2000a). Guest editor's introduction: The personal software process-Status and trends. *IEEE Softw., 17*(6), 71-75. doi: http://doi.ieeecomputersociety.org/10.1109/MS.2000.895171

Humphrey, W. S. (2000a). *The team software process (TSP)*. Carnegie Mellon University, Software Engineering Institute. Retrieved from http://www.sei.cmu.edu/reports/00tr023.pdf

Humphrey, W. S. (2009). *The Watts New? Collection: Columns by the SEI's Watts Humphrey*. Carnegie Mellon University, Software Engineering Institute. Retrieved from http://www.sei.cmu.edu/reports/09sr024.pdf

Humphrey, W. S., & Thomas, W. R. (2010). *Reflections on management: How to manage your software projects, your teams, your boss, and yourself*. Retrieved from http://www.ebooksx.com/

Humphrey, W. S., Kitson, D. H., & Kasse, T. C. (1989). The state of software engineering practice. *ICSE '89: Proceedings of the 11th International Conference on Software Engineering,* Pittsburgh, Pennsylvania, United States (pp. 277-285).

Ibrahim, A., & Choi, H. (2009). Activity time collection and analysis through temporal reasoning. In *the 11th International Conference on Advanced Communication Technology* (pp. 579-584). Phoenix Park, Korea.

IEEE Std 1012. (2004). IEEE standard for software verificiation and validation. *IEEE Std 1012-2004 (Revision of IEEE Std 1012-1998),* 0_1-110.

IEEE Std 1059. (1993). *IEEE guide for software verification and validation plans.*

IEEE. (1998). *IEEE/EIA 12207.0-1996 industry implementation of international standard ISO/IEC 12207: 1995 (ISO/IEC 12207) Standard for information technology software life cycle processes. IEEE/EIA 12207.0-1996* (pp. i-75).

Isaac, G., Rajendran, C., & Anantharaman, R. N. (2003). Do quality certifications improve software industry's operational performance?—Supplemental material. *Software Quality Professional, 6*(1).

Isacsson, P., Pedersen, G., & Bang, S. (2001). Accelerating CMM-based improvement programs: The accelerator model and method with experiences. *Software Process Improvement and Practice, 6,* 23–34. doi:10.1002/spip.133

ISO/IEC 12207. (2008). Systems and software engineering - Software life cycle processes. Geneva, Switzerland: International Organization for Standardization (ISO).

ISO/IEC 15288. (2008). Systems engineering - Systems life cycle processes. Geneva, Switzerland: International Organization for Standardization (ISO).

ISO/IEC 15289. (2006). Systems and software engineering - Content of systems and software life cycle process information products. Geneva, Switzerland: International Organization for Standardization (ISO).

ISO/IEC 24765. (2010). Systems and software engineering–Vocabulary, Geneva, Switzerland: International Organization for Standardization (ISO).

ISO/IEC 29110-2. (2011). Software engineering - Lifecycle profiles for Very Small Entities (VSEs) -- Part 2: Framework and taxonomy. Geneva, Switzerland: International Organization for Standardization (ISO).

ISO/IEC 29110-4-1. (2011). Software engineering - Lifecycle profiles for Very Small Entities (VSEs) -- Part 4-1: Profile specifications: Generic profile group. Geneva, Switzerland: International Organization for Standardization (ISO).

ISO/IEC PDTR 29110-5-1-1. (2011). Software engineering - Lifecycle profiles for Very Small Entities (VSEs) -- Part 5-1-1: Management and engineering guide: Generic profile group: Entry profile. Geneva, Switzerland: International Organization for Standardization (ISO).

ISO/IEC Std 15939. (2007). *Information Technology - Software engineering - Software measurement process.* Geneva, Switzerland: International Organization for Standardization.

ISO/IEC TR 10000-1. (1998). Information technology – Framework and taxonomy of international standardized profiles – Part 1: General principles and documentation framework. Geneva, Switzerland: International Organization for Standardization (ISO).

ISO/IEC TR 24774. (2010). Software and systems engineering — Life cycle management- Guidelines for process description. Geneva, Switzerland: International Organization for Standardization (ISO).

ISO/IEC TR 29110-5-1-2. (2011). Software engineering - Lifecycle profiles for Very Small Entities (VSEs) -- Part 5-1-2: Management and engineering guide: Generic profile group: Basic profile. Geneva, Switzerland: International Organization for Standardization (ISO).

ISO/IEC. (1998). *ISO/IEC TR 15504, Information Technology - Software process assessment - Parts 1-9.*

ISO/IEC. (2003-2006). *ISO/IEC 15504 Information Technology - Process assessment - Parts 1-5.*

ISO/IEC. (2004). *ISO/IEC 15504-1 Information Technology — Process assessment — Part 1: Concepts and vocabulary.*

ISO/IEC. (2008). *ISO/IEC 12207:2008, Information technology – Software life cycle processes.* International Organization for Standardization/International Electrotechnical Commission. Geneva, Switzerland: International Organization for Standardization (ISO).

ISO/IEC. (2010). *ISO/IEC DTR 29110-1: Software engineering - Lifecycle profiles for very small entities (VSE) -- Part 1: VSE profiles overview.* Geneva, Switzerland: International Organization for Standardization (ISO).

ISO/SPICE. (2003). *ISO/SPICE.* Retrieved March 24, 2006, from http://www.isospice.com

Iversen, J., Nielsen, P. A., & Norbjerg, J. (1998). *Problem diagnosis software process improvement.* Paper presented at the IFIP on Information systems: Current Issues and Future Changes. Retrieved March 24, 2006, from http://citeseer.ist.psu.edu/cache/papers/cs/12921/http:zSzzSzis.lse.ac.ukzSzhelsinkizSziversen.pdf/iversen98problem.pdf

Jain, M. (2009). *Delivering successful projects with TSP and Six Sigma: A practical guide to implementing team software process.* Retrieved from http://www.ebooksx.com/

Jiang, J., Klein, G., Hwang, H., Huang, J., & Hung, S. (2004). An exploration of the relationship between software development process maturity and project performance. *Information & Management, 41*, 279–288. doi:10.1016/S0378-7206(03)00052-1

Johnson, P. M., & Disney, A. M. (1999). A critical analysis of PSP data quality: Results from a case study. *Empirical Software Engineering, 4*(4), 317–349. .doi:10.1023/A:1009801218527

Johnson, D. L., & Brodman, J. G. (1997, Winter 1997). Tailoring the CMM for small businesses, small organizations, and small projects. *Software Process Newsletter, 8.*

Johnson, P. M., & Disney, A. M. (1998). The personal software process: A cautionary case study. *IEEE Softw., 15*(6), 85-88. doi: http://dx.doi.org/10.1109/52.730851

Johnson, P. M., Kou, H., Agustin, J., Chan, C., Moore, C., Miglani, J., et al. (2003). Beyond the personal software process: Metrics collection and analysis for the differently disciplined. *ICSE '03: Proceedings of the 25th International Conference on Software Engineering.* doi: http://dx.doi.org/10.1109/ICSE.2003.1201249

Jones, L., & Soule, A. (2002). *Software process improvement and product line practice: CMMI and the framework for software product line practice.* (Technical Report CMU/SEI-2002-TN-012). Carnegie Mellon University Software Engineering Institute.

Jorgensen, M., & Molokken, K. (2006). How large are software cost overruns? A review of the 1994 chaos report. *Information and Software Technology, 48*(4), 297–301. .doi:10.1016/j.infsof.2005.07.002

Jung, H. W., & Hunter, R. (2001). The relationship between ISO/IEC 15504 process capability levels, ISO 9001 certification and organization size: An empirical study. *Journal of Systems and Software, 59*(1), 43–55. doi:10.1016/S0164-1212(01)00047-4

Karagöz, N. A., & Grubu, A. Y. B. (2004). *Experiences from teaching PSP,* (pp. 58-63). Retrieved from http://trese.cs.utwente.nl/workshops/improq2004/Papers/workshopReport-Improq-2004.pdf

Kauppinen, M., Aaltio, T., & Kujala, S. (2002). Lessons learned from applying the requirements engineering good practice guide for process improvement. In *Proceedings of Seventh European Conference on Software Quality (QC2002)* (pp. 73-81). Helsinki, Finland.

Kautz, K. (1998). Software process improvement in very small enterprises: Does it pay off? *Software Process Improvement and Practice, 4*(4), 209–226. doi:10.1002/(SICI)1099-1670(199812)4:4<209::AID-SPIP105>3.0.CO;2-8

Kautz, K., & Nielsen, P. A. (2000). *Implementing software process improvement: Two cases of technology transfer.* Paper presented at the 33rd Hawaii Conference on System Sciences, Maui, USA.

Kautz, K., & Ramzan, F. (2001). *Software quality management and software process improvement in Denmark.* Paper presented at the 34th Hawaii International Conference on System Sciences, Maui, Hawaii, USA.

Keeni, G. (2000). The evolution of quality processes at Tata Consultancy Services. *IEEE Software, 17*(4), 79–88. doi:10.1109/52.854073

Kellner, M., Becker-Kornstaedt, U., Riddle, W., Tomal, J., & Verlage, M. (1998). Process guides: Effective guidance for process participants. In *the Fifth International Conference on Software Process* (pp. 11-25). Chicago, Illinois.

Kelly, D. P., & Culleton, B. (1999). Process improvement for small organization. *Computer, 32*(10), 41–47. doi:10.1109/2.796108

Khajenoori, S., & Hirmanpour, I. (1995). Personal software process: An experiential report. *Software Engineering Education, 895,* 131–145. doi:.doi:10.1007/3-540-58951-1_100

Khurshid, N., Bannerman, P. L., & Staples, M. (2009). Overcoming the first hurdle: Why organizations do not adopt CMMI. In *Proceedings of the International Conference on Software Process* (pp. 38-49). Vancouver, Canada.

Kirsch, L. J. (1997). Portfolios of control modes and IS project management. *Information Systems Research, 8*(3), 215–239. .doi:10.1287/isre.8.3.215

Kit, E. (Ed.). (1995). *Software testing in the real world: Improving the process.* Addison-Wesley.

Knauber, P., Muthig, D., Schmid, K., & Widen, T. (2000). Applying product line concepts in small and medium-sized companies. *IEEE Software,* 88–95. doi:10.1109/52.877873

Konsky, B. R. v., Ivins, J., & Robey, M. (2005). Using PSP to evaluate student effort in achieving learning outcomes in a software engineering assignment. *ACE '05: Proceedings of the 7th Australasian Conference on Computing Education,* (p. 42). Retrieved from http://portal.acm.org/citation.cfm?id=1082424.1082449

Krasner, H. (1999). The payoff for software process improvement: What it is and how to get it. In El Emam, K., & Madhavji, N. H. (Eds.), *Elements of software process assessment and improvement* (pp. 151–176). Los Alamitos, CA: IEEE Computer Society Press.

Kraut, R. E., & Streeter, L. A. (1995). Coordination in software development. *Communications of the ACM, 38*(3), 69–81. .doi:10.1145/203330.203345

Krishnan, M. S. (1996). *Cost and quality considerations in software product management* (Doctoral dissertation, Graduate School of Industrial Administration, Carnegie Mellon University).

Kuilboer, J. P., & Ashrafi, N. (2000). Software process and product improvement: An empirical assessment. *Information and Software Technology, 42*, 27–34. doi:10.1016/S0950-5849(99)00054-3

Kulpat, M., & Johnson, K. (2008). *Interpreting the CMMI: A process improvement approach* (2nd ed.). Germany: Auerbach Publications.

Kurniawati, F., & Jeffery, R. (2004). The long-term effects of an EPG/ER in a small software organization. In *the 15th Australian Software Engineering Conference* (pp. 128-136). Melbourne, Australia.

Laporte, C. Y., Alexandre, S., & Renault, A. (2008). The application of international software engineering standards in very small enterprises. *Software Quality Professional, ASQ, 10*(3), 4–11.

Laporte, C. Y., Alexandre, S., & O'Connor, R. V. (2008). A software engineering lifecycle standard for very small enterprises. In O'Connor, R. V., Baddoo, N., Smolander, K., & Messnarz, R. (Eds.), *Software process improvement* (*Vol. 16*, pp. 129–141). Berlin, Germany: Springer. doi:10.1007/978-3-540-85936-9_12

Laporte, C. Y. (2009). Contributions to software engineering and the development and deployment of international software engineering standards for very small entities (Doctoral dissertation, Université de Bretagne Occidentale, Brest).

Laporte, C. Y. (2010). Deployment Packages repository. Retrieved from http://profs.logti.etsmtl.ca/claporte/English/VSE/index.html

Laporte, C. Y., Alexandre, S., & O'Connor, R. A Software Engineering Lifecycle Standard for Very Small Enterprises, in R.V. O'Connor et al. (Eds.): EuroSPI 2008, CCIS 16, pp. 129–141

Laporte, C., & April, A. (2005, October 19-20, 2005). *Applying software engineering standards in small settings: Recent historical perspectives initial achievements.* Paper presented at the International Research Workshop for Process Improvement in Small Settings, Software Engineering Institute, Pittsburgh.

Laporte, C., Alexandre, S., & Renault, A. (2008). Developing international standards for very small enterprises. *IEEE Computer, 41*(3).

Laporte, C., Desharnais, J. M., Abouelfattah, M., Bamba, J. C., Renault, A., & Habra, N. (2005). *Initiating software process improvement in small enterprises: Experiments with micro-evaluation framework.* Paper presented at the SWDC-REK International Conference on Software Development, Rekjavick, Iceland.

Laryd, A., & Orci, T. (2000). *Dynamic CMM for small organizations.* Paper presented at the First Argentine Symposium on Software Engineering - ASSE 2000, Tandil, Argentina.

Lederer, A. L., & Prasad, J. (1995). Causes of inaccurate software development cost estimates. *Journal of Systems and Software, 31*(2), 125–134. .doi:10.1016/0164-1212(94)00092-2

Lee, C. (2005). Malaysia helps local developers deliver quality software. *ZDNET Software.* Retrieved March 4, 2011, from http://www.zdnetasia.com/malaysia-helps-local-developers-deliver-quality-software-39220761.htm

Leung, H. (1999). Slow change of information system development practice. *Software Quality Journal, 8*(3), 197–210. doi:10.1023/A:1008915509865

Levenson, N., & Turner, C. (1993). An investigation of the Therac-25 accidents. *IEEE Computer, 26*(7), 18–41.

Leveson, N. G., & Turner, C. S. (1993). An investigation of the Therac-25 accidents. *IEEE Computer, 26*(7), 18–41. .doi:10.1109/MC.1993.274940

Linscomb, D. (2003). Requirements engineering maturity in the CMMI. *The Journal of Defense Software Engineering.* Retrieved October 11, 2009, from http://www.stsc.hill.af.mil./crosstalk/2003/12/0312linscomb.html

Lions, P. (1996). *Ariane 5: Flight 501 failure - Report by the inquiry board.* Retrieved from http://sunnyday.mit.edu/accidents/Ariane5accidentreport.html

Lipke, W. H., & Butler, K. L. (1992). Software process improvement: A success story. *Crosstalk. The Journal of Defense Software Engineering, 38*, 29–31.

Lisack, S. K. (2000). The personal software process in the classroom: Student reactions (an experience report). *CSEET: Proceedings of the 13th Conference on Software Engineering Education & Training.* doi: http://dx.doi.org/10.1109/CSEE.2000.827035

Liu, A. Q. (2007). Motorola Software Group's China center: Value added by CMMI. *SoftwareTech, 10*(1), 18–23.

Lowe, D. E., & Cox, G.M. (1996). Implementing the capability maturity model for software development. *Hewlett- Packard Journal*, 1–11.

Lui, K. M., & Chan, K. C. C. (2006). Pair programming productivity: Novice-novice vs. expert-expert. *Int. J. Hum.-Comput. Stud., 64*(9), 915-925. doi: http://dx.doi.org/10.1016/j.ijhcs.2006.04.010

Macke, S., Khajenoori, S., New, J., Hirmanpour, I., Coxon, J., Ceberio, A., et al. (1996). An industry/academic partnership that worked: An in progress report. *CSEE: Proceedings of the 9th Conference on Software Engineering Education.* doi: http://doi.ieeecomputersociety.org/10.1109/CSEE.1996.491375

Mäkinen, T., Varkoi, T., & Lepasaar, M. (2000). *A detailed process assessment method for software SMEs.* Paper presented at the European Software Process Improvement SPI and Assessments (EuroSPI 2000).

Maletic, J. I., Marcus, A., & Howald, A. (2001). Incorporating PSP into a traditional software engineering course: An experience report. *CSEET: Proceedings of the 14th Conference on Software Engineering Education and Training.* doi: http://doi.ieeecomputersociety.org/10.1109/CSEE.2001.913825

Mali, P. (1978). *Improving total productivity: MBO strategies for business, government and not-for-profit organizations.* New York, NY: John Wiley and Sons.

Manish, A., & Kaushal, C. (2007). Software effort, quality, and cycle time: A study of CMM level 5 projects. *IEEE Transactions on Software Engineering, 33*(3), 145–156. doi:10.1109/TSE.2007.29

Marczak, S., Audy, J., & Sá, L. (2005). *Proposta e aplicação de um instrumento de acompanhamento da implantação do SW-CMM Nível 2.* Paper presented at the 4th Symposium on Software Quality, Porto Alegre, Brazil.

McCaffery, F., McFall, D., & Wilkie, F. G. (2005). Improving the express process appraisal method. *PROFES, 2005*, 286–298.

McCaffery, F., Taylor, P., & Coleman, G. (2007). Adept: A unified assessment method for small software companies. *IEEE Software Special Issue of "SE Challenges in Small Software Organizations*, (pp. 24-31).

McDonald, M., Musson, R., & Smith, R. (2008). *The practical guide to defect prevention.* Retrieved from http://www.ebook3000.com/The-Practical-Guide-to-Defect-Prevention_66621.html

McGarry, J. (Ed.). (2001). *PSM - Practical software measurement: Objective information for decision makers.* Addison-Wesley.

McGarry, J., Card, D., Jones, C., Layman, B., Clark, E., & Dean, J. (2002). *Practical software measurement: Objective information for decision makers.* Boston, MA: Addison-Wesley.

McGarry, F., & Decker, B. (2002). Attaining level 5 in CMM process maturity. *IEEE Software, 19*(6), 87–96. doi:10.1109/MS.2002.1049397

McGarry, F., Pajerski, R., Page, G., Waligora, S., Basili, V., & Zelkowitz, M. (1999). *Software process improvement in the NASA Software Engineering Laboratory.* (Technical Report CMU/SEI-94-TR-22). Carnegie Mellon University Software Engineering Institute.

McGibbon, T. (1996). *A business case for software process improvement.* Utica, New York: Data and Analysis Center for Software, Kaman Sciences Corporation.

McGibbon, T., Grader, M., & Vienneau, R. (2007). The DACS ROI dashboard-Examining the results of CMMI® improvement. *SoftwareTech, 10*(1), 30–35.

McGuire, E. G., & Randall, K. A. (1998). Process improvement competencies for IS professionals: A survey of perceived needs. *Proceedings of the 1998 ACM SIGCPR Conference on Computer Personnel Research*, (pp. 1-8).

McHale, J., & Wall, D. S. (2005). *Mapping TSP to CMMI*. Carnegie Mellon University, Software Engineering Institute. Retrieved from http://www.sei.cmu.edu/reports/04tr014.pdf

Mexican Standard. (2005). *NMX-059-NYCE-2005, Information Technology-Software-models of processes and assessment for software development and maintenance, part 01: Definition of concepts and products; Part 02: Process requirements (MoProSoft); Part 03: Guidelines for process implementation; Part 04: Guidelines for Process Assessment (EvalProSoft)*. Mexico: Ministry of Economy.

Microsoft. (2008). *Developing speech applications*. Microsoft Speech Technologies. Retrieved June 2009, from http://www.microsoft.com/speech/

Moore, C. A. (2000). Lessons learned from teaching reflective software engineering using the Leap Toolkit. *ICSE 2000: Proceedings of the 22nd International Conference on Software Engineering*. doi: http://dx.doi.org/10.1109/ICSE.2000.870464

Morisio, M. (2000). Applying the PSP in industry. *IEEE Softw., 17*(6), 90-95. doi: http://dx.doi.org/10.1109/52.895174

Na, K., Li, X., Simpson, J. T., & Kim, K. (2004). Uncertainty profile and software project performance: A cross-national comparison. *Journal of Systems and Software, 70*(1-2), 155–163. .doi:10.1016/S0164-1212(03)00014-1

Napier, N. P., Mathiassen, L., & Johnson, R. (2009). Combining perceptions and prescriptions in requirements engineering process assessment: An industrial case study. *IEEE Transactions on Software Engineering, 35*(5), 593–606. doi:10.1109/TSE.2009.33

NASA Software IV&V Facility. (2000, 31 August 2000). Software independent verification and validation. In *Program manager handbook*. Retrieved Jan 30, 2003, from http://www.ivv.nasa.gov/about/tutorial/PM_Handbook_v1.pdf

Nasir, M. H. N. M., & Yusof, A. M. (2005). Automating a modified personal software process. *Malaysian Journal of Computer Science, 18*(2), 11–27. Retrieved from http://ejum.fsktm.um.edu.my/ArticleInformation.aspx?ArticleID=337.

Nasir, M. H. N. M., & Sahibuddin, S. (2011). Addressing a critical success factor for software projects: A multi-round Delphi study of TSP. *International Journal of the Physical Sciences, 6*(5), 1213–1232.

Naur, P., & Randell, B. (Eds.). (1969). *Software engineering: Report on a conference sponsored by the NATO Science Committee*. Belgium: NATO Science Committee. Retrieved from http://homepages.cs.ncl.ac.uk/brian.randell/NATO/nato1968.PDF

Nazareth, H. R. D. S. (1998). *Curso básico de estatística*. São Paulo, Brasil: Ática.

Ngwenyama, O., & Nielsen, P., A. (2003). Competing values in software process improvement: An assumption analysis of CMM from an organizational culture perspective. *IEEE Transactions on Engineering Management, 50*(1), 100–112. doi:10.1109/TEM.2002.808267

Niazi, M., Wilson, D., & Zowghi, D. (2005). A maturity model for the implementation of software process improvement: An empirical study. *Journal of Systems and Software, 74*(2), 155–172. doi:10.1016/j.jss.2003.10.017

Niazi, M., Wilson, D., & Zowghi, D. (2006a). Critical success factors for software process improvement: An empirical study. *Software Process Improvement and Practice Journal, 11*(2), 193–211. doi:10.1002/spip.261

Niazi, M., & Shastry, S. (2003). Role of requirements engineering in software development process: An empirical study. In. *Proceedings of IEEE INMIC, 2003*, 402–407.

Niazi, M., & Babar, M. A. (2007a). *De-motivators for software process improvement: An analysis of Vietnamese practitioners' views*. Paper presented at the International Conference on Product Focused Software Process Improvement PROFES 2007, LNCS 4589.

Niazi, M., & Babar, M. A. (2007b). *Motivators of software process improvement: An analysis of vietnamese practitioners' views*. Paper presented at the International Conference on Evaluation and Assessment in Software Engineering (EASE 2007).

Niazi, M., & Staples, M. (2005). *Systematic review of organizational motivations for adopting CMM-based SPI*. Technical Report (No. National ICT Australia, PA005957).

Niazi, M., Hickman, C., Ahmad, R., & Babar, M. A. (2008). *A model for requirements change management: Implementation of CMMI level 2 specific practice.* Paper presented at the International Conference on Product Focused Software Process Improvement PROFES 2008, Italy, LNCS 5089.

Niazi, M., Wilson, D., & Zowghi, D. (2003). *Critical success factors and critical barriers for software process improvement: An analysis of literature.* Paper presented at the Australasian Conference on Information Systems (ACIS03), Perth, Australia.

Niazi, M., Wilson, D., & Zowghi, D. (2004). *Critical barriers for SPI implementation: An empirical study.* Paper presented at the IASTED International Conference on Software Engineering (SE 2004), Austria.

Niazi, M., Wilson, D., & Zowghi, D. (2006b). *Implementing software process improvement initiatives: An empirical study.* Paper presented at the The 7th International Conference on Product Focused Software Process Improvement, LNCS.

Nichols, W. R., Carleton, A. D., Humphrey, W. S., & Over, J. W. (2009). A distributed multi-company software project. *Crosstalk. The Journal of Defense Software Engineering, 22*(4), 20–24.

Nichols, W. R., & Salazar, R. (2009). *Deploying TSP on a national scale: An experience report from pilot projects in Mexico.* Carnegie Mellon University, Software Engineering Institute. Retrieved from http://www.sei.cmu.edu/reports/09tr011.pdf

Nidumolu, S. (1995). The effect of coordination and uncertainty on software project performance: Residual performance risk as an intervening variable. *Information Systems Research, 6*(3), 191–219. .doi:10.1287/isre.6.3.191

Nielsen, P. A., & Pries-Heje, J. (2002). A framework for selecting an assessment strategy. In Mathiassen, L., Pries-Heje, J., & Ngwenyama, O. (Eds.), *Improving software organizations: From principles to practice.* New Jersey: Addison-Wesley.

NMX-059-NYCE. (2005). Information technology-Software-models of processes and assessment for software development and maintenance. Part 01: Definition of concepts and products; Part 02: Process requirements (MoProSoft). Part 03: Guidelines for process implementation; Part 04: Guidelines for process assessment (EvalProSoft).

Nogueira, M. O., & Rocha, A. R. C. (2003). *Práticas relevantes em engenharia de software: Uma avaliação de especialistas.* Paper presented at the 2nd Symposium on Software Quality, Salvador, Brazil.

Northrop, L. (2002). SEI's software product line tenets. *IEEE Software, 19*(4), 32–40. doi:10.1109/MS.2002.1020285

Northrop, L. (2008). Software product line essential. Retrieved Dec 2009, from http://www.sei.cmu.edu/library/assets/spl-essentials.pdf

Oktaba, H., Felix, G., Mario, P., Francisco, R., Francisco, P., & Claudia, A. (2007). Software process improvement: The Competisoft project. IEEE Computer, 40(10).

Oldham, G., Putman, B., Peterson, M., Rudd, B., & Tjoland, K. (1999). Benefits realized from climbing the CMM ladder. *Crosstalk. The Journal of Defense Software Engineering, 12*(5), 7–10.

Orci, T., & Laryd, A. (2000, Nov. 2000). *Dynamic CMM for small organisations - Implementation aspects.* Paper presented at the European Software Process Improvement Conference-EuroSPI 2000, Copenhagen, Denmark.

Othman, M., Zain, A. M., & Hamdan, A. R. (2010). Review on project management and issues surrounding dynamic development environment of ICT project: Formation of research area. *International Journal of Digital Content Technology and its Applications, 4*(1). doi:10.4156/jdcta.vol4.issue1.10

Palza, E. (2005). *Facilitating measurement indicators in software improvements projects. Systems & Software Engineering Review.* Lima, Peru: Faculty of Systems & Computer Engineering, San Marcos University.

Palza, E. (2010). *Process and datamarts for V&V in critical projects.* Éditions Universitaires Européennes: Südwestdeutscher Verlag für Hochschulschriften Aktiengesellschaft & Co. KG.

Palza, E., & Upe, U. (2010). OpenUP - EPFC plugin for ISO 29110. Retrieved from http://investigacion.upeu.edu.pe/index.php/Portada#

Palza, E., Abran, A., & Fuhrman, C. (2003). Establishing a generic and multidimensional measurement repository in CMMI context. Paper presented at the 28th Annual IEEE/NASA Software Engineering Workshop, Greenbelt, MD, USA.

Palza, E., Levano, D., & Mamani, G. (2010). Creating a model for software project management in the context of small and medium enterprises (SMEs). Paper presented at the Software Engineering Process Group Conference SEPG 2010.

Palza, E., Sanchez, J., Abran, A., & Mamani, G. (2010). Implementing KPI with open source BI software in an academic department. Paper presented at the Computer Professional Conference /Software Maintenance and Evolution.

Paquette, D., April, A., & Abran, A. (2006). Assessment results using the software maintenance maturity model (S3M). *16th International Workshop on Software Measurement - (IWSM-Metrikom 2006)*, (pp. 147-160).

Paulk, M., Weber, C., Curtis, B., & Chrissis, M. (1994). *A high maturity example: Space shuttle onboard software, in the capability maturity model: Guidelines for improving software process*. California, US: Addison-Wesley.

Paulk, M. C. (1995). How ISO 9001 compares with the CMM. *IEEE Software*, *12*(1), 74–82. doi:10.1109/52.363163

Paulk, M., Weber, C., Curtis, B., & Chrissis, M. (1995). *The capability maturity model: Guidelines for improving the software process*. Addison-Wesley.

Paulk, M. C. (1995). How ISO 9001 compares with the CMM. *IEEE Software*, *12*(1), 74–83. doi:10.1109/52.363163

Paulk, M. C., Weber, C. V., Curtis, B., & Chrissis, M. B. (1995). The capability maturity model: Guidelines for improving the software process. In Institute, C. M. U. S. E. (Ed.), *The SEI Series in Software Engineering*. Reading, MA: Addison Wesley Longman Inc.

Paulk, M. C. (1998). *Using the software CMM in small organizations*. Paper presented at the Pacific Northwest Software Quality Conference and the Eighth International Conference on Software Quality.

Peter, J., & Rohde, L. (2007). Performance outcomes of CMMI®-based process improvements. *SoftwareTech*, *10*(1), 5–8.

Pettersson, F., Ivarsson, M., Gorschek, T., & Ohman, P. (2008). A practitioner's guide to light weight software process assessment and improvement planning. *Journal of Systems and Software*, *81*, 972–995. doi:10.1016/j.jss.2007.08.032

Philip, T., Schwabe, G., & Ewusi-Mensah, K. (2009). *Critical issues of offshore software development project failures*. Paper presented at the Thirtieth International Conference on Information Systems, Phoenix, Arizona.

Pikkarainen, M. (2006). *Agile assessment approach (based on the eight case experiences), Technical Report: D4.2_v1.0* (Technical Report): Technical Research Centre of Finland, VTT.

Pires, C. G., Marinho, F., Tellas, G., & Belchior, A. (2004). *A experiência de melhoria do processo do Instituto Atlântico baseado no SW-CMM nível 2*. Paper presented at the 3rd Symposium on Quality of Software, Brasilia, Brazil.

Pitterman, B. (2000). Telcordia Technologies: The journey to high maturity. *IEEE Software*, *17*(4), 89–96. doi:10.1109/52.854074

Point. (2004). *TSP tool development*. MSE Studio, Carnegie Mellon University. Retrieved June 2009, from http://dogbert.mse.cs.cmu.edu/mse2004korea/projects/point/index.html

Prechelt, L., & Unger, B. (2001). An experiment measuring the effects of personal software process (PSP) training. *IEEE Transactions on Software Engineering*, *27*(5), 465–472. doi:10.1109/32.922716

Pyzdek, T. (2003). *The Six Sigma handbook: The complete guide for greenbelts, blackbelts, and managers at all levels*. McGraw-Hill.

QuEST Forum. (2007). *TL 9000 quality system requirements: Measurements handbook* (Release 4). Kimball, R., & Ross, M. (Ed.). (2002). *The data warehouse toolkit: The complete guide to dimensional modeling.* John Wiley & Sons. Ferguson, R. (Ed.). (2002). *Special edition using Microsoft SharePoint portal server.* Indianapolis, IN: Que.

Ravichandran, T., & Rai, A. (2003). Structural analysis of the impact of knowledge creation and knowledge embedding on software process capability. *IEEE Transactions on Engineering Management, 50*(3), 270–284. doi:10.1109/TEM.2003.817278

Reo, D. (2002, April). *CMM for the right reasons* [PowerPoint slides]. Paper presented at the ASQF CMM Day, European Software Institute.

Richardson, I. (2002). SPI models: What characteristics are required for small software development companies? *Software Quality Journal, 10*, 101–114. doi:10.1023/A:1020519822806

Rickets, C. A. (2005). A TSP software maintenance life cycle. *Crosstalk. The Journal of Defense Software Engineering, 18*(3), 22–24.

Rico, D. F. (2004). *ROI of software process improvement: Metrics for project managers and software engineers.* J. Ross Publishing.

Robey, D. (2001). Blowing the whistle on troubled software projects. *Communications of the ACM, 44*(4), 87–93. .doi:10.1145/367211.367274

Rocha, A. R. C., Maldonado, J. C., & Weber, K. C. (2001). *Qualidade de software teoria e prática.* São Paulo, Brazil: Prentice Hall.

Rombach, D., Munch, J., Ocampo, A., Humphrey, W., & Burton, D. (2008). Teaching disciplined software development. *Journal of Systems and Software, 81*, 747–763. doi:10.1016/j.jss.2007.06.004

Rook, P. (1986). Controlling software projects. *Software Engineering Journal, 1*(1), 7–16. .doi:10.1049/sej.1986.0003

Rout, T. P., Tuffley, A., Cahill, B., & Hodgen, B. (2000, June 10 - 11, 2000). *The rapid assessment of software process capability.* Paper presented at the First International SPICE Conference, Limerick, Ireland.

RTI. (2002). *The economic impacts of inadequate infrastructure for software testing.* Research Triangle Park, NC: Author.

Runeson, P. (2001). Experiences from teaching PSP for freshmen. *Paper CSEET '01: Proceedings of the 14th Conference on Software Engineering Education and Training.* Retrieved from http://portal.acm.org/citation.cfm?id=794193.794906

Runeson, P. (2003). Using students as experimental subjects - An analysis of graduate and freshmen PSP student data. *Proc. Empirical Assessment in Software Eng.* Retrieved from http://citeseerx.ist.psu.edu/viewdoc/download?doi=10.1.1.99.6046&rep=rep1&type=pdf

Russwurm, W., & Meyer, L. (2000). Integrated evaluation procedure for software/hardware system development processes based on the software capability maturity model. *Software Process Improvement and Practice, 5*, 231–242. doi:10.1002/1099-1670(200012)5:4<231::AID-SPIP128>3.0.CO;2-#

Saint-Amand, D. C. H., & Hodgins, B. (2007). *Results of the software process improvement efforts of the early adopters in NAVAIR 4.0.* Naval Air Warfare Center Weapons Div., China Lake, CA. Retrieved from http://oai.dtic.mil/oai/oai?verb=getRecord&metadataPrefix=html&identifier=ADA482027

Sanders, M., & Richardson, I. (2007). Research into long-term improvements in small- to medium-sized organizations using SPICE as a framework for standards. *Software Process Improvement and Practice, 12*, 351–359. doi:10.1002/spip.319

Sangwan, R., Mullick, N., Bass, M., Paulish, D. J., & Kazmeier, J. (2006). Critical success factors for global software development. In *Global software development handbook* (pp. 9-20).

Sapp, M., Stoddard, R., & Christian, T. (2007). Cost, schedule and quality improvements at Warner Robins Air Logistics Center. *SoftwareTech, 10*(1), 10–13.

Sauer, C., & Cuthbertson, C. (2003, April 15). The state of IT project management in the UK 2002-2003. *Computer Weekly.*

Sawyer, P. (2004). Maturing requirements engineering process maturity models. In Maté, J., & Silva, A. (Eds.), *Requirements engineering for socio-technical systems* (pp. 84–99). Hershey, PA: Idea Group Inc.doi:10.4018/978-1-59140-506-1.ch006

Scheible, A., & Bastos, A. V. (2005). *CMM e comprometimento: Um estudo de caso na implantação do nível 2.* Paper presented at the 4th Symposium on Software Quality, Porto Alegre, Brazil.

Schneider, K., & von Hunnius, J.-P. (2003). Effective experience repositories for software engineering. In *the 25th International Conference on Software Engineering* (pp. 534-539). Portland, Oregon.

Schulmeyer, G. G. (2008). *Handbook of software quality assurance* (4th ed.). Artech House Publishers.

Schwalb, J. (2004, July). *Overview of the team software process & personal software process* [PowerPoint slides]. Paper presented at the Eight Annual PSM Users' Group Conference, Keystone, Colorado. Retrieved from http://www.psmsc.com/UG2004/Presentations/SchwalbJeff_PSMTSPBrief.pdf

Scott, L., Carvalho, L., Jeffery, R., D'Ambra, J., & Becker-Kornstaedt, U. (2002). Understanding the use of an electronic process guide. *Information and Software Technology, 44*(10), 601–616.

Scott, L., Carvalho, L., & Jeffery, R. (2002). A process-centered experience repository for a small software organization. In *the Ninth Asia-Pacific Software Engineering Conference* (pp. 603-610). Gold Coast, Australia.

SEBRAE. (2004). *Serviço de apoio às micro e pequenas empresas do Rio Grande do Sul.* Retrieved March 24, 2006, from http://www.sebrae-rs.com.br

SEI. (2002). *Process maturity profile of the software community.* Software Engineering Institute Carnegie Mellon University.

SEI. (2004). *Process maturity profile.* Software Engineering Institute Carnegie Mellon University.

SEI. (2008). *Process maturity profile.* Software Engineering Institute Carnegie Mellon University. Retrieved Oct 2008, from http://www.sei.cmu.edu/appraisal-program/profile/pdf/CMMI/2008MarCMMI.pdf

Shellenbarger, S. (2000). To win the loyalty of your employees, try a softer touch. *The Wall Street Journal, 26*(1).

Shen, W.-H., Hsueh, N.-L., & Chu, P.-H. (2006). *An experience report of applying the personal software process methodology.* International Conference on Software Engineering Research and Practice, (pp. 184-190). Retrieved from http://iec.cugb.edu.cn/WorldComp2006/SER4081.pdf

Shin, H., Choi, H.-J., & Baik, J. (2007). Jasmine: A PSP supporting tool. *ICSP '07: Proceedings of the 2007 International Conference on Software Process.* Retrieved from http://portal.acm.org/citation.cfm?id=1763239.1763248

Sillitti, A., Janes, A., Succi, G., & Vernazza, T. (2003). Collecting, integrating and analyzing software metrics and personal software process data. *EUROMICRO '03: Proceedings of the 29th Conference on EUROMICRO,* (p. 336). doi:http://doi.ieeecomputersociety.org/10.1109/EURMIC.2003.1231611

Singh, R. (1996). International Standard ISO/IEC 12207 software life cycle processes. *Software Process Improvement and Practice, 2*(1), 35–50. doi:10.1002/(SICI)1099-1670(199603)2:1<35::AID-SPIP29>3.0.CO;2-3

Sison, R., Diaz, D., Lam, E., Navarro, D., & Navarro, J. (2005). Personal software process (PSP) assistant. *APSEC '05: Proceedings of the 12th Asia-Pacific Software Engineering Conference,* (pp. 687-696). doi:http://dx.doi.org/10.1109/APSEC.2005.87

Sison, R., Diaz, D., Lam, E., Navarro, D., & Navarro, J. (2005). Personal software process (PSP) assistant. In *the 12th Asia-Pacific Software Engineering Conference* (pp. 687-696). Taipei, Taiwan.

Smite, D., & Borzovs, J. (2006). A framework for overcoming supplier related threats in global projects. In Richardson, I., Runeson, P., & Messnarz, R. (Eds.), *Software process improvement* (Vol. 4257, pp. 50–61). Berlin, Germany: Springer. doi:10.1007/11908562_6

SOFTEX. (2005). *Associação para Promoção da Excelência do Software Brasileiro.* Retrieved March 24, 2006, from http://www.softex.br/mpsbr

SOFTSUL. (2001). *Sociedade Sul-riograndense de Apoio ao Desenvolvimento de Software.* Retrieved March 24, 2006, from http://www.softsul.org.br

Software Engineering Institute. (2009). *Process maturity profiles*. Retrieved November 25, 2009, from http://www.sei.cmu.edu/cmmi/casestudies/profiles/pdfs/upload/2009SeptCMMI.pdf

Software Engineering Institute. (1996). *EPIC: An integrated product development capability maturity model*, version 0.9. Carnegie Mellon University, Software Engineering Institute. Retrieved from http://www.sei.cmu.edu

Software Engineering Institute. (2007). *Capability maturity model integration (CMMI.) version 1.2*. Carnegie Mellon University, Software Engineering Institute. Retrieved from http://www.sei.cmu.edu

Software Process Dashboard. (2009). *The software process dashboard*. The Software Process Dashboard Initiative. Retrieved September 2009, from http://www.processdash.com/

Sommerville, I., & Ransom, J. (2005). An empirical study of industrial requirements engineering process assessment and improvement. *ACM Transactions on Software Engineering and Methodology, 14*(1), 85–117. doi:10.1145/1044834.1044837

Sommerville, I., & Sawyer, P. (1997). *Requirements engineering: A good practice guide*. Chichester, UK: John Wiley and Sons.

Sommerville, I. (2003). *Engenharia de software*. São Paulo, Brazil: Addison-Wesley.

Standish Group International. (1995). *Chaos*. Standish Group International.

Standish Group International. (1999). *Chaos: A recipe for success*. Standish Group International.

Standish Group International. (2001). *Extreme chaos*. Standish Group International.

Standish Group International. (2009). *Chaos summary 2009: 10 laws of CHAOS*. Standish Group International.

Standish Group International. (2010). *Chaos summary for 2010*. Standish Group International.

Standish-Group. (2003). *Chaos - The state of the software industry*.

Staples, M., Niazi, M., Jeffery, R., Abrahams, A., Byatt, P., & Murphy, R. (2007). An exploratory study of why organizations do not adopt CMMI. *Journal of Systems and Software, 80*(6), 883–895. doi:10.1016/j.jss.2006.09.008

Staples, M., & Niazi, M. (2008). Systematic review: Systematic review of organizational motivations for adopting CMM-based SPI. *Information and Software Technology, 50*(7-8), 605–620. doi:10.1016/j.infsof.2007.07.003

Std, I. E. E. E. (1998a). *IEEE guide for developing system requirements specifications* (pp. 1233–1998). New York: The Institute of Electrical and Electronics Engineers, Inc.

Std, I. E. E. E. (1998b). *IEEE recommended practice for software requirements specifications* (pp. 830–1998). New York: The Institute of Electrical and Electronics Engineers, Inc.

Steinen, H. (1999). Software process assessment and improvement: Five years of experiences with BOOTSTRAP. In Emam, K. E., & Madhavji, N. H. (Eds.), *Elements of software process assessment and improvement* (pp. 57–76). California: IEEE Computer Society.

Suri, D., & Sebern, M. J. (2004). Incorporating software process in an undergraduate software engineering curriculum: Challenges and rewards. *CSEET'04: Proceedings of the 17th Conference on Software Engineering Education and Training*. doi: http://doi.ieeecomputersociety.org/10.1109/CSEE.2004.1276505

Swartz, A. J. (1996). Airport 95: Automated baggage system? *ACM SIGSOFT Software Engineering Notes, 21*(2), 79–83. .doi:10.1145/227531.227544

Taylor, A. (2000). IT projects: Sink or swim. *The Computer Bulletin, 42*(1), 24–26. .doi:10.1093/combul/42.1.24

Telesko, R., & Ferber, S. (2007). *Applying design patterns on processes*. Paper presented at the SEI SEPG European Conference.

Tingey, M. O. (1997). *Comparing ISO 9000, Malcolm Baldrige, and the SEI CMM for software: A reference and selection guide*. Upper Saddle River, NJ: Prentice-Hall, Inc.

Tomaso, C. D. (2008). *Analyse de contexte et évolution d'un outil expérimental de support aux évaluations de la maturité des processus de la maintenance: S3mAssess. Unpublished Mémoire de maître.* Belgium: Facultés Universitaires Notre-Dame de la Paix Namur.

Train, O., & Jacobson, R. (Eds.). (2000). *Microsoft(r) SQL Server(tm) 2000 analysis services step by step.* Microsoft Press.

Trechter, R., & Hirmanpour, I. (2005). Experiences with the TSP technology insertion. *Crosstalk. The Journal of Defense Software Engineering, 18*(3), 13–16.

TSPi. (2010). *Introductory team software process (TSPi).* Software Engineering Information Repository, Software Engineering Institute, Carnegie Mellon University. Retrieved January 2010, from http://www.sei.cmu.edu/tsp/tools/tspi/

tVista. (2009). *Web application to support the team software process.* Open Source Software Engineering Tools. Retrieved September 2009, from http://tvista.tigris.org/

Umphress, D. A., & Hamilton, J. A. (2002). Software process as a foundation for teaching, learning, and accrediting. *CSEET'02: Proceedings of the 15th Conference on Software Engineering Education and Training.* doi: http://doi.ieeecomputersociety.org/10.1109/CSEE.2002.995208

Varkoi, T., & Makinen, T. (2000). *Software process improvement initiation in small organisations.* Paper presented at the 3rd European Software Measurement Conference, FESMA-AEMES

Velden, M., Vreke, J., Wal, B., & Symons, A. (1996). Experiences with the capability maturity model in a research environment. *Software Quality Journal, 5,* 87–95. doi:10.1007/BF00419772

Villalón, J. A., Cuevas, A. G., San Feliu, G. T., De Amescua, S. A., García, S. L., & Pérez, C. M. (2002). Experiences in the application of software process improvement in SMES. *Software Quality Journal, 10*(3), 261–273. doi:10.1023/A:1021638523413

Vincent, L. (2008). *Méthode d'évaluation des processus de la maintenance du logiciel. Unpublished Mémoire de maître.* Belgium: Facultés Universitaires Notre-Dame de la Paix Namur.

Vu, J. D. (1997). *Software process improvement journey (from level 1 to level 5).* Paper presented at the 2nd Annual European Software Engineering Process Group Conference.

Walkerden, F. (1995). *A design for a software metrics repository (CAESAR Technical Report).* Sydney, Australia: Centre for Advanced Empirical Software Research, School of Information Systems, University of New South Wales.

Wallace, D. R., & Fujii, R. U. (1989). Software verification and validation: An overview. *IEEE Software, 6*(3), 10. doi:10.1109/52.28119

Wangenheim, C., Anacleto, A., & Salviano, C. F. (2004). *MARES - A methodology for software process assessment in small software companies. Technical Report: LQPS001_04E.* Brazil: LPQS - Universidade do Vale do Itajai.

Wangenheim, C., Varkoi, T., & Salviano, C. F. (2006). Standard based software process assessments in small companies. *Software Process Improvement and Practice, 11*(3), 329–335. doi:10.1002/spip.276

Ward, R. P., Laitinen, M., & Fayad, M. E. (2000). Thinking objectively - Management in the small. *Communications of the ACM, 43,* 113–116. doi:10.1145/353360.353377

Webb, D. (2000). Managing risk with TSP. *Crosstalk. The Journal of Defense Software Engineering, 13*(6), 7–10.

Webb, D. (2002). All the right behavior. *Crosstalk. The Journal of Defense Software Engineering, 16*(9), 12–16.

Webb, D., & Humphrey, W. S. (1999). Using the TSP on the TaskView Project. *Crosstalk. The Journal of Defense Software Engineering, 12*(2), 3–10.

Weissfelner, S. (1999). ISO 9001 for software organizations. In Emam, K. E., & Madhavji, N. H. (Eds.), *Elements of software process assessment and improvement* (pp. 77–100). California: IEEE Computer Society.

Wheeler, S., & Duggins, S. (1998). Improving software quality. *Paper presented at the Proceedings of the 36th Annual Southeast Regional Conference,* ACM.

Wiegers, K. (2003). *Software requirements* (2nd ed.). Redmond, CA: Microsoft Press.

Wiegers, K. E. (1996). Software process improvement: Ten traps to avoid. *Software Development, 4,* 51–58.

Wiegers, K. E., & Sturzenberger, D. C. (2000). A modular software process mini-assessment method. *IEEE Software, 17*(1), 62–69. doi:10.1109/52.819970

Wilkie, F. G., McCaffery, F., McFall, D., Lester, N., & Wilkinson, E. (2007). A low-overhead method for software process appraisal. *Software Process Improvement and Practice, 12*(4), 339–349. doi:10.1002/spip.321

Williams, L. (2001). Integrating pair programming into a software development process. *CSEET '01: Proceedings of the 14th Conference on Software Engineering Education and Training.* Retrieved from http://portal.acm.org/citation.cfm?id=794193.794899

Wilson, D. (2010). *New TSP paths: System engineering team uses TSP to manage software test product development* [PowerPoint slides]. Paper presented at the TSP Symposium, Pittsburgh, PA. Retrieved from http://www.sei.cmu.edu/tspsymposium/2010/proceedings.cfm

Wiredu, G. O. (2006). A framework for the analysis of coordination in global software development. *Proceedings of the 2006 International Workshop on Global Software Development for the Practitioner, Shanghai, China,* (pp. 38-44). doi:10.1145/1138506.1138516

Wohlwend, H., & Rosenbaum, S. (1994b). Schlumberger's software improvement program. *IEEE Transactions on Software Engineering, 20*(11), 833–839. doi:10.1109/32.368125

Wohlwend, H., & Rosenbaum, S. (1994a). Software improvements in an international company. *Proceedings of the 15th International Conference on Software Engineering.*

Xiaohong, Y., Percy, V., Huiming, Y., & Yaohang, L. (2008). A personal software process tool for Eclipse environment. Retrieved from http://abner.ncat.edu/yaohang/publications/eclipsepsp2.pdf

Yamamura, G. (1999). Software process satisfied employees. *IEEE Software,* (September/October): 83–85. doi:10.1109/52.795105

Yamamura, G. (1999). Process improvement satisfies employees. *IEEE Software, 16*(5), 83–85. doi:10.1109/52.795105

Yamamura, G., & Wigle, G. B. (1997a). SEI CMM level 5: For the right reasons. *Crosstalk. The Journal of Defense Software Engineering, 10*(8), 3–6.

Yamamura, G., & Wigle, G. B. (1997b). Practices of an SEI CMM level 5 SEPG. *Crosstalk. The Journal of Defense Software Engineering, 10*(11), 19–22.

Young, R. R. (2001). *Effective requirements practices.* Boston, MA: Addison-Wesley.

Zahran, S. (1998). *Software process improvement - Practical guidelines for business success.* Addison-Wesley.

Zahran, S. (1998). *Software process improvement: Practical guidelines for business success.* Reading, MA: Addison-Wesley.

Zahran, S. (2008). *Patterns for the enterprise process architecture.* Paper presented at the SEI SEPG European Conference.

Zarour, M., Desharnais, J.-M., & Abran, A. (2007). *A framework to compare software process assessment methods dedicated to small and very small organizations.* Paper presented at the International Conference on Software Quality - ICSQ'07.

Zhong, X., Madhavji, N. H., & Emam, K. E. (2000). Critical factors affecting personal software processes. *IEEE Softw., 17*(6), 76-83. doi: http://dx.doi.org/10.1109/52.895172

Zmud, R. W. (1980). Management of large software development efforts. *Management Information Systems Quarterly, 4*(2), 45–55. .doi:10.2307/249336

About the Contributors

Shukor Sanim Mohamed Fauzi serves as a Senior Lecturer at Faculty of Computer and Mathematical Sciences, Universiti Teknologi MARA, Malaysia. He received his Bachelor Science (Hons) specializing in Information Systems Engineering from the Universiti Teknologi Mara, and Master of Science (Computer Science - Real time Software Engineering) from the Centre for Advanced Software Engineering, Universiti Teknologi Malaysia. His research interests are in empirical software engineering, mining software repository, software configuration management, social network analysis, computer supportive collaborative work, and software process. He has authored and presented more than 40 papers in International and National conferences, journals, and book chapters and won several medals at national and international exhibition. In professional activity, he has involved in Technical Committee Software Engineering for Standard and Industrial Research Institute of Malaysia, a member of Software Process Improvement Network (SPIN) MSC Malaysia, Malaysia Software Engineering Interest Group (MySEIG), IEEE, ACM, and also IAENG. He also is a reviewer for several journals and committee member for international conferences.

Mohd Hairul Nizam Md Nasir received his Bachelor of Computer Science (Hons.) specializing in Software Engineering and Master's of Computer Science from University of Malaya in 2003 and 2005, respectively. He is currently serving as a Lecturer in the Department of Software Engineering, Faculty of Computer Science and Information Technology, University of Malaya. His area of specialization includes software process, software process improvement, project management, radio frequency identification, object oriented design and development, accessibility, and computing. He is also a member of IEEE Computer Society and Association for Computing Machinery, technical council of software engineering, technical committee on internet and technical committee on electronic commerce. As an active researcher, he has run several research projects and produced significant research output. He has published more than 60 scientific publications and won several medals at national and international exhibition.

Nuraminah Ramli is a Lecturer at Universiti Pendidikan Sultan Idris, Malaysia. She has Master of Sc (Comp. Sc-Real Time Software Engineering) from the Centre for Advance Software Engineering, University of Technology Malaysia. She also has a Bachelor's Degree in Computer Science, majoring in Software Engineering from the University of Putra Malaysia. Because of her interest in Software Process Improvement (SPI), she has pursued further research on the area.

Shamsul Sahibuddin is a Dean of Advanced Informatics School, University Technology Malaysia. He received his BSc in Computer Science from Western Michigan University, USA, MSc in computer science from Central Michigan University, USA, and PhD in Computer Science from Aston University, Birmingham, UK. He is member of the program committee for Asia -Pacific Conference in Software Engineering since 2003. His fields of specialization are computer supported cooperative work, computer network, and software quality. He is a member of ACM.

* * *

Alain Abran holds a Ph.D. in Electrical and Computer Engineering (1994) from École Polytechnique de Montréal (Canada) and Master degrees in Management Sciences (1974) and Electrical Engineering (1975) from University of Ottawa. He is a Professor and the Director of the Software Engineering Research Laboratory at the École de Technologie Supérieure (ETS) – Université du Québec (Montréal, Canada). He has over 15 years of experience in teaching in a university environment as well as more than 20 years of industry experience in information systems development and software engineering. His research interests include software productivity and estimation models, software engineering foundations, software quality, software functional size measurement, software risk management, and software maintenance management. He has published over 300 peer-reviewed publications and he is the author of the book "Software Metrics and Software Metrology" and a co-author of the book "Software Maintenance Management" (Wiley Interscience Ed.. & IEEE-CS Press). Dr. Abran is co-editor of the Guide to the Software Engineering Body of Knowledge – SWEBOK (see ISO 19759 and www.swebok.org), and he is the chairman of the Common Software Measurement International Consortium (COSMIC) – www.cosmicon.com

Rodina Ahmad has received her Bachelor degree of Computer Science and Mathematics from University of Hartford, Connecticut, USA. She pursued her Master of Computer Science in Rensselaer Polytechnique Institute and later her PhD from National University of Malaysia in the area of Information System. She teaches in Universiti Malaya for more than 15 years and is actively researching in the areas of Software Engineering and Information Systems.

Nur Aalyaa Alias received her Bachelor of Computer Science from Universiti Teknologi Mara, Malaysia in 2009. She is active researcher in Department of Advanced Research & Consultancy, Two Sigma Technologies, Malaysia. In a near future, she plans to further her study, majoring in business.

Ho-Jin Choi is a faculty member of the Dept. of Computer Science at Korea Advanced Institute of Science and Technology(KAIST), Daejeon, Korea. In 1982, he received a BS in Computer Engineering from Seoul National University, Korea, in 1985, an MSc in Computing Software and Systems Design from Newcastle University, UK, and in 1995, a PhD in Artificial Intelligence from Imperial College, London, UK. From 1982 to 1989, he worked as a Senior Engineer for DACOM Laboratory, Korea, and between 1995 and 1996, as a post-doctoral researcher at IC-PARC, Imperial College, London. From 1997 to 2002, he was a faculty member at Korea Aerospace University, then from 2002 to 2009, a faculty member at Information and Communications University(ICU), Korea, and since 2009 he has been with the Dept. of Computer Science at KAIST. Between 2002 and 2003, he visited Carnegie Mellon University(CMU), USA, and became an Adjunct Professor of CMU for the program of Master of Software Engineering(MSE). Between 2006 and 2008, he served as the Director of Institute for IT Gifted

Youth at ICU. His research interests include artificial intelligence, data mining, software engineering, and biomedical informatics.

Jean-Marc Desharnais has been working in the computer and software engineering fields for more than 30 years, as an analyst and project manager at the start of my career, and, most recently, as a software engineering consultant and professor. Since 1987, the expertise he has developed has mainly been in project management, specifically software measures for business applications. He has been, for 6 years, the Canadian representative at ISO SC/7 WG-6 (Quality measures) and the Editor of the Quality Measure Element standard (ISO/IEC 25021). He is also co-founder of COSMIC in 1998 and co-author of the COSMIC functional measure method. For 4 years he was full time Professor (docent) at ÉTS (École de Technologie Supérieure) in Montreal, Canada, from Fall 2008 through Spring 2009 as Lecturer at Middle East Technical University (METU) in Ankara, from Summer 2009 till December 2010 searcher at Bogaziçi University in Istanbul. He is currently Lecturer at Bogaziçi University and Adjunct Professor and Lecturer ÉTS. He has more than a hundred publications (see GELOG website), and his experience as a consultant is in many countries. His degrees are: Ph.D. in cognitive science, Master Business in Computing, Master Public Administration, Diploma in Administration, Bachelor in Sociology.

Abdul Azim Abd Ghani received B.Sc in Mathematics/Computer Science from Indiana State University in 1984 and M.Sc in Computer Science from University of Miami in 1985. He joined Universiti Putra Malaysia in 1985 as a Lecturer in Computer Science. He received his PhD in Software Engineering from University of Strathclyde in 1993. Currently he is a Professor at the Faculty of Computer Science and Information Technology, Universiti Putra Malaysia. He teaches software requirements engineering, software design, and software measurement. His research interests are software engineering, software measurement, software quality, and security in computing.

Salmiza Saul Hamid earned a Bachelor's degree in Computer Science from International Islamic University Malaysia in 2007. She is active researcher in Department of Advanced Research & Consultancy, Two Sigma Technologies, Malaysia. Currently she furthers her study at the Master level at the Faculty of Computer Science & Information Technology University of Malaya, Malaysia. Although she enjoyed her work, she felt that her range of future job opportunities would be broadened by further studies at Master's level.

Zarinah Mohd Kasirun received her BSc (CS) and MSc (CS) from National University of Malaysia (UKM) in 1989 and 1993, respectively. She obtained her PhD in the field of Requirements Engineering from University of Malaya in 2009. Currently, she is a Senior Lecturer in Software Engineering Department at the Faculty of Computer Science and Information Technology, University of Malaya. Her current research interests include requirements engineering, software quality, object-oriented software engineering and computer-supported collaborative learning.

Claude Y Laporte is a Professor, since 2000, at the École de Technologie Supérieure (ÉTS), an engineering school, where he teaches software engineering. His research interests include software process improvement in small and very small organisations and software quality assurance. He has worked in defense and transportation enterprises for over 20 years. He received a Master's degree in Physics from the Université de Montréal, a Master's degree in Applied Sciences from the École Polytechnique de Montréal and a Ph.D. from the Université de Bretagne Occidentale (France). He is the Editor of an ISO working group tasked to develop software life cycle standards ISO/IEC 29110 and guides for use in very small organisations. He is a member of IEEE, PMI, INCOSE and a member of the professional association of engineers of the Province of Québec (Ordre des ingénieurs du Québec). He is the co-author of 2 books on software quality assurance.

Mahmood Niazi is working at Keele University UK. He has done PhD from University of Technology Sydney Australia. Dr Niazi has spent more than a decade with leading technology firms and universities as a Process Analyst, Research Scientist, Senior Systems Analyst, Project Manager, Lecturer, and Professor. He has participated in and managed several software development and research projects. These have included the development of management information systems, software process improvement initiatives design and implementation, and several business application projects. Dr. Niazi has published more than 60 articles in peer reviewed conferences and journals. He is a Visiting Associate Professor at King Fahd University of Petroleum and Minerals Saudi Arabia and also Adjunct Professor at International Islamic University Pakistan.

Mustafa Kamal Mohd Nor is a Senior Lecturer at University of Malaya, Kuala Lumpur, Malaysia. He has several experiences working abroad and at local companies before joining UM in 1998. He taught mostly undergraduate courses and has published numerous papers. He also actively supervises many undergraduate and master level students. His research interests are ICT in small medium enterprises, Information Technology strategic planning, knowledge management, Information Systems development, and software development and management.

Josiane Brietzke Porto is a Project Manager in the IT industry and student of Master's degree in Business Administration in PUCRS (2011). She is specialist in Software Process Improvement in Federal University of Lavras (2008). She earned a Bachelor's in Computer Science in UNILASALLE (2005). She has experience in quality, development and software process improvement areas. She is a teacher of graduate degree in Computer Science and IT in UNISINOS. Her areas and research interests include software quality, software development process, project management, requirements engineering, people management, innovation projects, and e-learning.

Badariah Solemon is a Senior Lecturer at the College of Information Technology at Universiti Tenaga Nasional (UNITEN) in Malaysia. She has been involved in developing and teaching a number of subjects, including C/C++/Java programming, Software Engineering, and Requirements Engineering. Her research interests include requirements engineering, software process improvement, and software engineering education. She is currently a part-time PhD student at Universiti Teknologi Malaysia (UTM) that focuses at requirements engineering process improvement. At the same time, she enjoys providing software development consultancy services. Balancing formal theory and practical implementation is a principle that she plans to continue to practice in her future research and software development consultancy endeavors.

Edgardo Palza Vargas has more than 15 years of experience as Professor, Researcher, and Consultant. He has extensive experience in areas such as Software Quality, Statistical Analysis, MIS, and Business Management. As a consultant, Dr. Palza has implemented Business and IT solutions for organisations as Nokia, Ericsson Research Canada, John Hancock (USA), NASA IV&V, World Bank, Bombardier (Canada), Cirque du Soleil (Canada), CGI Inc. (Canada), etc. Dr. Palza has taken in different roles and responsibilities: Director, Manager, Business Architect, and others. He is Associate Professor at the Department of Software Engineering and Information Technology at Université du Québec – École de Technologie Supérieure. Dr. Palza current research activities covers artificial intelligence applied to management (health, finance, and marketing), business intelligence (data-mining/data-warehouse), statistics in management, performance management, project management, IT governance, and business strategies. He has published several books, book chapters, and articles in journals and international conferences.

Sami Zahran is one of the chief advocates of Software Process Improvement and its impact on organizations. He has over three decades of experience in the software industry assuming senior positions in large organizations including IBM, Digital Equipment (HP), ICL (Fujitsu), and the United Nations. He was trained in Software Process Improvement at the Software Engineering Institute, Carnegie Mellon University, and he is the author of a book on Software Process Improvement as part of the SEI Series on Software Engineering. Dr. Zahran regularly teaches courses on the subject and is an invited speaker at numerous international conferences and workshops.

Mohammad Zarour holds a Ph.D. in Software Engineering (2009) from École de Technologie Supérieure (ETS) – Université du Québec (Montréal, Canada), and Master's degree in Computer Science (1998) from University of Jordan. He is currently a Chief Technical Advisor at one of the UNDP programmes in King Abdul-Aziz City of Science and Technology, Riyadh, Saudi Arabia. He has over 5 years of experience in teaching in a university environment and also has several years of industry experience in information systems development. His research interests include software process assessment and improvement, software quality, and cost estimation. He has several peer-reviewed publications.

Index